Conflict in the Shared Household

Conflict in the Shared Household

Domestic Violence and the Law in India

Edited by
Indira Jaising
Pinki Mathur Anurag

OXFORD
UNIVERSITY PRESS

OXFORD
UNIVERSITY PRESS

Oxford University Press is a department of the University of Oxford. It furthers the University's objective of excellence in research, scholarship, and education by publishing worldwide. Oxford is a registered trademark of Oxford University Press in the UK and in certain other countries.

Published in India by
Oxford University Press
2/11 Ground Floor, Ansari Road, Daryaganj, New Delhi 110 002, India

First Edition published in 2019

ISBN-13: 978-0-19-948995-4
ISBN-10: 0-19-948995-5

Typeset in Adobe Jenson Pro 10.7/13.3
by The Graphics Solution, New Delhi 110 092
Printed in India by Replika Press Pvt. Ltd

Contents

Tables and Figures

Tables

Figures

Foreword

I am honoured to be asked to write the foreword to this very important book, *Conflict in the Shared Household: Domestic Violence and the Law in India*, and I am not just making a polite statement. This should be in the libraries of every court, police academy, and training centres, and more importantly this book must be read by judges, police officers, government officers, and the people's representatives—yes, I mean politicians.

At a meeting to remember Mr K.G. Kannabiran, Justice Zak Yakoob quoted Mr Kannabiran and it went something like this: that gender discrimination is the most ubiquitous injustice and permeates everywhere. I am not quoting verbatim, but I am sure you get the general trend. As I was reading the draft of this book I felt that it is such an entrenched virus that has spread so fully and I wondered if there is any antidote. What gets reinforced in these chapters is that the authorities who must be the bulwark against gender violence just do not act, they make the right statements but when it comes to action something holds them back. And yet when I close the book, I need not lose hope and I am thankful for that.

In the chapter 'The Long Road to Justice' (Monica Sakhrani, Trupti Jyhaveri Panchal, Radhika Chakravarty, and Manisha Kande) the women interviewed say, '*sarkari vakil main dum nahin hota*' (government lawyers don't have any strength) and that, '*court main jakar kaval perishani hi mili*' (one gets only trouble by going to court). Can there be a worse indictment of the justice delivery system? This chapter speaks of the implementation of the PWDVA; the authors have chosen the state of Haryana recording through interviews the multiple forms of violence experienced by women; the interim reliefs sought for and granted; the compensation claimed and granted; and so on. There are excellent charts to explain this. I am sure the sense of betrayal that women feel may vary in degrees from one state to another, but it is clear that women, our women, would generally choose not to approach the court. This chapter gives the reasons for it and explains why a unique law, the PWDVA, still lags behind in implementation because of fractured networks, lack of information, and tardy judicial proceedings.

The first chapter written by Indira Jaising, 'Unscrambling the Images', gives us a bird's-eye view of why and how this act was structured. In a matrimonial home the traditional bifurcation of duties was that the man would go out and earn and the woman would tend the home. So in some ways her right in the home should be traditionally recognized. Yet the tragic irony is that the concept of a shared household which came with this law is the first legislation of this kind, it is an amazingly empowering section. So the house she works for was something that she was not entitled to traditionally until this Act gave her the voice and the agency. I might say that this chapter gives a concise view of what we are going to read in the rest of the chapters.

The authors of each chapter have been candid in critiquing those judgments that failed to give effect to the whole purpose of this new law; which carved and threw away chunks of rights that were given to the women rendering those rights null, for example, the Taruna Batra case. The second chapter, by Uma Chakravarti, speaks of the very dangerous normalization of violence inflicted by the men on the women inside the home. Historically, socially, and culturally it was the norm and so just recently we saw what popular icons of sport said on a show while having coffee with a movie icon. This chapter tells us that wife battering has no bar—caste, class, nor social group; it is practised uniformly and that we are far from achieving equality that is our Constitution's aspiration. The subjugation of women as we see in this chapter seems to have the approval of religious text of all hues, and wife-beating is designed in trivial and fatalistic terms. Uma Chakravarti says that a special patriarchy unique to India exists because of compulsory marriages arranged by elders and the dispatch of the women to the marital homes; the return from which casts an indelible slur on the family and therefore had to be avoided even if it meant death by a 'stove burst'. The right to safety in her own home must become a non-negotiable right, and the earlier that courts and the police understand this the better it is for women.

To understand any law as Justice Aftab Alam has put in a totally different context—that of intellectual property—we must understand the 'how' and the 'why'. The third chapter deals with 'Mapping Legislative Changes', the 'why' of the law; Asmita Basu says, comes from the feminist engagement with law, reformed processes to address violence against women, and to promote women's equality. When you track the legislative changes, you cannot ignore the Mathura case, and it was at the same time that the Dahej Virodhi Manch was formed in Delhi to raise issues of dowry-related violence. This chapter deals with inherent limitation of criminal law and the impediments in implementation of the law. Some were infrastructure inadequacies but what is dismaying is the readiness with which judicial authorities presume 'misuse' of legal provisions by women. This chapter also examines why the options for leaving violent marriages is almost non-existent. The social and economic disadvantages that visit a woman when the marriage breaks down are so huge that the woman has no space for negotiations even if she has the agency. To quote from this chapter, however well-intentioned the law-makers may be, they come from an environment which is so male-drenched that 'non-implementation is written into the law'. The post of the protection officers is an innovation and they are intended to be the eyes and ears of the court or the outreach arm of the court. But did this happen? Please read the book.

The fourth chapter is about where the women will live. Traditionally, women have gone from the natal home to the marital home in India, and this chapter tells us how inheritance rights are inversely proportionate to the incidents of domestic violence. The Act was not intended to address just the violence between male and female partners but violence against all members residing together in a domestic relationship. The right to housing which is actually a facet of right to life is the space within which this domestic violence has to be located as this chapter delineates clearly. The invidious ways in which patriarchal attitudes are entrenched make it almost impossible for the women to get her right to housing secure. Men are traditionally considered as heads of the household and the acts of ownership were seldom being exercised by the women, hence, the violation of the right to adequate housing is an automatic fall-out of domestic violence. It is travesty of justice to treat the escape by women from a violent home as a voluntary exit; it is not choice but rather the absence of choice. It was with dismay that I read in practically every chapter, how courts have faltered in recognizing the experience of women. Then where do we go? If a woman had ownership rights in property, her power to negotiate is enhanced, and Pinki Mathur Anurag, in this chapter, argues that this would serve as a critical tool of protection. In this chapter and others, the authors use the word 'gender neutral' in connection to laws. I ask myself whether the phrase 'gender neutral' is right, or is 'gender equal' better? It is a question that I leave open. The right to residence under this Act is a right independent of the women's title in the household. The other conundrum faced by courts is whether this right to reside exists qua property owned by the in-laws. If the women's right to a safe life is recognized as a paramount right, then all pieces will fall into place.

Language is such a powerful tool for recognizing or negating rights. The fifth chapter, 'Of Keeps and Concubines', deals with relationships in the nature of the marriage. The dynamic of property rights is recognized only through male members of the family. Therefore, women who are in fraudulent marriages are left remediless though men might have exercised all the rights of a partner within a marriage against those women. Brototi Dutta argues in this chapter that the Indian Constitution recognizes right to equality and personal dignity and provides the basis for recognizing the dignity of women co-habitees, whether within a marriage or without. We have seen that there are peculiarly Indian conditions which make the practice multifaceted. This chapter deals with plural typographies of relationships and the women's vulnerabilities within such a relationship, and compares the right of co-habitees as recognized by English courts and Indian courts. *Velusamy v. Pachiamma*, narrowing the scope of the term 'relationship in the nature of the marriage', highlights the discomfort that society feels, and this includes the judge's feel, in expanding the ambit of legal protection to women in such relationships. The shadow of the Velusamy ruling appears reluctant to vanish. This Act's greatest contribution as explained in this chapter is to bring those women, whose relationships are 'in the nature of the marriage' into a right recognizing frame which is untouched by morality. This chapter argues that the recognition of rights of women in such relationships would be in consonance with the constitutional right to equality and dignity.

In the chapter 'Marital Rape', there is a tone of despair as Ajita Sharma writes 'till the State dithers from criminalizing marital rape, it cannot hope to protect and ensure women's fundamental human right to the life of dignity and reproductive and sexual rights'. It is a matter of interest and deep anguish that persons who will readily accept men and women as equal somehow cannot bring themselves to accept that marital rape is also rape. They seem to think that the family system would be stressed only if marital rape is made an offence. This chapter quotes from the 167th Parliamentary Standing Committee report on Home Affairs on the Criminal Law (Amendment) Bill 2012: 'it was therefore felt that if the marital rape is brought under the law the entire family system will be under great stress and the committee may perhaps be doing more injustice'. Isn't it ironic that when the committee speaks of family system and injustice they are not thinking of women in the family and the violent injustice done to her?

'Towards Uniformity of Rights' is interesting and important for more reasons than the simple fact that it speaks of harmonization of family law in India; it is the only chapter written by a male author, Saptarshi Mandal. This chapter highlights the Danial Latifi judgment. What is needed is an innovative judicial spirit, rooted in the Constitution, which must go beyond religious differences. Nothing illustrates how this can be done as a case decided and this case refers to a Delhi District Court judgment by Judge Hemani Malhotra, who uses an idea propounded under a statute governing Hindus, to grant relief to the Muslim petitioner in a case filed under a common law. Innovation in using the tool of substantive and procedural law is what women in a violent home need.

The importance of empirical analysis of the contours of jurisprudence in this difficult area can be ignored only at our peril and Aparna Chandra in her chapter 'Analysing Orders' has based her study on 7,000 orders viewed from various perspectives, like profile of users, types of violence and reliefs sought, reliefs granted, reliefs not granted, and reasoning for the same. This chapter alone is eloquent of the judicial attitudes, the concerns in obtaining relief, and how the patriarchal framework is so difficult to escape.

The last two chapters deal with nature of services available to women survivors and the changing contours of fiscal policy. In the end, whatever the law may be, it is the access that a woman has and the ease with which she is able to approach the source of relief that are important. As Devaki Jain puts it in her amazing book *The Journey of a Southern Feminist* (2018), 'Women value proximity, whether it is to a drinking water source, a fuel source, a crèche, a health centre, a court of justice or an office of administration ... if (they) are near, the chance of redress and effective action are greater.' We read about the one-stop crisis centres in 'Nature of Services Available to Women' by Padma-Bhate Deosthale and Sangeeta Rege; the setting up of the centres is not even half the battle. It is the facilities that are inbuilt into these institutions and the manner in which they really function. As regards the fiscal functions and budgets that are required to address violence against women, Kanika Kaul in 'Changing Contours of Fiscal Policy and Budgets' writes that henceforth policy decision in this domain must necessarily be informed by gender dimensions and that our programmes must be reoriented and budgets must reflect increased priority for women. For that, women's voices must be heard in the policymaking processes and they cannot remain passive bystanders.

This book would be very helpful in strengthening the idea of justice to women. I congratulate everyone who has contributed to this book. We must remember that justice is not done in courts alone; it inheres in every transaction of ours with another human being.

Justice Prabha Sridevan (Retd.)
Madras High Court
20 January 2019

Acknowledgements

The editors would like to acknowledge Asmita Basu's contribution to the planning and conception of this volume. She is one of those who has seen the PWDVA from the drafting board to the courts. We also thank Brototi Dutta and Tenzing Choesang, who along with Asmita Basu and the team at Lawyers Collective put in place a system of monitoring the implementation of the PWDVA. They created the resource that has enabled the identification of issues with the law.

We would like to express our heartfelt gratitude to all our contributors. You have made it possible for us to compile a volume covering a wide range of issues on domestic violence.

Our heartfelt thank you to Justice Prabha Sridevan (Retd.) for her insightful foreword.

The editorial team at Oxford University Press has been very supportive in ensuring the timely publication of this book.

We thank Ajita Sharma at the Lawyers Collective for her enthusiasm and support throughout the process.

Most of all, we thank the community of women's rights activists who contributed to the drafting of the law and have been monitoring it through its existence. And even more, the brave women who at the cost of being re-victimized have used the law, sometimes with success and sometimes they have come out of the court with tears in their eyes....

SECTION I

Causes and Consequences

1. *Unscrambling the Images*

Conflict in the Shared Household

Indira Jaising

'Now Touch His Feet and Go Home'

The idea of this book germinated on the 10th Anniversary of The Protection of Women from Domestic Violence Act (PWDVA) on 26 October 2016. The milestone needed to be marked. The law meant to provide a framework for equality by providing remedies to end violence when it occurred in the shared household. This collection of chapters intends to evaluate some of the concepts that shaped the framing of the law and its evaluation in the hands of judges.

As a lawyer representing women and an observer of the courts and their judgments, I have been struck by the moral indignation shown by judges when women are killed in the matrimonial home. Yet, simultaneously, it is the same judges who are in denial when a living woman complains of violence in the matrimonial home. Indeed, they go further, conjuring up the image of a 'scheming wife', 'the manipulating wife', a 'gold digger wife', and 'the wife who 'misuses the law'. This I call, 'concern for the dead, condemnation for the living'.[1] Hence, while convictions were quick to come under Section 304B of the Indian Penal Code (IPC)[2] for death in the matrimonial home, the antecedent violence was not addressed under Section 498A of the IPC[3] when the woman was alive. A woman who complained of violence was often told by judges, 'now touch his feet and go home'. There have been women who did that, if only to regain custody of their children, and never came back alive. While Section 498A of the IPC[4] has been given a bad name by constructing the image of a scheming wife, there was no alternative civil law, which a woman could use to address domestic violence. The PWDVA was an attempt to frame such a law, premised on the need for an equal relationship between the members of the family living in a shared household. Recognizing that not just wives, but mothers, daughters, and women in live-in relationships also needed protection from violence and from being rendered homeless, the law covers the household as a unit, not just the matrimonial relationship.

[1] Indira Jaising, 'Concern for the Dead, Condemnation for the Living', *Economic and Political Weekly* 49, 30 (2014): 34.

[2] Section 304B of the IPC Dowry death: (a) Where the death of a woman is caused by any burns or bodily injury or occurs otherwise than under normal circumstances within seven years of her marriage, and it is shown that soon before her death, she was subjected to cruelty or harassment by her husband or any relative of her husband for, or in connection with, any demand for dowry, such death shall be called 'dowry death', and such husband or relative shall be deemed to have caused her death. Explanation: for the purpose of this sub-section, 'dowry' shall have the same meaning as in section 2 of the Dowry Prohibition Act, 1961 (28 of 1961). (b) Whoever commits dowry death shall be punished with imprisonment for a term which shall not be less than seven years but which may extend to imprisonment for life.

[3] Section 498A of the IPC: Husband or relative of husband of a woman subjecting her to cruelty: whoever, being the husband or the relative of the husband of a woman, subjects such woman to cruelty shall be punished with imprisonment for a term which may extend to three years and shall also be liable to fine. Explanation: for the purpose of this section, 'cruelty' means: (*a*) any wilful conduct which is of such a nature as is likely to drive the woman to commit suicide or to cause grave injury or danger to life, limb, or health (whether mental or physical) of the woman; or (*b*) harassment of the woman where such harassment is with a view to coercing her or any person related to her to meet any unlawful demand for any property or valuable security or is on account of failure by her or any person related to her to meet such demand.

[4] See footnote 3.

Providing Definitions

Definitions go to the heart of any law; if they go wrong, the law goes wrong. For a country which has non-violence as its founding faith, it took more than 60 years to get a definition of domestic violence. The PWDVA, for the first time, sought to address the emotional and physiological trauma[5] faced by women in domestic situations. Sexual abuse[6] is included as a form of violence and it should include unwanted sex, making marital rape an actionable wrong, though it is excluded from the definition of rape under the IPC.

In this volume, we have not added to the literature of statistics on the functioning of the PWDVA, but focus on the main issues that have been litigated over the years: is the law universally applicable regardless of religion; have women in relationships in the nature of marriage been using the law; is marital rape addressed by this law; has the right to reside in the shared household found a foothold in jurisprudence; is the infrastructure to support women evolving; how does budgeting affect the implementation of a law?

When I started my legal practice in the 1960s, women could not frame the question of violence against them. When faced by a petition for divorce by their husbands, they would ask what would happen to their children if the divorce comes through, or they would have questions on how to get a divorce in an abusive marriage. Some women would ask the smart question of what their options are, but many women did not even realize and were not aware that there could be any options at all. Given that there is no law of community of property or equitable distribution of assets on the breakdown of a marriage, divorce in the Indian context meant civil death for most women. Women in violent marriages continue to resist divorce, knowing that there are no options for an honourable exit. Laws declaring the father to be the 'natural guardian'[7] terrorize women into fearing that they will lose custody

[5] Sub-section (iii) of Explanation I to Section 3 of the PWDVA states the following: (iii) 'verbal and emotional abuse' includes: (*a*) insults, ridicule, humiliation, name calling and insults, or ridicule especially with regard to not having a child or a male child; and (*b*) repeated threats to cause physical pain to any person in whom the aggrieved person is interested.

[6] Sub-section (ii) of Explanation I to Section 3 of the PWDVA states the following: (ii) 'sexual abuse' includes any conduct of a sexual nature that abuses, humiliates, degrades, or otherwise violates the dignity of woman.

[7] For example, see Section 6 of the Hindu Minority and Guardianship Act, 1956: 6. Natural guardians of a Hindu minor—The natural guardians of a Hindu,

of their children, the one thing they fear on the breakdown of marriage. I have known women who have gone underground with their infant children, never to be seen again when orders to give up custody of minor children were passed. Others have waited patiently till their children reached the age of discretion to exit a marriage. This fear has been often used, and continues to be used effectively, to keep women in a violent relationship from exiting on reasonable terms of separation. For many women, divorce has simply not been an option they could exercise, and yet there was no other exit option from a bad marriage. The PWDVA was intended to be an attempt to restore the measure of equality within a domestic relationship by creating conditions within which a woman could negotiate her options without fear of violence or of being rendered homeless. It is not, and never was, a law of equitable distribution of assets between the people in a domestic relationship. Such a law awaits enactment.

In 1984, Section 498A[8] of the IPC was enacted. There is a long history behind the criminal law on domestic violence coming into place. Preceding this powerful amendment, were cases of women dying in their matrimonial homes. The police were habitually recording these deaths as 'accidents' and the case files were closed without an investigation. It was the historic campaign of mothers of these women who died, and their demand for reopening the case file, which led to the enactment of Section 498A. Satya Rani Chaddha, who had lost her daughter in a so-called 'accident', was at the forefront of this campaign. Her daughter, Kanchan Rani, got married at a

---

minor, in respect of the minor's person as well as in respect of the minor's property (excluding his or her undivided interest in joint family property), are (*a*) in the case of a boy or an unmarried girl—the father, and after him, the mother: provided that the custody of a minor who has not completed the age of five years shall ordinarily be with the mother.

[8] Section 498A of the IPC, Husband or relative of husband of a woman subjecting her to cruelty: whoever, being the husband or the relative of the husband of a woman, subjects such woman to cruelty shall be punished with imprisonment for a term which may extend to three years and shall also be liable to fine. Explanation: For the purpose of this section, 'cruelty' means, (*a*) any wilful conduct which is of such a nature as is likely to drive the woman to commit suicide or to cause grave injury or danger to life, limb, or health (whether mental or physical) of the woman; or (*b*) harassment of the woman where such harassment is with a view to coercing her or any person related to her to meet any unlawful demand for any property or valuable security or is on account of failure by her or any person related to her to meet such demand.

young age and died within 10 months of marriage. She was pregnant at that time. Chaddha refused to believe it was an 'accident'. She wanted the police to record an FIR and to prosecute, but the police refused to do so.

Reports[9] show that in these cases of 'accidental' deaths, women were always in the kitchen, working on the kerosene stove. These 'accidents' were therefore termed as cases of stove bursts. This was the period when the polyester king, Dhirubhai Ambani, invented the polyester saree and women had switched over from wearing silks and cottons to polyester. Polyester was notorious for catching fire faster than cotton or silk. Hence, there were two villains at the crime scene—one was the kerosene stove and the other was the polyester saree. The social dynamics of the family, the deliberate abuse, and the dowry demands were not taken into consideration. It was Chaddha who brought these issues to the forefront of Indian legal history. Women like her made it the mission of their lives to ensure that other daughters did not die a similar death. Her long battle resulted in her son-in-law being convicted for abetting the suicide of this wife.[10] These campaigns finally led the government to introduce Section 498A IPC. This was a bold provision for several reasons. First, it introduced the concept of cruelty in marriages as a criminal offence and secondly, the definition was not limited to dowry demands or physical violence only, but extended to mental cruelty as well. It is a different matter that in its operation, the police understand the law to mean that it can only be used for prosecuting demands for dowry and insist that they be included in the FIR as a pre-condition for investigating the crime of cruelty. Section 304B IPC[11] was introduced thereafter, which defines dowry death. Both sections dealt with aspects of cruelty within

[9] Sharma et al., 'Accidental Burns in Indian Kitchens: Are They Really Accidental?', *Journal of Indian Academy of Forensic Medicine*, Vol. 28, no. 1 (2006); see also, Menon,'Dowry Deaths in Bangalore', *Frontline* 16, 17.

[10] *Subhash Chandra* v. *State*, II (2013) DMC 426.

[11] Section 304B of the IPC Dowry death: (*a*) Where the death of a woman is caused by any burns or bodily injury or occurs otherwise than under normal circumstances within seven years of her marriage, and it is shown that soon before her death, she was subjected to cruelty or harassment by her husband or any relative of her husband for, or in connection with, any demand for dowry, such death shall be called 'dowry death', and such husband or relative shall be deemed to have caused her death. Explanation: For the purpose of this sub-section,'dowry' shall have the same meaning as in section 2 of the Dowry Prohibition Act, 1961 (28 of 1961). (*b*) Whoever commits dowry death shall be punished with imprisonment for a term which shall not be less than seven years but which may extend to imprisonment for life.

marriage. While Section 498A addressed a woman's situation when she is alive, Section 304B addresses the situation when she is dead. Both sections were necessary, though they served a different purpose. After all, the aim of every law is to prevent crime, not just punish it after it happens. Section 498A was intended to prevent women from dying a 'dowry death'.[12]

Women were interested in keeping their marriage together but they wanted the abuse to stop. There was no law that addressed what happens within a marriage. There was a law that addressed how one marries and there was a law which addressed how one exits a marriage, but there was no law which addressed what happened between those two points of time. That was the background noise in my head for many years.

In 1994, the National Commission for Women, then headed by V. Mohini Giri and Padma Seth, asked me to create a draft law addressing domestic violence in the matrimonial home. The Lawyers Collective (LC) by then had already started working on a specific project on issues related to domestic violence.

The Need for a Civil Law and the Structure of the PWDVA

There were a lot of women who did not want to use the criminal law.[13] The absence of a civil law left them often without a remedy and rendered them homeless.

The major problem with criminal law is that the state vindicates the rights of the victim on her behalf. The survivor is cut out of the whole process of seeking justice. It is the prosecution which has the carriage of the proceedings and the burden of proving it. In civil law, by contrast, the woman never loses agency over decision-making. The rights of the survivors in a criminal trial are limited. There are constitutional guarantees under Article 20[14] to protect the rights of convicts, but the same paradigm cannot be used for the victims. There was therefore the need to put the victim centre stage and strengthen criminal remedies with additional civil remedies.

[12] Jaising, 'Concern for the Dead, Condemnation for the Living'.

[13] 498A IPC.

[14] Article 20 of the Indian Constitution: Protection in respect of conviction for offences: (*a*) No person shall be convicted of any offence except for violation of the law in force at the time of the commission of the act charged as an offence, nor be subjected to a penalty greater than that which might have been inflicted under the law in force at the time of the commission of the offence. (*b*) No person shall be prosecuted and punished for the same offence more than once. (*c*) No person accused of any offence shall be compelled to be a witness against himself.

There is no need to have a sharp divide between criminal and civil law. Both seek to achieve the same objective: to hold the wrongdoer accountable. It is the nature of relief that varies. Criminal law ends in conviction and incarceration of the accused, whereas civil law could provide monetary relief, custody of the children, and most importantly, residence orders. There is a line that divides criminal and civil remedies. The PWDVA does not delete the line. The civil and criminal reliefs in domestic violence can be concurrent, leaving it to the woman to select remedies most suited to her situation. At all times, the agency is with the women. She should have the right to choose what remedy she wants and which right she wants to exercise. The aim of the PWDVA was to tailor individual relief to the individual need of the woman based on her choice. Most importantly, for the first time, a married woman would have a stake in the shared household and feel a real sense of empowerment with the right to reside in the shared household.[15]

Within the women's movement there was a unanimous opinion that women were looking for a single-window clearance to deal with the issue of domestic violence. Women had to approach multiple forums for addressing their issues. Not every woman wanted a divorce: some just want to deal with the issue of custody; some wanted to deal with the issue of maintenance; some wanted a separation; and some just wanted the abuse to stop. There was not a single law, which addressed all these issues under a single forum. This was my motivation and driving force behind drafting the Domestic Violence Act; a woman should be able to choose her options without approaching multiple forums. Most importantly, it was necessary that the forum be accessible to women without having to pay a court fee. Hence, we situated the jurisdiction within the Magistrate's court, which we considered to be the most accessible forum for the survivors. The Magistrate was empowered to provide civil reliefs.

During the consultations, there was a felt need to extend the domain of the law to a multiplicity of household relationships and not just focus on marital relationships, to sisters who were denied access to the joint family home, mothers facing homelessness, and women in relationships in the nature of marriage. Given that marriage in India is not required to be registered, men

[15] Section 17 of the PWDVA: Right to reside in a shared household: (a) Notwithstanding anything contained in any other law for the time being in force, every woman in a domestic relationship shall have the right to reside in the shared household, whether or not she has any right, title, or beneficial interest in the same. (b) The aggrieved person shall not be evicted or excluded from the shared household or any part of it by the respondent, save in accordance with the procedure established by law.

in multiple marriages could deny to the 'second wife' any rights by simply saying that they never married her lawfully despite the fact that there were children from the 'second wife'. This, among other considerations, led to the inclusion of the provision giving rights to women in domestic relationships 'in the nature of marriage',[16] distinguishing them from women who were married in accordance with law.

Most importantly, this was a law of universal application regardless of the religion to which the woman belonged. It was the first attempt in the realm of family law to depart from the regime of 'personal laws' and recognize that women of all communities need protection from violence and had the right to reside in the shared household. Saptarshi Mandal traces the access to this law by Muslim women to establish its universal applicability in his chapter.

Challenges Faced in the Drafting and Enactment of the Law

Between 1998 and 2001, the LC started a dialogue within the women's movement on the need for a domestic violence legislation. A series of consultations were held throughout the country, women's groups were well-exposed to international conventions and hence there was a groundswell of opinion that there was a need for domestic violence legislation. Challenges were many—both at the stage of drafting and at the stage of it becoming the law. The definition of the 'respondent' was the most controversial. As originally drafted, a complaint could not be filed against a woman, including a mother-in-law. A contrary point of view was that if under Section 498A, a woman's parents-in-law could be prosecuted, there is no reason for the relatives of the husbands to be left out. This gave rise to the proviso to Section 2(q) of the PWDVA, which enables a complaint to be filed against a female family member of the male respondent.[17] Justice Rohinton Nariman seems to have missed the point.[18]

[16] Section 2(f) defines domestic relationship as follows: (f) 'domestic relationship' means a relationship between two persons who live or have, at any point of time, lived together in a shared household, when they are related by consanguinity, marriage, *or through a relationship in the nature of marriage*, adoption, or are family members living together as a joint family.

[17] Section 2(q) of the PWDVA: (q) 'respondent' means any adult male person who is, or has been, in a domestic relationship with the aggrieved person and against whom the aggrieved person has sought any relief under this Act: provided that an aggrieved wife or female living in a relationship in the nature of a marriage may also file a complaint against a relative of the husband or the male partner.

[18] *Hiral P. Harsora v. Kusum Narottamdas Harsora* (2016) 10 SCC 165.

The issue of gender-neutrality has always been a point of discussion from the inception of the law. For me, there was a complete rejection of dominant cultural, social, and political ideologies since the time I had seen women in my family get married according to those norms. Consultations during the drafting of the law with various women's organizations and empirical data revealed that the law had to be gender-specific due to the pervasive problem of gender inequality existing in the socio-cultural familial structures in India. Given the power relations in these structures, the men could use the domestic violence law to dispossess the women from home. Moreover, Article 15 of the Constitution of India empowers the state to take affirmative action and make special provisions for women and children.

Then comes the issue of gender-neutrality of the definition of the respondent. As mentioned above, during the consultations, it was felt that the new law had to be consistent with Section 498A IPC. Hence, under the PWDVA, an aggrieved woman could bring an action against a relative of the respondent.

The Supreme Court struck down 'adult male' from the definition of the respondent under Section 2(q) of the Act.[19] It stated: 'The classification of "adult male person" clearly subverts the doctrine of equality.' In a seeming attempt to do justice to women, he interpreted the definition of a 'respondent' to include all women, making it possible for a mother-in-law in a stand-alone application to file a complaint against her daughter-in-law for domestic violence. This was certainly not the intent of the law. Now, under the Nariman dispensation, a mother-in-law can file a collusive application against her daughter-in-law with her son, who she can say she has 'disowned' and seek to evict her from her home. The law has been made to stand on its head. Prior to this judgment, and as the definition stood, a mother-in-law could file a complaint against her daughter-in-law, provided she also made a complaint against her son stating that she was being ill-treated by them both. The judgment now enables the mother-in-law to act as a surrogate for her son, protect him, and exclude her daughter-in-law from the matrimonial home. In the name of gender neutrality, the judgment has reinforced patriarchal notions that the fight is always between a mother-in-law and a daughter-in-law. It has given the right to make anyone a respondent without making the male member a co-respondent and which goes against the spirit of the Act. The Supreme Court has overlooked the complicity between the mother and son in striking down the exception.

[19] *Hiral P. Harsora v. Kusum Narottamdas Harsora* (2016) 10 SCC 165.

The phenomenon of mothers 'disowning' their sons, only to deny the daughter-in-law access to the shared household, is now a familiar one, yet no court has said that this is 'misuse' of the law, while constantly mourning the fact that wives 'misuse' the law, a narrative constructed to protect the male privilege. On the other hand, adequate care was taken in the law to ensure that no woman should be rendered homeless even if that woman was a violent mother-in-law. No woman could be removed from a shared household.[20] The eviction of a woman regardless of her relationship to the woman complainant could not be sought as a relief.[21]

This shows how judges who appear to be progressive in making laws gender-neutral, end up disadvantaging the woman they seek to protect. This is the inability to see that the family is not an aggregation of the same interests, but that their rights have to be disaggregated and that is what the PWDVA seeks to do.

After this long exercise of meetings and consultations, the bill was submitted to the National Commission for Women, the Department of Women and Child Development, and other related departments. Thereafter, the National Democratic Alliance (NDA) propounded a bill called the 'Protection from Domestic Violence Bill, 2002' (hereinafter, GOI Bill) in the Lok Sabha. This meant that for the first time, there was some acknowledgement of the issue of domestic violence at the government level. However, the bill itself was a disappointment in terms of what it sought to do. The focus of the bill was the preservation of the family unit rather than stopping domestic violence against women. The critical issue of the definition of domestic violence was narrowed down to the scope of relief and sought inspiration from a 1939 law[22] which defined violence as conduct/assault habitual in nature, which made the life of

[20] Section 19 of the PWDVA states the following: (19) Residence orders: (a) While disposing of an application under sub-section (1) of section 12, the Magistrate may, on being satisfied that domestic violence has taken place, pass a residence order... (b) Directing the respondent to remove himself from the shared household;... Provided that no order under clause (b) shall be passed against any person who is a woman.

[21] Section 19 of the PWDVA states the following: (19) Residence orders: (*a*) While disposing of an application under sub-section (1) of section 12, the Magistrate may, on being satisfied that domestic violence has taken place, pass a residence order... (*b*) Directing the respondent to remove himself from the shared household;... Provided that no order under clause (b) shall be passed against any person who is a woman.

[22] Dissolution of Muslim Marriages Act, 1939.

the victim 'miserable'. A single act could not be termed as an act of domestic violence under the bill.[23] Terms such as 'cruelty' and 'misery' were not defined in the bill, leaving it vague and open to interpretation. Women in relationships other than legal marriages were excluded from the definition of an 'aggrieved person'. Section 4(2) of the bill allowed the respondent to take the plea of self-defence. The respondent could thus get away with brutally assaulting a woman on the pretext that such conduct was meant for his own protection or for the protection of his or even another person's property. The section was misplaced and betrayed mal-intent in protecting women form violence; after all, self-defence is available to the victim and not to the aggressor.

The 2002 bill had no provision granting a woman in an abusive relationship a right of residence. In the absence of any matrimonial or cohabitee property rights in India, the main aim of a prevention of domestic violence law must be to secure the right to reside for women. The bill also ignored the critical need for providing immediate interim relief and 'stop violence' orders nor did it provide a time frame for the proceedings to be completed. Further, it required mandatory counselling.[24]

Due to an obvious outrage against the bill, it was referred to the Parliamentary Standing Committee on Human Resource Development (HRD) for examination. The Committee invited comments and views on the bill from various stakeholders. The Parliamentary Standing Committee Report rejected the narrow definition of domestic violence.[25] The Committee stated that the primary concern was to provide relief to women in recognition of their right to live with dignity and therefore women outside marital relationships should also be covered by the Act.[26] Further, it struck

[23] The Protection from Domestic Violence Bill, 2001.

[24] For a detailed critique of the GOI bill, see Indira Jaising, 'Bringing Rights Home: Review of the Campaign for a Law on Domestic Violence', *Economic and Political Weekly* XLIV, 44 (2009): 54–5.

[25] Department-Related Parliamentary Standing Committee On Human Resource Development Hundred—Twenty-Fourth Report On The Protection From Domestic Violence Bill, 2002, available at http://164.100.47.5/rs/book2/reports/HRD/Report124th.htm

[26] Department-Related Parliamentary Standing Committee On Human Resource Development Hundred—Twenty-Fourth Report On The Protection From Domestic Violence Bill, 2002: '*Moreover, the issue of domestic violence is more proximate with the basic human rights of a woman to live a dignified life. Therefore, providing relief under the present Bill to a woman whose marriage is not legally valid won't be in conflict with the existing laws and will not give any legal sanction to the illegal marriages*'.

down the need for the plea of self-defence,[27] recognized the right to reside in a shared household, and asked for better enforcement mechanisms to be included in the Act.[28]

Despite the active involvement and campaigns by the women's organizations, there was no initiative from the government to reformulate the bill in terms of the suggestions made by the Standing Committee. In February 2004, with the dissolution of the Lok Sabha, the bill lapsed. It was during the election of 2004 that many non-governmental organizations (NGOs) suggested that the United Progressive Alliance (UPA) promise the enactment of the Domestic Violence Act in their common minimum programme, which they did.[29] After coming into power, the promise was redeemed with the enactment of the PWDVA.

While Uma Chakravarti traces the long history of inequality towards women and their exclusion from social spaces, Asmita Basu in her chapter traces the history of the engagement of women's movement with law reform on the subject.

In June 2005, the draft Protection of Women from Domestic Violence Bill received cabinet approval and the bill was tabled in the Parliament in July of that year. Certain members of the house expressed reservations regarding the inclusion of 'relationships in the nature of marriage' within the purview of protected categories of women under the law. It was said that the concept was alien to *Bharatiya sanskriti* (Indian culture), which would send across the wrong message to society. They need not be worried. In her chapter, Brototi

[27] Department-Related Parliamentary Standing Committee On Human Resource Development Hundred—Twenty-Fourth Report On The Protection From Domestic Violence Bill, 2002: '*It is of the considered opinion that there are sufficient provisions in the existing criminal and civil laws to take care of the right to defence and there is no need to provide the same in the Bill and unnecessarily overburden it*'.

[28] Department-Related Parliamentary Standing Committee On Human Resource Development Hundred—Twenty-Fourth Report On The Protection From Domestic Violence Bill, 2002: '*The Committee however, feels that there should be specific mention about the right to residence of the aggrieved person in matrimonial home in the Protection order passed by the Magistrate*'.

[29] National Common Minimum Programme of the UPA government, available at http://nceuis.nic.in/NCMP.htm: 'The UPA government will take the lead to introduce legislation for one-third reservations for women in vidhan sabhas and in the Lok Sabha. Legislation on domestic violence and against gender discrimination will be enacted'.

Dutta points out that Justice Katju in Veluswamy[30] held that women who are in live-in relationships are 'keeps'. Aside from the ambiguous moral judgment Katju J also forgets a central fact—only property, not humans of either gender—can be kept. Dutta deals with the law relating to conjugality tracing it back to almost a century of development.

Basu, working through the history of law reform, concludes that there has been an excessive reliance on criminal law at the cost of civil law. Sitting in the Parliament during the passage of the bill, we were amused at the fact that every political party fielded a woman Member of Parliament to support the bill, the maximum attendance of male MPs being when Jaya Prada addressed the Parliament on behalf of the Samajwadi Party in support of the bill. The bill was unanimously passed by the Lok Sabha on 22 August 2005 and by the Rajya Sabha on 24 August 2005. On 13 September, it received the assent of the president and the PWDVA, 2005 entered the statute book.

Domestic Violence Act: A Promise of Non-Discrimination

Article 15 of the Constitution[31] guarantees protection of women in one major way: it prohibits discrimination based on sex. In relation to domestic violence, we draw inspiration from the general comments by Committee on Elimination of Discrimination Against Women (CEDAW).[32] The guarantee of non-discrimination, most importantly, includes freedom from violence. The law on non-discrimination has been developed over time to include both direct and indirect discrimination. It also requires due-diligence on behalf of the state to prevent the occurrence of violence against women.

There are various limitations of the adversarial system. The judge does not play an active role, but is an umpire. The person who approaches the

[30] *D. Velusamy v. D. Patchaiammal* (2010) 10 SCC 469: 'If a man has a "keep" whom he maintains financially and uses mainly for sexual purpose and/or as a servant it would not, in our opinion, be a relationship in the nature of marriage'.

[31] Article 15 (1) of the Constitution states the following: (15) Prohibition of discrimination on grounds of religion, race, caste, sex, or place of birth. (a) The State shall not discriminate against any citizen on grounds only of religion, race, caste, sex, place of birth or any, of them.

[32] Convention on the Elimination of All Forms of Discrimination against Women, available at http://www.ohchr.org/Documents/ProfessionalInterest/cedaw.pdf.

court carries the whole burden of proving her case. The PWDVA has therefore been carefully crafted to eliminate such technical limitations. It has been placed in a civil jurisdiction, where judges are required to play an active role. The requirement of due diligence of the state was given shape by introducing the concept of protection officers. A state-mandated assistance to the survivor ensured that evidence could be collected and presented to the court without burdening the victim.[33] The protection officers were envisaged to be the eyes and ears of the court. The proactive role played by the protection officers ensured fair reporting and prevented husbands from lying in court about their assets. It was a remarkable departure from the adversarial

[33] Section 9 of the PWDVA lays down the duties of the protection officers: (9) Duties and functions of protection officers: (a) It shall be the duty of the protection officer—

(1) to assist the Magistrate in the discharge of his functions under this Act;
(2) to make a domestic incident report to the Magistrate, in such form and in such manner as may be prescribed, upon receipt of a complaint of domestic violence and forward copies thereof to the police officer in charge of the police station within the local limits of whose jurisdiction domestic violence is alleged to have been committed and to the service providers in that area;
(3) to make an application in such form and in such manner as may be prescribed to the Magistrate, if the aggrieved person so desires, claiming relief for issuance of a protection order;
(4) to ensure that the aggrieved person is provided legal aid under the Legal Services Authorities Act, 1987 (39 of 1987) and make available free of cost the prescribed form in which a complaint is to be made;
(5) to maintain a list of all service providers providing legal aid or counselling, shelter homes, and medical facilities in a local area within the jurisdiction of the Magistrate;
(6) to make available a safe shelter home, if the aggrieved person so requires and forward a copy of his report of having lodged the aggrieved person in a shelter home to the police station and the Magistrate having jurisdiction in the area where the shelter home is situated;
(7) to get the aggrieved person medically examined, if she has sustained bodily injuries and forward a copy of the medical report to the police station and the Magistrate having jurisdiction in the area where the domestic violence is alleged to have been taken place;
(8) to ensure that the order for monetary relief under section 20 is complied with and executed, in accordance with the procedure prescribed under the Code of Criminal Procedure, 1973 (2 of 1974);
(9) to perform such other duties as may be prescribed.

system. In the initial phases of the implementation of the Act, protection officers were meeting the survivors, drafting and filing the petitions, appearing and arguing the matter in courts. Specifically, in Andhra Pradesh, the government played a pioneering role in training, awareness programmes, and budget allocations.[34]

The problem arose in the limited role and power granted to the protection officer. The exclusive privilege of lawyers to appear in court denies the protection officer the right to appear and articulate their views, once they have conducted their investigation. It is therefore the need of the hour to enable better implementation by amending the Advocates Act, 1961 giving paralegals the power to address the court in matters of social legislations. The direct interaction with the survivor actually informs the protection officer of the true situation in the shared household.

It is imperative to understand that the law tries to bring about a synergy between NGOs, shelter homes, protection officers, and medical facilities to support the survivor. The roles are distinct yet complementary to each other in the ultimate aim of protecting and aiding the survivor. However, in an effort to defeat this coordinating role, in 2014, a circular was issued in Maharashtra that NGOs providing hands on support to women were prohibited from providing counselling or mediation services without the directions of the court. A writ petition was filed for setting aside this circular. Women's organizations opposed this circular and submitted a report contending that it is due to the support and services rendered by NGOs that women come forward to report domestic violence. The circular restricted the violated woman's avenues of using mechanisms provided by the law for redressal of her grievance. Counselling is a remedy in itself where women are offered a neutral, non-judgmental, safe place to decide their course of action. The Bombay High Court held the circular issued by the state of Maharashtra to be arbitrary and unreasonable and hence allowed the petition for quashing the circular.[35] A declaration of non-discrimination is therefore not enough; it is only when the state will play an active role in the implementation of beneficial legislations such as allocating a generous amount for gender initiative, initiating awareness, and training programmes, will the guarantee of non-discrimination be redeemed.

The synergy between service providers and state agencies has a long history within the women's movement. Beginning with a complete rejection

[34] Lawyers Collective, Staying Alive: Second Monitoring and Evaluation Report, 2008 on the Protection of Women from Domestic Violence Act, 2005, p. 24.

[35] *Dr Jaya Sagade v. State of Maharashtra* (2015) SCC On Line Bom 4777.

of the police and its role in stopping domestic violence, women's groups gradually developed a sense of self-confidence to coordinate their efforts with those of the police under Section 498A of the IPC and later the PWDVA. The coordination took multiple forms: some NGOs offered to operate out of the police station or be available on call, as in Rajasthan, others set up special cells within police stations using the authority of the police to mediate the conflict, as did Tata Institute of Social Sciences (TISS) in Mumbai. This latter pattern was replicated in many police stations across the country. However, in a bizarre distortion of institutional framework established by the autonomous women's movement, the Rajasthan government has outsourced this role of mediation within the police station to the Durga Wahini who, with their misogynist ideology, remain focussed on the subordinate role of a wife in a marriage, ensure that no legal action is taken and the woman who complains of violence is compelled to get back into gains of the last few decades. We now live in the era of one-stop crisis centres which ought to be professionally managed centres to deal with all forms of violence against women. Sangeeta Rege and Padma Bhate-Deosthali have traced the evolution of the one-stop crisis centres which have taken on the role of providing support services, establishing their lineage in the history of the movement which gave birth to women's centres providing legal services to women in distress.

Importance of the Concept of Shared Household

The first, and most common, manifestation of domestic violence is throwing out of the woman from the matrimonial home. The second most common was to kill her. Under Indian Law, a married woman had lesser right to reside in the shared household than a tenant or a trespasser. Section 6 of the Specific Relief Act[36] protected a person in possession of property

[36] Section 6 of the Specific Relief Act: Suit by person dispossessed of immovable property: (a) If any person is dispossessed without his consent of immovable property otherwise than in due course of law, he or any person claiming through him may, by suit, recover possession thereof, notwithstanding any other title that may be set up in such suit. (b) No suit under this section shall be brought,

(1) after the expiry of six months from the date of dispossession; or
(2) against the government;
(3) no appeal shall lie from any order or decree passed in any suit instituted under this section, nor shall any review of any such order or decree be allowed;

from being evicted except by due process of law. Section 17 of the Domestic Violence Act[37] was put in place to give a married woman and a woman in a relationship in the nature of marriage the same right to reside in the shared household. There is a long way to go before women get equal rights to matrimonial property. The Act was the first legislation of its kind to introduce the concept of shared household[38] and the right to residence of a woman in a shared relationship. The impetus for framing the law in such a manner was the tradition of joint family systems in India; several generations of a family could be living under the same roof. It also indicates that the economic conditions of India do not permit most married couples to have an independent home as soon as they marry.

The definition of 'shared household' is significant. It arose out of the need to delink the concept of ownership of property from the use of it for residential purpose. This is a very important distinction that runs through the fabric of law. People who have possession of property also have rights, although, they may not have ownership. Now, moving our focus very specifically to married women: Indian family structure is patrilocal in nature. After marriage, a woman leaves her natal home and comes into her husband's house. She does not enter her husband's home as a trespasser and it is not necessary for her to have ownership of that home. She has conjugal rights and by virtue

---

(5) nothing in this section shall bar any person from suing to establish his title to such property and to recover possession thereof.

[37] Article 20 of the Indian Constitution: Protection in respect of conviction for offences: (*a*) No person shall be convicted of any offence except for violation of the law in force at the time of the commission of the act charged as an offence, nor be subjected to a penalty greater than that which might have been inflicted under the law in force at the time of the commission of the offence. (*b*) No person shall be prosecuted and punished for the same offence more than once. (*c*) No person accused of any offence shall be compelled to be a witness against himself.

[38] Section 2(s) of the PWDVA: 'shared household' means a household where the person aggrieved lives or at any stage has lived in a domestic relationship either singly or along with the respondent and includes such a household whether owned or tenanted either jointly by the aggrieved person and the respondent, or owned or tenanted by either of them in respect of which either the aggrieved person or the respondent or both jointly or singly have any right, title, interest, or equity and includes such a household which may belong to the joint family of which the respondent is a member, irrespective of whether the respondent or the aggrieved person has any right, title, or interest in the shared household.

of those conjugal rights, she has a right to reside in the matrimonial home. Recognizing this very conjugal right of residence, the expression 'shared household' was defined in a way so as to delink ownership and possession. The words 'whether the respondent or the aggrieved person has any right, title or interest in the shared household' were added to the definition because the technical aspect of ownership cannot be allowed to defeat the purpose of the law and to decide on the right of residence.

The PWDVA was the first glimmer of recognition of the concept of 'shared household' and was an amazingly empowering section. Suddenly, a woman realized that she is entitled, she has rights, she has negotiating power, she has agency, and she has a voice that should be heard without the fear of being thrown out. In her chapter, Pinki Mathur Anurag links the right to residence with the right to adequate housing under international law, demonstrating that empowering effect of the right to reside for domestic violence survivors.

Going back to the concept of shared household, in the Taruna Batra[39] case, the daughter-in-law, Taruna Batra, was claiming a right of residence in a house, which was owned by her mother-in-law. It was an admitted fact that Taruna and her husband Amit Batra, were residing in the second floor of the house after their marriage. Taruna moved to her parent's house due to disputes with her husband. When she tried to move back into the matrimonial home, the locks had been changed. She managed to take possession of the house and filed for an injunction restraining her in-laws from interfering with her possession of the said property. The in-laws declared in their affidavit that their son was no longer residing with them and had moved to Ghaziabad, Uttar Pradesh. The Delhi High Court held that the mere change of residence of the husband would not change the matrimonial home. The Court further held that Taruna was entitled to reside on the second floor by virtue of her right to residence.[40] The Supreme Court overruled the decision of the High Court. The Supreme Court held that the house did not belong to her husband and therefore Taruna could not claim a right to live in that house.

That issue with the Supreme Court's ruling in the Taruna Batra case is that they failed to delink the concept of ownership from possession. The judge ignored the words 'whether the respondent or the aggrieved person has any right, title or interest in the shared household'. He went back to linking

[39] *S.R. Batra and Anr. v. Taruna Batra*, AIR 2007 SC 1118.

[40] *Smt. Taruna Batra v. S.R. Batra*, AIR 2005 Delhi 270.

the entitlement of residence to ownership, factoring in ownership as the single most important element to decide the right to reside in a shared space. He seemed to be suggesting that if the ownership of the property is with the parents-in-law, the daughter-in-law does not have a right to reside in that property. Further, the judge held that the phrase 'lived or has lived' in the definition of 'shared household' would lead to absurd results, with the woman claiming several places as her 'shared household' on the ground that she had lived there 'at some point of time' or the other.[41] Apart from completely going against the statute, the judgment does not make sociological, legal, or economic sense. The tragedy of the situation is that what the legislature achieved in the law, making a quantum shift from the concept of ownership and creating the right to residence, was erased by this judgment. In a subsequent case[42] before the Delhi High Court, although Justice Sikri was bound by the holding of the Taruna Batra case, he held that even if the daughter-in-law had no right of residence in the house that belonged to her in-laws, she could not be removed from the possession without due process of law.[43] It was a very progressive judgment, but it was manipulated to act against daughters-in-law. Hundreds of suits were filed by in-laws in civil courts stating that the property belonged to them and that they wanted to dispossess the daughter-in-law of the suit property. Parents-in-laws also put out ads in the newspapers declaring that they had disowned their sons. Husbands were also taking property on rent. These tactics were used just to produce evidence in court to prove that the son was no longer the member of the household. Once the husband moved out, it was easier for him to abandon the wife. This was due process and how it was manipulated to defeat the purpose of the legislation. This is how the Taruna Batra judgment rendered the due process a mockery of the law. Due process only works when the coordinate substantive provisions also work. After all, due process is in aid of substantive provisions and is not a standalone provision. There is a critical assumption for the success of due process, which is that the duties imposed by the substantive provisions and the rights enshrined in law are voluntarily respected by those upon whom the duty is cast. The law

[41] Jaising, 'Bringing Rights Home: Review of the Campaign for a Law on Domestic Violence'.

[42] *Smt. Shumita Didi Sandhu v. Mr Sanjay Singh Sandhu and Ors.* (2007) 96 DRJ 697.

[43] *Smt. Shumita Didi Sandhu v. Mr Sanjay Singh Sandhu and Ors*: '*However, statement of defendant No. 2 was recorded by the Court under Order X CPC where he stated that he or his wife had no intention to throw her out of the premises in question without due process of law. Therefore, while dismissing the applications of the plaintiff, it is ordered that the defendant Nos. 1 and 2 shall remain bound by the said statement*'.

comes in, when those on whom the duties are imposed do not honour the duties, and hopefully that should be an aberration and an exception to the rule. My critique of the Taruna Batra judgment is not just confined to the fact that the judgment itself is wrong because it ignored the letter of the law, but also that it gave birth to a manipulative process which subverted the law and enabled the due process provision to be misused in order to defeat the law. The critical link between the substantive law and due process was broken. When due process is used as a tool to manipulate the system and is misused, it ceases to be due process. It is the people who manipulate due process that misuse the law and not the women. Further, when the abuse of due process becomes a pattern, then it is time to recalibrate both the substantive and the due process provisions of the law. It is time to make course corrections and understand what is it in the due process provisions that made it possible for this provision to be misused, and the answer is not just in dealing with an isolated instance of misuse. It is no longer an isolated misuse once it becomes a pattern.

Luckily, many judges understood the dangers of the Taruna Batra judgment and went beyond the judgment, distinguishing the fact scenario from the Taruna Batra judgment.[44]

On Misuse

The provisions of laws are being overlooked and undermined in practice and women are constantly being accused of misusing the law. No court has defined misuse of Section 498A in specific terms. An obvious example of the misuse would be making relatives of the husband respondents in a cruelty case where the relatives are not residing in the same country and have nothing to do with the abuse. The problem with judgments, specifically the Arnesh Kumar[45] and more recently the Rajesh Sharma[46] rulings is that what is specific to one fact scenario has been generalized to state that all women misuse the law.

If an individual woman does misuse the law, it is within the power of the court to delete the name of the said relatives from the proceedings through a quashing petition. It is true that sometimes police and even lawyers

[44] Lawyers Collective, Staying Alive: 5th Monitoring and Evaluation 2012 on the Protection of Women from Domestic Violence, p. 169. Also detailed in Chapter 6.

[45] *Arnesh Kumar v. State of Bihar* (2014) 8 SCC 273.

[46] *Rajesh Sharma v. State of U.P.* (2017) SCC On Line SC 821.

encourage women to put a narrative which they think will work with the courts, such as dowry-demands.[47] They sometimes fail to understand that Section 498A goes beyond dowry demands and covers mental harassment too. In addition to this being the wrong legal strategy, it is unethical too. I have seen in my years of practice that the most credible narrative is when you stick to the basic facts because that is the true narrative. The judges understand that narrative.

Where the judges fail us, it is not because they do not understand that narrative, but it is the extraneous factors of bias which disappoint us. What they bring onto the table is their bias of the concept of marriage being sacred, of women's duty to be obedient and subservient to her husband and in-laws. It is pertinent that in cases like this, experts who understand sociology of the family, causes and consequences of domestic violence, and narratives of women be appointed as *amicus curiae*, which the court failed to do. The approach of the court undermined the functions of the protection officers and the police. It corrupted the jurisprudence of law. The judges relied upon the data of the National Crime Record Bureau (NCRB) of 2005, 2012, and 2013. Relying on the figures of the number of people arrested, convicted, and acquitted, it concluded that since the conviction rate is low, most of the cases registered under 498A are 'false'. These data do not give a clear picture as there can be a number of reasons for acquittal, such as poor investigation by the investigating officer, settlement through mediation, or intimidation of witnesses and the complainant herself.

It is nobody's case that if an individual woman has lied or has falsely implicated a relative of the husband, she should be supported or that the courts should decide in her favour. But to brand women as a class of liars is where the error lies. Section 498A questions patriarchy and this seems to be the response of the court, who take it as their moral duty to 'save the institution of marriage'. The misuse argument often spills over to the PWDVA. As there is no issue of arrest under the Act, the central issue revolves around property. This, again, is another stronghold of patriarchy: that property should remain in the hands of the male members of the family. The PWDVA becomes very critical in dismantling patriarchy. Woman's right to demand a fair share in the assets of the family is labelled as misuse. The basis of the argument is the same—the refusal to give up patriarchy.

[47] In cases where domestic violence did not specifically include or did not extend to demands for dowry.

***

It is indeed very encouraging to see that the PWDVA has been widely used; this is an indicator of its success. It has been an empowering legislation, particularly the right to residence provision. A few limitations of the usage of the law have emerged that it is being used primarily by married women and not all the other categories of women in domestic relationships that the Act seeks to protect. Monica Sakhrani and Tripti Panchal, in their chapter, explain their success and their disappointments with the law, in their own voice.

The other disappointment is that the protection officers are no longer working in an efficient manner as they were during the early years of implementation. The reasons lie in the negligence of the state towards specific gender initiatives. The government has failed to create a separate cadre of protection officers. Further, one cannot dissociate the role that patriarchy plays. For example, the rules state that counselling can only take place when an injunction is granted preventing the respondent from committing any act of violence.[48] The idea is that counselling can only take place when there is a level playing field and the level playing field can be created by this order restraining the respondent from committing further acts of violence. Survivors often complain that the protection officers often tell them to go back to the matrimonial home or to opt for conciliation.

Kanika Kaul explains in her chapter[49] that the inadequate nature of gender budgeting is one of the main contributors for non-implantation of the Act in letter and spirit. The state therefore has to take proactive measures in evolving the institutional structures and put a national action plan in place for the implementation of the Domestic Violence Act. There should be protocols and standard operating procedures put in place for shelter homes, protection officers, and NGOs to ensure elimination of bias.

The feminist movement has gone through several phases in its engagement with the state. The first phase saw a total rejection of the state

[48] Rule 14(3)of the PWDVA, 2006: The factors warranting counselling shall include the factor that the respondent shall furnish an undertaking that he would refrain from causing such domestic violence as complained by the complainant and in appropriate cases an undertaking that he will not try to meet, or communicate in any manner through letter or telephone, electronic mail or through any medium except in the counselling proceedings before the counsellor or as permissibly by law or order of a court of competent jurisdiction.

[49] Conclusion of this book.

machineries, including the police. Then it moved into a phase where they considered working with the institutions of the state. TISS social workers were placed within police stations in the mid-1990s, and they worked with the institution of states. The format was used differently in different states but the role was the same: to act as the first interface of interaction between the survivor and the police. The third phase has seen the elimination of the progressive women's alliances out of the police stations. They have been replaced by organizations such as the Durga Wahini. The driving force behind this is politics. The progressive forces of the women's movement are not being allowed to mould and shape the law. The one-stop crisis centres do not synergize with the existing structures in place. They end up adding to the burden of the survivor to repeat her narrative to yet another stakeholder in the system. In our search for a solution, we could be falling between stones.

In the midst of all this, the profile of the Indian woman is also changing; she is beginning to reject patriarchal norms and wants to get out from the marriage. More women are opting out of marriage by mutual consent, rather than clinging on to a violent relationship. The stigma of being divorced is slowly disappearing. Dignity for women is a more sought-after goal, rather than the status of being married. While this reality has changed, the mindset of the courts and other state functionaries is yet to follow suit.

2. *Some Thoughts on Domestic Violence*

Using Violence to Regulate a Patriarchal Family

UMA CHAKRAVARTI

If a wife, a son, or slave, a menial servant, or full brother has committed an offence, they may be beaten with a rope, or a split bamboo cane but only on the back of the body.[1]

The offence would be defined in terms of patriarchal and caste norms, because those would be the norms of Brahmanical society; the husband was a woman's God; obedience to him was the defining feature of a wife's daily conduct.

The drum, the uneducated, the animal, the shudra and the woman are deserving of beatings:

Popular saying attributed to Tulasidas, sixteenth-century devotee of Rama who wrote eight versions of the Ramayana.

[1] *The Laws of Manu*, trans. Wendy Doniger with Brian Smith (Delhi: Penguin Books, 1992), p. 184.

From nineteenth-century women's writings:

Narayanrao Tilak's account of his mother's death, the mother wrote poetry which the father hated:

> *Mother returned from her bath at the well with a heavy brass pot full of water for the cooking and her washing slung on her shoulder. Father was seated at the door. Mother said to him 'would you lift down the water pot from my head?' As the words fell on father's ears, like a tiger he assailed her. 'I am not your servant he cried'. Then he seized her by the throat and kicked her from behind. With an invocation to Ram she fell to the ground. The children were in a frenzy of terror at the sight and began to weep....*
>
> *For eight days mother never spoke a word except Ram, nor ate nor drank anything except water. On the eighth day leaving her husband a widower and the children to the care of the world, she passed away breathing Ram, Ram!*

The father was remorseful; he took his wife's ashes to the Godavari river but life went on: there were no consequences, legal or social, as we might see from the next generation's handling of conjugal relations. Thus, despite the account of Tilak's mother's death at the hands of his father, which devastated Narayan Tilak; he himself was quick to anger and acts of violence in that state: one day he was playing *Songtya*, a game, with his young wife and began to lose; his young wife was not exactly fearful at such a display of anger, laughing at the absurdity of the anger, at which Narayan Tilak became furious. In that state, he pushed her in the dark. Lakshmi fell down the flight of stairs till the landing broke her fall: she was seven months pregnant at the time.

Tilak, who normally wrote poetry, wrote a farce about his own temper after the fall. Lakshmi concludes the account of the violent end to the game in her autobiography with the words: 'It [the farce] was left half finished!'[2]

Another account from the nineteenth century comes from the famous young woman named Anandibai Joshi, who was the first woman to graduate as a doctor and was celebrated as the very embodiment of a perfect Hindu wife because she never said anything controversial in public. At the age of 21 she wrote thus of her relationship with her husband in a letter to him, describing the violence she experienced at his hands from the age of 10 when she was married off to him. However, she never spoke of the violence in public, thereby allowing his image of a loving and supportive husband to stand and circulate in the public sphere.

[2] Summarized from Lakshmibai Tilak, *I Follow After: An Autobiography* (Bombay: Oxford University Press, 1950), pp. 21–2, 52–3.

> I pleaded with you to end my existence. There is nothing in the law to stop such things against women, if there is any [law/rules] they work against women. Therefore, I had no option but to bear everything silently. A Hindu woman has no right to speak even a word against her husband or to advise him. She has only the 'right' to allow her husband to do what he wants and remain silent.[3]

Part I

In the year 1982, my ex-student, Nandita Haksar, and I went to the Santhal Parganas as part of a larger team to investigate a case of state repression against poor coal miners who were running a people's mine that had been bulldozed by the state. The coal miners had lost their livelihood and were subjected to all the measures a state takes to crush a movement of workers.

During the day, we investigated the incident where we talked to hordes of men who gave us an account of the political work they had done, or were doing, but there were hardly any women we met in these sessions. One night we asked our hosts to organize a meeting with the women; though somewhat surprised they did set up a meeting. We arrived after it was dark; with no lights, we could hardly see the women nor they us. The conversation we began with them was going nowhere.

Failing to get the conversation going Nandita fired a salvo: Do your men beat you? I waited with bated breath to hear the answer and was completely stumped when I heard someone say: 'Yes, when we make a mistake'. While I dithered, Nandita shot back: 'Do you beat them when they make a mistake?' Some women gasped, others giggled, and an excited chatter broke out. We then moved on to other issues but the explanation given by the woman for being subjected to violent action by the men and Nandita's response has stayed with me. In this way, many women think of the beatings and battering they receive and the violence that is routinely unleashed upon them is something they have precipitated: the rationalization of the violence is so sedimented that it has become the norm for men to be violent, and for women to be subjected to it, so there is little outrage, or resistance to it; everyone thinks it is the norm and so it must be alright. Men will be violent within the home (and outside too) and women will simply bear it, because that is how it has been and that is how it is going to be. All other forms

[3] Uma Chakravarti, *Rewriting History: The Life and Times of Pandita Ramabai* (Delhi: Kali for Women, 1998), p. 213.

of violence against women have become criminal acts; only violence within the home, perpetrated by men of the household (except for murder) especially since colonial times, has more or less stayed outside the purview of legal redress, both in colonial times and after independence too. After all, the infamous statement made by Judge Gidumal—on the equality of men and women in the eyes of the state and as guaranteed by the Constitution—were thrown into the dustbin when he stated that the the cold principles of constitutional law entering the bedroom was akin to 'letting loose a bull in a China shop'.[4] The sanctity of personal laws in constitutional freedoms has meant that religion-based ideologies of patriarchal control over women by fathers and husbands has sedimented the view that the domestic space was considered outside the purview of constitutional guarantees including the right to be safe from bodily harm.

It is clear then that historically, socially, and culturally, there has been a complete normalization of the violence men inflict upon women within the household: husbands, fathers, brothers all use violence when their self-assumed authority seems to be challenged. Since women live under the authority of the men of the family—as Manu so succinctly stated in the Dharmashastra attributed to him—in childhood, women live under the authority of the father, in marriage under that of the husband, and when widowed under that of the son, a woman can never be independent.[5] Since men have power over women, and that includes the right to use violence, women have internalized the normality of the violence as a consequence of having done something wrong, whether they are aware of it or not. Therefore, they

[4] *Harvinder Kaur v. Harmender Singh Chaudhar*, AIR 1984 Del. 66:'Introduction of constitutional law in the home is most inappropriate. It is like introducing a bull in a china shop. It will prove to be a ruthless destroyer of the marriage institution and all that it stands for. In the privacy of the home and the married life neither Article 21 nor Article 14 have anyplace. In a sensitive sphere which is at once most intimate and delicate the introduction of the cold principles of constitutional law will have the effect of weakening the marriage bond. That the restitution remedy was abolished in England in 1970 by Section 20 of the Matrimonial Proceedings and Properties Act, 1970 on the recommendation of the Law Commission headed by Justice Sharman is no ground to hold that it is unconstitutional in the Indian set-up. In the home, the consideration that really obtains is that natural love and affection which counts for so little in these cold courts. Constitutional law principles find no place in the domestic code' (*Harvinder Kaur v. Harmender Singh Chaudhary*, AIR 1984 Del. 66 at Para 33: 'Introduction of....)

[5] *The Laws of Manu*, p. 197.

do not speak about the violence as it is associated with some wrongdoing on their part. This was so until we came to a point when we, a new generation of women, began to question that violence. I can remember an incident from my adolescent days when my father, a normally mild-mannered man who never ever touched us ever in his life after we were no longer little girls, did occasionally display his temper when he perceived us to be 'recalcitrant' in some way. One day my sister said/did something that was perceived to be provocative, suggesting insubordination. My father lifted his hand to hit her, but as he did so, my sister suddenly grabbed his hand—while it was mid-air—and said with great firmness: 'Don't! I have now reached the age when no man has the right to touch me without my permission!' My father's raised hand froze in mid-air. Then it dropped and he went away without a word. Perhaps he was ashamed that my sister had to defend herself with such words in order to stop the demeaning beating of a young girl by a man under whose protective authority she lived, but who thought that he could only display his authority by raising his hand against her, because others too routinely did that.

I have never forgotten those words and my father[6] never again raised his hand against us. I have often recounted this incident to others to make

[6] My father was actually an incredibly unusual man: born in 1898 he had paid off the family debts and remained unmarried till the age of 36 so that he could end the family's debt-ridden condition while his brothers claimed their inability to do so because they were all married. Many years later he recounted to me his misery at not being able to ensure that his destitute sister and widowed mother could live a life of dignity because they stayed in the village home with other brothers and were dependent on them for even their basic necessities. This led him to be a champion of women's education and insisted that all his daughters studied and then worked so that they could stand on their feet and never ask for money from their husbands whether they lived with them or led their own lives independently though married. This has led me to feel outraged when women have to beg for maintenance—auratein kyuna pneshoharon ke tukdo par palen [why should women have to live on the pieces of food their husbands throw at them]; the state must give social security to all its citizens enabling them to live with dignity. He was furious with me for resigning my permanent job as a school teacher after I made a marriage of my own choice because my partner was doing fieldwork in a village and I thought I should be with him. He saw no reason for us to not have a vacation marriage so he wasn't into the notion of a romantic conjugality at all. He wrote me only a few letters, always on post cards, and the proudest of them was when I finished my PhD; the post card was addressed to Dr Uma Chakravarti, MA PhD. He thought any woman who had a job but did not seriously pursue her career was useless and dismissed them as mere cook masters so

the point about protective custody, and the normalization of the right to use violence against daughters, wives, sisters which have historically gone unchallenged. I am, therefore, outraged when I see newspaper headlines such as: 'Woman loses nose for disobedience', or 'Woman killed for refusing to heat food for husband'; but as the story proceeds, the newspaper report tells you that the woman whose nose was slashed by her husband wanted to stay on at her father's place for the wedding festivities of her sister. Or that an inebriated husband came home when his was wife was fast asleep and demanded that she heat the food or/and have sex with her. What the headline tells us instead is that the violence is about a recalcitrant woman who has *provoked* her husband in some way. It is no wonder, then, that the famous case of Kiranjeet Ahluwalia who was subjected to terrible violence by her husband, and killed him when he was asleep, was titled 'The Provoked Wife' when it came out as a film because all violence by men against women had been viewed as provocation by the wife; in this film, the title inverted the way violence was normally viewed. Unfortunately, unless the violence is extreme, or extremely brutal and sustained, it seems to deserve no attention or no remedy because cultural codes put a lid on male violence against women as a matter that is to be remedied in some way by family members if it gets too bad, so that the family can go on as before and still be regarded as the space where affective relations rule out power or conflictual material interests.

It was girls like my sister who changed the way the domestic space was viewed as the closed space, the 'inside the family' space, and thereby opened it up for re-inscription. They did that by demanding that the home must be subjected to the acid test of whether it was a space where a girl/woman had a right to be free of violence, a right to be free of bodily harm like every other space in the world. In the late 1960s and from then onwards, feminists across the globe brought the family under the scrutiny of public gaze. There were speaking sessions where feminists were able to dump the unwritten code of silence that was imposed on wives, daughters, sisters, even mothers and grandmothers, and laid bare the multiple types of physical harm they were routinely subjected to.

In an insightful study of domestic violence, based on documents in the Boston area comprising case records for a period stretching over 50 years,

---

he didn't believe that his daughters should only be housewives and reproducers of the family although I'm sure he didn't understand the feminist theories of unpaid domestic labour and social reproduction.

Linda Gordon,[7] a first-generation women's studies scholar, who is a very fine historian, plots the slow incremental way in which women sought the protection of the local officials in their town as they battled the violence of their husbands. The acts of violence included the battering of children and went all the way to demands that ranged from better housekeeping, good cooking, and sex on demand and of their choice from their wives. This way the batterers turned themselves into the aggrieved party rather than be seen as violent men displaying their power over women.

Nor was wife-battering a phenomenon associated with class,[8] or with social groups such as immigrant populations where it was tolerated as a male privilege to hit in order to 'punish' wives. Early feminists, drawing their views from suffragette campaigns for the vote, directly took on wife-beating as a political struggle to break the existing pattern of social beliefs in which 'though wife-beating was not considered legitimate, public discussion of it was also not considered legitimate'. They brought it into the open and showed how endemic it was even among women of considerable social standing. Myths about wife-beating as a consequence of drinking which placed it in a male culture of recreation and kept it defined in trivial and fatalistic terms were also demolished as struggles were launched to advocate for the 'right' not to be beaten. In the end, women's resistance showed local authorities and wider society the very real and endemic violence against women in the household. They sought the protection of the authorities first on behalf of their children and then on behalf of themselves as protectors of their children, asking for restraining orders and even interventions by the police to stay on in the home without being subjected to bodily harm.

[7] Linda Gordon, *Heroes of Our Own Lives: The Politics and History of Family Violence* (London: Virago Books, 1988), Chapter 8.

[8] In India too domestic violence and wife battering is not a phenomenon associated with the brutish lower classes and castes as some people like to argue: in recent years, we have seen a number of middle class women who have come out of bad marriages and described the cruelty they experienced at the hands of husbands or intimate partners: Rinki Bhattacharya the daughter of the sensitive film director Bimal Roy and was the wife of another sensitive director Basu Bhattacharya who also made sensitive films on the relationship between men and women in marriage, wrote about the violence within her marriage. More recently Meena Kandaswamy, the feminist writer, has written about the extreme cruelty she experienced in her marriage in *When I Hit You: Or a Portrait of the Writer as a Young Wife* (Juggernaut Books, New Delhi, India, 2017).

Building on such studies, the women's movement worldwide—especially in the northern world—have pushed for legislation and demanded shelter homes that would at least provide women with temporary reprieve. After years of such struggle, we feminists have shifted the way we think about domestic violence or intimate partner violence. In a powerful essay, the feminist jurist Rhonda Copelon[9] has extended the meaning of terror and torture to include intimate partner violence that normally stays hidden from public view. Copelon extends the way torture has an expanded dimension that is not confined to state violence against prisoners. Elaine Scarry's work on the body in pain opens up aspects of the relationship between the inflictor of pain and the person who experiences the pain. In her view, the infliction of mind-numbing pain affects the very notion of 'myself' and at the same time erases or denies for the rest of society the suffering of the person on whom the violence is directed. The infliction of pain turns the attributes of pain into the insignia of power.

Extending the arguments of Scarry, Copelon break down the conventional divide between the public and the private spheres and the contexts in which the 'political' is conventionally understood. She argues that domestic violence too falls under the rubric of torture and that torture need not, perhaps should not, be confined to acts committed by, or in the name of public authorities. Using the story of a couple—Molly and Jim—she challenges the conventional manner in which intimate violence remains on the margins is still considered different and less deserving of international condemnation than officially inflicted violence.

The story of Jim and Molly is terrifying: starting with battering, Jim proceeded to locking Molly up at home when he went out, name calling, shearing her hair, keeping her awake, knifing and threatening to kill the baby, till finally one day a desperate and sleep-deprived Molly killed Jim when she got the opportunity to do so.

Further, Copelon argues that domestic violence is not gender-neutral. Citing a UN report that says that violence against wives is a function of the belief, fostered in *all* cultures that men are superior to women and that the women they live with are their possessions and chattels whom they can treat as they wish. This is a widely held belief in society.

Treating domestic violence as akin to torture, Copelon points out that the defining feature of torture is that pain must be *intentionally* inflicted against the

[9] Rhonda Copelon, 'Intimate Terror', in *The Phenomenon of Torture*, ed. William E. Schulz (Philadelphia: University of Pennsylvania Press, 2007), pp. 180–91.

will of the victim. It is often claimed in cases of domestic violence that the batterer acted impulsively, or under a state of lack of control but such an explanation is a depoliticization of domestic violence against women and obscures the underlying dynamic of domination and subordination. The focus must be on the perpetrator's accountability in order to counter the traditional complicity of law and custom in giving license to violent impulses against women and relief for the woman suffering the violence. Domestic violence, like torture, seeks to intimidate not only the individual woman, but women as a class.[10] The goal of domestic violence is to 'domesticate' the wife, to terrify her into obedience, and to subject her will to the husband's will and to leave her without agency. Violence or the threat of it perpetuates the economic, social, and psychological dependency of a woman on a man—it is the perfect tool to position a woman within the household to use her labour—and thus allows the smooth reproduction of the household, that is, the social reproduction of the family based on women's labour: servicing the needs of its members, reproducing children and looking after them, and ensuring that the family is reproduced as a social unit that sustains the society and produces goods and services required by all. Historically, therefore, there has been the collusion between patriarchy, society, and the state in treating the family as a domain outside of the norms of governance that could have countered the power of men over women within the household. Violence enables men to *stay* in control.

Part II

Let us now look at the way jurisprudence on domestic violence evolved in the sub-continent during colonial times when laws began to be codified. Judgments were derived from Anglo Saxon law, from personal laws of religious communities, from customary laws differing widely based on caste among other kinds of derived legal regimes.[11]

Usha Ramanathan's powerful study of cases from the different courts of India:[12] clinical, sensitive, and sarcastic, according to the judgments

[10] Copelon, 'Intimate Terror', p. 185.

[11] I have in mind the Rakhmabai case where ecclesiastical laws from the Anglican church too could be an element in handling cases even in faraway India! See Uma Chakravarti, Chapter 3.

[12] Usha Ramanathan, 'Images (1920–1950) Reasonable Man, Reasonable Woman and Reasonable Expectations', in *Engendering Law: Essays in Honour of Lotika Sarkar*, ed. Amita Dhanda and Archana Parasher (Lucknow: Eastern Book Depot, 1999), pp. 33–70, 42–6.

delivered, give us an account of how the courts viewed wife-beating (the most common form of domestic violence as we have already seen in the earlier section) from the late colonial period and into post-Independence times. Beginning with the question 'Are there limits to judicial tolerance to a man venting his spleen on his wife', they went on to lay down judicial precedents for examining the ambit of the law on the penetration of legally defined norms in governing the household. It appears the courts believed there was. 'Small beatings' were not regarded as legal cruelty and the poorer classes were expected to beat their wives to chastise them, but not sufficiently so as to result in the wife's death. The lower rungs of the judiciary could even deny a decree for judicial separation to a 'wife whose hands were tied with a chain and her feet with a rope while she was kept hanging in a doorway because a few isolated acts of violence were not enough to constitute legal cruelty'. In a 1936 case, the sessions judge was inspired to set out a right of the husband to beat his wife for impertinence and impudence, though the high court fortunately overruled the sessions judge holding that there was no such unqualified right and the IPC did not provide for an exception in such cases. Some judges and lawyers sought to mould popular opinion on the subject even as others sought to iterate the right to beat a wife. Indeed, these debates inspired a book titled, *The Husband's Right to Beat His Wife*, which drew passages from the Manusmriti, the Holy Quran, and the Bible; its reviewer exhorted the bench, the bar, and laymen to read it as they would profit from it. But in the midst of all these debates on the right to beat and in what way this should be executed, the courts did draw a line in some ways: nose cutting was not exonerated as it was too vindictive and cruel. But that was the extent of relief provided by the courts until the women's movement of the late 1970s and the early 1980s changed the way we think, forcing society, the law, and the administration to re-think the public–private divide that had kept the household outside judicial scrutiny unless a woman had been killed as a consequence of the violence.

The flashpoint of the women's movement has been traced to the judgment on the Mathura case, the classic case of custodial rape. Unlike the women's movement in the West, where rape per se became the clarion call for resistance to the violence women faced in a patriarchal society, the Indian women's movement picked up on custodial rape as the flashpoint that triggered off the outrage that women and sensitive men felt about the patriarchal and class bias of the courts in redressing violence against women. But how and why did that happen in the way it did in the Mathura case? I have been arguing that the experience of the Emergency that India had just witnessed perhaps accounts for casting the state as the first culprit in the violence perpetrated on women. Here was violence in the public sphere, the police station that was meant to be the custodian of the rule of law and the protector of the people, yet it was here that gross violence had taken place against a minor who was from a marginalized location in society. All the anger against the Emergency, the anger against the rape—again in a thana[13]—in the case of Rameeza Bee, where civil rights groups had been active, now fed into the campaign against the judgment denying rape and casting the assault as consensual sex, even though Mathura was a minor at the time of the rape, as upheld by the judges. While the Supreme Court did not review its judgment, violence against women had become the site of women's resistance and their demands ultimately made for legislative changes in the rape law that was passed in 1983.

That was not all; once the movement took off, it was the beginning of a series of campaigns, and for women's groups to become active on other issues such as in street protests when the private sphere, the sacred marital home, suddenly became viewed as the most systematic location for the perpetration of violence against women. Delhi's dowry violence was the trigger for laying bare the working of culture, for marriage as an institution, for the violence within marriage, which was endemic and systemic, hit the women's movement. As the burnt bodies of young married women came out of their marital homes in the phenomenon called dowry deaths (attributed to stove bursts!),[14] the bubble of the benign home burst. Dowry deaths became the ground on which the women's movement cut its teeth and led it to unravel various masks that patriarchal society had carefully nurtured. Feminists then came to an understanding of a very indigenous patriarchy that was unique to India: here we had compulsory marriage (and therefore compulsory heterosexuality), arranged by the elders with the cultural norm that banned any scrutiny of the marital household, the home to which the daughter was sent, whether you liked it or not and from which you must never return even after

[13] Police station.

[14] At advocacy and lecture sessions, this led us as feminists to ask why stoves burst only in the hands of the daughters-in-law; so were the stoves partial to the lives of mothers-in-law? The ludicrousness of the explanation was brought home to the audiences at these sessions but they were used in the defense of the in-laws charged sometimes with abetment to suicide. It was rare to call dowry deaths dowry murders as that would castigate the great Indian tradition or how well Indian culture respected women.

death, irrespective of the degree of cruelty you experienced. All the energy then went into creating a legal regime that would punish the husband and the husband's family if a woman died within seven years of marriage and also spawned a host of institutions: special police stations, family courts, counselling groups, amongst others. There were street plays, sessions in colleges and *mohallas* (an area of a town or a village, a community), and women's groups began to go into the *bastis* (in India this refers to a specific area inhabited by poor people, a slum) to do advocacy work. However, the state never provided for shelters for women while they experienced violence so that they could exit a marriage before they ended up dead—especially since most natal homes did not accept the return of a daughter they had given away in marriage.

Stoves did not stop bursting; young wives did not stop dying, though once they died, the law swung into operation, and families that did not encourage their daughters to return home to build another life were quite willing to press charges of dowry-related violence upon the families where young women had been killed. So, the law swung into operation, but only *after* a woman died; there was no relief for the young woman while she was alive—neither from natal families, nor from the state—and the women's movement did not press hard enough for shelter homes for battered women, unlike countries like the UK and Canada and so women continued to live in their affinal homes till they learnt to resist, or till death took them. It was in this backdrop that the domestic violence legislation was put into place. I have never forgotten Indira Jaising's formulation at a panel discussion somewhere in Delhi: 'We need to give relief to a wife when she is still alive not redress her wrongs after she is dead!'

Has the battering of women ended since the Domestic Violence Act[15] came into operation? Surely not, but we have opened up the sacred home to see what really happens there: we have demanded that the matrimonial home should be one where a woman's right to be safe from bodily and mental harm is acknowledged, that women—wives, daughters, sisters, and mothers—can stay on at home and demand the right to not be beaten or subjected to cruelty, that women contribute labour to the running of the household and are not maintained by their husbands, instead they contribute labour to service men so that they can go back the next day to work—cooking, cleaning, washing, caring for children, in-laws, and anyone else that the house-owner includes

[15] Protection of Women from Domestic Violence Act, 2005.

in his family. The idea that men maintain women has been challenged by women, but it is still part of the patriarchal ideology and is widely reiterated by men, women, and children: '*meri bibi kaam nahi karti*' or '*my mother does not work*'. Let us be clear: the patriarchal household cannot be reproduced without the 'free' labour of women and patriarchy itself cannot be reproduced without violence whatever gloss we put upon it. Violence within the home will never end but it can be mediated: women's right to stay in the house is critical to her capacity to physically survive and launch her children into adulthood. The Domestic Violence Act seeks to do that. It must be allowed to do that. Women have a right to stay safe and productive on their own terms and feminists must stay alert to ensure that they can do so.

***

Before the Domestic Violence Act has made a noticeable impact on the remedies for violence within marriage or in the household, we are witnessing a 'backlash' from patriarchal society strongly committed to upholding the 'rights' of men who 'suffer' under the provisions of 498A, a provision that was intended to provide relief to women who were subject to mental and physical cruelty in the marital home. When it was enacted, the legislators seemed to have understood the need for this provision to prevent suicides and unnatural deaths of wives facing a dead-end situation in their lives. The backlash of men is now supported by the state, a state that is invested in upholding the patriarchal Hindu Indian family whose cultural codes require that there is a silence upon the violence inside the family and that all is well in this family structure. The courts too are colluding with the interests of men to stay in power, asserting their wills and whims upon women who must subscribe to the ideology of *pati-parmeshwar*.[16]

In recent days, we have been unimaginably hit by the terrible news of a young 10-year-old girl being raped by her uncle for months but who must now be punished for being a child who did not, in all likelihood, know what was being done to her because the courts have held that she cannot have an abortion. She and her parents must suffer the consequences of the child being a girl—it is the lordships who can decide as they think fit because the state owns the wombs of all women—they cannot have agency. While we are still reeling from that, we now have the judgment[17] which gives

[16] Translates to: 'My husband is my god'.

[17] *Rajesh Sharma & Ors. v. State of UP & Anr.*, on 27 July 2017.

the backlash on 498A, articulated through disgruntled men who have the backing of the state. Women are 'disgruntled wives' when a wife demands a share of the matrimonial home and the right to live without violence in it. As Jaising's article, 'Concern for the Dead, Condemnation for the Living', so succinctly points out, the advances in the law on domestic violence being made an actionable wrong is being whittled down by the court's articulation of concern that the institution of marriage needs 'protection as it is greatly revered in the country'. As Jaising argues, how does one explain the courts willingness to recognize injury to a dead wife but deny it to the living wife? Is it that the dead wife can claim no right to reside in the shared household whereas the living wife is cast as a disgruntled wife because she is claiming the right to live in that household?

While these are developments in the criminal law to counter 498A as a mechanism to protect women from violence and cruelty within the marital home, we need to be alert to the possibilities that civil remedy provided to the aggrieved wife, sister, daughter, who lives in the household under the power of men under the Domestic Violence Act is not similarly sought to be reversed by the workings of patriarchal and social power so rampant in our society which is ever so ready to resist the rights of women to live with dignity and without fear of bodily harm.

3. *Mapping Legislative Changes*

Asmita Basu

Globally, until the 1970s, 'domestic violence' remained largely unrecognized, as it was deemed to be a culturally acceptable 'private' matter not worthy of state intervention. In this time limited support, in terms of legal remedies and support services, was available for women facing violence within the home. However, by the end of the decade, due to massive mobilization by the international women's movement, domestic violence came to be regarded as the most insidious form of violence against women in all societies. Subsequently, with developments in international law, including the adoption of the Declaration on the Elimination of Violence Against Women in 1993, domestic violence came to be recognized as both a cause and consequence of women's unequal status in society.

As per international consensus, domestic violence may be a single act, or a series of acts of abuse committed on women within familial and intimate relationships. Fear and insecurity associated with domestic violence make it a long-term chronic condition that has substantial and cumulative effect on women's well-being as well as on their mental/physical/reproductive/sexual health. In a significant number of cases, the lack of available options, financial dependency, and fears of stigmatization impair women's ability to leave violent homes.

Understanding violence against women as being a function of discrimination means that addressing violence against women requires tackling of its root causes by promoting gender inequality and reducing women's vulnerability to violence. To address gender inequalities, the Constitution of India includes broad guarantees of equality rights for women: equality before the law and the equal protection law, as well as the right not to be discriminated on grounds of sex alone. Despite these guarantees, gender inequality remains the norm in India. According to the World Economic Forum's Gender Gap Report of 2016, India ranks second-last among 144 countries in the category of 'health and survival', which includes the issue of domestic violence. This points to the high level of vulnerability of Indian women to domestic violence.

To counter this, the Indian state has enacted a significant number of laws, mostly in response to the demands made by the Indian women's movement, to address violence against women and discriminatory practices in various areas. The universe of legal rights for women are prescribed under provisions in criminal law that penalize gender specific offences, provisions under civil law that regulate women's rights within the home, and special laws to address specific forms of violence against women/discriminatory practices such as laws prohibiting the practice of dowry, child marriages, indecent representation of women, sex selective abortions, sexual harassment at the workplace, and so on. However, a comprehensive law against gender-based discrimination, which binds both the private and public entities, is yet to be adopted.

The PWDVA is a special civil law aimed at the 'more effective protection of the rights of women guaranteed under the Constitution who are victims of violence of any kind occurring within the family'. The date 26 October 2016 marked the 10th anniversary of the enforcement of the PWDVA. In this chapter, we examine the trajectory of legal developments that culminated in the enactment of the PWDVA and the gaps in the legal regime that were sought to be overcome with the enactment of this law.

As with other legal developments, the PWDVA was enacted as a result of a sustained campaign, spanning nearly a decade, by the Indian women's movement. The LC, who drafted the law in consultation with the women's movement, spearheaded this campaign. The draft law was foregrounded in earlier feminist engagements on issues of violence against women starting from the 1970s. Hence, in order to understand the need for the law, it is essential to first examine feminist engagements with law reform processes to address violence against women of all forms and to promote women's equality within the home.

Women's Movements Engagement with Law on Violence against Women

The women's movement in India is said to have started in the 1920s by building on to the nineteenth-century social reform movement, which laid the foundation for women's equality through reforms in education and abolition of practices such as sati, child marriage, infanticide, and so on. In this section, we examine the history of the women's movement in three contexts:

- Reforms in criminal laws to address violence against women within the home,
- engagements in relation to the reform of 'personal' family laws, and
- engagements towards improving support for victim/survivors of violence.

In the pre-Independence days, women's organizations were linked to political parties and participated in numbers in India's freedom struggle. However, during this time, when nation-building was the focus of political activism, issues of women's emancipation were relegated to the cultural and spiritual realm, particularly in negotiations with the State.[1] Although the Congress and Communist party affiliated women's organizations and raised the issue of women's equal rights within marriages and inheritance, there was no major restructuring of familial relationships during this time.[2]

With the adoption of the Constitution, which guaranteed women's equal rights, there was no significant growth in the women's movement in the era immediately after India's Independence. In the early 1970s, the 'Towards Equality' Report (1974) by the Committee on the Status of Women in India was prepared to mark the UN Year of Women, 1975. This report provided a damning indictment of women's low position in Indian society and broke the complacency surrounding constitutional gains on women's equality rights. Pursuant to the report, a renewed debate on issues of women's rights

[1] Mary E. John, 'Politics of Quotas and the Women's Reservation Bill in India', Centre for Women's Development Studies (CWDS), New Delhi, 2011, available at http://www.cwds.ac.in/Politics%20of%20quotas%20and%20WRB-MJ-Ch.8.pdf..

[2] Anupama Roy, 'The Women's Movement', in *Oxford Companion to Politics in India*. Debates on the Hindu Code Bill is presented in the following sections.

resulted in the enactment of the Equal Remuneration Act, which recognized women's rights to equal pay for equal work, as well as the specific inclusion of women's developmental needs in national planning documents in the 1980s.[3]

The National Emergency of 1975–7 witnessed heightened mobilization on civil rights. This was also the period, which saw the formation of the autonomous women's groups in major cities across the country. These groups were 'women's only' groups, not linked to political parties, and by the 1980s included a range of support groups, agitational groups, grassroots groups, professional women's groups, research and documentation centres, and so on.[4] Autonomous feminist groups focussed on issues of gender, patriarchy, and control of women's sexuality, and particularly on issues of all forms of violence against women, such as rape, dowry deaths, sex selective abortions, and so on.

Following the furore in the wake of the Supreme Court's judgment in the Mathura rape case, the Forum against Rape, which later became the broader 'Forum against the oppression of women', was established in Mumbai, Maharashtra as a network of autonomous groups and to unify voices from the movement. During the same time, the Dahej Virodhi Manch was formed with 25 women's groups in Delhi to raise issues of dowry related deaths/harassment and demands for more stringent laws for prevention and redress.

The campaign against dowry and dowry-related violence had already begun in the mid-1970s, which was possibly the first time that the issue of violence within the home was brought into the public view. Agitations by feminist groups across the country were able to attract the attention of the state to growing incidents of so-called 'death by fire'. Such incidents were (and even now are) seen as accidents and not investigated properly. The campaign highlighted the difficulties in invoking the law in cases of dowry-related violence for a range of reasons. To illustrate, dying declarations by women were seldom treated as evidence against the husband and in-laws. Courts dismissed even cases that were registered on the basis of dying declarations on the ground of inadequate evidence. Thus, charges of murder or abetment to suicide could not be successfully invoked. Similarly, the police

[3] Gender and Economic Policy Discussion Forum; Gender and Affirmative Action; Briefing note 6, Forum VI, March 2013.

[4] Nandita Shah and Nandita Gandhi, *Issues at Stake* (New Delhi: Kali for Women, 1992).

would be reluctant to intervene, arguing that it was not the task of the police to intervene in 'family quarrels'.[5]

The campaign led to the Criminal Law (Second Amendment) Act, 1983, which introduced Section 498A in the IPC, 1870. Under this provision, 'cruelty' to the wife was made a cognizable, non-bailable offence punishable with imprisonment up to three years and a fine. Cruelty was defined as including both physical and mental cruelty or harassment by the husband/in-laws in relation to demands for dowry. The phraseology used in this provision encompassed a broad ambit, which could be used to address any form of 'cruelty' within marriages and was not limited to dowry-related harassment alone.

Shortly following the adoption of Section 498A, Section 304B was introduced in the IPC to create a new offence of 'dowry death'. This provision made it possible to prosecute the husband and in-laws if a woman died as a result of burns or under any other suspicious circumstances within seven years of marriage, *and* if it could be shown that she was subjected to cruelty or dowry-related harassment by the husband. Here it must be noted that the practice of giving and taking dowry had already been criminalized under the Dowry Prohibition Act of 1961 (DPA). Along with amendments to the IPC, changes were also affected to the DPA to improve its effectiveness. Additionally, during this period, women's police stations and family courts started functioning in response to demands made by the women's movement for more sensitive handling of cases of marital violence.[6]

However, applying these new provisions revealed that the focus on dowry-related violence during the campaign had been rather narrow and it distracted from other forms of everyday violence that women faced, which were not necessarily dowry-related. Further, the provision covered only married women and not the other unmarried women in domestic relationships—mothers, sisters, adopted daughters, widows, and so on—facing violence within the home. It also did not protect women from violence in intimate relationships that did not receive legal sanction of marriage.

The other problematic aspect of this provision was the definition of 'cruelty' itself. Cruelty was defined to mean any '*wilful conduct which could have driven the woman to commit suicide or caused grave injury to her or posed a danger to her life, limb or health (either mental or physical)*'. The definition was

[5] Indira Jaising, 'Bring Rights Home: Campaign for a Law on Domestic Violence', *Economic and Political Weekly* XLIV, 44 (2009).

[6] A. Suneetha and Vasudha Nagraj, 'Adjudicating (Un) Domestic Battles', *Economic and Political Weekly* 40(38) (2005).

worded in such vague terms that it was difficult to bring issues of sexual violence, economic violence, or even threats of violence within the ambit of the section. The experience with using this section showed that the evidentiary burden that had to be met under criminal law was so high that many forms of cruelty fell through the net. A woman had to prove that she was driven to contemplate suicide, or that her life was in danger before she could access the law.

A third significant concern was in relation to inherent limitations of criminal law. While criminalizing acts, cruelty played a significant role in socially delegitimizing the practice,[7] it did not offer any remedies to women in terms of meeting immediate needs of protection, shelter, monetary reliefs, and so on. Some of these reliefs could be obtained under existing civil laws such as divorces on grounds of cruelty under marriage laws, maintenance under personal laws as well as Section 125 of the Code of Criminal Procedure (CrPC), injunctive orders under the Code of Civil Procedure, and the Specific Reliefs Act, to name a few. However, these reliefs were limited as they involved protracted legal proceedings and hence were not available in a timely manner.

A significant concern with the civil law regime was the absence of the recognition of a woman's right to reside in the shared household. In law, the right to reside devolves on the person who holds property rights—for example, the person who owns the premises or whose name appears on lease deeds, and so on. In the prevailing patriarchal context, male members of the family usually hold property rights. Further, none of the personal laws, be it Hindu, Muslim, Christian, or Parsi, which govern rights within the family, make a clear declaration of a woman's right to reside in a shared household. Although the right to reside was recognized in common law and in cases decided by courts[8] as being part of women's right to maintenance, there was no statutory recognition of this right.

A persistent problem witnessed in cases of domestic violence is that women are thrown out of the homes and then the house is sold or rented to dispossess women indirectly. In the absence of a formal title over the property, women could do little to reside in a house that was owned by the husband or other male members. While it can be argued that the right to reside

[7] According to Nivedita Menon, as 'Law [was] seen as a legitimating discourse, it [was] believed, therefore, that legal criminalization would socially delegitimize a practice', 'Embodying the Self', in *Community, Gender and Violence*, Subaltern Studies XI, by Parthan Chatterjee and Pradeep Jeganathan (New Delhi: Permanent Black, 2000).

[8] *B. P. Achala Anand* v. *Appi Reddy* (2005) 3 SCC 313.

should be available to all women in domestic relationships and not limited to cases of domestic violence, it is in such cases that this right assumes added significance. The lacuna in the law, coupled with the lack of support from natal families and state sponsored shelter home services, resulted in increasing women's vulnerability to violence and adversely impacted their ability to leave a violent home for fear of destitution and homelessness.

Feminist engagements with the reform of personal laws have had a vexed history in India, which can be traced back to the colonial era. The colonial state applied separate religious family laws for different communities—Hindu, Muslim, Christian, and Parsi—although laws to meet administrative imperatives were secularized. There was no single or uniform body of religious laws and there were wide variations in customary practices, particularly among the Hindus.[9] The process of codification of Hindu laws by the British and its interpretation in civil colonial courts in line with prevailing Victorian-era common law constructs led to the preservation of the most patriarchal aspects of practices.[10] This was particularly evident in matters relating to the privileging of property ownership rights of male family members, and maintaining unequal rights of women in relation to inheritance, divorce, guardianship, matrimonial property. Reform of these colonial era laws and the adoption of a uniform civil code (UCC) applicable to all religions has consistently been opposed by orthodox sections of religious groups in both the pre- and post-Independence eras.

Debates on reforming the personal law regime must be viewed within a context of a perceived tension between individual women's rights and collective rights of minorities to their religion. Here it must be remembered that the Indian independence and the establishment of a sovereign republic took place within the context of a violent partition based on religious lines. In these circumstances, the right to religion adopted in the Indian Constitution has been understood as an attempt to secure rights of minorities to self-preservation. This context has had a significant influence on debates on religious family laws and particularly on debates on the adoption of a secular UCC.

The agenda for a UCC was part of the women's organizations' agenda from pre-Independence days. However, it was hijacked by the Hindu right wing in the controversy following the Supreme Court's judgment in the *Shah Bano* case in an attempt to '*establish majority norms as the ostensibly*

[9] Madhu Kishwar, 'Codified Hindu Law, Myth and Reality', *Economic and Political Weekly*, 29(33) (1994): 2145–61.

[10] Flavia Agnes, 'Women, Marriage and the Subjugation of Rights', in *Community, Gender and Violence*, Subaltern Studies XI.

neutral norms against which all others are judged'.[11] These developments have correspondingly changed how the women's movement has articulated its demand for a UCC over the years. According to Nivedita Menon, while there has been consistent support and attempts to reform religious family laws, there was also an attempt to bring about legislation that is not covered by either secular or personal '*thus avoiding a direct confrontation with communities and communal politics*'.[12] She cites the PWDVA as an example in this regard as it articulates the right to reside in cases of domestic violence, applies in addition to existing laws thus keeping the personal law regime intact.

The third aspect, that is essential for context setting, is feminist engagements with facilitating access to justice and support in individual cases. Other than campaigning for law reform and conscious raising activities in the 1980s, women's organizations in various cities across the country started providing a combination of support, such as feminist counselling services, legal aid, short stay facilities, in individual cases under the broad rubric of 'case-work'. By the 1990s, the overwhelming demand for such services caused a withdrawal of these groups from 'case-work' so that their limited resources could be used to raise emerging issues, seek state accountability, and influence policy changes.[13] However, 'case work' done by women's organizations led to the creation of a vast body of experiential knowledge. In fact, much of the implementation mechanisms provided for in the PWDVA are grounded in these practices of women's organizations.

Moreover, women's organizations strove hard for the effective implementation of laws by providing trainings and gender sensitizing the police, lawyers, and judiciary, as well as popularizing legal changes through legal literacy programmes.[14] There were a number of impediments in implementation of laws on violence against women, arising as a consequence of an overburdened and under-resourced justice system, the absence of a supportive structure (such as counselling, shelter, and medical facilities) for women

[11] Ratna Kapur, 'Communalising Gender, Engendering Community: Women, Legal Discourse and the Saffron Agenda', *Economic and Political Weekly*, 28(17) (1993).

[12] Kapur, 'Communalising Gender, Engendering Community'.

[13] Manisha Gupte, 'Why Feminism should Inform Our Routine Interventions in Domestic Violence', in *Feminist Counselling and Domestic Violence in India*, ed. Padma Bhate Deosthali, Sangeeta Rege, and Padma Prakash (CEHAT Routledge, 2013).

[14] Suneetha and Nagraj, 'Adjudicating (Un) Domestic Battles'.

seeking legal redress and the lack of recognition of women's equality rights within the family as a result of discriminatory personal laws.

Issues with Using Law to Address Domestic Violence

While inadequacies in the justice system are concerns for all litigants, women also face the added burden of confronting patriarchal attitudes of the law enforcement machinery and a hostile legal environment. These attitudes are manifest in refusals to record FIRs under Section 498A and diversions to police facilitated mediation (counselling) services, which often resulted in forced reconciliations.

Patriarchal attitudes are also reflected in the judgments of courts and higher judiciary, who have alleged frequent 'misuse' of Section 498A by women. To illustrate, the Supreme Court in *Arnesh Kumar* v. *State of Bihar*[15] observed that 'the fact *that Section 498A is a cognizable and non-bailable offence has lent it a dubious place of pride amongst the provisions that are used as weapons rather than shield by disgruntled wives. The simplest way to harass is to get the husband and his relatives arrested under this provision*'. Most recently, in July 2017, the Supreme Court in *Rajesh Sharma* v. *State of Uttar Pradesh*,[16] moved to prevent the 'misuse' of Section 498A and has emasculated the law by putting in place 'welfare committees' to scrutinize complaints filed by women before the police take cognisance of it.[17] This ruling appears to be based on an assumption that violence inflicted upon women is 'a mere figment of their imagination and that cases registered under the anti-dowry law-Section 498A—are false'.[18]

Allegations of misuse are also part of a strong lobby by men's rights groups from urban areas to amend the provision. These allegations are not based on any rigorous social science study or research, but on low conviction rates in cases reported under the provision. These arguments are the complex reasons behind the failure to prove such cases in courts. As per Indira Jaising, '*the misuse argument perpetuates patriarchal traditions of accusing women of manipulating*

[15] 2014 (8) SCC 273.

[16] See https://indiankanoon.org/doc/182220573/.

[17] Indira Jaising, 'Victim in the Dock', *Indian Express*, 2 August 2017, http://indianexpress.com/article/opinion/columns/victim-in-the-dock-law-of-cruelty-against-women-supreme-court-judgment-rajesh-sharma-and-ors-v-state-of-up-and-anr-4777931/.

[18] Flavia Agnes, 'Supreme Court's Judgment Ignores Lived Reality of Married Women', *Economic and Political Weekly*, 52(36) (2017): 16–19.

the law. In actuality, there is scope for the misuse of all laws, and yet the spotlight is turned on the most important contemporary development to prevent violence against women'.[19] However, there have been numerous moves to dilute Section 498A by making it compoundable and bailable,[20] instead of efforts to change prevailing patriarchal attitudes among law enforcement officials and the judiciary. It seems that the final blow has been delivered by the Supreme Court in the Rajesh Sharma case, which 'apart from giving a long rope to the accused to abscond [amounts to a] virtual privatisation of the policing function'.[21]

Under criminal law proceedings, women are dependent on public prosecutors who are not as involved in the case as private lawyers hired by the opposite party.[22] The need for hiring private lawyers arises when women claim their rights under civil law. However, women's lack of resources and social capital, when compared to men, limits their ability to hire good lawyers, produce witnesses and documentary evidence needed.[23] A majority of domestic violence cases involve multiple forums to access rights under civil family laws and criminal law. Other than excessive financial and time commitments due to multiplicity of forums and delays within courts, accessing free and quality legal representation is extremely difficult. This is despite the recognition of the right to free legal aid of all marginalized communities, including women, under the Legal Services Authorities Act, 1987.

In an effort to overcome excessive reliance on lawyers while accessing (civil) reliefs under family law, the Family Courts Act (FCA) was enacted in 1984. The FCA attempted to establish less formal mechanisms for speedy settlements of matrimonial disputes and limited the role of lawyers in arriving at these settlements. However, the FCA's focus on 'preservation of families', the lack of trained counsellors to guide settlement processes, and the increasing role of lawyers in proceedings, have severely hindered the achievement of the FCA's objectives.[24] In these circumstances, women's access to justice is

[19] Lawyers Collective, 'Only Her Word', Lawyers Collective monograph, 2004.

[20] Malimath Committee Report on Reforms of the Criminal Justice System, March 2003, Law Commission Report No. 243 on Section 498A, available at http://lawcommissionofindia.nic.in/reports/report243.pdf.

[21] Jaising, *Victim in the Dock*.

[22] Jaising, *Victim in the Dock*.

[23] Monica Sakhrani and Trupti Panchal, '*Quest for Justice: A Study of the Implementation of the Protection of Women from Domestic Violence Act, 2005* (Mumbai: MWCD/TISS, 2015).

[24] Flavia Agnes and Audrey D'Mello, 'Protection of Women from Domestic Violence', *Economic and Political Weekly* L, 44 (2015). Review of Women's Studies.

rendered hugely cumbersome. Moreover, state-sponsored services, such as shelter homes and medical facilities, which are crucial to sustain women in their quest for justice, were, and continue to be, grossly inadequate to meet the demand.

The existence of discriminatory family law provisions also influences outcomes and use of legal strategies in cases of domestic violence. A 2006 ethnographic study conducted by Srimati Basu in Family Courts and Women's Grievance Cells of the Police in Kolkata found that '*when judges, counsellors and police dealt with [cases under Section 498A], they were often not managing/punishing violence per se, but rather negotiating a range of issues related to the social and economic entitlements of marriage*'. Options for leaving violent marriages are also linked with social and economic entitlements available upon the breakdown of marriages. As Jaising argued during the campaign for the PWDVA, '*[t]he breakdown of a marriage in our society with its attendant discrimination means virtual civil death for a woman*'.[25]

Most countries around the world have adopted 'community of matrimonial property' laws/provisions to determine economic entitlements and division of matrimonial property based on the principle of 'contributions', both economic and non-economic, during the course of the marriage. In India, however, economic entitlements are limited to the right to maintenance, which is determined by applying principles of 'need' and 'fault'. Application of such principles in practice perpetuate gender stereotypes of males being primary breadwinners and are grounded in notions of sexual purity of women.[26] Here too, claims to the limited right to maintenance in courts involve protracted and multiple legal proceedings, not only to obtain orders but also to get court orders enforced.

In the context of domestic violence, Jaising observed in the early stages of the campaign for the PWDVA, that

> *[V]iolence is used by the abuser as a tool of blackmail, as a method of coercing her to give up her claims to her property, to her assets and to her children, all of which are often in the control of the man. Given the repeated violence, the abuser will have achieved his aim of getting rid of his liabilities by driving the woman to such a point that she will agree to walk out of the house in destitution and desperation, giving up all claims only to be free from the violence ... the matrimonial laws of this*

[25] Indira Jaising, 'Comparing the Government of India Bill 2001 with the Lawyers Collective Draft', in Lawyers Collective, 'Only Her Word', 2004.

[26] Flavia Agnes, 'Conjugality, Property, Morality and Maintenance', *Economic and Political Weekly* XLIV, 44 (2009).

> *country do not contain any significant rights to matrimonial property for women, so that on the breakdown of a marriage, the woman has to literally leave with empty hands. Given that there is often no record of her own property such as stridhan or gifts, she often has to leave without her own belongings as well. This is very often the reason why women stay on in bad marriages, knowing that on exit they must go with empty hands.*[27]

It was in this context that the need for a civil law on domestic violence was identified. The campaign was towards bringing in a law, which would be responsive to the need of equalizing familial relationships and serve to overcome the hurdles identified above. Hence, as per the proposal of the LC, minimum attributes that the law would have to incorporate were:[28]

- A declaration of basic intent of the law, namely, the object of preventing domestic violence.
- A clear and unambiguous statement of the right to be free from domestic violence and the recognition of domestic violence as a violation of the human rights of women.
- The definition of domestic violence, which captures women's experience of abuse with some degree of precision.
- The definition of the shared household so that rights can be protected within that household.
- The relief that can be given to protect the woman from violence.
- The infrastructure available to victims of violence that can make the remedy accessible.
- Clarity and simplicity of court procedures.
- Monitoring of the functioning of the law, is it serving its intended purpose?
- Providing a coordinated response to domestic violence by recognizing the role of other agencies such as NGOs, the medical profession, shelter homes, and the police in assisting the prevention of domestic violence.

Campaign for a Civil Law on Domestic Violence

The involvement of the LC in the campaign for a civil law on domestic violence began in 1993, when the National Commission for Women (NCW) requested the LC to prepare a draft bill on domestic violence. In response,

[27] Jaising in LC, 'Only Her Word: Campaign for a Civil Law on Domestic Violence', New Delhi, 2004.

[28] Jaising in LC, 'Only Her Word'.

the LC proposed three laws for simultaneous adoption to effectively tackle domestic violence—a law on emergency civil reliefs in cases of domestic violence, a law on the community of matrimonial property, and an anti-sex discrimination law—which would apply both to the private and public sectors. However, given the urgency in cases of domestic violence, discussion on the law on domestic violence was prioritized and the draft of a law was presented to NCW in 1994.

However, a more focussed campaign began later in 1998. The first step in the campaign was to recognize the concept of 'domestic violence', which was much broader than the definition of 'cruelty' under Section 498A, as legal tender. Hence, the legal community was specifically targeted to build consensus, sensitize members on the seriousness of the issue of domestic violence, inadequacies in legal remedies, and the demands of the women's movement towards ensuring the safe passage of the bill. Hence, a colloquium on domestic violence, 'Empowerment through Law', involving lawyers, academics, activists, and appellate judges was organized in Delhi to flag off the campaign. At the colloquium, a draft prepared by the LC based on the UN Model Framework on Legislation on Domestic Violence was discussed extensively and given more concrete shape.[29]

The draft law was then discussed at consultations organized across the country, and often in collaboration with local women's groups, and revised several times on the basis of inputs received. Even in these wider consultative processes, special efforts were made to seek inputs. This consultative process served a number of purposes: first, it aided consensus building on the content of the draft law, second, greater consensus meant that there was more lobbying for the adoption of the bill at local levels. Consultations also meant that the draft of the bill was informed by lessons from practice. The draft bill that emerged out of these consultations aimed at recognizing domestic violence as a violation of women's human rights and providing civil reliefs to survivors in cases of domestic violence. It had the following features:

- Definition of domestic violence.
- Broad coverage of women in all domestic relationships.
- Recognition of the right to reside.
- Range of civil reliefs to respond to the needs of women survivors.
- Judicious mix of criminal and civil procedure to ensure.

[29] Indira Jaising, 'Bringing Rights Home: Review of the Campaign for a Law on Domestic Violence', *Economic and Political Weekly*, 44(44) (2009): 50–7.

- A mechanism to facilitate a woman's access to court orders and other supportive services.

Definition of Domestic Violence

The bill adopted a broad definition of domestic violence. Given the wide acceptance and rationalization of domestic violence as being part of marital and other domestic relationships,[30] it was essential to first identify specific forms of conduct that constitute domestic violence, the experience of using Section 498A showed that it was extremely difficult to convince judges of the existence of domestic violence within a relationship. Although the term 'cruelty' under Section 498A included aspects of both physical and mental cruelty, it was difficult to bring the subtleties of everyday violence in intimate relationships within the ambit of the law. Even when judges were convinced of the existence of 'cruelty', they tended to play down the possible impact of it and often asked women to 'forgive and forget'.

In order to reign in judicial subjectivity in determining what constitutes domestic violence and to counter trivializing discourses that downplay the severity and seriousness of violence at home, the LC draft included the unnamed aspects of everyday violence. Thus, the definition of domestic violence included a range of harms, injuries, and threats caused by physical, sexual, verbal, emotional, and economic abuse. Each aspect was further defined by illustrations. The point of providing such an extensive definition was not to put a seal on the conceptualization of 'violence', but to indicate that certain forms of behaviour must be seen as an exercise of sexual power and hence must be condemned.

Coverage of the Law

A consensus among the movement was that the law should cover not only matrimonial relationships but all other women in the home. Hence, a new definition of 'domestic relationships' was adopted to include all relationships based on consanguinity, marriage, adoption, and even relationships in the

[30] 54 per cent of women surveyed under the National Family and Health Survey 3, believed that it is justifiable for husbands to beat their wives under certain circumstances—such as disrespecting in-laws, neglecting household responsibilities in any manner, and so on. International Institute for Population Sciences (IIPS) and Macro International, 'National Family Health Survey (NFHS-3), 2005–6: India', Volume I. IIPS, Mumbai, 2007.

nature of marriage. Including intimate relationships outside the marital context within the scope of the law was necessary in view of the absence of compulsory registration of marriages in India, which leaves a majority of women outside the domain of legal protection. The site of violence—the home—was also brought into the purview of the law by defining the 'shared household' in relation to residence, instead of property rights. This also increased the scope of the site of violence, which was earlier limited to the matrimonial home.

During the course of the consultations, a much-debated issue was whether the proposed law should be gender neutral and extend its protection to men facing violence within the home. The wide consensus was that the bill had to be gender-specific in nature since the objective was to protect women by countering historical disadvantage. Hence, a gender-neutral law would defeat the purpose of a law on domestic violence. Further, given the skewed power relations within the home, men could use a gender-neutral law against women.

This meant that the definition of 'aggrieved women' (those eligible to file complaints under the law) would be confined only to women and the definition of 'respondent' would include only men. Later, the definition of 'respondent' further worked on to bring it in line with Section 498A by including female relatives of male respondents. This meant that violence by women against women in same-sex relationships was left out of the ambit of the law. This also meant that while daughters-in-law could bring cases against mothers-in-law, mothers-in-law could file complaints against daughters-in-law only as an adjunct to complaints filed against the son.

There were also suggestions to include domestic workers within the ambit of the law. Given that the relationship of domestic workers within the home is that of an employer–employee, which is different from domestic relationships based on intimacy or through family, it was felt that domestic workers can be better accommodated in laws relating to sexual harassment and regulation of the informal sector.

Right to Reside

The most important aspect of the bill was the recognition of the right to reside to guard against illegal dispossession. As mentioned earlier, the right to reside must be distinguished from the broader right to property. The draft law recognized the rights of women to reside in the shared household, even in the absence of a formal title over it and irrespective of ownership patterns. The law did not create a substantive right over property for women, but provided a safeguard against illegal dispossession. Thus, the objective of the law was to provide 'due process' protection to women in domestic relationships.

Reliefs under the Law

In keeping with the understanding that women facing domestic violence require holistic support, which cannot be met through a criminal proceeding or a divorce petition, the reliefs were designed to respond to the needs of victim/survivors and included:

- *Protection Orders* in the form of civil injunctive reliefs to stop and prevent acts of domestic violence, as well as acts adversely affecting the legitimate rights and interests of victim/survivors.
- *Residence Orders* to prevent victim/survivors' illegal dispossession and prevent any acts that impact on her peaceful occupation of the shared household.
- *Orders for Monetary Reliefs* to reimburse actual expenses incurred due to domestic violence (for example, medical expenses, loss of earnings) as well as maintenance in the form of an appropriate lump sum payment or monthly payments for the woman as well as for her children.
- *Orders granting Temporary Custody* of children.
- *Compensation Orders* for mental trauma and emotional distress caused to the victim/survivors as a result of acts of domestic violence.

Recognizing the need for emergency court orders, the proposed bill also included provisions on interim and exparte orders. Moreover, cognizant of delays associated with court processes, the proposed law put in a deadline of 60 days for the application to be disposed off by the courts.

Mix of Criminal and Civil Procedure

The PWDVA is primarily a civil law, as it provides for civil remedies in cases of domestic violence. The breach of a court order is deemed to be an offence. From the very beginning, the PWDVA was envisaged to work in addition to Section 498A and other criminal provisions (for example, Section 125 CrPC) and other civil laws (for example, family laws). The idea was to create multiple options for women, even while reducing the multiplicity of forums. Hence, a woman could decide on whether she wanted to pursue civil remedies under PWDVA or criminal proceedings under Section 498A, or both simultaneously. On the other hand, an application for any PWDVA remedies could be added in any pending proceedings filed by the woman. For instance, a protection order could be sought in a pending Section 498A proceeding, or during the course of a divorce or maintenance proceedings.

Another important decision that was taken during the consultations was to choose the Magistrate's courts as the forum to which all applications under the PWDVA would lie. Magistrates' courts already had the jurisdiction to deal with applications under Section 125 of CrPC. Further, Magistrates' courts, being at the sub-district level, were considered to be more easily accessible for women. Selecting Magistrates' courts as the appropriate forum also meant that the comparably more efficacious criminal procedure would be applied in cases under the PWDVA. However, to ensure timely disposal of cases, the proposed law also recognized the power of Magistrates' to devise their own procedures. This meant that Magistrates', or any other court, could use principles from both the civil and criminal procedure codes, while dealing with PWDVA complaints.

Finally, another procedural innovation introduced by the law was simple formats for recording complaints—Domestic Incident Reports (DIR) and filing petitions. DIRs were considered to be the civil equivalent of FIRs used to initiate criminal proceedings. However, unlike FIRs, solely recording DIRs did not trigger off legal processes. It was meant to create an evidence base of complaints, which a survivor could rely on in any proceedings in the future. A protection officer or a service provider could record a DIR. Once recorded, copies of the DIR are to be sent to the police and the court. In cases where the aggrieved woman wished to initiate court proceedings, a protection officer would file the DIR along with an application in a prescribed format in court. If the aggrieved woman could not afford legal representation, the court would provide free legal aid to the women under the Legal Services Authorities Act, 1987. However, the recording of a DIR was not made a prerequisite for filing an application for reliefs in courts. Hence, women could approach courts directly for reliefs.

Mechanism to Facilitate a Woman's Access to Justice

Although India has enacted a number of laws on women's rights, effective implementation has been an issue. According to Jaising, a reason for ineffective implementation is that '*non-implementation is written into the law*'. To illustrate, the DPA penalizes both the giver[31] and taker of dowry. When

[31] Although the giver of dowry has a comparably limited liability.

both are criminally liable, it is unlikely that either will complain of the offence. The DPA also mandated the appointment of Dowry Prohibition Officers (DPOs), vested with the charge of ensuring the implementation of the DPA. However, the appointment of DPOs has not been adequate and these officers have played a limited role in the enforcement of the DPA.

Bearing this context in mind, the PWDVA ensured women's direct access to courts for reliefs. However, recognizing that the entire justice delivery system is largely inaccessible to women, the proposed law recommended the appointment of protection officers, who would be the link between the aggrieved woman and the legal system. To ensure accountability and efficiency of protection officers, they were placed under the direct supervision of the court. Hence, a twofold role of protection officers was envisaged under the law. First was to assist women in accessing the court and other available support services (such as legal aid, medical aid, shelter homes, counselling centres, and so on). Second was to assist the court during the course of the proceedings, particularly to collect evidence and make enquiries, as also to assist with the enforcement of orders. The office of the protection officer was inspired by the casework undertaken by autonomous women's groups, as well as by experience of special cells of the TISS. Thus, protection officers were meant to be the 'eyes and ears' of the court or in other words, the 'outreach arm' of the court, who would help the aggrieved woman gather evidence to support her case in court.

During the consultations, there was a discussion on who should be appointed as protection officers. There was a proposal to appoint police officers as protection officers. However, this proposal was not accepted by most of the women's organizations, since this was a civil law and thus the police were not the appropriate authorities. There was also an apprehension that including the police directly in the law would increase state power and cause unnecessary interventions in the domestic sphere. Since the law would act in addition to other laws, the role of the police in cases of domestic violence was already outlined and implicated as per the CrPC.

Protection officers were meant to be supported by 'service providers'. In another innovative move, the draft law proposed the *recognition*, as opposed to appointment, of service providers. Recognizing service providers was towards providing legal protection to women's organizations, NGOs, and other registered bodies providing support to women facing violence. Organizations eligible for registration as service providers include those proving legal aid, medical, financial, counselling, or other assistance to women. Registered service providers were also given the power to record DIRs and initiate legal proceedings on behalf of women.

Finally, the law provided for the notification of *Medical Facilities* and *Shelter Homes*. Existing public and private medical facilities, such as hospitals, clinics, nursing homes, and shelter homes, including short stay homes, could be notified under the law. Upon notification, such facilities would be duty bound to provide services to aggrieved women. Given that state-sponsored services are vastly inadequate to meet the need of domestic violence survivors, the idea was to increase the scope of services available to survivors, by including private sector service providers through notification.

The mechanism (Figure 3.1) under the proposed law was to act in a coordinated manner with other entities implicated in the issue of domestic violence, namely, the police and courts. In order to facilitate coordination, the law vested the duty of informing survivors of their rights, including those recognized under the proposed law, on a number of key stakeholders including the police and the court. Further, obligations to facilitate inter-departmental coordination and preparing protocols for coordinated service delivery were included as duties of the central and state governments.

In order to ensure effective implementation, the proposed law included provisions on dedicated funds required for implementation and National Rapporteurs to collect data on domestic violence and to monitor legal

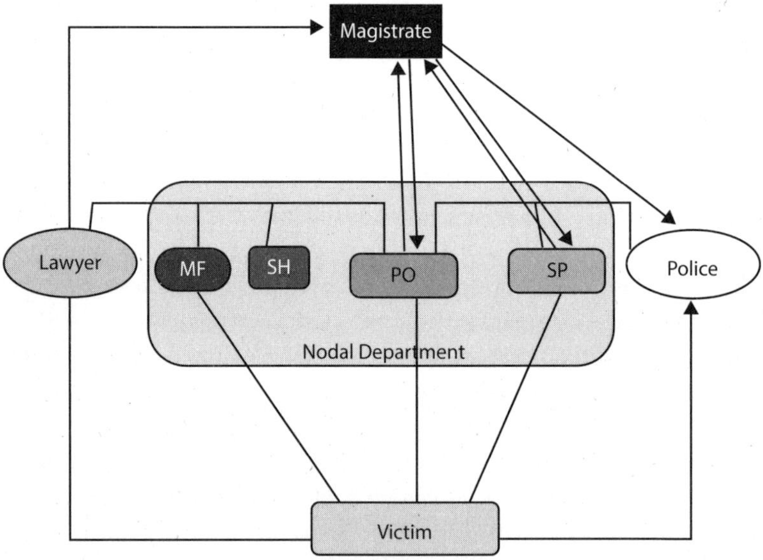

Figure 3.1 Mechanism under the proposed law.
Source: http://lawcommissionofindia.nic.in/reports/report243.pdf at p. 9

implementation. Overall, the objectives behind the law was to create avenues to justice and enabling environments that were responsive to the needs of women.

Milestones in the Campaign

In the period 1998–2001, the draft law prepared by the LC underwent several revisions based on inputs received during the consultations. Another significant development during this period was the concluding observations made by the CEDAW committee on India's progress report in 2000. One of the recommendations of this report was for the government to '*strengthen law enforcement and introduce reforms proposed by the NCW and women activists in regard to the law on rape, sexual assault and domestic violence*'.[32] This development provided significant impetus to the campaign for adopting a law on domestic violence. During this time, although the LC draft bill was submitted to the government for adoption, in 2001 the NDA government of the time introduced its own version of the bill.

The government draft had a number of serious lacunae. First, the definition of domestic violence was vague and inadequate and only included habitual assault and acts that *made the life of an aggrieved person miserable by cruelty*. The bill contained no declaration of rights or prescriptions for remedies. Instead, it provided for joint mandatory counselling for both parties to preserve marriages. It also included a clause, which allowed a plea of self-defence to the man by recognizing that men had the right to use violence to defend themselves and their property. According to the LC's critique of the bill, this was a ploy to '*undo the main provision as a man [could] always say that he was trying to get out or a scuffle, a fight between himself and his wife and his mother and caused the injury complained of, not intentionally, but to protect himself*'.[33] Overall, it was observed that the government's bill did not '*give any indication that the commitment to securing the right to life and liberty of women [of India] was its driving force*'.[34]

This bill was widely opposed by the women's movement. As a result of the pressure exerted by the movement, the government bill was referred

[32] Committee on the Elimination of Discrimination Against Women, 'Concluding Observations: India', 2000, available at https://www1.umn.edu/humanrts/cedaw/india2000.html.

[33] Committee on the Elimination of Discrimination Against Women, 'Concluding Observations'.

[34] Committee on the Elimination of Discrimination Against Women, 'Concluding Observations'.

to a Parliamentary Standing Committee of the Ministry of HRD. The Parliamentary Standing Committee was chaired by Arjun Singh. A number of women's organizations made submissions before the Committee, including the LC. The Committee agreed with most of the submissions made by the LC, including expanding the coverage of the law to include non-marital relationships, deletion of provisions relating to self-defence, and mandatory counselling. In its report in 2002, the Committee also recommended that the scope of orders under the law be strengthened.

Before the government could act on the recommendations of the Standing Committee, there was a regime change in 2004. The Common Minimum Program adopted by the UPA government included the enactment of a law on domestic violence. The LC convened a meeting of representatives of key women's groups across the country who were part of the campaign and the consultative process. A delegation from this meeting met with Arjun Singh, who was the minister of HRD, to hand over a copy of the bill. The bill received cabinet approval in May 2005 and was subsequently passed in the Parliament as the PWDVA, 2005.

Due to the long and concerted campaign that preceded its enactment, there was an overwhelming consensus on the need for the law when it was introduced in the Parliament in September 2005. Debates in the Parliament were mostly rhetorical highlighting the paradox of women being 'worshipped as goddesses' in the Hindu religion, while being subjected to violence within the home and outside.

Overall, the parliamentary debates revealed the protectionist urge of lawmakers rather than their commitment to promoting women's equality rights. The response of the then Minister of State (HRD), Kanti Singh, to the issues raised by MPs is particularly revealing of the contradictory views on using law to address domestic violence:

> Despite unanimity on this Bill, one question is arising in the minds of many people. Many of them are apprehensive that the bill may also disturb the cordial relationship between a husband and wife and create a chasm in the relationship and obstruct the smooth function [sic] of the family and matters might end up promoting the tendency of washing one's dirty linen in public, However, I would like to submit that any woman who has patience, courage and strength, would never prefer to approach courts for scuffle with her husband and other trivial discords in the family. This is the reason that there is so much increase in domestic violence.[35]

[35] Parliamentary debates accessed from the Parliament Library on the debates on the Domestic Violence Bill, 2005.

Despite the quality of parliamentary debates, the enactment of the PWDVA marked a significant victory for the women's movement and symbolized the hope for more equal domestic relationships. Over the years, there have been massive increases in cases filed under the PWDVA. This indicates its success, particularly when compared to other laws on women's rights, for example, the Prohibition of Child Marriage Act, that are poorly implemented. Interactions with lawyers indicate that that the law is useful because of the comprehensiveness of the *definition* of domestic violence and the *scope of reliefs* provided in it; and that it allows women direct access to courts. While there are gaps in implementation, the PWDVA, is, in most part, a model legislation that has inspired similar laws in our neighbouring countries. In our current milieu, where the Section 498A is being severely diluted, this law assumes an added significance. One can only hope that the Indian State takes cue from the spirit that the PWDVA embodies—that women, as equal citizens, have the right to a violence-free home—to strengthen laws to protect women's rights within the home.

SECTION II

Critical Issues

4. *'But ... Where Will I Live?'*

Domestic Violence and the Right to Reside

PINKI MATHUR ANURAG

Domestic violence is one of the most prevalent forms of violence against women in the private sphere[1] and has received due acknowledgement in international forums as a serious human rights violation.[2] The prevalence of domestic violence violates a multitude of rights: one of the most significant amongst these is the right to housing. The chapter deals in essence with women's unequal rights to housing, and draws on the related concepts of security of tenure and ownership rights to explore the interlink

[1] R. Copelon, 'Intimate Terror: Understanding Domestic Violence as Torture', in *Human Rights of Women, National & International Perspectives*, ed. R. Cook (Philadelphia: University of Pennsylvania Press, 1994), p. 116.

[2] CEDAW Recommendation No. 19 on Violence Against Women U.N. Doc. (CEDAW/C/L.1/Add.151992); Declaration on the Elimination of Violence Against Women, U.N. GAOR, 3rd Comm., 48th Session, Res. 48/104, U.N. Doc. A/48/629 (1994) (1992); Declaration on the Elimination of Violence Against Women, U.N. GAOR, 3rd Comm., 48th Session, Res. 48/104, U.N. Doc. A/48/629 (1994).

between housing rights for women and domestic violence, and is grounded in the reality that the protection of right to housing enhances and positively impacts women's negotiating capacity in dealing with domestic violence.

Domestic violence, as the term suggests, is violence that takes place within the privacy of the home and at once shatters the right to live somewhere in 'security, peace, and dignity', which form the pillars of the right to adequate housing[3] guaranteed under international law. The chapter begins with a brief note on the right to adequate housing under international law, presenting an overview of the components of the right to adequate housing and examining the dynamics of domestic violence as being in breach of these components. While pausing briefly on the assorted factors responsible for lack of security of tenure which result in forced evictions due to domestic violence, an attempt has been made to examine the correlation between tenancy rights, inheritance rights, and domestic violence and to establish that security of tenure in the form of right to housing, and a right to reside acts as a shield against domestic violence.

Studies have sufficiently established inheritance rights and domestic violence as being inversely related to each other. Indeed, inheritance rights are considered the most comprehensive means of insuring security of tenure.[4] Studies also indicate inheritance as being the primary source of ownership of house and land for women.[5] In the absence of de facto inheritance rights and discriminatory customary practices governing ownership patterns for women in most parts of the world, it becomes imperative that the next best steps that can be taken to ensure security of tenure for women be examined. One such step is to recognize and protect the right to reside,[6] irrespective of ownership or title for all members of the household, especially the women.

[3] General Comment No. 4 on the Right to Adequate Housing, adopted by the U.N. Committee on Economic, Social Cultural Rights, U.N. Doc. E/C.12/1991/4 (1991) at para 7 Note, also the working definition of the right to adequate housing developed by the Special Rapporteur on Adequate Housing Miloon Kothari: 'as the right of every woman, man, youth and child to gain and sustain a secure home and community in which to live in peace and dignity'.

[4] With the exception of state sponsored forced evictions or evictions due to war, natural calamities, and so on, ownership of property remains the most comprehensive guarantee in securing tenure, irrespective of gender.

[5] As against self-acquired ownership of house or land.

[6] In the context of women's right to reside, while the right is directly or indirectly recognized under several legislations relating to women in all states, in this chapter the term 'right to housing' has been used to indicate a right to reside, independent of legal right in property.

Laws addressing domestic violence, without exception, recognize the need to create a distance between the victim[7] and the perpetrator and in most cases, provide for protection, restitution, and alternatives to a violent home in the form of state-run shelters and safe homes.[8] The PWDVA, 2005[9] goes a step further[10] to articulate the right of survivors to continue to reside in the household, irrespective of title or ownership, to the exclusion of the perpetrator.[11] Focusing on the essential components that best represent the objectives behind the articulation of the right to residence under PWDVA, the discussion on jurisprudence under the right to housing, developed over a decade,[12] examines whether the courts have adequately protected the right to residence under the PWDVA and upheld the spirit fundamental to the provision.

Domestic violence is not just a phenomenon between male and female partners but extends to violence against all members residing together in a domestic relationship.[13] Since the aim is to examine housing rights of women in the context of domestic violence, the scope of this chapter is limited to the study of domestic violence where the victim is female and the perpetrator male, but extends beyond intimate partner relationships to other relationships such as son–mother, brother–sister, nephew–aunt, that exist within the house. The chapter concludes with the premise that in the absence of de facto ownership rights in property,[14] security of tenure for women must be ensured through a guarantee that they cannot, under any circumstances, be dispossessed from the shared household[15] and that such a guarantee will act

[7] The terms survivor and victim have been used interchangeably throughout the chapter, both refer to the woman who has suffered or continues to suffer from domestic violence.

[8] Further discussed in the section on select domestic violence laws from Asia.

[9] PWDVA, 2005, the Civil law for addressing Domestic Violence in India.

[10] Under the PWDVA, provisions for Shelter Homes (Section 6) exist in addition to the right to residence and not only as a substitute for the right to residence.

[11] PWDVA Section 17 and 19.

[12] The PWDVA was enacted in the year 2005 and came into force in 2006.

[13] PWDVA, Section 2(f) defines Domestic Relationship as: 'a relationship between two persons who live or have, at any point of time lived together in a shared household, when they are related by consanguinity, marriage or through a relationship in the nature of marriage, adoption or are family members living together as a joint family'.

[14] In natal and/or matrimonial property.

[15] PWDVA, Section 2(s) Definition of Shared Household discussed in detail n. 77.

as an essential empowering tool for women dealing with the phenomenon of domestic violence.

Locating Domestic Violence within the Right to Housing under International Law

The right to adequate housing finds explicit mention in a wide variety of international instruments;[16] Article 11 (1) of the International Covenant on Economic, Social and Cultural Rights (ICESCR) contains, however, the most comprehensive,[17] legal provisions related to the right to adequate housing.[18] The essential components of 'adequacy' identified by the Committee on Economic, Social, Cultural Rights (CESCR) as comprising the right to adequate housing are: legal security of tenure,[19] availability of services, materials, facilities and infrastructure,[20] affordability,[21] habitability,[22] accessibility,[23] location,[24] cultural adequacy,[25] thereby widening the scope of the right

[16] Article 25 (1) The Universal Declaration of Human Rights; Article 5 (e) (iii) The Convention on the Elimination of All Forms of Racial Discrimination; Article 27 The Convention on the Rights of the Child; Article 14 (2) (h) and 16 (1) (h) The Convention on the Elimination of All Forms of Discrimination Against Women and Article 21 The Convention Relating to the Status of Refugees. The Habitat II Conference held in 1996 in Istanbul was a vital step towards action.

[17] The right to adequate house under ICESCR, from the perspective of women, is further strengthened under General Comment No. 4 by the statement of the Committee on Economic, Social, Cultural Rights (CESCR), 'in particular, enjoyment of this right ... is not to be subjected to any form of discrimination' General Comment No. 4, with the exception of state sponsored forced evictions or evictions due to war, natural calamities, and so on, ownership of property remains the most comprehensive guarantee in securing tenure, irrespective of gender, at para 6.

[18] S. Leckie, 'The Human Right to Adequate Housing', in *Economic, Social, Cultural Rights, A Textbook*, in A. Edi, C. Krause, and A. Rosas, 2nd revised edition (Dordrecht/Boston/London: Martinus Nijhoff Publishers, 2001), p. 153. See also General Comment No. 4 at para 3: 'Although a wide variety of international instruments address the different dimensions of the right to adequate housing, Art 11(1) is the most comprehensive and perhaps the most important of the relevant provisions.'

[19] General Comment No. 4, para 8 (a).

[20] General Comment No. 4, para 8 (b).

[21] General Comment No. 4, para 8 (c).

[22] General Comment No. 4, para 8 (d).

[23] General Comment No. 4, para 8 (e).

[24] General Comment No. 4, para 8 (f).

[25] General Comment No. 4, para 8 (g).

and extending it beyond the concept of a house, simply, as a place to live. From among the list of standards associated with the right to adequate housing under ICESCR, the prevalence of domestic violence violates at the very least, the accepted standards of adequacy, habitability, and legal security.

Domestic violence takes the form of verbal, physical, sexual, psychological, and economic abuse.[26] Abuse takes place on a continuing basis and is rarely a matter of sporadic incidents. If adequate housing is understood as ensuring to its occupants a life of security, peace, and dignity, the inadequacy of a house where domestic violence abounds cannot be a matter of debate. The woman suffering domestic abuse systematically loses all sense of security, peace, and dignity and lives instead, in fear, oppression, and humiliation,[27] and with it, she loses her right to adequate housing as guaranteed under Article 11(1) of ICESCR.

It has been accurately pointed out that the 'adequacy' concept must go beyond the seemingly material safety standards developed by the CESCR in General Comment No. 4 to include the dangers posed by domestic violence. Closely related to the concept of adequacy is the standard of habitability, which has been interpreted as a 'guarantee' of the 'physical safety' of occupants. Domestic violence turns the home into a hostile space, as physical safety of the victim cannot be guaranteed; this directly breaches the adequacy and habitability requirements implicit within the right to adequate housing.[28]

Legal security of tenure is regarded as the cornerstone of the right to housing and accords the occupants 'protection from forced eviction, harassment and other threats'.[29] Since men are traditionally seen as heads of households,[30] security of tenure in almost all cases is guaranteed to men to the exclusion of

[26] Economic abuse is a type of domestic violence under some of the domestic laws and is significant within the context of this chapter. Economic abuse includes inter alias controlling finances, either own or of the victim's, preventing access to earnings, alienating personal belongings or household goods, denial of finances for basic necessities. Though economic violence is not as visible as physical or psychological violence it has the effect of excess control over the victim's life and can have serious psychological and physical impact over a period of time.

[27] G. Paglione, 'Domestic Violence and Housing Rights: A Reinterpretation of the Right to Housing', *Human Rights Quarterly* 28 (2006): 126.

[28] Paglione, 'Domestic Violence and Housing Rights', p. 132.

[29] General Comment No. 4, at para 8 (a).

[30] L. Farha, 'Women and Housing', in *Women and International Human Rights Law, Volume 1*, ed. K.D. Askin and D.M. Koenig (New York: Transnational Publishers, Inc. Ardsley, 2000), p. 511.

women. This dynamic ensures that women are either *de jure* or *de facto* prevented from buying, inheriting, or owning property as a result of discriminatory laws or by customs regulating inheritance laws and access to property. In the absence of legal rights in the home where she resides, the domestic violence survivor is forced to remain in an abusive relationship because if she leaves in order to escape the violence, she risks homelessness.[31] The Special Rapporteur on Adequate Housing has acknowledged that 'domestic violence is a key cause of homelessness and presents a real threat to women's security of person and tenure' and that 'women continue to live in violent relationships because they face homelessness if they resist domestic violence'.[32] It is indeed the tragic reality of domestic violence that best brings to fore the issues related to the right or the absence thereof to women's right to adequate housing.

Leilani Farah[33] visited India in 2016 with the objective of examining the housing and homeless conditions of vulnerable groups in light of legislation, policies, and programmes. The Report on her mission to India[34] records: the Special Rapporteur's meetings with women who had fled violent households revealed that few housing options for these women had left them 'destitute, living on the roadside'.[35] She notes that violence against women is fundamentally linked to the right to adequate housing, as indicated by the CESCR in its General Comment No. 4, and that under the international commitment to combat domestic violence, 'one essential measure would be to mainstream the links between domestic violence and the right to adequate housing at all levels of government'.[36]

[31] While homelessness is several definitions, the UN interpreted homeless to include 'those sleeping without shelter, in constructions not meant for habitation and in welfare institutions'. For the purpose of the Chapter, it is in this sense that the term homeless has been used.

[32] Women and Adequate Housing, Study by the Special Rapporteur on Adequate Housing as a Component of the Right to Adequate Standard of Living and on the Right to Non-Discrimination, Miloon Kothari, in accordance with Commission Resolution 2002/49, U.N, ECOSOC, Comm'n on Human Rights, 59th Sess., Agenda Item 10, U.N. Doc.E/CN.4/2003/55 (2003).

[33] UN Special Rapporteur on Adequate Housing, 2014–17.

[34] Report of the Special Rapporteur on adequate housing as a component of the right to an adequate standard of living, and on the right to non-discrimination in this context, on her mission to India, 10 January 2017, available at https://documents-ddsny.un.org/doc/UNDOC/GEN/G17/002/82/PDF/G1700282.pdf?OpenElement.

[35] Report of the Special Rapporteur on adequate housing, p. 16.

[36] General Comment No. 4, p. 16.

In linking domestic violence to the right to adequate housing, two distinct approaches can be traced. While one directs its energy in understanding domestic violence as the cause of the violation of the right to housing, the second approach studies inadequate housing conditions as a cause of domestic violence and other forms of violence. Both approaches point us to a sort of dual violation of human rights since the right to adequate housing and domestic violence appear to be entwined under both. In a study conducted in Sri Lanka, single-room houses were provided by the British for plantation workers over 100 years ago, and even today more than three families live under one roof, domestic violence is reported to be frequent,[37] and poor living conditions, lack of privacy are cited as the reasons for the violence. Several studies indicate that homeless women suffer the most severe kind of abuse and violence.[38] The present chapter has been restricted to the study of domestic violence as a violation of the right to adequate housing.

Domestic Violence as Forced Eviction

Forced evictions are a grave human rights issue[39] and represent a prima facie violation of the right to adequate housing, as being 'incompatible' with the provisions of ICESCR.[40] It would be unfair and incorrect to state however, that only women are affected by forced evictions or that domestic violence is the primary cause of forced evictions. Armed conflicts, internal strife, communal violence, conflicts over land rights, development projects such as dams, land acquisition measures, and even sporting events like the Olympic Games are some known causes of forced evictions which take the face of refugee movements, mass exodus, internal displacements, and forced population transfers.[41] Irrespective of the factors responsible, it has been

[37] 'Interlinkages between Violence against Women and Women's Right to Adequate Housing', Proceedings of the Asia Regional Consultation on The Interlinkages between Violence against Women and Womens Right to Adequate Housing, 2003, available at http://www.hic-sarp.org/documents/Interlinkages_VAW&RAH.pdf, p. 24.

[38] See S. Chaudhry, A. Joseph, and I. Prakash Singh, 'Violence and Violations: The Reality of Homeless Women in India', 2014, available at http://hlrn.org.in/documents/Violence_and_Violations_Homeless_Women_in_India_2014.pdf

[39] General Comment 7 on Forced Evictions, U.N. GAOR, U.N. ECOSOC, Comm'n on Human Rts., 16th Session, U.N. Doc. E/C.12/1997/4 (1997) at para 1.

[40] Chaudhry, Joseph, and Prakash Singh, 'Violence and Violations'.

[41] General Comment No. 7, paras 5, 6, 7.

established that women along with other vulnerable groups 'suffer disproportionately from forced evictions'.[42]

Domestic violence, in the absence of security of tenure in the form of ownership or tenancy rights for women, is a major cause of forced evictions. Stated simply, in most societies, women's access to property is through their relationships to men such as husbands, fathers, brothers, sons, and other male relatives and when these relationships come to an end as a result of dispute, death, or divorce, women lose their home, land, or property by forcible eviction.[43] Forced evictions caused by domestic violence which result in loss of home for the survivor can strike in two ways: in some cases women leave home to escape violence and in other cases they are thrown out the house by the abuser and are thus rendered homeless. While the second scenario qualifies easily as a case of forced eviction by private persons, the first case may not immediately appear as falling under the category of forced eviction, as it is often argued that the woman in these cases made a conscious decision and exercised choice in leaving the house. Courts have often denied the right to residence for women who 'chose' to leave a violent home. A closer and a more sensitive glance at the situation will make it apparent however, that the decision to leave a violent home was not out of 'choice' but rather the absence of it.

G. Paglione appropriately calls an approach that labels a situation where the woman escapes a violent home at the cost of being rendered homeless voluntary, an 'unrealistic and deceptive' approach.[44] Choice must necessarily be accompanied with the existence of reasonable alternatives and in most cases, for the domestic violence survivor, the only alternative to leaving is to remain in a violent home. In the face of intense physical and mental violence, when the woman leaves, it is a case of a compulsory act of survival and not one of choice.[45] Lack of choice is, however, not the only commonality between traditional forms of forced evictions and those due to domestic violence. Women who are forced to leave their homes by violent partners or by circumstances created by them are victims of the same process as in the case of persons coercively removed from their homes by state agents. The situation of the evictor and that of the process of eviction share the common

42 General Comment No. 7, para 10.

43 Paglione, 'Domestic Violence and Housing Rights', p. 135.

44 Paglione, 'Domestic Violence and Housing Rights', p. 138.

45 Paglione, 'Domestic Violence and Housing Rights', p. 138.

features of coercive removal, intimidation, threats to life, loss of possessions, and unavailability of an alternate place to go.[46]

In a situation of domestic violence, the plight of women goes to the very heart of the definition of forced evictions in General Comment No. 7 as 'the permanent or temporary removal against the will of individuals, families and/ or communities from the homes and/or land which they occupy, without the provision of, and access to, appropriate forms of legal or other protection'.[47] It requires little analysis to appreciate that when women have no legal title in the property by way of ownership or tenancy rights, the law clearly tilts in favour of men who have the legal right of possession. It is indeed ironic that law prohibits evicting a tenant, say in the case of arrears in payment, unless a proper procedure under law is followed, while a wife or a mother who has no legal rights in the property can be evicted without following any procedure of law and this is indeed the stark reality of domestic violence that a wife, mother, sister or daughter has fewer rights in the home where she resides than a tenant has under the law.[48]

Egyptian law, to provide just one example, limits a woman's right to adequate housing post-divorce to the period during which she has physical custody of the children, rendering both childless women and those who no longer retain custody of their children perpetually at risk of homelessness. Under Egyptian law, women do not obtain a share of, or legal title to, the marital home. Instead, the marital home is viewed as the exclusive property of the husband, both in marriage and divorce. Save having custody of children, women have no entitlement to the marital home upon divorce; the husband is only required to provide 'adequate independent accommodation for his young children by his divorced wife and for the wife who has custody of the children'.[49] Thus, women who have spent years maintaining and contributing to the marital home are left with no right to live in the house.

46 Paglione, 'Domestic Violence and Housing Rights', p. 139.

47 General Comment No. 7, para 5.

48 This is an analogy that has been articulated by Indira Jaising (Senior Advocate at the Supreme Court of India, former Additional Solicitor General) at various forums on domestic violence and best represents the spirit behind the Right to Residence under the PWDVA, the civil law addressing domestic violence against women in India.

49 A. Browne and S. Bassuk, 'Intimate Violence in the Lives of Homelessness and Poor Housed Women', *American Journal of Psychiatry* 67, 2 (1997): 261–78; See also, 'Egypt Situation Report on Violence Against Women', available at http://www.euromedrights.org/wp-content/uploads/2017/03/Factsheet-2017-VAW-Egypt-EN.pdf.

Forced evictions thus takes place in various ways and each time the loss of home caused by family members takes the face of domestic violence and must thus be prevented not only as a right under the right to housing but also as the human right to a life free of violence. The threat or act of being evicted from one's home is a violation of security of tenure and at the same time it is a form of domestic violence in itself. Because a victim of domestic violence leaves her abusive home multiple times before she finally escapes the violence, she and her children may experience multiple periods of homelessness and several episodes of eviction.

Domestic Violence and Inheritance Rights

Women's ownership of property extends their capacity, negotiation power, and enhances their ability to address vulnerabilities and serves therefore as a critical tool of protection against domestic violence. Though ownership rights may not always ensure protection against forced evictions, especially in cases where such eviction is part of a larger scheme of discrimination and is carried out by state actors, in the case of homelessness due to domestic violence where the abuser, a private party, is directly responsible, ownership rights in property can considerably enhance protection for the rightful owner.

Ownership over immovable assets by women has emerged as a significant area that must be incorporated within any discourse seeking to impact women's economic and social security and must be seen as enhancing their capacity to deal with risk, in this case domestic violence. Analysis of research, drawing attention to the significance of focusing on women's ownership of house or land or both in gender sensitive social protection policies, must therefore form an integral part of any discussion aimed at examining domestic violence as a violation of the right to adequate housing and as a cause of forced eviction and homelessness.

Studies indicate inheritance as the principal source of ownership of home or land for women,[50] despite wide-scale discrimination under inheritance laws and customary practices governing women's inheritance rights. The key issue with equal inheritance rights for women is not always inequalities in law; even where law ensures equal inheritance rights between the sexes, a

[50] International Centre for Research on Women, Property Ownership and Inheritance Rights of Women for Social Progress, 'The South Asia Experience-Synthesis Report of Three States', available at www.icrw.org/docs/2006_propertyrights-southasia.pdf.

complicated social and cultural dynamics operates that perpetuates the role of a man as 'protector'. This guise of the male protector kept alive and thriving by society ensures that women are kept out of property rights. This isolation in both law and its implementation operates in a way that asserts control over women's autonomy, bodies, and labour and 'enrich' their 'protectors'.[51] Such segregation and general apathy towards women's right to property at all levels—courts, administration, and the society in general—also operates to ensure that women do not often pursue legal remedies for property rights violations in states where such remedy exist in the first place.[52] The Special Rapporteur for Adequate Housing in her Report on India[53] identifies women as being especially vulnerable to 'multiple discrimination' in the access, control, ownership, and inheritance of housing, land, and property.[54] In India, inheritance practices continue to deny women title to housing, land, and property despite equal rights created under the Hindu Succession (Amendment) Act, 2005.[55]

Kenya is not the only example, but a striking one, of a state where women have unequal property rights under both law and custom. Women are systematically excluded from inheriting and are evicted from their lands and homes by family members in order to keep them away from inheriting. When relations end by way of death, divorce, or separation, the women lose their home, land, livestock, money, and household goods. This is a classic example of forced eviction due to blatant denial of inheritance rights, both in the natal and matrimonial home of a woman from rural Kenya.[56]

Pacific Island nations do not, similarly, provide secure joint ownership for married women and this seriously impacts their ability to leave a violent

[51] 'Human Rights Watch, Double Standards: Women's Property Rights Violations in Kenya', 2002, p. 2, available at http://www.hrw.org/reports/2003/kenya0303/kenya0303.pdf>.

[52] 'Human Rights Watch, Double Standards'.

[53] Report of the Special Rapporteur on adequate housing, para 54: 'Certain inheritance practices continue to be used to deny women title to housing, land and property despite the fact that, under the Hindu Succession (Amendment) Act, 2005, daughters and sons have equal rights'.

[54] An observation also made in 2014 by the Committee on the Elimination of Discrimination against Women, CEDAW/C/IND/CO/4-5, para 32 and 33.

[55] The Hindu Succession (Amendment) Act, 2005, No. 39 of 2005 [5 September 2005], available at http://www.hrln.org/admin/issue/subpdf/HSA_Amendment_2005.pdf.

[56] 'Human Rights Watch, Double Standards', pp. 17–18.

home.[57] Practices related to inheritance are not always uniform through any state. A woman in the Cook Islands shared that her village was divided into two parts, one side was a swampy area, the land rights over this part were held by women; since this area was an important source of food, women were seen as providers and there was little domestic violence on the swampy side; while there was a high level of domestic violence on the side where land rights were not held by women.[58]

A study conducted in Kerala, India,[59] aimed at studying interlinks between property ownership and domestic violence. The report established that women's ownership of property not only reduces the incidents of domestic violence but also enhances women's choices in escaping domestic violence.[60] It is important to note that Kerala is a state with exceptionally high female literacy levels, life expectancy, and health indicators and exhibits a striking similarity in the pattern of ownership of property between men and women, with approximately 36 per cent of men and women each owning either land, house, or both. This was reported to be a direct consequence of equality in inheritance rights of sons and daughters over paternal property.[61]

The women who owned property stated explicitly that owning property has protected them from potential violence and ownership of property enhanced, in their opinion, their status in the marital family, as the property they own contributes to economic security of the family as a whole.[62] Propertied women also noted that possession of a house gave them confidence that they will be able to take care of themselves and the children in case of a future emergency, independent of support from the husband, and that they would not tolerate violence at home 'in case it occurred' and 'would seek alternatives'.[63]

[57] 'Our Land, Our Home, Our Culture, Our Human Rights,' Proceedings of the Pacific Regional Consultation on 'Women's Rights to Adequate Housing and Land,' in cooperation with the UN Special Rapporteur on Adequate Housing at Fiji, 2004, Housing and Land Network, Habitat International Coalition, South Asia Regional Programme, New Delhi, India, 2006, available at http://www.hic-sarp.org/documents/fiji%20report.pdf.

[58] 'Our Land, Our Home, Our Culture, Our Human Rights,' p. 24.

[59] A part of the 'South Asia Experience-Synthesis Report of Three States,' 'The South Asia Experience-Synthesis Report of Three States,' pp. 10–36.

[60] The findings are based on a survey of 502 women who are married or were married at some point.

[61] 'The South Asia Experience-Synthesis Report of Three States,' p. 10.

[62] 'The South Asia Experience-Synthesis Report of Three States,' pp. 14–24. Note here that in some cases property serves as a source of income for the family.

[63] 'The South Asia Experience-Synthesis Report of Three States,' p. 15.

Among the women who owned property and faced domestic violence, 58 per cent of the women left the marital home and did not return, as compared to this, just 6 per cent left and did not return from those who did not own property and had faced domestic violence. On the other extreme, the study reports that 81 per cent of women not owning property and experiencing violence did not leave the marital home as compared to 29 per cent who owned property but did not leave a violent matrimonial home. Among the women who left and did not return, they either owned a house (37 per cent) or both a house and land (62 per cent). All those women who owned both a house and land did not return to a violent home. Clearly, for this group not only was there a place to reside but also a means to earn income from the land. The women who did not own any property and face violence shared through personal testimonies that ownership of property, especially a house, would have protected them from violence and provided them with the option to leave the violent home.[64]

That women who own property are more likely to leave a violent relationship is evident from the research findings discussed in this section; it would be interesting to delve into what happens after the women take the decision to leave. In the present study, all the women who owned property continue to reside in their own homes after leaving the marital home, while a large majority of women without any property, who left violent homes and did not return, continue to live with their parents or relatives.[65] This clearly indicates that ownership rights are not just significant at the stage of decision-making but continues to be a source of security and sustenance. Clearly, ownership rights can provide permanent protection to women in domestic violence, providing them with choices.

Domestic Violence Legislations and the Right to Reside

While all legislations on domestic violence take into account the requirement for alternate safe spaces or shelters as an emergency measure[66] or in the form of or as a part of protection orders,[67] laws do not in every case

64 'The South Asia Experience-Synthesis Report of Three States', p. 22.

65 'The South Asia Experience-Synthesis Report of Three States', p. 23.

66 Article 26, Law of Domestic Violence Prevention and Control, Socialist Republic of Vietnam, Law No: 02/2007/QH12 provides for 'temporary domicile and other essential support'.

67 Article 29 (3), Domestic Violence Law of the People's Republic of China: Personal safety protection order may include: (3) 'ordering the subject of the

explicitly create a 'right to reside' in the household where the victim currently lives. This is true even in cases where ouster orders[68] are provided for; in most cases these form a part of the protection order. A brief review of laws addressing domestic violence in select countries from Asia[69] clearly reflects the trend that laws take into account: the need for protecting the victim by providing for shelters or safe homes in order to create a distance between the perpetrator and the victim. These provisions appear at best to be an emergency measure of a temporary nature and do not in any way provide for housing rights of a more permanent nature.[70]

Domestic violence legislation in Cambodia[71] is a gender-neutral law that provides protection to all 'persons living under the roof of the house who are dependents of the households'.[72] There exists a provision for moving the perpetrators from the scene if requested by the victims to do so. The victim can however be removed from the scene for their safety even where such a request is not made,[73] as a temporary measure. In addition, the perpetrator can be prohibited from 'destroying the property' or instructed not to sell the victims' or the victims' relatives joint property, prohibition from approaching or entering the house shared together or at a place the victim resides and the place of work without taking permission of the victim or the authorities in charge and for taking legitimate measures that are necessary to protect the safety of the victims and the household members or

---

application to move out of the applicant's residence' such an order can be made for up to six months at a time. Japan: Act on the Prevention of Spousal Violence and the Protection of Victims (Act No. 31 of 2001) residence rights discussed under Protection orders, Chapter IV of the Act.

[68] Article 10, Act on Protection of Victims of Domestic Violence 2007: 'order forbidding a perpetrator of domestic violence from entering his/her family's residence or going closer to any family member, as well as setting forth the childcare arrangements'.

[69] Though all existing domestic violence laws in Asia were consulted, only findings from those laws that refer to the point of study have been included in this section.

[70] With the exception of laws addressing domestic violence in Sri Lanka and Singapore.

[71] Law on the Prevention of Domestic Violence and the Protection of Victims, 2005.

[72] Article 3, Law on the Prevention of Domestic Violence and the Protection of Victims, 2005.

[73] Article 13, Law on the Prevention of Domestic Violence and the Protection of Victims, 2005.

persons involved.[74] The action to 'protect the safety and welfare of victim or to preserve the properties of the victim' as temporary measure allows for wide discretion.[75] Under a protection order, the perpetrator could be prohibited from approaching the house shared,[76] this provision is akin to an ouster order. The Elimination of Violence in Households, 2004, Indonesia is also a gender-neutral law, the law explicitly recognizes though that 'victims of violence in households are mostly women',[77] it does not mention dispossession or create a right to reside in the household. The law provides for a 'safe house'[78] belonging to the government or an 'alternate dwelling place'.[79] In South Korea, the domestic violence law contains detailed provisions on 'Protection Facilities'[80] for domestic violence victims, but does not refer to the home and the right of the woman to reside there.

The domestic violence law in Malaysia[81] grants the 'right of exclusive occupation to any protected person of the shared residence'[82] by excluding the person against whom the order is made, regardless of whether the shared residence is solely owned or leased or jointly owned or leased by the parties. This is made conditional, however, by a clause that stipulates that the court shall not make an order excluding the person against whom the order is made from the whole of a shared residence, that is solely or jointly owned or leased by him, unless, 'it is satisfied that there is no other way to secure the personal safety of any protected person for the time being and

[74] Article 14, Law on the Prevention of Domestic Violence and the Protection of Victims, 2005.

[75] Article 24, Law on the Prevention of Domestic Violence and the Protection of Victims, 2005.

[76] Article 25, Law on the Prevention of Domestic Violence and the Protection of Victims, 2005.

[77] Law of the Republic of Indonesia, Number 23 of Year 2004 Regarding Elimination of Violence in Households, p. 2.

[78] Law of the Republic of Indonesia, Number 23 of Year 2004, elucidations to the Act, it defines a safe house as a temporary dwelling place to provide protection to the victim in accordance with designated standards.

[79] Article 22 (d) Law of the Republic of Indonesia, Number 23 of Year 2004.

[80] Act on the Prevention of Domestic Violence and Protection, and so on, of Victims. Thereof, Republic of Korea, Act No. 5487, 31 December 1997, Amended 2006, Article 7–2 detail provisions with respect to Protection Facilities.

[81] The Domestic Violence Act, 1994 (as at 1997), available from APWLD 2003 (International Law Book Services), at apwld@apwld.org.

[82] Section 1 Protection Order, The Domestic Violence Act, 1994.

such order must be revoked if a suitable alternative residence is found for the protected person'.[83] It has been noted that despite nine years of lobbying by the women's movement, the act was passed without an 'unconditional ouster clause', on the rationale that a man should have a right to stay in his house. As a result, while the law recognizes the need for an alternative residence, usually in the form of shelters for the victim, courts are reluctant to pass orders for removal of the man who has a title in the property. In the absence of the ouster clause, women continue to live in homes with the abuser who, in most cases, treat the protection order as a mere piece of paper.

Provisions under the domestic violence law in Sri Lanka[84] that protect the women's right to reside in her home are similar in nature and coverage to those under the PWDVA.[85] As in the case of most domestic violence laws, these provisions form a part of protection orders.[86] Among other reliefs, protection orders can be passed preventing the respondent from occupying the shared residence,[87] restraining him from 'selling, transferring, alienating or encumbering the matrimonial home so as to place the aggrieved person in a destitute position'.[88] A clause attached to this section, stipulates however that

> in imposing any prohibition referred to the subsection the Court shall have regard to the need for the accommodation of the aggrieved person or the children (if any) of the aggrieved person and the children (if any) of the respondent; any hardship that may be caused to the respondent or to any other person as a result of the making of the Order.[89]

The Singapore Women's Charter[90] provides and articulates the right to residence under the provision for protection orders: 'A protection order[91]

[83] Section 4 Protection Order.

[84] Prevention of Domestic Violence Act, No. 34 of 2005, Sri Lanka, http://www.childprotection.gov.lk/Child_Related_ACTs/Prevention%20of%20Domestic%20Violence%20Act%20No.%2034%20of%202005.pdf.

[85] Discussed in detail in the next section.

[86] Prevention of Domestic Violence Act, No. 34 of 2005, Sri Lanka, section 11.

[87] Prevention of Domestic Violence Act, No. 34 of 2005, Sri Lanka, section 11 (e).

[88] Prevention of Domestic Violence Act, No. 34 of 2005, Sri Lanka, section 11 (1).

[89] Prevention of Domestic Violence Act, No. 34 of 2005, Sri Lanka, section 11 (1).

[90] Singapore Women's Charter, Chapter 353, Part VII, Protection of Family.

[91] Singapore Women's Charter, Chapter 353, Part VII, Protection of Family, section 5.

may, where the court is satisfied on a balance of probabilities that it is necessary for the protection or personal safety of the applicant, provide for such orders as the court thinks fit having regard to all the circumstances of the case, including any one or more of the following orders:

> The granting of the right of exclusive occupation to any protected person of the shared residence or a specified part of the shared residence by excluding the person against whom the order is made from the shared residence or specified part thereof, regardless of whether the shared residence is solely owned or leased by the person against whom the order is made or jointly owned or leased by the parties.'[92]

All protective legislation reflects the felt needs of the victims and experiences of civil society, which are essentially specific to cultural and customary practices. This is especially true with respect to legislations on families, women, and children. Provisions related to right to residence in this section must be read with this in mind.

The Scope of the Right to Residence under PWDVA

Direct forcible eviction or the creation of circumstances that prevent the survivor from enjoying the benefits that accrue from the home have been appropriately defined under the PWDVA as a type of domestic violence under the category of economic violence.[93] The PWDVA seeks further to

[92] Singapore Women's Charter, Chapter 353, Part VII, Protection of Family, section 5 (a).

[93] PWDVA, General Comment No. 4 on the Right to Adequate Housing, adopted by the U.N. Committee on Economic, Social Cultural Rights, U.N. Doc. E/C.12/1991/4 (1991), section 3 (iv): 'economic abuse' includes (*a*) deprivation of all or any economic or financial resources to which the aggrieved person is entitled under any law or custom whether payable under an order of a court or otherwise or which the aggrieved person requires out of necessity including, but not limited to, household necessities for the aggrieved person and her children, if any, *stridhan* (voluntary gifts given to a woman before or after her marriage (distinct from dowry in that it has no element of coercion), that a woman has absolute right over, property, jointly or separately owned by the aggrieved person, payment of rental related to the shared household and maintenance; (*b*) disposal of household effects, any alienation of assets whether movable or immovable, valuables, shares, securities, bonds, and the like or other property in which the aggrieved person has an interest or is entitled to use by virtue of the domestic relationship or which may be reasonably required by

articulate and protect the right to residence[94] in the shared household,[95] both directly and indirectly. This is done in recognition of the fact that in the absence of any title for the women in the shared household, the courts can, at the very least, establish that the domestic violence survivor has a right to reside in the space she calls home and that she is protected from being evicted and rendered homeless as a result of domestic violence. Direct recognition of the right to residence under the PWDVA is further strengthened and sought to be protected under the provisions for reliefs,[96] provided sometimes as a part of a protection order, but in most cases as a standalone relief known as the residence order.[97]

---

the aggrieved person or her children or her stridhan or any other property jointly or separately held by the aggrieved person; and (*c*) prohibition or restriction to continued access to resources or facilities which the aggrieved person is entitled to use or enjoy by virtue of the domestic relationship including access to the shared household.

[94] PWDVA, General Comment No. 4 on the Right to Adequate Housing, adopted by the U.N. Committee on Economic, Social Cultural Rights, U.N. Doc. E/C.12/1991/4 (1991), section 17: 'every woman in a domestic relationship shall have the right to reside in the Shared Household, whether or not she has any title or beneficial interest in the same'.

[95] PWDVA, Section 2 (s) Definition of Shared Household: 'shared household' means a household where the person aggrieved lives or at any stage has lived in a domestic relationship either singly or along with the respondent and includes such a household whether owned or tenanted either jointly by the aggrieved person and the respondent, or owned or tenanted by either of them in respect of which either the aggrieved person or the respondent or both jointly or singly have any right, title, interest, or equity and includes such a household which may belong to the joint family of which the respondent is a member, irrespective of whether the respondent or the aggrieved person has any right, title, or interest in the shared household.

[96] PWDVA provides for 'reliefs' under Section 18,19, 20, 21, and 22 in the form of Protection Orders, Residence Orders, Monetary Reliefs, Custody Orders, and Compensation Orders, respectively.

[97] PWDVA, Section 19 (1) Residence Orders: While disposing of an application ... the Magistrate may, on being satisfied that domestic violence has taken place, pass a residence order (*a*) restraining the respondent from disposing or in any other manner disturbing the possession of the aggrieved person from the shared household, whether or not the respondent has a legal or equitable interest in the shared household; (*b*) directing the respondent to remove himself from the shared household; (*c*) restraining the respondent or any of his relatives from entering any portion of the shared household in which the aggrieved person resides; (*d*) restraining the respondent from alienating or disposing off the shared household or encumbering

The right to reside in a matrimonial home for women and children and elderly parents[98] has always existed in India under personal laws[99] and penal provisions,[100] as an essential component within the right to maintenance[101] or as a part of alimony settlement at the time of divorce. The need for protecting the right of vulnerable members of a household has therefore always been recognized under the law and by courts alike. How then, one may ask, are the right to reside and relief for residence orders under the PWDVA distinct from the provisions under laws in existence prior to the enactment of the PWDVA? Residence orders are passed both as interim orders to provide protection against dispossession and as final orders establishing and ensuring continuity of residence in the shared household for the domestic violence survivor. Residence orders under the PWDVA are intended to provide quick relief to women, taking away, at the bare minimum any immediate threat of being thrown out of the home.[102]

The primary purpose of the residence order under the PWDVA is to ensure that the domestic violence survivor be granted the right to continue residing in the shared household[103] and in certain circumstances the abuser

---

the same; (*e*) restraining the respondent from renouncing his rights in the shared household except with the leave of the Magistrate; or (*f*) directing the respondent to secure same level of alternate accommodation for the aggrieved person as enjoyed by her in the shared household or to pay rent for the same, if the circumstances so require.

[98] Section 125, Criminal Procedure Code, 1973 provides for Order for maintenance of wives, children, and parents.

[99] Hindu Adoptions and Maintenance Act, 1956, Hindu Married Women's Right to Separate Residence and Maintenance Act, 1946, Muslim Women (Protection of rights on divorce) Act, 1986, Section 125 Criminal Procedure Code.

[100] Section 125, Criminal Procedure Code, 1973 provides for Order for maintenance of wives, children, and parents.

[101] In *B.P. Achala Anand v. S. Appi Reddy and Another*, MANU/SC/0100/2005 (2005) 3 SCC 313A; the Supreme Court decided that under the provisions of Hindu Adoption and Maintenance Act, 1956, a Hindu wife is entitled to be maintained by her husband and is entitled to remain under his roof and protection. She is also entitled to a separate residence if by reason of the husband's conduct or by his refusal to maintain her in his own place of residence or for other just cause she is compelled to live apart from him, this forms a is a part of the wife's right to maintenance.

[102] PWDVA, Section 19 (1) (a), Section 1 Protection Order, The Domestic Violence Act, 1994.

[103] If she desires to do so.

be removed from the household, irrespective of ownership or tenancy rights in the shared household.[104] Provision for removal of the abuser from the home in which he has proprietary or tenancy rights, which are in almost all cases superior to those held by the abused, necessitated that the special circumstances created by domestic violence, should, to a reasonable extent, tilt the law in favour of the abused. Residence orders can be passed in the form of restraining orders to ensure that the survivor is not thrown out of the house and that the abuser does not alienate his rights in the household in order to defeat the rights of the survivor. It is this all-encompassing understanding of the complex nature of domestic violence, the vulnerability of the survivor pitted against the position of power exerted by the abuser, that the right to residence and residence orders seek to address.

The right under the PWDVA differs from right to reside as part of right to maintenance under laws prior to the enactment of the PWDVA, also in that the PWDVA provides for a relief distinct and in addition to monetary[105] and compensatory reliefs.[106] A separate right to residence was created with detailed provision protecting the right to ensure that courts deliberate on special circumstances surrounding the nature of the shared household, the woman's residence needs and deliver judgments that are mindful of the unique situation of all the members of the shared household.

In appreciation of the fact that domestic violence is not a phenomenon between intimate partners alone and that in the absence of title in property, other female members of the household such as the mother, an aunt, or a sister residing in a domestic relationship in the shared household with the abuser, often face domestic violence in the form of removal or threats of removal from the house, the PWDVA provides that while a Stop Violence Order[107] may be passed against a female member of the household if she commits acts of domestic violence against another female member, no order for removal from the household can be passed against her. This special

[104] In most cases however, the women is required to demonstrate that she has been dispossessed, and in cases where she has left the home on her own to escape domestic violence, courts are often reluctant to pass residence orders. See I. Jaising and M. Sakhrani (eds), *Lawyers Collective, Law on Domestic Violence a Manual for Users*, second edition (New Delhi: Universal Law Publishing Co. Pvt Ltd, 2007).

[105] PWDVA, Section 20.

[106] PWDVA, Section 22.

[107] PWDVA, Protection Orders under Section 18 have the effect of a Stop Violence order and are commonly referred to as such.

clause[108] provides protection to all female members of the house from being rendered homeless and is an unequivocal recognition of the vulnerability of every woman to forced evictions.[109]

Domestic violence continues unabated as the victim is caught in a cycle of dependence in the home where she lives. The location of the home, furthermore, assumes significance for women as it determines proximity from schools and the place of work. Even in rare cases where an alternative is possible, for instance with the natal family, this may not always be a practical solution as it may entail moving to a different city or village, especially in light of the fact that this can at best be a temporary solution. Women are in most cases reluctant to move, most women want to continue to reside in their homes, they simply want the home to be violence free. Right to residence in the shared household where the woman resides must therefore be ensured, even if this entails removal of the abuser from the household. The spirit of the law is to ensure that the perpetrator of violence be made to leave the house and not the victim. In the absence of a right to reside, independent of a title in the house, it is the victim who is forced to leave the shared household.

The nature and composition of a shared household in India is not always simple; often, the person in whom the title of the household vests, is not necessarily the direct perpetrator of violence. Sons continue to reside with their parents after marriage, even when the shared household is not a joint family property.[110] It is not uncommon for a married son to be residing with his wife in a home that is the self-acquired property of both or either of his parents, where the son has no share in the title to the house.

[108] PWDVA, 2005, Clause to Section 19 (b): Provided that no order under clause (b) shall be passed against any person who is a woman. Section 19 (b): directing the respondent to remove himself from the shared household.

[109] An interesting situation emerges; a woman can be arrested as an abuser but cannot be ousted out of the house on the basis of a complaint. This is done to ensure that the eviction clause is not used by one woman against the other as a form of domestic violence. Also, a woman member accused of committing domestic violence can be directed under Section 19 (c) be restrained from entering any portion of the shared household.

[110] Broadly refers to property jointly held by all members of the Hindu undivided family: ancestral property acquired through inheritance or property self-acquired through joint funds. For the purposes of the present discussion, joint family property would imply that the husband or male partner of the domestic violence survivor has a right or title in the property jointly with other members of the shared household.

It is this multifaceted nature of the joint family system[111] and the Indian household that further complicates the question of right to reside and courts are confronted frequently with cases where the definition of the shared household requires deliberation. The PWDVA provides a right to reside in the shared household; courts must therefore establish whether the woman has a legitimate right to reside based on the claim made by her that she seeks residence in a home, which is her shared household, within the intended parameters of the definition of a shared household under the PWDVA.

A comprehensive, all-encompassing definition of a shared household under the PWDVA is intended to protect women's right to reside, irrespective of ownership or tenancy rights; the right is framed on the foundation of factum of residence, not just in the present but also in the past. A typical scenario to elucidate this point would be the case of a newly married couple residing in a home that is either a joint family home or is exclusively owned by the husband's parents. At a later date, for reasons of profession or otherwise, the couple may discontinue to reside with the parents and seek residence elsewhere. The definition of shared household under the PWDVA is worded such that the home where the couple has resided at 'any point in time' is covered under the definition of shared household. That the woman has a right to reside in the shared household has never been disputed by courts, it is with respect to the right to reside in a 'particular household' claimed to be a shared household that has resulted in varied, and at times contradictory, judgments by courts in India.

Jurisprudence on the Right to Residence under PWDVA

That courts in India have upheld the right to reside in a household that must qualify as 'adequate' under the right to housing,[112] is clear from several judgments in favour of the domestic violence survivor and her right to adequate housing, granted as part of right to residence under the PWDVA. The Delhi High Court viewed with displeasure the order of a lower court

[111] A joint family may consist of all or some persons lineally descended from a common ancestor, including their wives and daughters. While the common ancestor is necessary for bringing a joint family into existence, this is not necessary for its continuance. The death of common ancestor does not mean that the joint family comes to an end; the joint family ends only though acts of its members, such as partition of ancestral property.

[112] Under the ICESCR, discussed in earlier sections of the chapter.

confining the residing rights of the aggrieved woman[113] to the annex of the shared household and denial of her use of the kitchen, calling such an order as one emanating from a 'feudal and archaic attitude' noting that 'in relegating her to the outhouse' the wife has been treated 'as if she where a mere chattel'.[114] The High Court, while appreciating that in a case such as this one, where the household is large enough to accommodate both parties and ensure that a distance between them can be maintained, noted that decent and adequate living arrangements and facilities must be ensured for the wife. Similarly, where the aggrieved woman had been provided residence in the same premises as her alcoholic husband and his second wife by the family court,[115] the High Court of Bombay directed the husband to provide alternate residence comprising two flats on a different floor of the same residence complex where the husband lived, in light of the fact that the husband had adequate means to do so.[116] Clearly, due respect was shown by the court in ensuring that arrangements for adequate housing are provided keeping in mind both physical and emotional comfort of the woman,[117] noting further, that 'if the husband can offer the wife no alternative accommodation to reside there peaceably, he would be required to be stopped from living in such a matrimonial home with his second wife'.[118]

Jurisprudence under PWDVA demonstrates sensitivity towards housing requirements of women, and courts have taken into consideration several factors such as safety and comfort and adjudicated based on the facts of each case. The two cases discussed in the preceding paragraph adequately demonstrate this sensitivity. The case of a 63-year-old woman survivor of

[113] PWDVA, Section 2 (a) defines Aggrieved Person as 'any woman who is, or has been, in a domestic relationship with the respondent and who alleges to have been subjected to any act of domestic violence by the respondent'.

[114] *Natasha Kohli* v. *Mon Mohan Kohli*, 172 (2010) DLT 516 (2010) 119 DRJ 44 (Delhi H.C.) (24 September 2010), para12.

[115] Family Courts were constituted in several cities in India under the Family Courts Act, 1984 with the objective to promote conciliation and secure speedy settlement of disputes relating to marriage and family affairs and matters connected therewith.

[116] *Sabah Sami Khan* v. *Adnan Sami Khan* (2011) 1 MhLj 427 (Bombay High Court) (21 October 2010).

[117] *Sabah Sami Khan* v. *Adnan Sami Khan*, para 24: 'She is expected to reside there peaceably and without the intrusion of a second wife or the domestic violence otherwise caused by an errant husband'.

[118] *Sabah Sami Khan* v. *Adnan Sami Khan*, para 17.

domestic violence will further validate the point. In this case, the Supreme Court modified the order of the high court giving due consideration to the woman's apprehension for her safety while residing alone in a rented accommodation.[119] The Supreme Court directed that she be provided with a right of residence in the home where the husband is presently residing by way of relief under Section 19 of the PWDVA. The residence order passed in her favour provided her with a 'suitable portion' of the house along with 'all amenities required to make the residential premises suitably habitable, including furniture chosen by the aggrieved woman in order to enable her to live with dignity in the shared household'.[120] In addition to the residence order, protection order and monetary relief was also provided to ensure her safety and to provide for her expenses.

Right to residence under the PWDVA was intended as a right independent of the woman's title in the household, whether proprietary or tenancy. A comprehensive definition of shared household[121] was provided for two primary reasons: first, to ensure that right to residence is not confused with property rights and secondly to accommodate the complex nature of the Indian household. Jurisprudence indicates, however, that while courts acknowledge and understand that the woman rarely, if ever, has a legal title in the home where she resides, ownership or tenancy rights over the shared household and who these rights belong to continues to dictate, either directly or indirectly, the right to reside in the shared household under the PWDVA for the aggrieved woman. While the fact of residence in the shared household, present or in the past, was intended as being the sole determinant of the right to reside, courts continue to debate if such a right exists against the husband exclusively or does it extend to a residence belonging to the husband's parents. The debate persists; the following cases will demonstrate that courts are reluctant to pass residence orders in favour of the woman where the house belongs exclusively to the parent/s-in-law and is not a joint family property.

The Supreme Court ruling in the notoriously infamous case of *S.R. Batra v. Taruna Batra*[122] (*Batra* v. *Batra*) was unambiguous in holding that a

[119] *V.D. Bhanot* v. *Savita Bhanot*, AIR 2012 SC 965, I (2012) DMC 482 SC (7 February 2012).

[120] *V.D. Bhanot* v. *Savita Bhanot*, para 11.

[121] PWDVA, Section 2 (s) Definition of Shared Household.

[122] *S.R. Batra* v. *Taruna Batra* (2007) 2 ALD 66 (SC), A (2007) SC 1118 (Supreme Court) (15 December 2006).

woman cannot claim a house as her shared household if the house belongs exclusively to the mother-in-law and the husband has no right in it, unless, the house is a joint family property. The aggrieved woman's claim was further weakened by the fact that the husband no longer resided in this house. Supreme Court noted that the wife has claimed residence in this house because she and her husband had resided on the second floor of this house after marriage. When dispute arose between the couple, the husband filed for divorce and moved out of the house. The wife started living with her parents. The judgment notes that the right to claim residence in every such house where the husband and the wife have 'lived together in the past',[123] 'would lead to chaos and would be absurd. It is well settled that any interpretation which leads to absurdity should not be accepted'.[124] This judgment impacted several right to residence cases adversely, women were denied the right to reside in homes belonging exclusively to the in-laws even though they had resided in these homes after marriage.

Courts have recognized, however, that at the stage of passing interim order as an emergency relief, the question of ownership of the shared household would be premature. The Delhi High Court did not find it appropriate to apply the ratio in *Batra* v. *Batra* in determining urgent interim relief.[125] In this case, the aggrieved woman had been thrown out of the house along with her minor daughter. The shared household was owned exclusively by the father-in-law. The Delhi High Court restored the woman to the portion of the house she had previously occupied and directed that she be allowed the use of the kitchen and be provided with a duplicate key to the house. The Supreme Court's narrow interpretation of the definition of household[126] was found inapplicable in deciding urgent interim relief.

Yet again, in a case where the mother-in-law was seeking an injunction restraining her daughter-in-law from entering the house which was exclusively owned by her, the Delhi High Court allowed the daughter-in-law to

[123] Act on the Prevention of Domestic Violence and Protection, and so on, of Victims. Thereof, Republic of Korea, Act No. 5487, 31 December 1997, Amended 2006, Article 7–2 detail provisions with respect to Protection Facilities.

[124] Act on the Prevention of Domestic Violence and Protection, and so on, of Victims. Thereof, Republic of Korea, Act No. 5487, 31 December 1997, Amended 2006, Article 7–2 detail provisions with respect to Protection Facilities, para 20.

[125] *Nidhi Kumar Gandhi* v. *The State* (2010) Cr.L.J. (NOC) 79, 157 (2009) DLT 472, II (2009) DMC 647 (Delhi High Court) (16 January 2009).

[126] In *Batra* v. *Batra*, PWDVA, Section 22.

continue residing in the house till such time that alternate arrangements could be made, on grounds that 'there is no reason to conclude that the definition of shared household does not extend to a house which is owned by a mother-in-law or any other female relative, 'since they are encompassed under the definition of "respondent"[127] under 2(q)'.[128] The High Court chose to deliberate on the factual matrix of the case distinguishing the facts from those in the *Batra* v. *Batra,* stating that in the case the dispute had not emanated from an application under PWDVA; secondly, the wife in the said case was not an occupant of the property at the time of filing; and finally, the court did not directly consider the definition of respondent or domestic relationship, and, moreover, failed to explore the link between these two concepts and the definition of shared household. According to the Delhi High Court, each of these three distinctions establish that the husband's title or interest in the property is not relevant in determining the factum of shared household.[129] This is a very progressive judgment where the High Court read the different provisions of the PWDVA together and accorded a just interpretation in favour of both the daughter-in law and the mother-in-law. The mother-in-law's health was also taken into consideration in granting residence to the daughter-in-law in the shared household temporarily, ensuring that she was not left without shelter till such time that the husband provided alternate accommodation for her, while at the same time, respecting the mother-in-law's right to exclusive residence in her home.

Courts have acknowledged that if the husband's title in the shared household alone was to establish the wife's right to reside, 'every husband will simply alienate his property in favor of somebody else after a dispute has arisen and would take a stand that the house where they last resided is not a shared household and therefore the wife is not entitled to seek for residence in the shared household'.[130] Bombay High Court, in a case with similar facts, challenged the sale deed whereby the husband had transferred his rights in

[127] PWDVA, Section 2 (q): 'respondent' means any adult male person who is, or has been, in a domestic relationship with the aggrieved person and against whom the aggrieved person has sought any relief under this Act: provided that an aggrieved wife or female living in a relationship in the nature of a marriage may also file a complaint against a relative of the husband or the male partner.

[128] *Eveneet Singh* v. *Prashant Chaudhri*, I (2011) DMC 239 (Delhi High Court) (20 December 2010).

[129] *Eveneet Singh* v. *Prashant Chaudhri*, para 16, 17.

[130] *P. Babu Venkatesh* v. *Rani*, AIR 2008 (NOC) 1772 (Madras High Court) (25 March 2008).

the house to frustrate the wife's claim to residence, stating that the husband has an undivided interest in the house after the death of his father, if the father were to die intestate.[131] The wife therefore has a claim to residence in the house and this must be deemed to be her shared household.

The Delhi High Court generated significant debate on the applicability of the concepts of matrimonial home, shared household, and the right of residence for a wife in the matrimonial home, shared household, or some other place in *Sandhu* v. *Sandhu*;[132] it was held that in the backdrop of facts and circumstances of the case,

> the property in question cannot be considered to be a shared household because neither the wife nor the husband has any right, title or interest or equitable right in the same and that the property belongs exclusively to the father-in-law and nor is it a joint family property, it does not, therefore, fall within the expression of shared household as defined under the PWDVA.[133]

It was emphasized further that 'the right of residence which a wife undoubtedly has does not mean the right to reside in a particular property. It may, of course, mean the right to reside in a commensurate property. But it can certainly not translate into a right to reside in a particular property'.[134]

Right to reside independent of the woman's title is unambiguous, the strength of her right, however, continues to be based in most cases on her husband's title in the family property or ownership or tenancy rights in his independent property. Jurisprudence demonstrates that passing of residence order in favour of the applicant is viewed in light of protection for her, but only where it does not lead to an abrogation of the right of the owner of property. Claims against husband continue to be stronger, and in claims to reside in a property owned by the in-laws, courts appear to be struggling with balancing conflicting rights.

***

Domestic violence clearly breaches the right to adequate housing since it violates the very basis of adequacy: security, peace, dignity, and the standard

131 *Rajkumar Rampal Pandey* v. *Sarita Rajkumar Pandey* (2008) 6 Bom CR 831, AIR 2009 (NOC) 1013 (Bombay High Court) (26 August 2008), para 17.

132 *Shumita Didi Sandhu* v. *Sanjay Singh Sandhu*, II (2010) DMC 882 (Delhi High Court) (26 October 2010).

133 *Shumita Didi Sandhu* v. *Sanjay Singh Sandhu*, para 47.

134 *Shumita Didi Sandhu* v. *Sanjay Singh Sandhu*, para 49.

of habitability. In some cases, it also violates the prohibition against forced evictions. The centrality of securing women's right to adequate housing as a vital step in the fight against domestic violence needs be recognized urgently. Empowerment through right to adequate housing by way of ownership rights through equal inheritance rights qualitatively improve women's position in negotiating for a life free of violence.

Let us always remember that intimate relationships are not simple. In most cases, emotional dependence on the abuser is far greater than economic dependence, and women caught in this cycle of dependence go through stages of denial about the abuse. Herein lies the most vital difference between violence at home and other forms of violence committed by a person who is in most cases a stranger to the victim. A decision with regard to initiating a complaint against a stranger cannot be equated with a complaint or a claim against a family member. In most cases, the woman simply wants a space free of violence where she can think through her decision with regard to the relationship, which is, despite the abuse she suffers, not an easy one to make. This may never be possible while she is trapped within a violent home. Mechanisms dealing with domestic violence must cater to the woman's immediate and long-term needs, one such need is a place to live safely with her children in a home from where she cannot be evicted.

No mechanism dealing with domestic violence is complete unless it addresses the vital question: 'But ... where will I live?'. In the absence of equal property rights for women, right to reside assumes greater significance. While impediments to women's ownership rights must be addressed, and until this can be secured, passing of residence orders should be the norm. The Special Rapporteur on right to housing has recognized the significant provision related to right to residence. The India report recognizes that while implementation of the PWDVA has been a problem, 'the PWDVA is human rights-oriented, providing women in a domestic violence situation with security of tenure through the right to reside in their home and barring the violent household member from remaining on the premises'.[135] Violations to adequate housing caused by domestic violence have been appropriately addressed by creating the right to reside under the PWDVA and it is hoped that a more stringent and sensitive implementation of this right will empower women to fight domestic violence and homelessness that can result from it.

[135] Report of the Special Rapporteur on adequate housing, Para 66.

Bibliography

Statutes

Act on the Prevention of Domestic Violence and Protection, etc of Victims Thereof, Republic of Korea, Act No. 5487, Dec 31, 1997, Amended 2006.

Cambodia: Law on the Prevention of Domestic Violence and the Protection of Victims, 2005.

Convention on the Elimination of All Forms of Discrimination Against Women, GA Res. 34/180, 18/12/1979, Entered into force: 3/9/1981. For text, see I. Brownlie and G.S. Goodwin-Gill, *Basic Documents on Human Rights* (Oxford, Oxford University Press, 5th edition, 2006), pp. 388–99.

International Covenant on Economic, Social and Cultural Rights, GA Res. 2200 A (XXI), Entry into force: 3/1/1976. For text, see I. Brownlie and G.S. Goodwin-Gill, Basic Documents on Human Rights (Oxford, Oxford University Press, 5th edition, 2006), p. 348–57.

Japan: Act on the Prevention of Spousal Violence and the Protection of Victims (Act No. 31 of 2001) residence rights discussed under Protection orders, Chapter IV of the Act.

Law of the Republic of Indonesia, Number 23 of Year 2004 Regarding Elimination of Violence in Households.

Law of Domestic Violence Prevention and Control, Socialist Republic of Vietnam, Law No: 02/2007/QH12.

Protection of Women From Domestic Violence Act, 2005, Lawyers Collective, Women's Rights Initiative, Print Graphics, New Delhi, 2007.

Prevention of Domestic Violence Act, No. 34 of 2005, Sri Lanka, available at http://www.childprotection.gov.lk/Child_Related_ACTs/Prevention%20of%20Domestic%20Violence%20Act%20No.%2034%20of%202005.pdf.

Singapore Women's Charter, Chapter 353, Part VII, Protection of Family https://www.hsph.harvard.edu/population/domesticviolence/singapore.dv.htm.

The Domestic Violence Act, 1994(as at 1997), available from APWLD 2003 (International Law Book Services), at apwld@apwld.org.

Cases

Ms. A.T. v Hungary, Communication No.: 2/2003 (View adopted on 26 January 2005, 32nd Session), Committee on Elimination of Discrimination against Women under Article 7, Para 3 of the Optional Protocol to the Convention on the Elimination of All Forms of Discrimination against Women.

B.P. Achala Anand v. S.Appi Reddy and Another, MANU/SC/0100/2005\2005 (3) SCC 313A.

Eveneet Singh v. Prashant Chaudhri, I (2011) DMC 239 (Delhi H.C.) (20 December 2010).

Natasha Kohli v. Mon Mohan Kohli, 172 (2010) DLT 516, 2010 (119) DRJ 44 (Delhi H.C.) (24.09.2010).
Nidhi Kumar Gandhi v.The State, 2010 Cr.L.J. (NOC) 79, 157 (2009) DLT 472, II (2009) DMC 647 (Delhi H.C.)(16.01.2009).
P. Babu Venkatesh v. Rani, AIR 2008 (NOC) 1772 (Madras H.C.) (25.03.2008).
Rajkumar Rampal Pandey v. Sarita Rajkumar Pandey, 2008 (6) Bom CR 831, AIR 2009 (NOC) 1013 (Bombay H.C.) (26 August 2008).
Sabah Sami Khan v. Adnan Sami Khan, 2011 (1) MhLj 427 (Bombay H.C.) (21 October 2010).
Shumita Didi Sandhu v. Sanjay Singh Sandhu, II (2010) DMC 882 (Delhi H.C.) (26 October 2010).
S.R. Batra v. Taruna Batra 2007 (2) ALD 66 (SC), A 2007 SC 1118 (Supreme Court) (15 December 2006).
V.D. Bhanot v. Savita Bhanot, AIR 2012 SC 965, I (2012) DMC 482 SC (7 February 2012).

Documents

Declaration on the Elimination of Violence Against Women, adopted 20th December 1993, GA Res. A/Res/48/104, U.N. GAOR, 48th Sess., 85th plen. Mtg.,U.N. Doc. A/Res/48/104 (1993).
CEDAW Recommendation No. 19 on Violence Against Women. U.N. Doc. CEDAW/C/L.1/Add.15 (1992).
General Comment No. 4 on the Right to Adequate Housing, U.N. ESCOR, Comm'n on Hum. Rts., 6th Sess., U.N. Doc. E/C.12/1991/4 (1992).
General Comment 7 on Forced Evictions, U.N. GAOR, U.N. ESCOR, Comm'n on Hum. Rts., 16th Sess., U.N. Doc. E/C.12/1997/4 (1997).
A Framework to Underpin Action to Prevent Violence Against Women, 2015 UN Women, http://www.unwomen.org//media/headquarters/attachments/sections/library/publications/2015/prevention_framework_unwomen_nov2015.pdf?vs=5223.
Report of the Committee on the Elimination of Discrimination Against Violence, U.N. GAOR CEDAW, 44th Session, Supp. No.38, Un Doc. A/44/38 at 81 (1992).
Report of the Special Rapporteur on adequate housing as a component of the right to an adequate standard of living, and on the right to non-discrimination in this context, on her mission to India, 10 January 2017, available at https://documents-ddsny.un.org/doc/UNDOC/GEN/G17/002/82/PDF/G1700282.pdf?OpenElement.
Report of the Special Rapporteur on Adequate Housing as a Component of the Right to an Adequate Standard of Living, Mr Miloon Kothari, U.N. ESCOR, Comm'n on Hum. Rts., 60th Sess., Agenda Item 10, U.N. Doc. E/CN.4/2004/48 (2004).

Report of the Special Rapporteur on Adequate Housing as a Component of the Right to an Adequate Standard of Living, Mr Miloon Kothari, U.N. ESCOR, Comm'n on Hum. Rts., 61st Sess., Agenda Item 10, U.N. Doc. E/CN.4/2005/48 (2005).

Report of the Special Rapporteur on Adequate Housing as a component of the Right to an Adequate Standard of Living, Mr Miloon Kothari, pursuant to Implementation of G A Res. 60/251 of 15 March 2006, entitled 'Human Rights Council', Human Rights Council, 4th Sess., Agenda Item 2, GA Res. A/HRC/4/18 (2007).

Women and Adequate Housing, Study by the Special Rapporteur on Adequate Housing, as a Component of the Right to an Adequate Standard of Living, and the Right to Non-Discrimination, Mr Miloon Kothari, U.N. ESCOR, Comm'n on Hum. Rts., 61st Sess., Agenda Item 10, U.N. Doc. E/CN.4/2005/43 (2005).

Women and Adequate Housing, Study by the Special Rapporteur on Adequate Housing, as a Component of the Right to an adequate Standard of Living, and the Right to Non-Discrimination, Mr Miloon Kothari, U.N. ESCOR, Comm'n on Hum. Rts., 62st Sess., Agenda Item 10, U.N. Doc. E/CN.4/2006/118 (2006).

Women and Adequate Housing, Study by the Special Rapporteur on Adequate Housing as a Component of the Right to Adequate Standard of Living and on the Right to Non-Discrimination, Miloon Kothari, in accordance with Commission Resolution 2002/49, U.N. ECOSOC, Comm'n on Human Rights, 59th Sess., Agenda Item 10, U.N. Doc.E/CN.4/2003/55 (2003).

Research

A. Edi, C. Krause, A. Rosas, *Economic, Social, Cultural Rights, A Textbook* (Martinus Nijhoff Publishers, Dordrecht/Boston/London, 2nd revised edition, 2001).

D. Elson, J. Gideon, 'Organising for Women's Economic and Social Rights: How useful is the International Covenant on Economic, Social and Cultural Rights?', *Journal of Interdisciplinary Gender Studies*, Vol. 8 No. 1, (2004), pp. 133–54.

C.G. Bowman, *Domestic Violence: Does the African Context Demand a Different Approach?*, Paper 139, Cornell: Cornell Law faculty Publications, 2003.

D.Q. Thomas, M.E. Beasley, 'Domestic Violence as a Human Rights Issue', *Human Rights Quarterly* 15 (1993): 36–62.

R. Pain, 'Everyday Terrorism: Connecting Domestic Violence and Global Terrorism', *Progress in Human Geography*, 38(4) pp. 531–50, Durham University, Online Library http://dro.dur.ac.uk/12511/1/12511.pdf.

G. Paglione, 'Domestic Violence and Housing Rights: A Reinterpretation of the Right to Housing', *Human Rights Quarterly* 28 (2006), 120–47.

G. Ni Carthy, *The Ones Who Got Away, Women who left abusive partners* (The Seal Press, Seattle, Washington, 1987).

H. Charlesworth, C. Chinkin, *The Boundaries of International Law: A Feminist Analysis* (Manchester University Press, Manchester, 2000).

I. Jaising (ed) Men's Laws Women's Lives, A Constitutional Perspective on Religion, Common Law and Culture in South Asia (Women Unlimited, Kali for Women, New Delhi, 2005).

I. Jaising, M. Sakhrani (ed) The Lawyers Collective, Law of Domestic Violence, A Users Manual For Women, 2nd Edition (Universal Law Publishing Co. Pvt Ltd, New Delhi, 2007).

International Centre for Research on Women, *Property Ownership and Inheritance Rights of Women for Social Progress, The South Asia Experience-Synthesis Report of Three States, www.icrw.org/docs/2006_propertyrights-southasia.pdf.*

K.D. Askin, D.M. Koenig (eds) *Women and International Human Rights Law, Volume 1& 2* (Transnational Publishers, Inc. Ardsley, New York, 2000).

L.B. Cattaneo, *What Is Empowerment Anyway? A Model for Domestic Violence Practice, Research, and Evaluation,* George Mason University Lisa A. Goodman Boston College https://www.researchgate.net/profile/Lauren_Cattaneo/publication/274867069_What_Is_Empowerment_Anyway_A_Model_for_Domestic_Violence_Practice_Research_and_Evaluation/links/552df3e40cf29b22c9c50fc8/What-Is-Empowerment-Anyway-A-Model-for-Domestic-Violence-Practice-Research-and-Evaluation.pdf.

M. Craven, *The International Covenant on Economic, Social and Cultural Rights, A Perspective on its Development* (Clarendon Press, Oxford, 1995).

M. Nussbaum, J. Glover (eds) *Women, Culture and Development, A Study of Human Capabilities* (Clarendon Press, Oxford, 1995).

'*Our Land, Our Homes, Our Culture, Our Rights*', Proceedings of the Pacific Regional Consultation on Women's Rights to Adequate Housing and Land, in cooperation with the UN Special Rapporteur on Adequate Housing, Nadi, Fiji, October 2004 at http://www.hic-sarp.org/documents/fiji%20report.pdf.

P. Hunt, *Reclaiming Social Rights: International and Comparative Perspectives* (Aldershot, Dartmouth, 1996).

Proceedings of the Asia Regional Consultation on 'The Interlinkages between Violence against Women and Womens Right to Adequate Housing', 2003 at *<http://www.hic-sarp.org/documents/Interlinkages_VAW&RAH.pdf>*.

S. Schechter, *Women and Male Violence, The Visions and Struggles of the Battered Women's Movement* (South End Press, Boston, 1982).

S. Chaudhry, A. Joseph, I. Prakash Singh, *Violence and Violations: The Reality of Homeless Women in India,* 2014, available at http://hlrn.org.in/documents/Violence_and_Violations_Homeless_Women_in_India_2014.pdf.

5. *Of 'Keeps' and 'Concubines'*

Rights of Cohabitees under Domestic Violence Act

Brototi Dutta

If a man has a 'keep' whom he maintains financially and uses mainly for sexual purpose and/or as a servant it would not, in our opinion, be a relationship in the nature of marriage.' No doubt the view we are taking would exclude many women who have had a live in relationship from the benefit of the 2005 Act, but then it is not for this Court to legislate or amend the law.

—A Division Bench of Supreme Court of India in *Velusamy* v. *D. Patchaiammal* (2011)

Individual dignity and privacy are inextricably linked in a pattern woven out of a thread of diversity into the fabric of a plural culture. Privacy of the individual is an essential aspect of dignity. Dignity has both an intrinsic and instrumental value. As an intrinsic value, human dignity is an entitlement or a constitutionally protected interest in itself. In its instrumental facet, dignity and freedom are inseparably intertwined, each being a facilitative tool to achieve the other.

—Constitution Bench of Supreme Court of India in *Justice K.S. Puttaswamy (Retd.) & Anr.* v. *Union of India & Ors.* (2017)

In 2011, the Supreme Court in its judgment in *Velusamy* v. *D. Patchaiammal*[1] limited the scope of the expression 'relationship in the nature of marriage' under Section 2(f) of the PWDVA and interpreted it as co-terminus with 'common-law marriage'. This is while the Court acknowledged that by clearly establishing two distinct categories, namely, relationship of 'marriage' and 'relationship in the nature of marriage', the Parliament had intended that the enactment protect and benefit women in both these relationships. Despite this, the Supreme Court went on to enumerate the essential ingredients of a 'common law marriage' to be considered the test for a 'relationship in the nature of marriage'. It also noted that not all 'live-in relationships' would amount to 'a relationship in the nature of marriage' *in the way it is intended under the Act* (emphasis supplied). What is worth noting is that the litigation in this case was not even a case under the PWDVA; the claim was of maintenance under the Hindu Marriage Act but the Court went a step further taking upon itself the responsibility of clarifying what it noted, had given rise to legal ambiguity because of the lack of a clear statutory definition of 'relationship in the nature of marriage'.

The question that begs an answer is to what extent, and more importantly, to what effect has the Supreme Court in Velusamy succeeded in addressing this apparent ambiguity in the statute. As lawyers and practitioners engaged in domestic violence litigation are well aware, by restrictively interpreting 'relationship in the nature of marriage' under the Act to mean a 'common law marriage' or 'marriage-like' relationship, the Court has without a doubt, excluded women in a diverse range of cohabiting relationships from seeking legal remedies against domestic violence. In fact, it has left those women who are already most vulnerable—women who are in fraudulent marriages or are 'second wives'—without a remedy in law. I would like to take this argument further to say that by transposing what is essentially a family law non-statutory category such as 'common law marriage' into the PWDVA, Velusamy (and its successors) has watered down a violence against women (VAW) legislation and negated its zero-tolerance approach to violence within intimate domestic relationships. While courts in India and elsewhere have always been fiercely protective of 'marriage' as an institution within the sphere of personal and family laws, use of such a value-laden judicial approach that idealizes 'marriage' and matrimonial relationships, and therefore, constructs a category of deserving women in the context of a domestic violence law is extremely problematic. Instead, the more appropriate legal

[1] *Velusamy v. D. Patchaiammal,* AIR 2011 SC 479 (Supreme Court of India).

criterion on the basis of which a woman should be able to seek protection from domestic violence is 'cohabitation'. This is clearly what was envisaged in the PWDVA, with 'aggrieved person' under the Act defined as one who is or has been in a 'domestic relationship' with the perpetrator, in a 'shared household'. Hence, it is the factum of residence or cohabitation in a shared household, whether current or past, which is the source of the rights and access to remedies under the PWDVA. In arguing for recognition of a cohesive framework of 'cohabitees' rights, I use examples from the development of cohabitees' rights in English law and in Scotland, and some state jurisdictions in the United States. Heterosexual cohabitation and the law have had a distinctly uncomfortable and often ambivalent relationship; Rebecca Probert (2004),[2] for instance, sums up the moral discomfort and resultant trajectory of development that cohabitees' rights in English law has taken since the sixteenth century such:

> *The policies adopted by the courts and the legislature can be seen as inspired by different—and sometimes conflicting—concerns. Equating cohabitants to married couples in the context of state benefits protects the public purse, as does the rule that fathers are economically responsible for their children, no matter what their legal status. Allowing a cohabitant a share in the other's home might have the effect of relieving the public purse but conflicts with the desire to protect marriage and property rights. Alongside such concerns are those laws that focus on the intention of the individual.*

In comparison, while its former colonies and common law countries like Canada and South Africa imported legal doctrines such as 'constructive trust' to cohabitees' rights, they also expanded the scope of available legal protections significantly. Domestic violence and legal obligations towards children of the relationship are particular areas that have witnessed a greater inclination for legal and policy reform, although more often than not, couched within a protectionist framework. An important development, both within policy and academic enquiries, has been the shift away from the 'form' of the relationship to its 'function'.[3] This approach has allowed the questioning of the heterosexual normative institution of marriage, and that

[2] Rebecca Probert, 'Cohabitation in Twentieth Century England and Wales: Law and Policy', *Law and Policy* 26, 1 (2004).

[3] Indira Jaising and Lawyers Collective, 'Staying Alive: Third Monitoring & Evaluation Report on the Protection of Women from Domestic Violence Act, 2005', The Lawyers Collective (2009).

a cohabitation relationship serves the functions that a 'family' is meant to serve. What such an approach does is also to refashion the narrative—where legal eligibility to contract a marriage or marriage-like relationship—does not regulate whether a woman is entitled to legal protections that would otherwise be available to an otherwise stable cohabiting relationship. This is particularly significant in the Indian context where second wives and women in *de facto* marriages have little legal protection,[4] even in situations of domestic violence, only by virtue of their ineligibility to contract a valid marriage.

In this Chapter, I argue therefore, that although several high courts and even the Supreme Court in its subsequent decisions, have distinguished the facts of Velusamy, it is important that one moves towards a more nuanced understanding of 'relationship in the nature of marriage' under the Act to recognize the rights of 'cohabitees' to protection from violence within such intimate cohabiting relationships. In doing so, we may be in a position to move towards a more inclusive and pluralistic framework within which to view women in violent domestic relationships. Adopting a more radical position, I further argue that any framing of an *opposite sex intimate relationship* in the manner of a marriage, for example, 'relationship in the nature of marriage' or 'common law marriage' or 'de facto marriage' is always something *less than a marriage*, and likely, therefore, not to lead one to the desired equality outcome; such a framing may ensure the legal rights and obligations but not the 'status' accorded to a marital relationship. I use the example of the *marriage equality* movement in the United States, particularly the strategies used, to emphasize that although the shift in the language of advocacy from civil unions to marriage equality was a consciously developed political strategy in the context of same-sex rights, for our purposes, it needs to be distinguished from opposite-sex cohabiting relationships. In fact, this very distinction provides the basis on which to co-opt the tools and strategies, including the rights-language framing used by marriage equality advocates to develop the legal framing of cohabitees' rights in India. It is my argument that the Indian Constitution, in its framing of equality and personal dignity, already provides the language and the framework for such a project, with international human rights law and its recognition of personal autonomy and choice in marriage, providing an

[4] Mary E. John, 'Women and Feminism in China and India', *Economic and Political Weekly*, Vol. 40 no. 16, 2005; Uma Chakravarti, 'Of Meta-Narratives and 'Master' Paradigms: Sexuality and the Reification of Women in Early India' (New Delhi: Centre for Women's Development Studies, 2009).

important counterfoil. Ideologically, this enquiry aligns itself to feminist critiques of marriage and family.[5] Anupama Rao notes this discomfort that has defined Indian feminist movement's engagement within questions of law's envisioning of family and marriage:

> For feminists, the family has often functioned as a way into questions of sex, gender, and sexuality, because the family—as a form, as a structure—is a significant point of contact between the interior world of intimacy and privacy, and the regulatory regimes of state. The family, as idea or ideal type, is a capacious and complex entity that regulates intimacy and emotion, as well as material outcomes. On the one hand, the family is a space where desires are expressed, a space of affect and emotion. Simultaneously, the family is a legislating or governing entity, centrally involved in adjudicating rights and apportioning resources. It is precisely the uncertain status of the family as an affective space as well as an accumulative entity, which has produced multiple critiques of the family, as well as attempts to reform it.[6]

Cohabitation, Marriage, and Individual 'Dignity'

The world over, there is growing documentation of cohabiting relationships although national approaches to recognition and regulation of cohabitation continue to show little harmony.[7] According to estimates, by 2031, one in four couples will be cohabiting outside marriage in the UK; cohabitation outside marriage, both as a step towards marriage and as an alternative to marriage, increased by almost 41 per cent in 2010, from the 2000 Census.[8] Although reliable large-scale data from both Asia and Africa is sparse, there

[5] Anupama Rao, 'Value, Visibility, and the Demand for Justice', Vol. 40 no. 8, *Economic and Political Weekly*, 2005.

[6] Anupama Rao, *EPW*, 2005.

[7] A briefing paper for Hague Conference on Private International Law notes that some states do not have a registered partnership scheme while others have. Among the latter, some reserve their registered partnership schemes exclusively for opposite-sex partners, others exclusively for same-sex partners, and yet others allow for both. Permanent Bureau, Hague Conference on Private International Law, Update on the Developments in Internal Law and Private International Law Concerning Cohabitation Outside Marriage, Including Registered Partnerships, The Hague, March 2015.

[8] Permanent Bureau, Hague Conference on Private International Law, Update on the Developments in Internal Law and Private International Law Concerning Cohabitation Outside Marriage, Including Registered Partnerships, The Hague, March 2015.

is some evidence to suggest change in attitudes, leading to greater acceptance of cohabiting relationships.[9]

Legislating on the rights of cohabitees, however, continues to remain fraught with challenges because of lack of a universally recognized definition of 'cohabitation', amongst others. In its ordinary usage, the term 'cohabitation' refers to coexistence or living together in any kind of living arrangement. It traces its origin in the Latin word *cohabitare* meaning to live together or to coexist. The Oxford Dictionary defines 'cohabitation' as *the state of living together and having a sexual relationship without being married.*[10] Family Law (Scotland) Act, 2006 enumerates elements that the courts must consider in deciding whether a relationship constitutes 'cohabitation', (*a*) length of the cohabitation (past or present); (*b*) nature of their relationship during that period; and (*c*) nature and extent of any subsisting or prior financial arrangements during the period of cohabitation. The elements enumerated under the Scottish law therefore, underscore stability and duration of the relationship as the determining markers from which legal rights and obligations arise.

Cohabitation is an essential component of marriage, with certain rights predicated on continued cohabitation of the parties such as the wife's right to claim maintenance under personal laws, provision of restitution of conjugal rights in case of desertion by the other party. Thus, while marriage is not a precondition for cohabitation, traditional family law has viewed continued cohabitation as an important marker of legal rights and status of marriage.

History of Cohabitation in India

A look at the history of cohabitation in India highlights its local roots and variations, debunking ideas that it is an alien 'western' concept. For instance, ancient texts and legal documents refer to *anuloma* (a male of a superior varna/caste/class marrying a female of an inferior varna/caste/class (hypergamous marriage) and *pratuloma* (a female of a superior varna/caste/class marries a male of an inferior varna/caste/class) marriage. Customary laws and practices across the country recognized varied forms of cohabiting relationships. It was only with British Empire's modernizing project that concepts such as 'monogamy' and spousal privilege became part of our legal

[9] Permanent Bureau, Hague Conference on Private International Law, Update on the Developments in Internal Law and Private International Law Concerning Cohabitation Outside Marriage, Including Registered Partnerships, The Hague, March 2015.

[10] Available at: https://en.oxforddictionaries.com/definition/cohabitation (last accessed 20 October 2017).

landscape, which located gender inequality at the very heart of the 'conjugal-family ideal'.[11] The IPC, 1860, which is based on English law, criminalized bigamy,[12] bigamy with concealment of existing marriage,[13] and fraudulent marriage, that is, ceremony performed which has no legal validity.[14] In 1955, the Hindu Marriage Act was enacted, which declared 'bigamy' as a matrimonial offence.[15] Despite these, customary laws in various parts of India continue to recognize cohabiting relationships outside marriage;[16] these relationships are as diverse in form and coverage, as the protections that they provide to the parties in such relationships. One example that has been oft cited in discussions around customary practices including child marriage, is the *nata-pratha*[17] that is practised primarily amongst the Gujjar and Bhil communities of Rajasthan and Madhya Pradesh. Nata-pratha refers to a relationship in which traditionally an already married couple can live together, outside of their marriage, without performing any rituals. It has been suggested that this practice was intended to ease separation norms in an otherwise rigid framework governing marriage; it offered an avenue to women who had been deserted by their husbands and widows to enter into an intimate relationship.[18] Among the Garasiyas of Rajasthan, long-term relationships are common; the wedding takes place only when the couple can afford it. Till it was banned in 1983,[19] *maitri karar* or friendship agreements

[11] Mytheli Sreenivas. *Wives, Widows, and Concubines: The Conjugal Family Ideal in Colonial India* (Contemporary Indian Studies). Bloomington:Indiana University Press, 2008.

[12] Section 494, Indian Penal Code, 1860.

[13] Section 495, Indian Penal Code, 1860.

[14] Section 496, Indian Penal Code, 1860.

[15] Section 17, Hindu Marriage Act, 1955.

[16] Ethnographic Atlas of Indian Tribes.

[17] In *Atma Rao v. Smt. Shantidevi* (1997) Cr. L.R. (Raj.) 753, the Rajasthan High Court held that a marriage entered into as per nata-pratha is a valid marriage in law.

[18] Annie Zaidi, 'What India's Old and Unusual Marriage Customs Tell Us about a Woman's Consent', *Daily O*, 2015, available at: https://www.dailyo.in/politics/child-marraige-natha-pratha-divorce-dowry-women-consent-inheritence/story/1/4683.html.

[19] In exercise of the powers conferred by sub-section (1) of Section 22-A of the Registration Act, 1908 (Act XVI of 1908), in its application to the State of Maharashtra, the Government of Maharashtra hereby declares that the registration of a document purporting, or operating to effect a contract popularly known as 'Companionship Contract' or *Maitri Karar* is opposed to public policy (GNR & FD RGN-1081/CR-410/81-M1 dated 8 June 1983). Pratiksha Baxi, 'Feminist Contributions to Sociology of Law: A Review', *Economic and Political Review* 43, 43

had wide social acceptance in Gujarat. These agreements were mostly used by women who enter into a relationship with a married man to secure a contract that guarantees financial support to the woman and their children by setting on the terms of their partnership. Pratiksha Baxi points out that '*(t)hese forms of intimate relations are not second marriages legally and seem to have an eye on the potentiality of criminal complaints of rape or abduction, which is suggested by the emphasis on consent in the drafting of such contracts*'.[20] While there may be differences of opinion on the impact of such customary practices on women,[21] the reality is that these do exist, and in their rejection of monogamous marriage as an inviolable monolith, provide a space for examining sexuality, desire, and women's choice in marriage and conjugality. Thus, there are plural typographies of relationships, which need to be acknowledged and the woman's vulnerabilities within such relationships recognized. To bring these diverse practices within the omnibus category of 'marriage' or 'marriage like' runs the risk of essentializing these practices, and imposing a qualifying criterion such as that affirmed by the Velusamy judgment. More importantly, it trivializes the fact of domestic violence—with morality determining which woman is deserving of the law's protection.

The concept of individual dignity and personal autonomy is inherent in the understanding of cohabitees' rights, particularly in the context of domestic violence. As in the case of marriage, our attention has almost exclusively focused on addressing legal issues emanating from breakdown of a cohabiting relationship. This can be counterproductive as it allows us to continue to be ambivalent towards recognition of rights during the subsistence of the relationship: '*Issues and analysis on it often centre on property distribution in the event of breakup of the relationship. There seems to be a dearth of discussion of its*

(2008). Maharashtra Registration Rules, 1961 specify that 'for the purpose of the notification the expression "Companionship Contract" or "maitri Karar" means a contract (by whatsoever name called) between a male and a female, whether either or both of them married or not, the consideration or object of which is forbidden by law, immoral or opposed to public policy'.

[20] Baxi, Pratiksha. 2008. 'Feminist Contributions to Sociology of Law: A Review', *Economic and Political Weekly* XLIII (43): 79–85, 25 October.

[21] Features, 'Towards Oblivion', *The Hindu* (18 June 2000), available at: http://www.thehindu.com/2000/06/18/stories/13180619.htm; 'Nata Pratha, a Tradition That Allows Men and Women to Live With Person of Their Choice', *The Citizen*, 10 May 2017; available at: http://www.thecitizen.in/index.php/en/NewsDetail/index/9/10641/Nata-Pratha-a-Tradition-That-Allows-Men-and-Women-to-Live-With-Person-of-Their-Choice.

intrinsic nature, centering on the very essence of being, the integrity of the parties and their dignity as humans'.[22]

The state's obligation to provide an *immediate and effective* response to domestic violence includes within its ambit, ensuring effective and easy access to justice, and once the aggrieved woman approaches the court, her claim be considered keeping in view the object of the law and without any bias.

> States are not only required to guarantee that no person is arbitrarily deprived or his or her life. They are also under a positive obligation to protect and prevent violations to this right, through the creation of the conditions that may be required for its protection. In the case of Leslie, Katheryn and Rebecca Gonzales, the State had a reinforced duty of due diligence to protect them from harm and from deprivations of their life, with special measures of care, prevention and guarantee.[23]

Once the fact of domestic violence is established to the prima facie satisfaction of the court, immediate and adequate relief(s) must be granted to prevent future violence. As Indira Jaising notes:

> We must then change the discourse on violence and discrimination against women; ensure that "zero tolerance for violence against women" is understood to mean a measurable and concrete State obligation to provide immediate response. And it is this right to immediate and effective State response to violence against women which is immediately realisable and not subject to progressive realisation, based on availability of resources.[24]

International human rights instruments such as the ICCPR, the CEDAW, as well as jurisprudence of treaty bodies also establish the right to freedom in marriage and family life.

Inherent in the recognition of individual dignity and choice in marriage and family life, is plurality of kinds of families—which has been used most effectively by the marriage equality movement. In 1999, the Vermont

[22] Nwudego Nkemakonam Chinwuba, 'Cohabitation: Human Dignity and One Aspect of Gender Insensitivity', *The International Journal of Human Rights* 14, 4 (July 2010): 624–34.

[23] Inter-American Commission on Human Rights in its Report No. 80/11, in Jessica Lenahan (Gonzales) et al., (2011). Jessica Lenahan case referred here was a landmark opinion delivered by the Inter-American Commission on Human Rights. Please cite as Jessica Lenahan (Gonzales) v. United States (Inter-Am. Comm'n H.R., Report No. 80/11 (2011)).

[24] Indira Jaising, Beijing+20 India CSO National Consultation (2014).

Supreme Court in *Baker* v. *State*[25] famously held that '*denying the rights and benefits of marriage to same-sex couples violated the Vermont Constitution*'. This was the first time that rights violation of same-sex couples was successfully argued by the lesbian, gay, bisexual, transgender (LGBT) advocates in the United States, and the subsequent enactment of the law recognizing civil unions in the state was celebrated by activists as having, 'accorded to lesbian and gay couples the *full equality* and protection we deserve and have long been denied'[26] (emphasis added). However, as Douglas Nejaime observes, by the time the New Jersey Supreme Court ruled in *Lewis* v. *Harris* in 2005, the trajectory of LGBT engagement with the law had changed substantially, from focusing on civil unions/domestic partnerships to demanding complete marriage equality.

> The constitutionalization of relationship recognition and the turn to courts facilitated—and ultimately required—the move from equality to inequality in framing civil unions and domestic partnerships. Once advocates were able to show the shortcomings of civil unions and domestic partnerships—that those regimes failed to satisfy equality mandates issued by courts—they could shift the frame from equality to inequality.[27]

This was predicated on the fact that the earlier strategy of using legal tools such as the Vermont Constitution's 'common benefits clause' to seek legal protections and rights did not automatically lead to status recognition because '[t]hrough civil marriage, the State confers a *status*, which plugs into a common social vocabulary and carries powerful personal and cultural weight'.[28] The conversation, thus, shifted to framing of 'civil marriage' as the only possible measure of complete constitutional equality.

History of marriage equality movement in the United States, therefore, provides us with important entry points for strategizing on legal recognition of 'cohabitation'. In the context of the marriage equality movement, the challenge was to bridge the gap between provisioning of legal protections and

25 *Baker* v. *State*, 744 A.2d 864 (Vt. 1999).

26 Press Release, Nat'l Ctr. for Lesbian Rights, Vermont Legislature, 'Governor Approve Landmark Legislation for Gays and Lesbians' (27 April 2000), available at: http://www.nclrights.org/site/PageServer? pagename=press_vermont.

27 Douglas Nejaime, 'Framing (In)Equality for Same-Sex Couples', *60 UCLA L. Rev. Disc. 184.*

28 Douglas Nejaime, 'Framing (In)Equality for Same-Sex Couples', *60 UCLA L. Rev. Disc. 184.*

privileges for same-sex relationships and social recognition of such unions, which was considered by LGBT advocates to be unattainable till such unions remained *less than a marriage*. The rationale was that such unions will always be discriminatory in favour of opposite sex married couples. In our case though, the legal framing of cohabiting relationships has already been taking place within the framework of marriage—*'common law marriage'*, *fe dacto marriage*, or *'relationships in the nature of marriage'*. Thus, it is the legal-institutional form of marriage, with its attendant qualifying conditions, that is the source of discrimination against certain women (those who are unable to fulfill the qualifying conditions of legally valid marriage). The strategy must therefore be distinct from the marriage equality movement, to argue for rights of cohabitees' outside the framework of marriage, and positioning it nonetheless as a constitutional equality and dignity issue.

Recent developments in our constitutional jurisprudence, including the Right to Privacy judgment, has given us a renewed opportunity to engage with the issue of marriage and cohabitation.

'Cohabitation' in English Law: History and Development

In the United Kingdom, cohabiting relationships that confer legal rights have not been defined exhaustively. As Barlow and James note: *'Broadly speaking inclusion has been reserved almost exclusively (at least until very recently) for the most marriage-like relationships, where a man and woman are living together "as husband and wife" usually within a shared household, often for a minimum prescribed period of time and where there is or has been sexual intimacy'*.[29] Unlike civil partnership, which confers certain statutorily granted rights to the parties, 'cohabitation' by itself does not automatically entail any legal consequences; the same is true for 'common law marriages'. While it continues to be used widely to refer to heterosexual marriage-like cohabiting relationships, there is no legal category of 'common law marriage' in English law.[30]

A morality-driven attack on cohabitation is not new and was a key concern in Edwardian England. What is interesting though is that it was used

[29] Anne Barlow and Grace James, 'Regulating Marriage and Cohabitation in 21st Century Britain', *The Modern Law Review* 67, 2 (March 2004).

[30] Catherine Fairburn, 'Common Law Marriage and Cohabitation', *Briefing Paper, No. 03372*, House of Commons Library, United Kingdom, 9 March 2017, available at: www.parliament.uk/commons-library.

as a basis for arguments by advocates of marriage and divorce reform as early as 1909, when advocates deposing before the Royal Commission on Divorce cited the prevalence of cohabitation among those who were unable to obtain a divorce to argue for granting the right to divorce. Thus, Probert notes, 'The argument that reform was necessary to allow such relationships to be legalized rested on *a negative view of cohabitation*....'[31] (emphasis added). At the same time, cohabitation outside marriage had no legal status, and cohabitees were stigmatized as much in the realm of law and policy, as in the society. Thus, in a case involving the question of arrears of rent, Judge Darling of the British Privy Council said, 'I do not think that it makes any difference whether the defendant is a common prostitute or whether she is merely the mistress of one man'.[32] However, as Probert points out, during the same time, in another case,[33] the court equated the rights of the cohabitee with that of the wife, and allowed her the benefit of the deceased partner's will. Hence, at the beginning of the twentieth century, as the legal system and the courts started to engage with the question of 'cohabitation', the approach appears to have been to respect the prevailing laws relating contract, trusts, succession, and certain welfare entitlements as long as the intent of such provision was not to secure cohabitation,[34] while circumventing conferring any legal status on the cohabiting relationship itself. With World War I, there was a clear shift with the law recognizing the dependant 'unmarried wife', necessitated primarily by the concern that not doing so would bring down the morale of the soldiers—gains made during a morally ambivalent time in the nation's history. In the aftermath of the war, this policy continued to some extent,[35] although the emphasis was on a child-centric approach and reference to 'unmarried wives' disappeared from legal and policy narratives.

Interestingly, contestations on the issue continued to be fought chiefly in relation to rights of women in *de facto* versus *de jure* marriages, particularly

[31] Probert, 'Cohabitation in Twentieth Century England and Wales'. In re Brown (1910) 26 TLR 257, as cited in Probert, Rebecca. 'Cohabitation in Twentieth Century England and Wales.

[32] *Upfill* v. *Wright* (1911) 1 KB 506.

[33] In *re Brown* (1910).

[34] Barton, Chris. 1985. *Cohabitation Contracts: Extra-marital Partnerships and Law Reform*. Aldershot, UK: Gower.

[35] See the discussion on the Unemployed Workers' Dependants (Temporary Provision) Act 1921, Widows' Orphans' and Old Age Contributory Pensions Act, Unemployment Insurance Act 1927 in Probert, 'Cohabitation in Twentieth Century England and Wales'.

as inheritance entitlements of the cohabiting female partner was challenged by the de jure wife. In various cases[36] that were agitated before the courts during this time, the provision made for the cohabitant was upheld at the expense of the 'legal family', driven in part by the judiciary's discomfort with leaving the cohabiting woman and her children destitute, although cohabitees were still denied positive rights.[37]

The 1970s marked a watershed for cohabitees' rights in English law with the courts applying the equitable remedy of 'constructive trust'[38] to explicitly recognize the rights of cohabitees in the family home, and by extension, parties' intention to enter into informal cohabiting relationships. In the landmark, *Cooke* v. *Head*,[39] Lord Denning expanded its scope to lay down the basis for a 'new model' constructive trust principle.[40] It introduced within English law (at least for some time), indirect non-financial contributions as the basis for inferring common intention of the parties to establish a constructive trust. For women in informal cohabiting relationships, it was the law finally recognizing the iniquitous and vulnerable situation they were in. In subsequent decisions,[41] however, this doctrinal formulation was rolled back to the earlier position in *Gissing* v. *Gissing*,[42] with 'constructive trust' interpreted as being limited to indirect financial contributions.[43]

Given this complex history of 'cohabitation' in English law, it is hardly a surprise that the current approach of the law and courts to reforms in

[36] In Re Joslin (1941); Re Charman (deceased) 1951, bequeathing of (part of) the deceased's estate in favour of the cohabiting family was challenged by the legally married wife as per the Inheritance (Family Provision) Act, 1938. The Court in both cases, declined to interfere with the distribution of estate.

[37] Probert, 'Cohabitation in Twentieth Century England and Wales'.

[38] A 'constructive trust' is a legal fiction that is used as a remedy for unjust enrichment. Hence, there is no trustee, but the constructive trust orders the person who would otherwise be unjustly enriched to transfer the property to the intended party. Thus, it is a remedy in equity, available at https://www.law.cornell.edu/wex/constructive_trust.

[39] *Cooke* v. *Head* (1972) 2 All ER 38.

[40] Lord Denning fully developed his arguments in favour of the 'new model' constructive trust doctrine in *Eves* v. *Eves* (1975) 3 All ER 368.

[41] *Burns* v. *Burns* (1984) 1 All ER 244; *Springette* v. *Defoe* (1992) 2 FLR 388.

[42] *Gissing* v. *Gissing* (1970) UKHL 3.

[43] See Gary Watt, 'Equity and Trusts Law Directions' (Oxford: Oxford University Press, 2012).

this area continue to remain 'piecemeal and context-specific'.[44] The current position in English law remains that unless specifically agreed upon between the parties, the rules relating to ownership of property in general apply to opposite sex cohabiting partners. The court decides the share in the property based on rules relating to trusts (including constructive trust) or proprietary estoppel. Although this leaves opposite sex cohabitees in an iniquitous position compared to married couples at the time of divorce or at dissolution of a civil partnership, application of the rules of constructive trust ensure that one party (most likely the woman) may be found to have a beneficial (or equitable) interest in the property even where the property is in the sole name of the other party, or have a higher share even though the property was in joint name.[45,46] In such cases, courts take into consideration the apparent intentions of the parties,[47] but the length of time the partners have cohabited is not necessarily relevant. A surviving cohabitant has no automatic rights of inheritance on the partner's estate, although she may make a claim under family provision legislation, if no provision (or inadequate provision) has been made for them either by will or as per intestacy rules. However, such a claim is only limited to a reasonable provision of maintenance.[48] Cohabitation agreements are also entered into, which are likely to be given due consideration by the courts.

Application of the 'constructive trust' rule has however not been without its share of criticism,[49] with the possibility that its strict application may lead to victimizing the party (again, most likely a woman) who is no longer in the family home or the 'shared household'. This is particularly significant in the Indian context since women in cohabiting relationships, especially those who are in de facto marriages, in bigamous or fraudulent marriages, rarely have an explicit share in the property, and in situations of domestic violence, are forced to leave their 'shared household'. Part IV of the Family Law Act, 1996, which provides for rights to the family home in case of domestic violence, addresses this concern to an extent by empowering the court to pass

[44] Probert, 'Cohabitation in Twentieth Century England and Wales.'

[45] *Stack v. Dowden* (2007) UKHL 17 (House of Lords), see concurring judgment by Lord Hope.

[46] Fairburn, 'Common Law Marriage and Cohabitation.'

[47] *Stack v. Dowden* (2007) UKHL 17.

[48] Fairburn, 'Common Law Marriage and Cohabitation.'

[49] BBC News, 'Court Rules on Unmarried Couples' Property Rights,' 9 November 2011, available at: http://www.bbc.com/news/uk-15651540.

an 'occupation order' in favour of a cohabitee,[50] in addition to a married spouse or civil partner.[51] The 'occupation order' is of a similar nature as the 'residence orders' envisaged under the Indian PWDV Act, 2005; depending on whether the applicant cohabitee is in occupation or not, the court can grant her protection from being dispossessed, or restore her into the dwelling house, or order the respondent to leave the house or restrict his rights, amongst others.[52] Significantly, it also extends the law's protection to any woman who may claim an occupation order against a spouse who '*is, or has at any time during the marriage been, married to more than one person*'.[53] As a result of the restrictive judicial interpretation of 'relationship in the nature of marriage' under the PWDV Act, 2006, the provisions under the UK Family Law Act, 1996 governing rights of cohabitees over the dwelling house in case of domestic violence thus marks a distinct advance and provides specific directions for future advocacy efforts in the Indian context.

Status of 'Cohabitees' in Indian Law

How the law and courts in India have treated cohabiting intimate partner relationships has often been shaped by its form and to how close it reaches the 'marriage' or 'marriage-like' ideal. As I propose to argue in this section, very rarely have the courts relied on constitutional equality arguments to recognize and expand the scope of rights for those who do not qualify for accommodation within the 'marriage-like' cohabiting relationship categories. Even when the judiciary was brave enough to expand horizons, it ended up speaking in conflicting voices and narratives. As for the law, before the PWDV Act, it recognized women in cohabiting relationships (that is, live-in relationships or common law marriages) only to such extent that these did not conflict with the rights of the wife in a legally valid marriage. In 2003, Justice Malimath Committee, which was tasked with reviewing and suggesting '*comprehensive reform*' of the criminal justice system, in its Report recommended inclusion of 'a woman who was living with the man as his wife for a reasonably long period, during the subsistence of the first marriage' in the definition of 'wife' under Section 125 CrPC, which would then entitle her to

[50] Cohabitants under the British law include both opposite sex and same sex cohabiting partners. See Section 62, Part IV, Family Law Act, 1996.

[51] Section 36, Part IV, Family Law Act, 1996.

[52] Sub-section (3), (4), and (5) of Section 36, Part IV, Family Law Act, 1996.

[53] Section 63 (5), Part IV, Family Law Act, 1996.

claim maintenance from the male partner. Justifying the recommendation, the Committee noted that '*quite often the man marries the second wife suppressing the earlier marriage. In such a situation the second wife can't claim the benefit of Section 125 for no fault of hers. The husband is absolved of his responsibility of maintaining his second wife. This is manifestly unfair and unreasonable*'.[54] But as Anuja Agrawal observes:

> The object of focus here is not all non-marital adult heterosexual relationships but only that between a married man and his second wife, particularly one who has been cheated into believing that she is marrying an unmarried man. By adding the clause 'during the subsistence of the first marriage', the report has left little room for any speculation regarding the objective of the recommendation.[55]

Thus, the Committee's recommendation clearly falls short of understanding the breadth of cohabiting intimate (non-marital) relationships that continue to remain outside legal protection. As noted earlier in this chapter, patterns of cohabiting intimate heterosexual relationships in India are unique, in as much as they cannot be oversimplified as 'live-in relationships' or 'common law marriages' but also because some are categories created because of the complex plural legal regime governing marriage and divorce. I will attempt to address this argument shortly.

Like several other recommendations provided by the Committee, the Central government did not act upon the proposed inclusion of the 'second wife' under Section 125 CrPC. In Maharashtra, however, a proposal was moved which sought to bring 'a woman who was living with a man like his wife for a reasonably long period' within the definition of 'wife' under Section 125 CrPC. Although the proposal remained on paper, media reports quoted officials of the Maharashtra government stating that the proposed 'amendment would cover the interests of women involved in polygamous or live-in relationships'.[56] The proposal recognized the right of the any woman to

[54] Committee on Reforms of Criminal Justice System: Report, Vol. I, Government of India, Ministry of Home Affairs, March 2003, p. 189 (hereinafter Justice Malimath Committee Report).

[55] Anuja Agrawal, 'Law and "Live-in" Relationships in India', *Economic and Political Weekly* xlviI, 39 (2012): 50.

[56] 'Govt to Legalize Live-In Relations in Maharashtra, 09 October 2008, available at: https://www.oneindia.com/2008/10/09/govt-to-legalise-live-in-relations-in-maharashtra.html.

maintenance, whether *she knowingly or unknowingly* entered into a relationship with a married man[57] (emphasis added).

Before undertaking a closer analysis of the manner in which courts have shaped rights of cohabitees under certain specific laws, I want to return to personal laws which have added to the complexity of non-marital cohabiting relationship patterns. Hindu codified law lays down certain conditions of a valid marriage, one of which is that neither party should have a spouse living at the time of such marriage.[58] Thus, the law prohibits a bigamous marriage, which if violated, renders it void *ab initio*.[59] This scheme is complicated by another provision in the statute,[60] which prescribes that a Hindu marriage must be solemnized according to *customary rites and ceremonies of either party*. Except *saptapadi*,[61] a statutory listing of such *shastric* or customary rites has not been provided; there is little consensus on the essential ceremonies or customary rites that make 'solemnization of marriage' under codified Hindu law complete. Over the years, courts have however, adopted a case by case approach for deciding whether 'solemnization' is complete, depending on ceremonies or rites of a marriage practiced within the community to which either parties belong.[62] Many women enter into and stay in relationships without realizing that their marriage is not considered legally 'solemnized'

[57] *Times of India*, 'Maharashtra to Legalise Live-In Relationships', 09 October 2008, https://timesofindia.indiatimes.com/india/Maharashtra-to-iegalise-live-in-relationships/articleshow/3575090.cms.

[58] Section 5 (i), Hindu Marriage Act, 1955.

[59] Section 11, Hindu Marriage Act, 1955.

[60] Section 7, Hindu Marriage Act, 1955.

[61] Sub-section (2) of Section 7, Hindu Marriage Act, 1955 states: Where such rites and ceremonies include the saptapadi (that is, the taking of seven steps by the bridegroom and the bride jointly before the sacred fire), *the marriage becomes complete and binding when the seventh step is taken* (emphasis added). In G. *Lakshmi* v. *Garikapte Subba Rao* (1989) 1 ALT 503, the court held that non-performance of other ceremonies do not render a marriage void, *if* saptapadi *has been proved* to have been completed (emphasis added).

[62] *S. Nagalingam* v. *Sivagami*, AIR 2001 SC 3576 (Supreme Court of India) noted that saptapadi is an essential ceremony for a valid marriage only in cases where it was admitted by the parties that as per the form of marriage applicable to them that was an essential ceremony. In an earlier judgment of Andhra Pradesh High Court in *Ramlal Agarwal* v. *Shantadevi* I (2000) DMC 640, *kanyadan* (Ceremonial offering of the bride to the groom, performed ordinarily by the bride's father, during the Hindu marriage ceremony) was held to be no longer an essential ceremony of a valid marriage under the Hindu Marriage Act, 1955.

(and therefore, *no marriage at all*) because essential ceremonies or customary rites have not been performed. Such relationships fall into *void/voidable* marriages, and depending on the men's rea of male partner, may be labelled as a *fraudulent marriage*.

Significantly though, the law creates a rebuttable presumption of marriage if there is continued cohabitation between the parties.[63] Courts have relied on this evidentiary rule to uphold the rights of women in 'common law marriages' to maintenance and residence, and in favour of legitimacy of children.[64] However, it still leaves Hindu women in bigamous or 'second marriages' outside the scope of legal protections. There are no essential religious ceremonies of marriage under Muslim law (since marriage is a contract and not a sacrament) and a Muslim male may contract upto four marriages. However, unlawful conjugation is prohibited,[65] and under Sunni law, acts as a relative impediment making the marriage *irregular*.[66,67] Muslim law also creates a presumption in favour of marriage where there has been prolonged and continual cohabitation between the parties if there are no other impediments to such marriage.[68] Lack of a national law on

[63] Section 114, Indian Evidence Act, 1872. In *Tulsa* v. *Durghatiya* (2008) 1 SCR 709 (Supreme Court of India), the Supreme Court reiterated the presumption of valid marriage if the partners have lived together for a long time as husband and wife, and observed that to prove the contrary would attract a heavy burden of proof.

[64] *Badri Pasad* v. *Dy. Director, Consolidation*, AIR 1978 SC 1557 (Supreme Court of India); *Parayankandiyal Eravath Kanapravan Kalliani Amma* v. *K. Devi* (1996) 4 SCC 76 (Supreme Court of India); *Ranganath* v. *Eknath*, AIR 1996 SC 1290; *Sobha Devi* v. *Setti Gandhara Swami*, AIR 2005 SC 800 (Supreme Court of India); *Kalpana Biswas* v. *Sukamal Biswas @ kamal* (2004) 1 CHN 93 (Chhattisgarh High Court); *Reema Aggarwal* v. *Anupam* (2004) 3 SCC 199.

[65] The prohibition is that a man may not have at the same time two wives who are so related to each other by consanguinity, affinity, or fosterage, that if either had been a male, they could not have lawfully intermarried. The rule against unlawful conjugation however, operates only during subsistence of first marriage.

[66] An irregular or *fasid* marriage can be made valid by removing the impediment. Flavia Agnes, *Family Law: Marriage, Divorce, and Matrimonial Litigation*, Volume 2 (New Delhi: Oxford University Press, 2011).

[67] Under Shia law, all impediments render a marriage void. Indira Jaising, *The Lawyers Collective, Law of Domestic Violence*, second edition (Universal Law Publishing Co., 2007), p. 68.

[68] Jaising, *The Lawyers Collective*, p. 69.

compulsory registration of marriages[69] further compounds vulnerability of women in marriages which are not 'solemnized' or where no proof of marriage exists—a grim reality for many women with limited formal/functional education and legal literacy. This is despite a landmark judgment of the Supreme Court in 2006,[70] which held that registration of marriages shall be compulsory and issued directions to states to frame rules for compulsory registration of marriages. Although some states have made rules regarding registration of marriages, irrespective of one's personal laws,[71] weak implementation is built into these laws given that failure to register does not render a marriage invalid.[72] Similar is the case with personal laws. The Hindu Marriage Act, 1955 provides only for optional registration of marriages, and specifically declares that '*validity of any Hindu marriage shall in no way be affected*' by non-registration.[73]

In this backdrop of complex and often iniquitous operation of personal laws, political apathy, and ineffective implementation of laws including marriage registration provisions, it is important to examine how the judiciary in India has viewed the rights of women in cohabiting relationships. The key areas in which this enquiry is situated includes case law under the PWDV Act, 2006, and on maintenance under personal laws and under the secular Section 125 CrPC.

[69] Registration of Birth and Deaths Act, 1969 does not include registration of marriages within its ambit. The old Births, Deaths and Marriages Registration Act, 1886, which remains in force despite the 1969 law, merely provides for transmission and maintenance of records received from marriage registrars under different personal laws and the Special Marriage Act. See Law Commission of India, Report No. 211, 'Laws on Registration of Marriage and Divorce—A Proposal for Consolidation and Reform', 2008. In 2012, a proposed bill seeking to amend the law was introduced and passed in the Rajya Sabha. However, the bill remained pending in the Lok Sabha. See, http://www.prsindia.org/uploads/media/Registration%20of%20births%20and%20deaths/Registration%20of%20Births%20and%20Deaths%20(Amendment)%20bill,%202012.pdf.

[70] *Smt. Seema v. Ashwani Kumar*, AIR 2006 SC 1158.

[71] As per available information, till date, registration of marriages is compulsory under Bombay Registration of Marriages Act, 1954 (amended 1977); Karnataka Marriages (Registration and Miscellaneous Provisions) Act, 1984; The Himachal Pradesh Registration of Marriages Act, 1997; The Andhra Pradesh Compulsory Registration of Marriages Act, 2002.

[72] Law Commission of India, Report No. 211, 'Laws on Registration of Marriage and Divorce'.

[73] Section 8, Hindu Marriage Act, 1955.

PWDVA and Cohabitation

While studies of use and implementation of the PWDV Act, 2006, over the years show that married women continue to be its most common users,[74] it is the claims of women in 'relationship in the nature of marriage' that has been contested before the courts in India. Before examining the case law on this issue, however, it is important to reiterate the intent behind this provision at the time the law was drafted. This provision was specifically incorporated to bring those women into the law's ambit who otherwise had no legal claim under personal laws. A common example is of a woman who believes that she is married, but when the relationship breaks down, comes to know that it is not recognized by law as essential ceremonies of the marriage were not performed. Another example is of a 'second wife' who is unaware of the existence of her husband's previous marriage. Thus, women face domestic violence in relationships that may not have received the legal sanction of marriage, and this law was intended to extend protection to women in various forms of 'relationships in the nature of marriage', including live-in relationships; relationships that may not be recognized by law as marriage, including fraudulent or bigamous marriages; and common law marriages. Jaising highlights the urgent need for expanding the Act's protective ambit to women who are in relationships that are not recognized as valid marriage thus: '*Including relationships outside the marital context within the scope of this law was necessary in view of the absence of compulsory registration of marriages in India, which leaves a majority of women outside the domain of legal protection. Hence, the term "matrimonial relationship" was replaced with "domestic relationship"*'.[75]

In the initial years, after the Act came into force, courts interpreted 'relationship in the nature of marriage' in a manner in which it was intended. Thus, in *Aruna Parmod Shah* v. *Union of India* (2008), which was the first constitutional challenge to the Act on the basis that its provisions jeopardize rights of the legally wedded wife, the Delhi High Court held there is '*no*

[74] Lawyers Collective, 'Staying Alive', fifth Report on Implementation of Protection of Women from Domestic Violence Act, 2006, 2011, Lawyers Collective (2011); Monica Sakhrani and Trupti Jhaveri Panchal, 'Quest for Justice: A Study of the Implementation of the Protection of Women from Domestic Violence Act, 2005', TISS, September 2014.

[75] Jaising, Indira. 2009. 'Bringing Rights Home: Review of the Campaign for a Law on Domestic Violence', *Economic & Political Weekly*, Vol. XLIV No. 44. pp. 50–7, 31 October.

reason why equal treatment should not be accorded to wife as well as woman who has been living with a man as his common law wife or even his mistress. Like treatment to both, DOES NOT, in any manner, derogate from the sanctity of marriage'[76](emphasis added).

In *Velusamy* v. *D. Patchaiammal* (2011),[77] the Supreme Court interpreted the meaning of 'relationship in the nature of marriage' under Section 2(f) of the Act to be co-terminus with 'common-law marriage', thus narrowing its scope to exclude relationships which did not have the elements of a legally valid marriage. The Court noted that *not all 'live-in relationships' will amount to 'a relationship in the nature of marriage' in the way it is intended under the PWDVA* (emphasis added), and went on to enumerate the essential ingredients of a 'common law marriage' to be used also as the test for 'a relationship in the nature of marriage'. To appreciate the problematic nature of this judgment, it is also important to understand the facts of this case. The respondent-wife filed for maintenance under Section 125 CrPC in 2001 (that is, even before the PWDVA came into force), claiming that they were married and had lived together in her father's home. The appellant argued that he was legally married to one Lakshmi and that this earlier marriage had not been dissolved. As such, the respondent had no claim under Section 125 CrPC. The lower courts, however, found in favour of the respondent. When the matter reached the Supreme Court, it pointed out that whether the appellant's earlier marriage had been dissolved was an issue of fact and remanded the case back to the trial court to hear evidence of the alleged first wife. Thus, although the case did not directly relate to claims under the PWDV Act, 2005, the Court went on to circumscribe the protected categories under 'relationship in the nature of marriage' and took it upon itself to provide an 'authoritative decision' as to its meaning. More importantly, the judgment brings to fore, the apparent discomfort with expanding the ambit of legal protection to the 'other woman' irrespective of whether she is a victim of domestic violence.

To understand the reasons for this discomfort, one must go back to Hindu personal law. Monogamy is at the heart of codified law on Hindu marriage, and the wife's legal rights and entitlements flow from a strict adherence to the norm of 'sexual purity', which lead to further disentitlement of the 'second wife' while the man, who often fraudulently enters into

[76] *Aruna Parmod Shah* v. *Union of India* (2008) 102 D.R.J. 543 (Delhi High Court) (7 April 2008).

[77] *Velusamy* v. *D. Patchaiammal*, AIR 2011 SC 479 (Supreme Court of India).

such a marriage, is able to defeat her claim to maintenance or residence. As Flavia Agnes notes:

> It is strange that matrimonial misconduct or 'guilt' can be flagrantly invoked by a husband to defeat the woman's economic claim, without any adverse criminal or civil consequences visiting him during court proceedings. This type of flouting of a legal mandate and its subsequent invocation to gain financial edge against a vulnerable person can take place only within a blatantly sexist social order.[78]

In *Indra Sarma* v. *V.K.V. Sarma* (2013),[79] the Supreme Court laid down specific guidelines to determine whether a particular case meets the test of 'relationship in the nature of marriage'. The court's discussion of 'live-in relationships' and how certain forms of 'live-in relationships' would not fall under the rubric of 'relationship in the nature of marriage' as provided under Section 2(f) of the PWDV Act, 2006 makes for interesting reading. This was a case of a married man cohabiting with his unmarried former colleague (aggrieved person) for 14 years. As a result of their relationship, the aggrieved woman went through three abortions, and when the relationship broke down after 14 years, she was left without any financial support. She filed a petition under the PWDV Act, 2006 seeking maintenance and compensation. The Supreme Court ruled out that the relationship would fall under 'relationship in the nature of marriage' although it may qualify as a live-in relationship mainly on the basis that she entered into the relationship '*knowing well that he was a married man with a wife and children, hence, was a party to an adulterous and bigamous relationship*'. The Court went on to distinguish between a live-in relationship simpliciter and one that qualifies as a 'relationship in the nature of marriage' on this very basis. What was most disturbing is that it set a dangerous precedent by stating that she had committed an intentional tort, by interfering in the marital relationship of the man, and intentionally alienating him from his legally wedded wife and children. While arguably, the court's preoccupation with protecting the interests of the legitimate 'family' could be understood, to accuse the 'other' woman of committing an intentional tort, is to paint the man as an innocent victim—a foolish simpleton at best who was wiled away from his wife and family by a scheming woman—for 14 long years. Let us now look at what the Court, based on a long line of judicial rulings in India and in common law, reiterated

78 Flavia Agnes, 'Conjugality, Property, Morality and Maintenance', *Economic and Political Weekly* xliv, 44 (2009): 61.

79 *Indra Sarma* v. *V.K.V. Sarma* (2013) 14 SCALE 448 (Supreme Court of India).

as essential ingredients of a relationship that qualifies as 'relationship in the nature of marriage'. As in the earlier case of Velusamy, the Supreme Court listed the following:

1. Duration of relationship—case to case determination necessary.
2. They are or have been in a 'shared household'.
3. Pooling of resources and financial arrangement.
4. Domestic arrangements, with the woman being responsible for household.
5. Sexual relationship.
6. Children.
7. Socialization, that is, the essential common law marriage attribute that the parties must have held out to be husband and wife in society.
8. Common intention and conduct of the parties, which we have seen earlier in this Chapter, is an essential attribute of the 'constructive trust' principle.

If we were to now examine these ingredients in relation to the facts of this case. There was no dispute that the parties cohabited in a shared dwelling house, that is, a shared household for 14 years. While the court did not think that there was sufficient evidence of pooling of resources and financial arrangement because there was no joint bank account, the appellant alleged that he reneged on his promise to help start a business. Since the parties were admittedly in a cohabiting relationship, with the court finding that the appellant had alienated the man from his legal family, there can hardly be a dispute that there was a domestic arrangement. They had a sexual relationship, with the parties agreeing that there were three abortions. Of course, there were no children; those who work with abandoned women and domestic violence victims know that they have little reproductive autonomy, and implicitly coercing them to have abortions fits the pattern quite easily. I am not arguing here that this is what happened, but it is likewise unjust to reach the conclusion that because there were abortions, the parties did not have a 'relationship in the nature of marriage'. As to holding out as husband and wife, the court noted that the legal wife and parents of the man disapproved of the relationship. Is it any wonder then that he was cautious about social appearances? The court's reasoning validates Agnes' critique that a husband may flagrantly invoke a matrimonial 'fault' to defeat the rights of the aggrieved woman.

It is this kind of conflation of statutory protection against violence against women with rights that flow from married status that is problematic. While the judicial approach to claims to maintenance under personal laws operates within the framework of whether the marriage is 'valid' or in a fact situation like Indra Sarma, whether it qualifies as 'marriage-like', the case of a cohabiting woman's claim under PWDVA is qualitatively different. PWDVA, 2006 is a 'stop violence law' and provides reliefs that are 'transitionary' in nature; it recognizes rights of a woman in a 'domestic relationship'[80] that are essential to stop violence from occurring and restore her to a position from where she can make an informed choice about her future course of action. As such, the right to be free from violence is not a qualified right that ought to vest in a woman who faces domestic violence, only if she meets the criteria of a 'marriage'. It may thus, be argued that every woman must have recourse against domestic violence, irrespective of whether she is the 'second wife', and an abusive partner must not be allowed to use 'bigamy' as a tool to defeat her right to be protected from such violence. So far as her right directly conflicts with the 'first wife's' rights, such as in case of claim for maintenance or residence under the law, the courts must give her the appropriate remedy based on a judicial consideration of the facts of the case. This is the reason why Supreme Court's judgment in Velusamy, using the standard of 'common law marriage' to limit the scope of 'relationship in the nature of marriage', is inherently problematic. To move away from this narrative therefore, it is important that we bring back the focus to 'cohabitation' and a woman's vulnerability to violence that arises precisely from the fact of such 'cohabitation'. In re-enlarging the ambit of statutory protection in situations of domestic violence, one must go beyond the existing formulation of 'relationship in the nature of marriage' in the law to recognize the plurality of relationships and families.

Maintenance under Section 125 CrPC and Personal Laws

A married Hindu woman is entitled to maintenance under Section 18 of the Hindu Adoptions and Maintenance Act, 1956 (HAMA) in addition to that which is available to women from all religious communities under the secular provision of Section 125 CrPC. However, this right to maintenance under Hindu law is rescinded if the wife remarries or if she is 'living in adultery'.[81] Maintenance under the law is intended to protect the wife from vagrancy and can be directly traced to the 'poor laws' of Britain; it is

[80] Section 2(f), Protection of Women from Domestic Violence Act, 2006.

[81] Section 18(3), Hindu Adoptions and Maintenance Act, 1956.

founded on the understanding that so long as the wife does not violate the norms against sexual promiscuity, she is entitled to the husband's protection. The Court's discourse, following the law's narrative, is therefore, mired in the language of 'sexuality' and 'morality', within which women claiming their rights in the domestic sphere have been viewed as either 'good litigant' and deserving of reliefs, or as a 'bad litigant' and therefore, undeserving and censured. As Agnes notes, '*Securing an order of adequate maintenance can be an extremely humiliating experience as a high degree of sexual morality surrounds the question of maintenance. Curiously, the core of this economic dispute does not revolve around questions of financial arrangements of the family unit, but hinges upon issues of sexual mores*'.[82] While we are concerned with maintenance claims of women in cohabiting intimate relationships in this chapter, this brief digression highlighting the sexual morality-laced genesis and evolution of provisions on wife's maintenance, particularly Section 125 CrPC, was necessary to set the context for the apparent tension in judicial approach(es) on the subject.

Over the years, claims of maintenance of women in void/voidable marriages has been recognized by courts.[83] In the 2005 judgment *Rameshchandra Daga v. Rameshwari Daga*,[84] the Supreme Court recognized that a wife whose marriage has been declared null and void under the HAMA would still be entitled to claim maintenance under the Act, because to not do so would be to force her into destitution. Cohabitation for a considerable period of time and existence of children were also relied upon to draw a presumption of marriage or 'marriage-like' relationship, thereby upholding the woman's right to maintenance under Section 125 CrPC.[85] While this judicial approach expanded the categories of cohabitees who could now

82 Agnes, *Conjugality, Property, Morality and Maintenance*, p. 60.

83 In *Dwarika Prasad Satpathy v. Bidyut Prava Dixit* (1999) 7 SCC 675 (Supreme Court of India), the court held that standard of proof for marriage under section 125 CrPC is not as strict as required in a trial for bigamy under section 494 IPC. In such cases, failure to complete certain essential rites cannot be used to contend that there was no valid marriage. The court concluded that Section 125 CrPC cannot be used to defeat the rights of destitute women and children. See Jaising, The Lawyers Collective, p. 88.

84 *Rameshchandra Daga v. Rameshwari Daga* (2005) 2 SCC 33 (Supreme Court of India).

85 *Mallika and Anr. v. P. Kulandi* (2001) I DMC 354 (Madras High Court); *Kartick Roy v. Prabitra Roy* (2004) 2) CHN 435 (Calcutta High Court); *Pradeep Kumar Gupta v. Smt. Kanti Devi* (2003) I DMC 265 (Jharkhand High Court).

claim maintenance under the secular law, at the deeper level, the emphasis was on the provision's protectionist objective to prevent vagrancy and destitution of women, and not on the fact of the de facto relationship which ought to entitle women in such relationships to certain legal rights. Besides, the courts continued to clearly distinguish 'second marriages' and deny maintenance claims of women in such marriages. Thus, in *Somabhai Bhatiya* v. *State of Gujarat*,[86] the Supreme Court refused to recognize the 'second wife's' right to maintenance under Section 125 CrPC since the husband had sufficient proof as to the validity of his first marriage. Since the PWDVA (and before and after Velusamy and Indra Sarma), one can notice a subtle shift in the judiciary's treatment of women cohabitees in 'second marriages' or in fraudulent marriages in relation to the right to maintenance.

The Supreme Court dealt with the issue of rights of women in technically defective marriages in *Chanmuniya* v. *Virendra Kumar Singh Kushwaha*.[87] The judgment was delivered in 2010, the same year as Velusamy, where the Court held that *a broad and expansive interpretation should be given to term 'wife' to include even those cases where a man and woman have been living together as husband and wife for a reasonably long period of time, and strict proof of marriage should not be a precondition for maintenance under S. 125 CrPC.* Significantly, the Court located such an interpretation as a just application of the constitutional principles of social justice and *dignity of the individual* (emphasis added). Although it referred the issue of interpretation of 'relationship in the nature of marriage' under the PWDVA to a larger bench, undoubtedly, it was a landmark ruling for its emphasis on a woman's dignity as the source of her rights in an intimate cohabiting relationship. The judgment was somewhat lost in the outrage and debates around the Velusamy ruling.[88]

In an interesting and sparsely discussed judgment,[89] the Tripura High Court held that although a decree of divorce under the HAMA cannot be granted where the parties were in a common law marriage. Before the court, the female partner argued that there was no valid marriage since necessary

[86] *Somabhai Bhatiya* v. *State of Gujarat*, AIR 2005 SC 1809 (Supreme Court of India).

[87] *Chanmuniya* v. *Virendra Kumar Singh Kushwaha* (2011) 1 SCC 141 (Supreme Court of India).

[88] Flavia Agnes, 'The Concubine and Notions of Constitutional Justice', *Economic and Political Weekly* xlvi, 24 (June 2011): 32.

[89] *Chandan Debnath* v. *Suniti Debnath* (2014) SCC Online Tri 74 (Tripura High Court).

ceremonies or customary rites were not performed; the male partner asked for divorce on the ground that they had cohabited as husband and wife for 10 years. Discussing a much-publicized single judge Madras High Court judgment,[90] referred to by the male partner, to suggest that prolonged sexual relationship raises a presumption of marriage, the Court held that this was a rebuttable presumption, especially in cases where marital status is challenged *by one of the parties and not by a third party*. The Court observed that live-in relationships are '*now a well recognised part of our social system*', and elsewhere, '*live-in relationships are to be dealt with in accordance with Protection of Women from Domestic Violence Act, 2005 and not under the Hindu marriage Act*'. There is no dispute that the HAMA lays down specific requirements for a valid marriage, and where such requirements are not met, a decree of divorce under the Act cannot be granted. However, the Court's reasoning that presumption in favour of marriage is weak when it is challenged by one of the parties is hugely problematic; is the court suggesting that a male cohabitee is not likely to challenge such presumption to avoid maintenance claims of the female cohabitee? The long line of case law clearly suggests otherwise. It appears that the Court was persuaded by what it referred to as an attempt by the male partner to claim alimony; '*The first issue that troubles us is—why does the appellant want decree of divorce?*'

In 2014, the Supreme Court in *Badshah* v. *Urmila Badshah Godse*,[91] once again upheld the right of a woman in a bigamous marriage to claim maintenance under Section 125 CrPC. Despite this, Velusamy appears to have done significant damage to the scope of Section 125 CrPC. Agnes notes, '*the adverse publicity of the Velusamy ruling has made it impossible to claim rights in magistrates' courts as the courts decline to entertain these applications*'.[92]

Other Common Law Jurisdictions: Some Examples

Common law jurisdictions like Scotland, Ireland, Canada, and Australia have made important advances towards recognition of rights of heterosexual non-marital cohabitees. I have referred to the Family Law (Scotland) Act, 2006, which allows cohabitants of both same sex and opposite sex to make claims against each other in case of relationship breakdown or death. These

[90] *Aysha* v. *Ozir Hassan* (2013) 5 MLJ 31 (Madras High Court).

[91] *Badshah* v. *Urmila Badshah Godse* (2014) 1 SCC 188 (Supreme Court of India).

[92] Flavia Agnes and Audrey D'Mello, 'Protection of Women from Domestic Violence', *Economic and Political Weekly* I, 44 (2015): 82.

claims are limited though, and do not bring them on an equal footing with married couples and civil partners.[93] A leading case from Scotland, which interpreted the scope of rights under the 2006 Act is *Gow* v. *Grant*.[94] The case involved a claim by Mrs Gow for financial provision following breakdown of a longstanding cohabiting relationship based on the fact that she had sold her home to move into Mr Grant's property, and as a result lost future earnings from appreciation in its value. She was awarded financial relief based on the principle of fairness. The matter reached the Supreme Court after a successful appeal by Mr Grant in the lower appellate court. The Supreme Court looked into the objectives behind the 2006 Act, and noting the clear economic disadvantage between the parties, concluded that 'the emphasis was very much on fairness between cohabiting couples, despite the absence of the words "fair and reasonable" in the section'.[95]

The Civil Partnership and Certain Rights and Obligations of Cohabitants Act, 2010 of Ireland defines 'cohabitant' as *one of 2 adults (whether of the same or the opposite sex) who live together as a couple in an intimate and committed relationship and who are not related to each other within the prohibited degrees of relationship or married to each other or civil partners of each other*.[96] The Act recognizes entitlements of dependant cohabitees under the social welfare legislation,[97] and the right to apply for orders such as maintenance orders, property adjustment orders, and pension adjustment orders and other related orders such as attachment of earnings orders. The dependant cohabitee can also apply for proceeds from the estate of the deceased cohabitant.[98]

Canada recognizes 'common law' relationships but the scope and application varies within the country since these are regulated by provincial laws/rules. British Columbia is considered to have the most progressive legal regime governing common law relationships, with the Family Law Act,

[93] Fairburn, 'Common Law Marriage and Cohabitation', p. 23.

[94] *Gow* v. *Grant* (2012) UKSC 29.

[95] Fiona Sasan, 'Cohabitees and the Principle of Fairness', *The Journal of the Law Society of Scotland*, 13 August 2012, available at: http://www.journalonline.co.uk/Magazine/57-8/1011519.aspx.

[96] Section 172(1), Civil Partnership and Certain Rights and Obligations of Cohabitants Act, 2010.

[97] Department of Employment Affairs and Social Protection, Government of North Ireland, available at: http://www.welfare.ie/en/Pages/Cohabitation.aspx#1

[98] Citizens Information, Ireland, available at: http://www.citizensinformation.ie/en/birth_family_relationships/problems_in_marriages_and_other_relationships/redress_scheme_for_cohabiting_couples.html.

2013[99] granting equal rights to such relationships as for married couples in matters of property division, health insurance, government benefits, inheritance, and spousal support.[100] Common-law relationships in British Columbia are referred to as 'marriage-like relationships' that lasted at least one or two years. The rules are inconsistent in other provinces. Ontario, Canada, entitles 'common law' partners to claim spousal support but does not grant property rights. In Nova Scotia, Canada, claims for spousal support is allowed once the parties have been in a common-law relationship for two years. However, the province also allows *Domestic Partnership Declaration*, which provides many of the same rights as married couples. Quebec is the only province in Canada which does not recognize a 'common-law' but refers to such relationships as 'de facto spouses' with limited rights.[101]

Australia recognizes 'de facto relationships' between same-sex or opposite sex partners. The federal law defines a 'de facto relationship', including current and former partners, who are not related or married to each other.[102] Partners in 'de facto relationships' have the same rights as married couples in terms of custody of children, dealing with financial disputes, and spousal support. However, to claim these rights, one has to discharge a higher burden to prove that the relationship qualifies as a 'de facto relationship', meet qualifying criteria of at least two years in most cases, and there are stricter timelines for filing such claims. These have led to widespread criticism, especially by advocates of marriage equality in the context of same-sex de facto relationships.[103]

Beyond Marriage and Morality: Towards Recognizing Cohabitees' Right to Protection from Domestic Violence

Due diligence obligation under international law: State obligation to provide an *immediate and effective* response to domestic violence includes within its

[99] Melanie Patten, *The Canadian Press*, February 2016, available at: https://globalnews.ca/news/2511460/common-law-couples-can-be-woefully-ignorant-of-their-rights-lawyer/.

[100] http://family.findlaw.ca/article/a-primer-on-common-law-marriage-rights-in-canada/.

[101] Melanie Patten, *The Canadian Press*.

[102] Section 4AA, Family Law Act, 1975.

[103] Hannah Robert and Fiona Kelly, 'Marriage v. De Facto Partnerships in Australia: The Legal Differences Explained', *The Guardian*, 21 September 2017, available at: https://www.theguardian.com/australia-news/2017/sep/21/marriage-v-de-facto-partnerships-in-australia-the-legal-differences-explained.

ambit, ensuring effective and easy access to justice, and once the aggrieved woman approaches the Court, her claim be considered keeping in view the object of the law and without any bias. Once the fact of domestic violence is established to the prima facie satisfaction of the court, immediate and adequate relief(s) must be granted to prevent future violence.

State obligation to protect women from domestic violence was realized with the enactment of the PWDVA, 2005. The Act broke new grounds by institutionalizing the support system that is critical to women negotiating violence within intimate relationships—the protection officer, service provider, right to shelter, and legal assistance. It deftly negotiated the complex questions of property and personal laws by recognizing a right to residence in the shared household, which accrues only from the status of the intimate or 'domestic relationship' that is ultimately based on past or continuing cohabitation. For the purposes of a discussion on cohabitees' rights, PWDVA's greatest contribution has been to bring women in 'relationships in the nature of marriage' in our public discourse on violence within the 'private' sphere. In doing so, the Act brought 'domestic relationships' defined solely by cohabitation in a shared household into the secular domain, and pierced the veil of *morality* from discussions on violence against women. It recognized that any woman, irrespective of whether she was in a legally valid marriage, has at the very minimum, a right to protection from domestic violence. The only limitation being that she must have cohabited in a 'shared household' or shared residence with the perpetrator of such violence. The Supreme Court in Velusamy has, therefore, done great disservice to women who are in abusive intimate relationships or are vulnerable to such violence.

So what is next for women in intimate relationships who are currently outside the ambit of protection of PWDVA and other laws? Given that any attempt to expand legal protections for women with reference to 'marriage' or 'marriage like relationships' is fraught with the danger of always excluding some women, there is a need to engage in discussions around rights of 'cohabitees'. Such discussions must necessarily be had within the framework of constitutional notions of equality and justice, and preventing a 'morality' based framing. Agnes maintains, 'the question that we need to ask is not whether Hindu marriages ought to be monogamous, or even, serially monogamous, but rather, whether we are bound by a constitutional duty and obligation to protect the rights of a large number of poor and destitute women who, wittingly or unwittingly, are trapped within technically defective marriages'. While recognizing that addressing dependency of vulnerable women in void/voidable, fraudulent, bigamous, and other multitude of patterns of cohabiting intimate relationships is necessary, my argument is that our framing must go beyond destitution and economic support. The principle of individual dignity is a powerful and often underutilized one; in the context of women in heterosexual cohabiting intimate relationships, it must be used to secure rights in relation to maintenance, residence, and others by virtue of the fact of such relationship.

In relation to legal protections on the issue of domestic violence first, and then with maintenance or other personal laws, this engagement is likely to be an organic one, given the Indian State's constitutional and due diligence obligations. The statutory recognition of cohabitees' rights, thus, would be an affirmation of the pluralities of relationships within the Indian constitutional narrative of individual dignity and personal autonomy.

6. *Marital Rape As Domestic Violence*

A Case for Criminalizing Marital Rape

Ajita Sharma

While patriarchy casts a dark shadow over most aspects of marriages in India, the issue that has been completely left out from the purview of law is the cruelty and violence inflicted upon the married woman by her husband in the form of forced sexual intercourse. The wife's consent to sexual intercourse within the marriage is an assumption reinforced by society and the legislature alike. Marriage seen as a sacrament, a revered union, thus becomes a violent space for women. While domestic violence[1] is now accepted as encompassing all forms of physical, sexual, verbal, emotional, and economic abuse; forced sexual intercourse by the husband has been specifically granted legal sanction and protection under penal laws in India,[2] thereby rendering the wife's consent irrelevant.

[1] The most comprehensive definition of 'domestic violence' in India is under § 3(a) of the PWDVA, No. 43 of 2005, INDIA CODE (2005) that includes physical, sexual, verbal, emotional, and economic abuse within itself.

[2] In India, rape by a husband in marriage is not a criminal offence, as the IPC retains the exception that exempts marital rape as given in Exceptions 2 to § 375

This chapter argues in favour of recognizing forced sexual intercourse within marriage (marital rape) as a crime in India. The arguments in favour have been made by rebutting the forcefully held misconceptions that continue to be put forth as justifications for exempting marital rape as an offence. The institution of marriage as a sanction for sex completely negates the consent of the wife. This has the effect of condoning acts in the nature of domestic violence and must be seen as a serious violation and a form of gender discrimination that negates the dignity, personal autonomy, and bodily integrity of married women. The chapter vehemently argues that the legal provision in the form of Exception 2 to Section 375[3] of the Indian Penal Code, 1860,[4] (the exception) that protects marital rape, is in direct contravention of constitutional[5] and international[6] guarantees, and that the exception severely impacts married women's safety within the private sphere. The marital rape exception takes away a married woman's right to legal protection and allows sexual violence to go unpunished.

The chapter studies the existing legal provisions on spousal sexual violence to assess the possible legal remedies available to women in cases of rape by her husband. The Protection of Women from Domestic Violence Act, 2005 (PWDVA) includes sexual violence as a type of domestic violence within the definition.[7] The accepted concept of cruelty under criminal law, divorce

---

of the IPC. Also: Statutory Resolution dated 21 March 2013 in Session 228 of the Rajya Sabha on the issue of 'Disapproving the Criminal Law (Amendment) Ordinance, 2013 and The Criminal Law (Amendment) Bill, 2013'.

[3] Indian Penal Code, No. 45 of 1860, INDIA CODE (1860) § 375 exception 2 as amended by the Criminal Law (Amendment) Act, No. 13 of 2013, INDIA CODE (2013) and the recent judgment of the Supreme Court in *Independent Thought* v. *Union of India*, 2017 SCC OnLine SC 1222 read as: Exception 2- Sexual intercourse or sexual acts by a man with his own wife, the wife not being under 18 years of age is not rape.

[4] Hereinafter referred to as 'IPC'.

[5] The said principles are guaranteed under the Constitution of India under the fundamental right to equality (Article 14) and to live life with dignity (Article 21).

[6] A law protecting marital rape is in clear violation of internationally principles of bodily integrity, integrity of person; gender discrimination based, in this case, more specifically to marital status. Relevant international principles are laid down under the International Covenant on Civil and Political Rights (ICCPR), ICESCR, further strengthened under the CEDAW.

[7] Protection of Women from Domestic Violence Act, No. 43 of 2005, INDIA CODE (2005), § 3. Definition of domestic violence. For the purposes of this Act, any act, omission or commission or conduct of the respondent shall constitute domestic

laws, and Section 377 IPC[8] will also be analysed in this context. The intent is to identify the parameters of sexual abuse within a marriage. In most cases of domestic violence by the husband forced sexual intercourse exists and must therefore be treated at par with other acts of domestic violence; even though marital rape is not specifically recognized as a crime under the penal laws of the country.

The detrimental social and health impact of marital rape on women demonstrates, through the data available, that marital rape impacts health and safety of women in the same way as rape by a stranger. Work with domestic violence victims at hospitals and counselling centres has demonstrated without a doubt that marital rape is never a matter of an isolated incident, it forms a part and parcel of the cycle of abuse suffered by women in their marriage. Consent as a primary requirement will be examined in the context of existing domestic violence provisions and under the rape laws to establish that the absence of consent must necessarily constitute a form of spousal sexual violence and be treated at par with rape as defined by the law. An exception to rape that renders consent irrelevant cannot be anything short of unconstitutional.

Protecting Marital Rape: Underpinnings of the Marital Rape Exception

The law is not simply silent on consent as a primary requirement for sexual relations within a marriage, it goes a step further and sanctions it

---

violence in case it, (a) harms or injures or endangers the health, safety, life, limb or well-being, whether mental or physical, of the aggrieved person or tends to do so and includes causing physical abuse, sexual abuse, verbal and emotional abuse and economic abuse; …Explanation: I. 'For the purposes of this section, "sexual abuse" includes any conduct of a sexual nature that abuses, humiliates, degrades or otherwise violates the dignity of woman'.

[8] Indian Penal Code, No. 45 of 1860, INDIA CODE (1860) § 377: Unnatural offences: Whoever voluntarily has carnal intercourse against the order of nature with any man, woman or animal, shall be punished with imprisonment for life, or with imprisonment of either description for a term which may extend to ten years, and shall also be liable to fine. Explanation: Penetration is sufficient to constitute the carnal intercourse necessary to the offence described in this section. On 6 September 2018 in *Navtej Singh Johar v. Union of India*, Writ Petition (Crl.) No. 76 of 2016, a five judge Constitution bench unanimously held § 377 IPC unconstitutional 'in so far as it criminalises consensual sexual conduct between adults of the same sex'.

under Exception 2 to Section 375 IPC.[9] Rape committed within a marriage can only be punishable in two cases: where the wife is a minor[10] and when spouses are living separately under a decree of judicial separation.[11] The punishment prescribed for cases of marital rape during subsistence of a judicial decree of separation is, however, lower than the punishment for rape under Section 376[12] IPC. Law clearly demonstrates permissiveness

[9] The Criminal Law (Amendment) Act, No. 13 of 2013, INDIA CODE (2013), § 375 Exception 2 (retained from the earlier provision § 376 IPC) reads: 'Sexual intercourse by a man with his own wife, the wife not being under fifteen years of age, is not rape.' In 2017, the *Supreme Court in Independent Thought* v. *Union of India*, 2017 SCC OnLine SC 1222 has struck down the exception to marital rape for a minor wife below 18 years of age, holding the exception as arbitrary and ultra vires. The court held that the said exception was defeating the purpose of the Prohibition of Child Marriage Act, No. 6 of 2007, INDIA CODE (2006) which is to discourage child marriages as it is a harmful practice. The exception was found to be in violation of international conventions to which India is a signatory. Further, the court held that the said exception in the IPC was contrary to the provisions of the Prevention of Children from Sexual Offences Act, No. 32 of 2012, INDIA CODE (2012) ('POCSO Act') as: Firstly, it is statutory rape if a man above 18 years of age had sex with the minor, thus, the willingness or consent of the minor below the age of 18 years for having sex is rendered irrelevant and inconsequential; secondly, raping a child is an offence, and a child is defined as any person below the age of 18 years and thirdly, § 5 of POCSO Act defines 'aggravated penetrative sexual assault' and clause (n) states that 'Whoever being a relative of the child through blood or adoption or marriage or guardianship or in foster career having a domestic relation with a parent of the child or who is living in the same or shared household with the child, commits penetrative sexual assault on such child'. Therefore, child's husband can be held guilty for penetrative sexual assault as well as non-penetrative sexual assault. Moreover, § 42-A of the POCSO Act states that the provisions of the Act will override the provisions of any other law to the extent they are inconsistent, hence the provisions of POCSO Act overrides § 375 IPC and its Exception 2.

[10] See note 9. *Independent Thought* v. *Union of India*, 2017 SCC OnLine SC 1222.

[11] Indian Penal Code, No. 45 of 1860, INDIA CODE (1860), § 376-B (Sexual intercourse by husband upon his wife during separation): Whoever has sexual intercourse with his own wife, who is living separately, whether under a decree of separation or otherwise, without her consent, shall be punished with imprisonment of either description for a term which shall not be less than two years but which may extend to seven years, and shall also be liable to fine.

[12] Indian Penal Code, No. 45 of 1860, INDIA CODE (1860), § 376 (Punishment for rape): Rigorous imprisonment for a term which shall not be less than ten years, but which may extend to imprisonment for life, which shall mean imprisonment for the remainder of that person's natural life, and shall also be liable to fine. See note 11.

in favour of the husband and the institution of marriage. The absence of criminal liability for committing marital rape by the husband with his wife, save the two provisions mentioned above, has remained unchanged since its adoption during the pre-constitutional era.[13] The exception to marital rape in the IPC was inserted in Clause 359 of Macaulay's Draft Penal Code[14] and was retained in the final version of Section 375[15] after deliberations by the Select Committee in the 1960s version of the IPC. The exception is thus reflective of the prevailing social mores in India and other parts of the world at that time. Today, penal laws in several states[16] recognize the consent of the wife as being essential to sexual intercourse based on the principle that marriage is a 'partnership of equals'.[17]

While the original definition of rape and the punishment prescribed for rape has undergone several amendments,[18] lack of criminal liability for marital rape has been retained despite objections and serious concerns voiced by the women's movement and legal luminaries over the years. So far, the amendments to the exception have only been with respect to the age of the wife, where

[13] K.I. Vibhute, 2001. 'Rape and the IPC at the Crossroads of the new millennium: Between Patriarchist and Gender Neutralist Approach', Indian Law Institute, 43: 1.

[14] K.I. Vibhute, Rape' and the IPC at the Crossroads of the new millennium.

[15] Exception to § 375 (Rape) as it stood in the final version of IPC in 1960: 'Exception—Sexual intercourse by a man with his wife, not being under ten years of age, is not rape.'

[16] Countries where Marital Rape is a crime: Poland, Czechoslovakia, Sweden, Norway, Australia, Italy, Slovenia, Belgium, Israel, Portugal, Canada, New Zealand, Austria, Republic of Ireland, England and Wales, Netherlands, Switzerland, United States, South Africa, France, Cyprus, Finland, Luxembourg, Macedonia, Colombia, Germany, Croatia, Chile, Namibia, Liechtenstein, Zimbabwe, Serbia, Papua New Guinea, Bosnia and Herzegovina, Turkey, Cambodia, Liberia, Greece, Nepal, Thailand, Mauritius, Ghana, Malaysia, Rwanda, Suriname, Nicaragua, Sierra Leone, South Korea, Bolivia, Samoa, Tonga; this chapter will only look at laws from some of these commonwealth countries or/and those that have complied with the international law principles.

[17] UK judgment of Reg. v. Roberts [1986] Crim. L.R. 188, where Lord Lane, CJ relied on R. v. Clark held: 'marriage in modern times is regarded as a partnership of equals and no longer one in which the wife must be the subservient chattel of the husband.'

[18] § 375 Exception 2 was further amended by the Criminal Law Amendment Act 43 of 1983 and expanded the definition of rape but retained the exception of marital rape.

the age of consent was increased to 15 years.[19] In the early 1980s, marital rape was one of the issues taken up during the campaigns on rape law reforms. The Law Commission had recommended that the marital rape exemption must be removed; the government however rejected the recommendations; the Criminal Law Amendment Act, 1983, was passed with no changes to the provision on marital rape.[20] Subsequent Law Commission reports have also rejected any proposal to repeal the marital rape exception on grounds that it would amount to 'excessive interference with the marital relationship'.[21]

The inclusion of marital rape within the definition of rape by removing the exception to marital rape[22] was fiercely advocated once again post the Nirbhaya incident[23] in 2013 by Justice J.S. Verma in the Report of

[19] The age of consent was increased from 10 years to 15 years by Act 43 of 1983, § 3, for § 375 and § 376 (w.e.f. 25-12-1983) and was retained by Criminal Law Amendment Act, 2013.

[20] Ratna Kapur, 'Challenging the Liberal Subject: Law and Gender Justice in South Asia', in Maitrayee Mukhopadhyay and Navsharan Singh (eds). GENDER JUSTICE, CITIZENSHIP AND DEVELOPMENT, p. 116 (Maitrayee Mukhopadhyay et al., 2007), https://books.google.co.in/books?id=fgg2TN-687EC&pg=PR3&dq=ratna+kapoor+%2B+marital+rape&source=gbs_selected_pages&cad=3#v=onepage&q=ratna%20kapoor%20%2B%20marital%20rape&f=false.

[21] Law Commission of India, Review of Rape Laws, 172nd Report, 2000, Chapter 3, p. 14 and 205th Report, 2008.

[22] Justice K.S. Verma (Retd) et al., 'Report of the Committee on Amendments to Criminal Law', 23 January 2014, pp. 117, 79: 'the exception for marital rape be removed' and 'the law ought to specify that: (a) A marital or other relationship between the perpetrator or victim is not a valid defence against the crimes of rape or sexual violation; (b) The relationship between the accused and the complainant is not relevant to the inquiry into whether the complainant consented to the sexual activity and (c) The fact that the accused and victim are married or in another intimate relationship may not be regarded as a mitigating factor justifying lower sentences for rape'; http://www.prsindia.org/uploads/media/Justice%20verma%20committee/js%20verma%20committe%20report.pdf.

[23] It was the Nirbhaya incident on 16 December 2012, where a female physiotherapy intern was beaten and gang raped in Delhi and died 13 days later while undergoing emergency treatment in Singapore for brain and gastrointestinal damage from the assault. This incident led to a nationwide protest for immediate changes in laws relating to rape and sexual assault. On 22 December 2012, the Central Government appointed a Committee under auspices of Justice J.S. Verma, former Chief Justice of India to submit a report suggesting amendments to the criminal law. The report was submitted on 13 January 2013 and based on the same, the Criminal Law (Amendment) Act, 2013 was enacted.

the Committee on Amendments to Criminal Law[24] (Verma Committee Report). The Amendment was passed with the exception remaining intact, save the provision with respect to rape in a marriage during legal separation.[25] The Criminal Law Amendment Act of 2013 has brought about significant changes: the definition of rape has been amended to include forced oral and anal sex, insertion of objects into mouth, both anal and vaginal, and the age of consent has been raised to 18 years.[26] The recommendations on marital rape by the Verma Committee Report were not implemented at the time the amendments were drafted in March 2013.[27] Instead, the government relied on a report prepared by a parliamentary committee[28] opposing the removal of the exception on marital rape. The 167th Parliamentary Standing Committee Report on Home Affairs on the Criminal Law (Amendment) Bill, 2012 ('Parliamentary Standing Committee's Report') states:

> The Committee felt that if a woman is aggrieved by the acts of her husband, there are other means of approaching the court. In India, for ages, the family system has evolved, and it is moving forward. Family is able to resolve the problems and there is also a provision under the law for cruelty against women. It was, therefore, felt that if the marital rape is brought under the law, the entire family system will be under great stress and the Committee may perhaps be doing more injustice.[29]

Subsequently, in 2014, the Special Rapporteur on Violence Against Women also recommended the amendment of Section 375, IPC, to include a definition of marital rape as a criminal offence.[30] She stated that not fully

[24] Verma (Retd) et al., '*Report of the Committee on Amendments to Criminal Law*'.

[25] See note 11.

[26] See note 9.

[27] The Criminal Law (Amendment) Act, No. 13 of 2013, INDIA CODE (2013); http://indiacode.nic.in/acts-in-pdf/132013.pdf.

[28] Rajya Sabha Parliamentary Standing Committee on Home Affairs, One Hundred and Sixty Seventh Report on the Criminal Law (Amendment) Bill, 2012, http://www.prsindia.org/uploads/media/Criminal%20Law/SCR%20Criminal%20Law%20Bill.pdf.

[29] Rajya Sabha Parliamentary Standing Committee on Home Affairs, One Hundred and Sixty Seventh Report on the Criminal Law (Amendment) Bill, 2012.

[30] Human Rights Council, 'Report of The Special Rapporteur on Violence Against Women, Its Causes and Consequences', Rashida Manjoo, 26th Session, A/HRC/26/38/Add.1, 2014. 78(c) which reads: 'Amend the Criminal Law

adopting the recommendations of the Justice Verma Committee was a lost opportunity.[31] In 2015, the Pam Rajput Committee was also appointed by the current government to study the status of women in India; the committee strongly recommended that marital rape be criminalized and argued that marriage does not presume consent.[32] Despite these recommendations, the lawmakers have taken no action against marital rape. The result of the protection of marital rape exception is that the judiciary[33] has consistently used it to acquit husbands accused of committing marital rape. The protection of marital rape has grave implications on the issue of domestic violence in India as it essentially restricts a woman from making a formal complaint against her husband for forced sexual intercourse. The effect of the exception is that if a husband has sexual intercourse with his wife against her will and without her consent, he cannot be held liable for committing rape on her. While the definition of domestic violence includes forced sex within a marriage, the penal law precludes it from being viewed as an offence.

(Amendment) Act, 2013 and in particular review the provisions that provide for the death penalty in section 376A; include a definition of marital rape as a criminal offence; expand the scope of protection of the law and include other categories of women, including unmarried women, lesbian, transgender and intersex women, religious minorities and underage citizens; and define gang rape as multiple crimes requiring appropriate punishment (§ 376D IPC)'.

[31] Human Rights Council, 'Report of The Special Rapporteur on Violence Against Women, Its Causes and Consequences' in 50 which reads: '50. However, the laws that were adopted did not fully reflect the recommendations of the Verma Committee. The opportunity to adopt a holistic approach to violence against women, including addressing the root causes and consequences of such violence, was lost. In fact, the Criminal Law (Amendment) Act failed to: criminalize existing beliefs and practices linked to chastity; protect women with disabilities, unmarried women, lesbian, gay, bisexual and transgender persons, religious minorities, and girls below 18 years of age from sexual violence; or recognize marital rape as a criminal offence.'

[32] Pam Rajput Committee, 'Report of the High Level Committee on the Status of Women in India, Submitted to the Ministry of Women and Child Development, Government of India', 2015; http://wcd.nic.in/sites/default/files/Vol%20I.compressed.pdf.

[33] In *State v. Vikash*, decided on 7 May 2014 by the Special Fast Track Court, Dwarka, New Delhi (Unique Case ID No. 02405R0349722013), the Additional Sessions Judge held that sexual intercourse between a legally wedded husband and wife is not rape even if it is forced; https://indiankanoon.org/doc/100624392/.

Marital Rape As Domestic Violence: Impact on Health

Domestic violence was recognized as a serious health concern by the World Health Organisation (WHO) in 1993.[34] It is therefore pertinent to look at the data available on the effects of marital rape on women's health and safety and to locate it within the regular cycle of domestic violence. Global estimates published by WHO indicate that about one in three women world-wide report that they have experienced some form of physical and/or sexual violence by their intimate partner during their lifetime.[35] The National Family and Health Survey-IV of 2015–16[36] similarly reports that nearly one out of three married women have experienced some form of spousal violence by their husband. According to the International Institute for Population Sciences,[37] nearly one out of 10 wives reported experiencing spousal sexual violence in the form of forced sexual intercourse or other sexual acts. The Report further indicates that amongst married women who experienced physical or sexual violence, 36 per cent report cuts, bruises, or aches; 9 per cent report eye injuries, sprains, dislocations, or burns; 7 per cent report deep wounds, broken bones, broken teeth, or other serious injury; and 2 per cent report severe burns. Notably, 38 per cent women experiencing physical or sexual violence report having suffered at least one of these groups of injuries. Additionally, a large majority of women who experienced only sexual violence[38] never spoke to anyone about the violence (85 per cent), and only 8 per cent have ever sought help after suffering sexual violence where no other physical injury was reported. It is plainly evident from the data that forced sexual relations and sexual violence rarely exist in isolation, they form an integral part of the regular unabated cycle of spousal domestic violence impacting women's health and well-being in much the same way as any other type of domestic violence.

[34] WHO Factsheet on 'Violence against Women: Intimate Partner and Sexual Violence against Women' (November 2016); http://www.who.int/mediacentre/factsheets/fs239/en/.

[35] WHO Factsheet on 'Violence against Women'.

[36] National Family Health Survey-IV (Factsheet) of 2015–16 (conducted during 20 January 2015 to 4 December 2016) by 14 Field Agencies and gathered information from 601,509 households, 699,686 women, and 103,525 men; http://rchiips.org/nfhs/pdf/NFHS4/India.pdf.

[37] International Institute for Population Sciences (IIPS) and Macro International of September 2007, National Family Health Survey (NFHS-3), 2005–6: India: Volume I; https://dhsprogram.com/pubs/pdf/frind3/frind3-vol1andvol2.pdf.

[38] Sexual violence, when not accompanied by other forms of physical violence.

Among several independent studies conducted in 2015, in the crisis counselling centre operated by Society for Nutrition, Education and Health Action (SNEHA)[39] in the Dharavi area,[40] out of 664 cases of domestic violence 159 reported marital rape.[41] These numbers are supported by their counselling centres at the KEM Hospital and Sion Hospital[42] where out of 218 cases of domestic violence 64 reported marital rape.[43] The numbers must be seen in light of the fact that women have approached hospitals after suffering injuries due to domestic violence; they are usually reductant to mention sexual violence including marital rape, they have approached the hospital for other injuries resulting from domestic abuse. As a married woman in India, women are socialized into believing that sex and marriage go hand in hand. Under these circumstances when women specifically report marital rape, it must be understood that the incidents are grave and are necessarily impacting women physically and mentally for them to specifically mention marital rape. It also demonstrates that marital rape is an integral part of domestic violence.

Empirical studies report about the brutality of the violence inflicted upon the women survivors of marital rape and sexual violence. A study conducted

[39] SNEHA is an NGO working in the field of women's health. It targets four large public health areas: Maternal and Newborn Health, Child Health and Nutrition, Sexual and Reproductive Health, and Prevention of Violence against Women and Children; http://www.snehamumbai.org/

[40] Dharavi is one of the top-five largest slum in the world with an estimated population of 1 million, located in Mumbai, India as per the United Nations World Cities Report, 2016; http://wcr.unhabitat.org/main-report/

[41] Roli Srivastava, 'Marital Rape: The Statistics Show How Real It Is', *The Hindu*, 30 June 2016; http://www.thehindu.com/news/cities/mumbai/Marital-rape-the-statistics-show-how-real-it-is/article14410173.ece.

[42] KEM Hospital and Sion Hospitals operate in Maharashtra. KEM Hospital is the largest Non-Governmental Organization in the Pune District of Maharashtra. The Hospital is a 550-bedded, tertiary-level teaching institution, serving not only people of the city itself, but also a large populace coming from the surrounding urban and rural areas. KEM also runs a secondary level Rural Hospital at Vadu, which serves a rural population of about 68,000 people through a network of health centres; http://www.kemhospital.org/index.html. Lokmanya Tilak Municipal Medical College, Sion Mumbai is a 1462-bedded hospital which also operates in Dharavi, Mumbai.

[43] Dharavi is one of the top-five largest slum in the world with an estimated population of 1 million, located in Mumbai, India as per the United Nations World Cities Report, 2016; http://wcr.unhabitat.org/main-report/.

at Dilaasa Counselling Centre[44] during the period of 2001–12 surveyed a total number of 1,991 registered married women. It was reported that 58 per cent of women had visited the crisis centre for complaints such as injuries, abortion, miscarriage, prolapsed uterus, and so on, due to the sexual violence they faced at home. The vast majority, 91 per cent, reported that they were suffering from mental health consequences from the trauma suffered; of these 26 per cent women had attempted suicide and 31 per cent women reported that they lived with constant fear, which in turn has heath consequences in the long run.

Health consequences of sexual abuse and marital rape include both physical (both short term and long term) and psychological.[45] Physical health consequences include severe abdominal pain, burning micturition, sexual dysfunction, menstrual disorders, urinary tract infections, unwanted pregnancy, miscarriage of an existing foetus, pelvic inflammatory disease, infertility, unsafe abortion, mutilated genitalia, and self-mutilation as a result of physiological trauma.[46] While short-term psychological effects reported include fear, shock, physical and emotional pain, intense self-disgust, powerlessness, worthlessness, feeling of humiliation, shame, apathy, denial, revenge,[47] numbing, withdrawal, and inability to normally function in daily lives,[48] long-term psychological effects include depression, chronic headaches, feelings of vulnerability, loss of control, emotional distress and anxiety, impaired sense of self, nightmares, self-blame, social phobia,[49] mistrust, avoidance, post-traumatic stress disorder, chronic mental disorders,

[44] CEHAT is a research centre of Anusandhan Trust which is involved in research, training, service and advocacy on health and allied themes; http://www.cehat.org. CEHAT conducted an empirical research in hospitals and counsellors in Mumbai within the period of 2001–14 and set up a hospital based crisis centre (Dilaasa, A Hospital Based Crisis Counselling Department for Women Facing Violence) in Mumbai as a collaboration between CEHAT and Municipal Corporation of Mumbai (BMC); http://www.cehat.org/researchareas/project/1489666774.

[45] CEHAT, 'Manual for Medical Examination on Sexual Assault' (2012); http://www.cehat.org/go/uploads/Publications/R83Manual.pdf.

[46] CEHAT, 'Manual for Medical Examination on Sexual Assault'.

[47] WHO Guidelines for medico-legal care for victims of sexual violence; http://apps.who.int/iris/bitstream/10665/42788/1/924154628X.pdf.

[48] WHO Guidelines for medico-legal care for victims of sexual violence.

[49] WHO Guidelines for medico-legal care for victims of sexual violence.

sleeplessness, eating disorders, sexual dysfunction, feeling of committing suicide or endangering their lives in other ways.[50,51]

Additionally, there is a direct linkage between marital rape and women's ability to protect themselves from HIV/AIDs from forced sex with an infected partner; and women's inability to negotiate condom usage.[52] The WHO guidelines for medico-legal care of victims of sexual assault[53] stress on the psychological consequences of sexual assault, stating that these consequences have the potential to 'influence and radically alter a person's entire life course'.[54] Even though the available data suggest that marital rape affects a woman the same way as it affects her when rape is committed by a stranger,[55] if not more, it should be noted that in a marital setting, a wife is vulnerable to continuous verbal, emotional, and physical violence apart from sexual abuse when she resides with her husband. This only suggests that women, within the context of marriage, are even more prone and vulnerable to violence and rape because of their inability to leave the space where abuse is taking place or to seek help. This situation is worsened by the fact that the victims most often do not realize the extent, severity, and magnitude of the act of forced sex.

Right to health is recognized as a fundamental right in India and is enshrined in a number of international instruments including ICESCR and CEDAW. It is thus imperative that the state take adequate measures in furtherance of this right and recognize that sexual violence and marital rape violates this right. The state under its international obligations is required not only to implement laws for the elimination of discrimination and protection of survivors of sexual violence but also ensure that appropriate physical and mental health services are made available, accessible, and are of good quality.[56] The exception of marital rape violates the right of health. Moreover,

[50] WHO Guidelines for medico-legal care for victims of sexual violence.

[51] Sana Contractor et al., 'Responding to Sexual Assault: A Study of Practices of Health Professionals in a Public Hospital', CEHAT (2011); http://www.cehat.org/go/uploads/Publications/R81%20SexualAssaultStudy.pdf.

[52] 'India Second NGO Shadow Report on CEDAW', Coordinated by National Alliance of Women released in November 2006; http://pldindia.org/wp-content/uploads/2013/06/CEDAW_-Second-Shadow_report_2006.pdf.

[53] WHO Guidelines for medico-legal care for victims of sexual violence.

[54] Contractor et al., 'Responding to Sexual Assault'.

[55] WHO Guidelines for medico-legal care for victims of sexual violence; Contractor et al., 'Responding to Sexual Assault'.

[56] CEHAT, 'Manual for Medical Examination for Sexual Assault.

apart from the constitutional provisions, constitutional morality forbids the state to sanctify a tradition or custom that is no longer sustainable and thus, the magnitude and the adverse effects of marital rape cannot and should not be used as an excuse by the state from legitimizing the right of the wife to seek justice under the criminal justice system for flagrant violations against her body.

Marriage as a sacrament[57] has historically projected immense burden on the wife to protect marriage and continues to do so, in this case, in the guise of forced sexual relations. Traditions have held marriage as the only validated space for a woman's existence.[58] Women are socialized into believing marriage to be the most significant and final phase in their lives.[59] While men are seen as naturally and biologically active, assertive, and aggressive in sexual affairs and are deemed to possess uncontrollable sexual desire. In such a situation 'sex' is seen as a wifely duty; there is really little scope for women's understandings of independent consent. 'For the husband and the society, he represents, sexual violence serves multiple functions including its use as a socially sanctioned strategy to punish women; a tactic to assert masculinity and maintain a patriarchal social order; a method to "resolve" domestic conflicts; and a male behaviour to take sexual pleasure.'[60] Women's

[57] Rajya Sabha debate (Session 235, 29 April 2015), in a written reply by Haribhai Parthibhai Chaudhary (Minister of State in the Ministry of Home Affairs) to the Unstarred Question No. 656 asked by Shrimati Kanimozhi on the issue of 'Women subjected to marital rape', the said Minister stated that, '(d) It is considered that the concept of marital rape, as understood internationally, cannot be suitably applied in the Indian context due to various factors e.g. level of education/illiteracy, poverty, myriad social customs and values, religious beliefs, mind-set of the society to treat the marriage as a sacrament, etc.'

[58] Dorothy E. Roberts, 'The Meaning of Gender Equality in Criminal Law', *Journal of Criminal Law and Criminology* 85 (1,8) (1994–5): Dominant sexual ideologies and power structures in the society play an essential role in the state's construction of intimate relations including marriage.

[59] Ratna Kapur, 2005. *erotic justice: law and the new politics of post-colonialiasm*, (London: Glass House Press), 36; Ratna Kapur has argued that women's sexuality is entrenched in dominant cultural perceptions of being 'good women' who maintain the integrity of the family, are submissive to dominant norms and are therefore submissive to their husbands.

[60] 'Rape: How Women, the Community and the Health Sector Respond, WHO Sexual Violence Research Initiative', published in 2007; http://www.svri.org/sites/default/files/attachments/2016-02-17/Rape%20how%20women%20community%20and%20health%20sector%20respond.pdf.

experiences of trauma and pain caused by sexual violence remains invisible. Inherent unequal power relations[61] ignore the woman's autonomy over her body. Women therefore, often comply to sex because it is understood to be a marital obligation and as the right of their husbands.[62]

Women's reluctance to discuss experiences of sexual violence in general and especially in cases of rape by their husband is understandable. International[63] and national studies[64] indicate the following as reasons for underreporting of marital rape:

> Loyalty to the husband and the sanctity of the family which is guarded by the safekeeping of the family secrets; unwillingness to accept their own victimization as it could be emotionally too painful to acknowledge that one is being betrayed or mostly because the wife lacks the economic resources, social support or job skills that could enable her to leave the relationship; reluctance to label the experience as 'rape' for reasons such as fear, feelings of guilt and responsibility for abuse; misunderstandings about a woman's role in marriage and marital responsibilities; uncertainty and ambiguity regarding what constitutes normal sexual relations and what constitutes 'forced' sexual relations etc.

Stigma attached to women survivors of marital rape and sexual violence is another reason for underreporting.[65] This is further substantiated by reports from police, hospitals, and counselling centres approached by survivors; that by the time women facing marital rape gather the courage to report these incidents to the police,[66] delayed action results in loss of

[61] Gayle Rubin, 1998. *Thinking Sex: Notes for a Radical Theory of The Politics of Sexuality*, in Culture, Society, and Sexuality, (New York: Routledge) 143, 143–152 (Peter Aggleton and Richard Parker eds. 2006): Gayle Rubin has argued that sex is always political. Moreover, sexuality is always manoeuvered by political motives which are both deliberate and incidental. Further, certain sexual acts are encouraged and other acts are oppressed and penalized into organized systems of power and this distinction of legitimizing or criminalizing certain acts of sexual nature is based on prevalent dominant ideologies.

[62] Kapur, *Erotic Justice*.

[63] Patricia Mahoney et al., 'Sexual Assault in Marriage: Prevalence, Consequences, and Treatment of Rape'; http://www.ncdsv.org/images/nnfr_partnerviolence_a20-yearliteraturereviewandsynthesis.pdf.

[64] Contractor, et al., 'Responding to Sexual Assault'.

[65] CEHAT study, where an empirical research in hospitals and counsellors was done in Mumbai within the period of 2011–14.

[66] This was also reiterated in the Justice Verma Committee report stating that: 'A large number of women still fail to report rapes to the police because they fear

medical evidence, causing further agony. A hospital-based study stated that when women who have been forced against their will to have sexual intercourse or perform other sexual acts within marriage, they approach citing complains of severe body pain or other physical ailments, but despite being users of medical services they do not explicitly identify rape as the reason for visiting the hospital.[67]

Counselling centres also narrate similar experiences with marital rape: women often do not seek the counsellors' services right after an episode of sexual violence,[68] they initially restrict themselves to describing only the physical, emotional, and economic abuse by their husbands and it is only after gaining trust of their counsellors that they gather courage to speak out. Absence of injury does not indicate willingness or consent, lack of resistance can be attributed to 'fear of being killed, feeling completely numbed or shocked when assaulted or being rendered unconscious during the assault'.[69] Such instances highlight women's hesitation to speak out on sexual abuse.[70] Studies have also suggested that since women experiencing marital rape reside within close proximity of their husband, perpetual victimization

---

embarrassing and insensitive treatment by the doctors, the law enforcement personnel and/or the cross-examining defense attorneys. The fear has to be allayed from the minds of women so that if and when this crime is committed, the victim may promptly report the matter to the police and on a charge-sheet being submitted, the trial may proceed speedily without causing any embarrassment to the prosecutrix who may come in the witness-box without fear psychosis.'

[67] Padma Deosthali et al., 'Establishing Dilaasa: Documenting the Challenges', CEHAT, 2005; http://www.cehat.org/go/uploads/Dilaasa/estdil.pdf.

[68] Dr Rekha Davar, Head of gynaecology at J.J. Hospital says: 'Very rarely do patients tell us about marital rape. In a few cases, we see injuries and probe them. They are not aware this is wrong'. Also, Roli Srivastava, 'Marital Rape: The Statistics Show How Real It Is', *The Hindu*, 30 June 2016; http://www.thehindu.com/news/cities/mumbai/Marital-rape-the-statistics-show-how-real-it-is/article14410173.ece.

[69] Sukhada Tatke, 'Many Rape Survivors Wipe Off Evidence: Study', *THE HINDU*, 11 September 2013; http://www.thehindu.com/news/national/many-rape-survivors-wipe-off-evidence-study/article5113801.ece.

[70] 'Other forms of domestic violence such as broken bones and cuts are easily visible, but women won't utter a word about sexual violence within marriage, even when they're bleeding and can barely walk', said a spokesperson from Vimochana, a Bangalore-based women's organization. Also, Anahita Mukherjee, 'Not-a-Rape Rape', *Times of India*, 10 May 2015; https://timesofindia.indiatimes.com/home/sunday-times/deep-focus/Not-a-rape-rape/articleshow/47219344.cms.

potentially leads to trauma where victims experience shock, denial, disbelief, fear, confusion, and withdrawal.[71]

Instead of protecting violent marriages as revered institutions in society, the State should acknowledge women's silent suffering from sexual violence in order to counter the inherent disability women face in reporting acts of marital rape. Till the State dithers from criminalizing marital rape, it cannot hope to protect and ensure women's fundamental human rights to a life of dignity, and reproductive and sexual rights.

Rebutting the Justifications for Inclusion of the Marital Rape Exception

The Parliamentary Committee has been consistent in its arguments in favour of retaining the marital rape exception. In this section, the commonly propagated arguments will be countered in order to render them frivolous and unjust. The Constitution of India guarantees to all its citizens equality before the law and equal protection of law.[72] The marital rape exception in the IPC systematically violates both these articles by leaving the married woman without legal recourse for an offence that systematically affects her quality of life.

'Marriage Sanctions Sex': An Outdated Understanding of Consent

Proponents against criminalization of marital rape often argue that marriage sanctions sex. Moreover, only when there is a judicially recognized strain in the marital relationship that a wife is assumed to have revoked her consent to sexual intercourse with her husband, in every other case her consent is assumed.[73] Consent in the context of rape, as defined in IPC, implies an unequivocal voluntary agreement to participate in a particular sexual

[71] 'Other forms of domestic violence such as broken bones and cuts are easily visible, but women won't utter a word about sexual violence within marriage, even when they're bleeding and can barely walk', said a spokesperson from Vimochana, a Bangalore-based women's organization. Also, Anahita Mukherjee, 'Not-a-Rape Rape', *Times of India*, 10 May 2015; https://timesofindia.indiatimes.com/home/sunday-times/deep-focus/Not-a-rape-rape/articleshow/47219344.cms

[72] Right to Equality under Article 14 and right to life and personal liberty under Article 21.

[73] Kapur, *Erotic Justice*; https://www.google.co.in/search?tbo=p&tbm=bks&q=isbn:1135310548.

act.[74] The provision further clarifies that the absence of resistance to the sexual act will not imply consent. The objective behind the definition of consent is to make the woman the subject of law.[75] The marital rape exception seems to suggest that married women are either incapable of giving consent or their consent to sex is presumed upon marriage.

The concept of 'presumed consent' within marriage can be traced back to the Lord Matthew Hale's declaration[76] that 'a husband cannot be guilty of raping his lawful wife since at the time of marriage by their mutual matrimonial consent and contract the wife gives up her autonomy to her husband which she cannot retract'.[77] In addition to the Hale's Declaration dating back to the seventeenth century, two other theories of 'implied consent' subsequently developed, namely, the unities theory and the separate spheres theory.[78] The 'unities theory' derived from the doctrine of coverture considered husband and wife as 'one' under law. It legitimized 'propertization' of women through marriage, as it barred a woman's legal existence during the period of marriage or in the very best consolidated her rights with her husband's. The woman, as a result, lost her identity as a person and she could not naturally claim any rights against her husband.[79] This theory was replaced by the 'separate spheres' theory, under which men inhabited the public realms of politics while women inhabited the private realm of family, and in this way, gender-specific roles were assigned.[80] Women were no longer considered naturally inferior, but naturally different. This ideology shaped

[74] Consent is defined in Explanation 2 of § 375 IPC: An unequivocal voluntary agreement by words, gestures or any form of verbal or non-verbal communication, communicates willingness to participate in the specific sexual act: Provided that a woman who does not physically resist to the act of penetration shall not by the reason only of that fact, be regarded as consenting to the sexual activity.

[75] Latika Vashist, 'The Terms of Consent: On the Farooqui Verdict', *The Hindu*, 5 October 2017; http://www.thehindu.com/opinion/op-ed/the-terms-of-consent/article19797667.ece.

[76] Matthew Hale's Declaration is given in Historia Placitorum Coronae ('Pleas of the Crown').

[77] MATHEW HALE, 'PLEA OF THE CROWNS', 629 (1736); R. Augustine, 'Marriage: The Safe Haven for Rapists', 29 *Journal of Family Law* 29 (3) (1991): 559.

[78] Anonymous, 'To Have and to Hold: The Marital Exemption and the Fourteenth Amendment', 99 *Harvard Law Review*, 99(6) (1986): 1255 at 1257; https://www.ncjrs.gov/App/Publications/abstract.aspx?ID=108745.

[79] Anonymous, 'To Have and to Hold'.

[80] Anonymous, 'To Have and to Hold'.

the notion that any legal intrusion upon the woman's sphere constituted an illegitimate public invasion of the private sphere and explained why law does not interfere with the family. This resulted in the absence of laws restraining male power and subordination of women especially with regard to spousal sexual violence.

The obvious logical fallacy in these theories is that they do not have applicability in current times. The importance of sexual intercourse in a marriage continues to be regarded as vital by law and the persistent lack of it constitutes as cruelty under Section 498A IPC, as iterated in *Sumar Kumar* v. *Sudhir Kumar*,[81] where the court held that 'continuous cessation of marital intercourse or total indifference on the part of the spouse towards marital obligations would also lead to cruelty'.[82] Courts in India have repeatedly held that 'sex plays an important role in marital life and cannot be separated from other factors which lend to matrimony a sense of fruition and fulfilment'[83] and 'sex is the foundation of marriage and marriage without sex is an anathema'.[84] However, there may be instances where a wife withdraws herself from the society of her husband without any reasonable cause and denies her husband sexual intercourse; the remedy for such withdrawal provided by law to the aggrieved spouse is restitution of conjugal rights under respective personal laws.[85]

[81] *Sumar Kapur* v. *Sudhir Kapur* (2009) 1 SCC 422.

[82] *Sumar Kapur* v. *Sudhir Kapur* (2009) 1 SCC 422, at 34.

[83] *Dastane* v. *Dastane* (1975) 2 SCC 326, at 56.

[84] In the landmark judgment of *Nijhawan* v. *Nijhawan* (1973) SCC OnLine Del 52, the Delhi High Court held in P. 964 that, 'Sex is the foundation of marriage and marriage without sex is an anathema. Willful denial of sexual intercourse without reasonable cause would amount to cruelty'. This is reiterated in subsequent judgments including *Parveen Mehta* v. *Inderjeet Mehta* (2002) 5 SCC 706, and *Reshma Rakesh Kadam* v. *Rakesh Vijay Kadam* (2013) SCC OnLine Bom 1546.

[85] One example is § 9 of the Hindu Marriage Act, 1955 (relating to marriage among Hindus): 'Restitution of Conjugal rights: When either the husband or the wife has, without reasonable excuse, withdrawn from the society of the other, the aggrieved party may apply, by petition to the district court, for restitution of conjugal rights and the court, on being satisfied of the truth of the statements made in such petition and that there is no legal ground why the application should not be granted, may decree restitution of conjugal rights accordingly. Explanation: Where a question arises whether there has been reasonable excuse for withdrawal from the society, the burden of proving reasonable excuse shall be on the person who has withdrawn from the society'.

The courts have, however, distinguished the remedy of restitution of conjugal rights as aimed at cohabitation and consortium from being merely sexual intercourse.[86] In *Saroj Rani v. Sudarshan Kumar Chadha*,[87] the Supreme Court provided reasoning for this distinction that while it is true that sexual relations constitute an important element in the conception of marriage, it is also true that sexual intercourse does not constitute its whole content of marriage and nor could the remaining aspects of the matrimonial consortium be said to be wholly unsubstantial or of trivial character.[88] Thus, the court clarified its position that 'courts do not and cannot enforce sexual intercourse between a married couple'.[89] This suggests that despite owing sexual obligations towards each other, neither the wife nor the husband can be forced to have sexual intercourse against their consent and will within their marriage.

Further, one may also refer to the fact that courts have held that 'persistent'[90] and 'wilful denial of sexual intercourse without reasonable cause'[91] would amount to cruelty as a ground for divorce, to mistakenly suggest that sexual intercourse is a binding obligation of the spouse towards the other spouse demanding sex. Here, an important distinction is necessary to be made which is that even if denial of sexual intercourse has been construed as mental cruelty, there is no remedy available in law to force sexual relations between a wife and a husband, for persistent and wilful denial of sex under personal law is to seek divorce[92] and thus there is no binding obligation on the spouse to have sexual intercourse at the other spouse's demands. Thus, in case a wife does not wilfully engage in sexual intercourse on several occasions, her husband at most can seek divorce or annulment of marriage on account of non-consummation of marriage.

Moreover, this understanding of women is very different from the one understood by Hale and other subsequent theories which only understand women as properties of their husbands. In the Indian context, this clear

[86] *Saroj Rani v. Sudarshan Kumar Chadha* (1984) 4 SCC 90, at 11.
[87] *Saroj Rani v. Sudarshan Kumar Chadha* (1984) 4 SCC 90.
[88] *Saroj Rani v. Sudarshan Kumar Chadha* (1984) 4 SCC 90, at 11.
[89] *Saroj Rani v. Sudarshan Kumar Chadha* (1984) 4 SCC 90.
[90] *Samar Ghosh v. Jaya Ghosh* (2007) 4 SCC 511, at 75.
[91] *Samar Ghosh v. Jaya Ghosh* (2007) 4 SCC 511, at 86, and 11.
[92] One such case where the court has granted divorce for perpetual denial of sexual intercourse is *Vidhya Viswanathan v. Kartik Balakrishnan* (2014) 15 SCC 21, where the court held that denial of sexual intercourse by wife for a long time without sufficient reason amounts to 'mental cruelty'.

distinction is further clarified by various laws giving property rights,[93] economic rights,[94] and the laws regarding marriage[95] and adoption,[96] and so on, which have been enacted in India to give rights to women to reflect this change. In this regard, Justice Lokur in *Independent Thought* v. *Union of India*,[97] has aptly made a pertinent observation that 'it must be remembered that those days are long gone when a married woman or a married girl child could be treated as subordinate to her husband or at his beck and call or as his property'.[98] He further stated that constitutionally, a female has equal rights as a male and no statute should be interpreted or understood to derogate from this position and 'if there is some theory that propounds such an unconstitutional myth, then that theory deserves to be completely demolished'.[99]

Similarly, in *Joseph Shine* v. *Union of India*,[100] in a unanimous decision by a five judge bench, the Supreme Court held that 'the court cannot conceive of women still being treated as property of men'[101] and 'a statutory provision belonging to the hoary past which demeans or degrades the status of a

93 An example of granting property rights to women is the enactment of the Hindu Succession (Amendment) Act, 2005 where the gender discriminatory provisions under the Hindu Succession Act, 1956, were removed to include rights of a daughter to have same rights in the coparcenary property as a son.

94 An example of granting economic rights to women is the Equal Remuneration Act, 1976, which provides for payment of equal remuneration to men and women for the same work or work of a similar nature.

95 An example being the PWDVA, 2005 which seeks to provide emergency relief to women in the form of protection orders, residence orders, and monetary relief and compensation orders.

96 The Personal Laws (Amendment) Act, 2010, which had amended the Guardians and Wards Act, 1890, and the Hindu Adoptions and Maintenance Act, 1956, where now 'mother' is now included as a 'guardian' along with the father and the provision which incapacitated a married woman from taking in adoption on the basis of her marital status stands amended.

97 *Independent Thought* v. *Union of India* (2017) SCC OnLine SC 1222.

98 *Independent Thought* v. *Union of India* (2017) SCC OnLine SC 1222, at 85.

99 *Independent Thought* v. *Union of India* (2017) SCC OnLine SC 1222.

100 *Joseph Shine* v. *Union of India*, Writ Petition (Crl) No. 194 of 2017. In this judgment, the Supreme Court abolished Section 498 of the Indian Penal Code which criminalized adultery.

101 *Joseph Shine* v. *Union of India*, Writ Petition (Crl) No. 194 of 2017, at 3 of the then Chief Justice of India Dipak Mishra's opinion who wrote it on behalf of Justice Khanwilkar and himself.

woman obviously falls foul of modern constitutional doctrine and must be struck down on this ground also'.[102] Justice Dr D.Y. Chandrachud specifically held that a woman, by marriage, consents in advance to sexual relations with her husband is 'offensive to liberty and dignity'[103] and 'curtailing the sexual autonomy of a woman or presuming the lack of consent once she enters a marriage is antithetical to constitutional values'.[104]

Therefore, the understanding that married women are incapable of giving consent or the presumption that consent is assumed upon marriage is a flawed one, as neither the legal provisions pertaining to marriage reflect the requirement of sexual intercourse nor understanding women as property is applicable to the women in India. Thus, at this point, it is essential to note that consent is what establishes that the interaction including sex is between equals in power. Without consent, a marriage results in an unequal relation between husband and wife. Hence, consent should be the standard of respect and dignity of the individual, which must be used as a legal threshold to decide whether a violation of rights has taken place.

In the international arena, the case that changed the law on marital rape and brought consent as the focal point of an investigation in rape cases, irrespective of the relationship between the plaintiff and the defendant was in 1991 in *R* v. *R*,[105] where Justice Keith noted that non-inclusion of marital rape had no legal basis, since sexual intercourse was no longer confined to marriage and the basis of the exemption therefore; the word 'unlawful' as a concept had now been eroded. The court noted that the common law is capable of evolving in the light of changing social, economic, and cultural developments, and that Hale's proposition[106] simply reflected the state of affairs at the time when these were enunciated. It was noted that along with a change in the status of women, 'one of the most important changes is that marriage is in modern times regarded as a 'partnership of equals', and it is no longer one in which the wife must be the 'subservient chattel of the

[102] *Joseph Shine* v. *Union of India*, Writ Petition (Crl) No. 194 of 2017, at 26 of Justice R.F. Nariman's opinion.

[103] *Joseph Shine* v. *Union of India*, Writ Petition (Crl) No. 194 of 2017, at 44 of Justice Dr D.Y. Chandrachud's opinion.

[104] *Joseph Shine* v. *Union of India*, Writ Petition (Crl) No. 194 of 2017, at 44 of Justice Dr D.Y. Chandrachud's opinion.

[105] [1991] UKHL 12.

[106] Hale's proposition is that 'a husband cannot be guilty of raping his lawful wife since at the time of marriage by their mutual matrimonial consent and contract the wife gives up her autonomy to her husband which she cannot retract'.

husband'.[107] The court rejected Hale's proposition as one that in modern times any reasonable person must regard as quite unacceptable.

Similarly, in Canada, the provision[108] which denied criminal liability for marital rape were repealed in 1983.[109] In 2011, the Canadian Supreme Court decision in *R.* v. *J.A.*,[110] the Supreme Court iterated that there is no defence of implied consent to sexual assault. The issue was the consent to sexual activity in case of spousal sexual assault while they are asleep or unconscious. By a majority judgment it was held that the relationship between the accused and the complainant does not change the nature of the inquiry to be conducted into whether the complaint consented to the sexual activity. The defendant husband cannot argue that the complainant's consent was implied by the relationship between them.

Even South Africa criminalized marital rape in 1993, reversing the Hale's principle by the Prevention of Family Violence Act, 1993.[111] Further, the Criminal Law (Sexual Offences and Related Matters) Amendment Act, 2007,[112] provides that marital or other relationship between the perpetrator or victim is not a valid defence against the crimes of rape or sexual violation. While marital rape is recognized as a crime, there is a risk that judges might regard marital rape less seriously than other cases of rape and may grant lenient sentences. In response to this danger, the South African Criminal Law (Sentencing) Act of 2007[113] now provides that the relationship between the victim and the accused may not be regarded as 'substantial and

[107] *R.* v. *R.* (1991) UKHL 12.

[108] The Canadian Criminal Code, 1892 (RSC 1985, c C-46).

[109] § 143 of the Canadian Criminal Code, 1970, was repealed in 1983 which read as: 'A man commits rape when he has sexual intercourse with a female person who is not his wife ... without her consent'.

[110] 2011 SCC 28.

[111] § 5 of the South African Prevention of Family Violence Act, 1993 reads as: 'Notwithstanding anything to the contrary contained in any law or in common law, a husband may be convicted for rape of his wife'.

[112] § 56(1) of the South African Criminal Law (Sexual Offences and Related Matters) Amendment Act 2007.

[113] § (3) (A) of the South African Criminal Law (Sentencing) Act of 2007 states that: When imposing a sentence in respect of an offence of rape the following shall not constitute substantial and compelling circumstances justifying the imposition of a lesser sentence:

... (iv) any relationship between the accused and the complainant prior to the offence being committed.

compelling circumstance', justifying a deviation from legislatively required minimum sentences for rape.

In Australia, the marital rape immunity was abolished in all jurisdictions in 1976 by the legislature and changes were made in the Criminal Law Consolidation Act 1935 of South Australia. In 1991, Justice Brennan stated that the 'common law fiction' pertaining to marital rape has always been offensive to human dignity and incompatible with the legal status of a spouse. The same was reiterated in subsequent case laws including *PGA v. The Queen*,[114] where the court held that the legal status of a spouse is irreconcilable with the archaic concept of irrevocable consent.

Thus, a mere existence of marital relationship cannot be taken to suggest consent as it violates the right to equality. In creating a category of assumed consent, the law makers reinforce male privilege in the domain of sexual consent on dominant perceptions of the woman's behaviour and reactions. Presumption of consent due to the factum of marriage in contrast with the existence or absence of consent as the primary requirement in establishing guilt in cases of rape under law, unjustly discriminates on the basis of marital status.

Limitations on the Right to Marital Privacy and Protecting the Institution of Marriage

Right to marital privacy and unwarranted intrusion of the State with private lives is used to justify non-interference with sexual relations between individuals in a marriage. It is essential to note that in recognizing the need for legal intervention in domestic violence, the threshold from public to private violence has already been crossed, marital rape clearly indicates discord and violence in a marriage. By allowing marital rape to go unpunished and by sanctioning it without fear of reprisals, the State allows a common form of spousal domestic violence to go unpunished.

In *Naz Foundation* v. *Government of NCT Delhi*,[115] the High Court of Delhi held that morality is not a compelling state interest and clarified the scope of consent within sexual intercourse and its relation to human dignity in upholding the right to equality and dignity of persons engaged in adult private consensual sexual relations. The court drew implicit linkages between 'consent' and 'dignity' by emphasizing the fact that 'at the root of

[114] *PGA* v. *The Queen* (2012) HCA 21.

[115] *Naz Foundation* v. *Government of NCT Delhi* (2009) SCC OnLine Del 1762.

dignity is the autonomy of the private will and a person's freedom of choice and of action'.[116]

The observations in *Justice K.S. Puttaswamy* (Retd.) v. *Union of India*[117] are significant. It was held that privacy is a fundamental right and that it is an integral part of right to life and personal liberty under Article 21 of the Constitution, and

> patriarchal notions still prevail in several societies including our own and are used as a shield to violate core constitutional rights of women based on gender and autonomy. As a result, gender violence is often treated as a matter of 'family honour' resulting in the victim of violence suffering twice over–the physical and mental trauma of her dignity being violated and the perception that it has a cause an affront to 'honour'. Privacy must not be utilised as a cover to conceal and assert patriarchal mind-sets.[118]

It was correctly noted that 'privacy safeguards individual autonomy and recognizes the ability of the individual to control vital aspects of his or her way of life and personal choices governing a way of life are intrinsic to privacy'.[119] Since individual dignity cannot be divorced from the concept of marriage, personal autonomy and the right to consent and bodily integrity must be protected by the State.

In the recent judgment in *Joseph Shine* v. *Union of India*,[120] Justice Dr D.Y. Chandrachud rejected the argument justifying the denial of sexual agency of women in order to preserve the sanctity of marriage. He said, 'Marriage in a constitutional regime is founded on the equality of and between spouses. Each of them is entitled to the same liberty which Part III guarantees. Each of them is entitled to take decisions in accordance with his and her conscience and each must have the ability to pursue the human desire for fulfilment'.[121] He further holds that 'familial structures cannot be regarded as private spaces where constitutional rights are violated' and

[116] *Naz Foundation* v. *Government of NCT Delhi* (2009) SCC OnLine Del 1762, at 26.

[117] *Justice K.S. Puttaswamy* (Retd.) v. *Union of India* (2017) SCC OnLine SC 996.

[118] *Justice K.S. Puttaswamy* (Retd.) v. *Union of India* (2017) SCC OnLine SC 996, at 371.

[119] *Justice K.S. Puttaswamy* (Retd.) v. *Union of India* (2017) SCC OnLine SC 996, at 459(F).

[120] *Joseph Shine* v. *Union of India*, Writ Petition (Crl) No. 194 of 2017.

[121] *Joseph Shine* v. *Union of India*, Writ Petition (Crl) No. 194 of 2017, at 35 of Justice Dr D.Y. Chandrachud's opinion.

'to grant immunity in situations when rights of individuals are in siege, is to obstruct the unfolding vision of the Constitution'[122] and hence it becomes imperative to 'intervene when structures of injustice and persecution deeply entrenched in patriarchy are destructive of constitutional freedom'.[123] He also said 'the sexuality of a woman is part of her inviolable core' and 'neither the state nor the institution of marriage can disparage it'.[124]

The Parliamentary Committee stands firm in their belief that 'for ages the family system has evolved' and 'family is able to resolve the problems'[125] and that 'the entire family system will be put under great stress'[126] if the exception to marital rape were to be removed, 'it would be doing more injustice'.[127] This argument fails to recognize the difference between the family system and the union of marriage. In *Independent Thought* v. *Union of India*,[128] Justice Lokur says, 'marriage is not institutional but personal—nothing can destroy the "institution" of marriage except a statute that makes marriage illegal and punishable'.[129] It is further stated that a divorce may destroy a

[122] *Joseph Shine* v. *Union of India*, Writ Petition (Crl) No. 194 of 2017, at 50 of Justice Dr D.Y. Chandrachud's opinion.

[123] *Joseph Shine* v. *Union of India*, Writ Petition (Crl) No. 194 of 2017, at 51 of Justice Dr D.Y. Chandrachud's opinion.

[124] *Joseph Shine* v. *Union of India*, Writ Petition (Crl) No. 194 of 2017, at 61 of Justice Dr D.Y. Chandrachud's opinion.

[125] *Justice K.S. Puttaswamy* (Retd.) v. *Union of India* (2017) SCC OnLine SC 996.

[126] Political party, Bharatiya Janta Party member, Sumitra Mahajan: 'India had a joint family system and the elders act as buffer and provide counselling in case of marital problem'. See, Lok Sabha debates anti-rape bill, views differ on age of consent dated 19 March 2013; https://www.ndtv.com/india-news/lok-sabha-debates-anti-rape-bill-views-differ-on-age-of-consent-516709.

[127] Rajya Sabha debate in Session 240 (4 August 2016), where in a written reply by Shri Dilip Kumar Tirkey (Minister of State in the Ministry of Women and Child Development) to the Unstarred Question No. 2139 asked by Shrimati Krishna Raj on the issue of 'Marital rape under law', the said Minister stated that, 'The Parliamentary Standing Committee deliberated the amendments to section 375 of IPC including the issue of marital rape and observed that if the marital rape is brought under the law, *the entire family system will be under great stress and the Committee may perhaps be doing more injustice*'.(emphasis mine). The same point was reiterated by Shrimati Sanjay Gandhi (Minister of Women and Child Development) to the Unstarred Question No. 1433 asked by Shri Avinash Pande in Session 239 of the Rajya Sabha on 5 May 2016.

[128] *Independent Thought* v. *Union of India* (2017) SCC OnLine SC 1222.

[129] *Independent Thought* v. *Union of India* (2017) SCC OnLine SC 1222, at 94.

marriage, but it does not have the potential of destroying the institution of marriage or the family system and that, by this logic, divorce and judicial separation should be prohibited if no distinction exists between the 'institution of marriage' and 'marriage'.

Misuse Argument

The State's presumption of the likelihood of harassment of husbands at the hands of their wives is yet another argument against recognizing marital rape as a crime.[130] The misuse argument casts its shadow over protection from marital rape in much the same way as with every gender-specific law, especially laws addressing violence against women.[131] This argument of widespread abuse by wives however cannot be sustained, as 'misuse' should not be construed to precede 'concerns of misuse'.[132] Concerns pertaining to misuse tend to 'pre-judge' a case without a proper hearing.[133] In doing so, they obstruct access to justice for women sexually abused by their husbands. Although false reports of rape are no more common than any other crimes,[134] the law-makers ignore the plight and claims of the married woman raped by her husband. Moreover, the aggrieved wife's conduct in her husband's home cannot be seen as a violation of traditional sex role norm to disbelieve her claim or even blame her for justifying the rape.

This misuse argument can largely be said to have stemmed from the allegations of misuse by wives with respect to the law of cruelty under Section 498A of the IPC, where cases have been labelled as 'false' at the time of

[130] Anonymous, 'Criminalising Marital Rape May Destabilise the Institution of Marriage, Centre Tells HC', *The Hindu*, 29 August 2017; http://www.thehindu.com/news/national/criminalising-marital-rape-will-destabilise-marriage-govt-tells-hc/article19581512.ece.

[131] Bindu N. Doddahatti, 'The Dangerous, False Myth that Women Routinely Misuse Domestic Cruelty Laws', *The Wire*, 11 August 2017; https://thewire.in/166766/section-498a-domestic-cruelty-laws/.

[132] 'India Second NGO Shadow Report on CEDAW', Coordinated by National Alliance of Women.

[133] 'India Second NGO Shadow Report on CEDAW', Coordinated by National Alliance of Women.

[134] Sanjoy Ghosh, 'Supreme Court Order on Domestic Abuse Cases is a Step Back for Women's Rights Law', *The Wire*, 31 September 2017; https://thewire.in/163011/supreme-court-domestic-abuse-dowry/; and Doddahatti, Doddahatti, 'The Dangerous, False Myth that Women Routinely Misuse Domestic Cruelty Laws'.

closure of the case.[135] However, in a recent study,[136] this popular notion was strongly contradicted and criticized. It was found that women facing violence use this legal provision to leverage for negotiating an end to violence within the space of her husband and marital family.[137] However, the negotiation and reconciliation processes involved right from filing an FIR to pursuing the case in the judicial system often lead such women to turn into hostile witnesses where they retract their case due to compromise or settlement being effected, and in turn such cases are closed as 'false' cases.[138]

It is already known that women do not wish to prosecute because of the insensitive treatment they face between the family, police, hospital staff, and the judiciary. Hence, it is only when they exhaust their social and community based interventions to stop domestic violence that they approach the state to challenge the violence that they are facing and to create a violence free space in which negotiation can take place for 'residence, financial support and mental well-being'.[139] However, when women approach the police, they are faced with preconceived notions and bias towards saving the family structure and women's honour and to effectuate a compromise in cases of domestic violence, rather than advocating for her safety and well-being.[140] Through these socio-legal processes of 'compromise', the woman complainant is presented as a 'hostile witness' and this then becomes imbedded in public discourse evidencing that women are generating 'false' cases to misuse the law, projecting the woman survivor as the one at fault.[141, 142] Thereafter,

[135] Doddahatti, Doddahatti, 'The Dangerous, False Myth that Women Routinely Misuse Domestic Cruelty Laws'.

[136] Study was undertaken by the Resource Centre for Interventions on Violence Against Women, at the Tata Institute of Sciences, Mumbai. This study traces the journey of women whose cases are closed as 'false', interrogates the discourse of misuse and advocate for social services and connections between women-centric laws to address marital violence.

[137] Anjali Dave et al., 'In Search of Justice and Care: How Women Survivors of Violence Navigate the Indian Criminal Justice System', *Journal of Gender Based Violence*, vol. 1 (2017): 79–97.

[138] Dave et al., 'In Search of Justice and Care'.

[139] Dave et al., 'In Search of Justice and Care'.

[140] Pratiksha Baxi, 'Justice is a Secret: Compromise in Rape Trials', *Contributions to Indian Sociology*, vol. 44–3 at 207–33.

[141] Baxi, 'Justice is a Secret', p. 140.

[142] 'Mediation is impermissible for non-compoundable offences, such as rape or marital cruelty under Section 498A IPC, however hostile witness and false cases are produced through the invisibilized processes undertaken by the state itself in

women return to the same patterns of violence and further stigmatization in the absence of police interventions and the closure of the case comes at a great 'personal and a social cost' where women are ridiculed by the community and violence from their families.[143]

In *Savitra Devi* v. *Ramesh Chand*,[144] the court remarked that 'before, parting I feel constrained to comment on the misuse of the provision of Section 498A/ 406 IPC to such as extent that it is hitting at the foundation of marriage itself and has proved to be not so good for the health of society at large'.[145] Subsequently, in *Sushil Kumar Sharma* v. *Union of India*,[146] the Supreme Court also honed the issue of misuse and stated that misuse of Section 498A IPC

> is a new legal terrorism can be unleashed. The provision is intended to be used as a shield and not as an assassin's weapon. If the cry of 'wolf' is made too often as a prank, assistance and protection may not be available when the actual 'wolf' appears. There is no question of the investigating agency and courts casually dealing with the allegations. They cannot follow any straitjacket formula in the matters relating to dowry tortures, deaths and cruelty.

Further, in *Arnesh Kumar* v. *State of Bihar*,[147] the court stated that

> the fact that Section 498A is a cognisable and non-bailable offence has lent it a dubious place of pride amongst the provisions that are used as weapons rather than shield by disgruntled wives. The simplest way to harass is to get the husband and his relatives arrested under this provision. In a quite number of cases, bedridden grandfathers and grandmothers of the husbands, their sisters living abroad for decades are arrested.[148]

Subsequent decisions[149] of the Supreme Court also labelled women misusing the provision of cruelty. More so, the Supreme Court in its recent

---

contravention to the aim sought to be achieved through the legislation', Baxi, 'Justice is a Secret', p. 140.

143 Baxi, 'Justice is a Secret', p. 140.

144 *Savitra Devi* v. *Ramesh Chand* (2003) SCC OnLine Del 483.

145 *Savitra Devi* v. *Ramesh Chand* (2003) SCC OnLine Del 483, at 21.

146 *Sushil Kumar Sharma* v. *Union of India* (2005) 6 SCC 281.

147 *Arnesh Kumar* v. *State of Bihar* (2014) 8 SCC 273.

148 *Arnesh Kumar* v. *State of Bihar* (2014) 8 SCC 273, at 4.

149 Such as *Preeti Gupta* v. *State of Jharkhand* (2010) 7 SCC 667; and *Ramgopal* v. *State of Madhya Pradesh* (2010) 13 SCC 540.

judgment in *Rajesh Sharma* v. *State of Uttar Pradesh*[150] assumed that women 'misuse'[151] the law and for this reason provided guidelines[152] to prevent misuse of cruelty against women where welfare committees, consisting of paralegals, volunteers, social workers, retired persons, wives of working officers, and other citizens who are found suitable and willing have been put in place to scrutinize a complaint by a woman before the police take cognisance of it. Moreover, the court has held that the police must ensure that every complaint under Section 498A IPC is referred to the welfare committee, which within one month will prepare a report, give its opinion, and send it back to the police.[153] Further, 'till the report of the committee is received there will be no arrest'.[154] Thus, given the attitude of the police officials at the ground level, which reflects the lack of respect of rule of law, it is quite certain that the object of the provisions will be lost and the accused is given more leeway to abscond delaying the process of justice and relief for the woman. It also completely ignores the fact that the aggrieved woman approaches the police and the judicial system as a last resort[155] to stop the violence. Further, appointing welfare committees drawn from civil society is their potential to become non-state vigilante groups.[156]

Moreover, this judgment relies upon the data of the NCRB to come to the conclusion that since the conviction rate is low, most of the cases registered under Section 498A IPC are false.[157] These data give an inaccurate picture as

150 *Rajesh Sharma* v. *State of Uttar Pradesh* (2017) SCC OnLine SC 821.

151 *Rajesh Sharma* v. *State of Uttar Pradesh* (2017) SCC OnLine SC 821, at 14, the court stated: 'This Court had earlier noticed the fact that most of such complaints are filed in the heat of the moment over trivial issues. Many of such complaints are not bona fide. At the time of filing of the complaint, implications and consequences are not visualized. At the time of filing of the complaint, implications and consequences are not visualized. At times, such complaints lead to uncalled for harassment not only to the accused but also to the complainant. Uncalled for arrest may ruin the chances of settlement'.

152 *Rajesh Sharma* v. *State of Uttar Pradesh* (2017) SCC OnLine SC 821, at 18.

153 *Rajesh Sharma* v. *State of Uttar Pradesh* (2017) SCC OnLine SC 821.

154 *Rajesh Sharma* v. *State of Uttar Pradesh* (2017) SCC OnLine SC 821.

155 Dave et al., 'In Search of Justice and Care'.

156 Indira Jaising, 'Victim in the Dock', *The Indian Express*, 2 August 2017; http://indianexpress.com/article/opinion/columns/victim-in-the-dock-law-of-cruelty-against-women-supreme-court-judgment-rajesh-sharma-and-ors-v-state-of-up-and-anr-4777931/.

157 *Rajesh Sharma* v. *State of Uttar Pradesh* (2017) SCC OnLine SC 821, 7.

there can be a number of reasons for acquittal, such as poor investigation by the investigating officer, settlement through mediation, or intimidation of witnesses and the complainant herself.[158] The court does not consult any expert evidence or women studies centre; hence, this judgment is based on police data alone.[159] Thus, it is pertinent to note that since the police power is limited to finding evidence, insufficient evidence does not render the complaint false.

In the subsequent judgment in Social Action Forum for *Manav Adhikar* v. *Union of India*,[160] the Supreme Court rightfully accepted that the social welfare committees have no role to play during investigation, and prescribing duties to the social welfare committees will tantamount to judiciary overreaching its power as it is the Parliament who makes the law. However, the Court has only done an incomplete task in correcting its error in its previous judgment. The Court has in fact further underlined its anxiety that 'the abuse of the penal provision [referring to Section 498A IPC] has vertically risen'[161] and has gone on to suggest that 'it is obligatory on the part of the legislature to bring in protective adjective law and the duty of the constitutional courts to perceive and scrutinize the protective measure so that the social menace is curbed'.[162]

Hence, the judiciary is equally responsible for propagating this argument as the patriarchal mindset and the prevailing bias against women are reflected through the judicial pronouncements repeatedly. In this regard, the available data on marital rape cannot be ignored and outweigh the allegations or concerns of misuse of the provision criminalizing marital rape. A presumption of harassment of the husband cannot legitimize the right of the wife to seek justice from the criminal justice system for violations against her body.

[158] Jaising, 'Victim in the Dock'.

[159] Jaising, 'Victim in the Dock'.

[160] Social Action Forum for *Manav Adhikar* v. *Union of India*, Writ Petition (C) No. 73 of 2015. In this judgment, the Supreme Court modified the directions issued in *Rajesh Sharma* v. *State of Uttar Pradesh* (2017) SCC OnLine SC 821 concerning the investigation of offences under Section 498A IPC.

[161] Social Action Forum for *Manav Adhikar* v. *Union of India*, Writ Petition (C) No. 73 of 2015. In this judgment, the Supreme Court modified the directions issued in *Rajesh Sharma* v. *State of Uttar Pradesh* (2017) SCC OnLine SC 821 concerning the investigation of offences under Section 498A IPC.

[162] Social Action Forum for *Manav Adhikar* v. *Union of India*, Writ Petition (C) No. 73 of 2015. In this judgment, the Supreme Court modified the directions issued in *Rajesh Sharma* v. *State of Uttar Pradesh* (2017) SCC OnLine SC 821 concerning the investigation of offences under Section 498A IPC.

Ambiguity on the Definition of Marital Rape: 'No' Means 'No'

The law does not define what constitutes marital rape, and hence 'what may appear as marital rape to a wife, may not appear so to others'[163] is yet another argument given to justify the marital rape exemption. This argument is fallaciously rooted in conventional morality[164] and completely undermines the dignity and personal autonomy of the aggrieved women. Clearly, the components of rape are already listed in the definition of rape under Section 375 IPC, which is currently applicable to all unmarried women who have been raped against their will or without consent; or with their consent by threatening to kill or hurt them or any person they care/know; when they are unable to communicate consent, and so on. In terms of health, rape affects a married woman in the same way as it affects an unmarried woman. The same components easily apply in case of marital rape as well. Therefore, consent and the evidentiary[165] requirements must be exactly the same as in rape.

Hence, any sexual activity between the spouses must be based on consent which is freely given when she feels unconstrained of her physical and moral power to act in a manner she wanted.[166] Consent is a voluntary and conscious acceptance of what is proposed to be done by another and is different from submission which is an act of helpless resignation in the face of inevitable compulsions, as also held in *Rao Harnarain Singh* v. *State*.[167] The Court has clarified that 'a mere act of helpless resignation in the face of inevitable compulsion, quiescence, non-resistance, or passive giving in, when volitional faculty is either clouded by fear or vitiated by duress, cannot be deemed to be "consent" as understood by law'.[168]

Tested from this standpoint, concepts such as 'consent' and 'coercion' must be infused with real meaning and marital rape be made an offence. The courts in such, as in the *State of U.P.* v. *Chhoteylal*,[169] have in the past

[163] Sohini Sengupta, 'Debate over Marital Rape: Talks of Morality Empty without Equal Rights for Women', *FIRST POST*, 31 August 2017; http://www.firstpost.com/india/marital-rape-debate-talks-of-morality-are-empty-without-equal-rights-for-women-3989857.html.

[164] Sengupta, 'Debate over Marital Rape'.

[165] § 114-A, Indian Evidence Act, No. 1 of 1872, INDIA CODE (1872).

[166] *Rao Harnarain Singh* v. *State* (1958) Crl.L.J 563, 7.

[167] *Rao Harnarain Singh* v. *State* (1958) Crl.L.J 563. The said rule is reiterated in *State of U.P.* v. *Chhoteylal* (2011) 2 SCC 550.

[168] *State of U.P.* v. *Chhoteylal* (2011) 2 SCC 550, 7.

[169] *State of U.P.* v. *Chhoteylal* (2011) 2 SCC 550, 7.

relied on the definition given in dictionaries, such as the Jowitt dictionary which defines consent as a conscious act carried out freely and intentionally. It states that the word 'consent' has been explained as an act of reason accompanied with deliberation, the mind weighing, as in a balance, the good or evil on either side.[170] Prior to this too, the Court had also held in the case of *State of Himachal Pradesh* v. *Mango Ram*[171] that consent for the purpose of Section 375 IPC requires voluntary participation by the victim not only after the exercise of intelligence based on the knowledge of the significance and moral quality of the act, but after having fully exercised the choice between resistance and assent.[172] Whether consent existed or not has to be ascertained on the basis of the facts of a given case.[173] This is seen as the landmark decision on sexual consent in India.

The standard of respecting the dignity of the individual must be used as a legal threshold to decide whether violation of rights has taken place. Indeed, guidance in this direction has already been provided in the recent landmark judgment of *Navtej Singh Johar* v. *Union of India*,[174] where the Supreme Court of India clarified the scope of 'consent' within sexual intercourse and its relation to human dignity in upholding the right to equality and dignity of persons engaged in adult private consensual sexual relations. The Court read down the archaic penal provision of Section 377 IPC that led to criminalization of adult private consensual penile non-vaginal sexual acts.

Justice Dipak Mishra in the context of Section 377 IPC very pertinently held that the essence of dignity is our constitutional duty to 'allow the individual to behave and conduct himself/herself as he/she desires and allow him/her to express himself/herself, of course, with the consent of the other. That is the right to choose without fear. It has to be ingrained as a necessary pre-requisite that consent is the real fulcrum of any sexual relationship'.[175] Moreover, Justice Dr D.Y. Chandrachud in his separate opinion held that the 'right to intimacy emanates from an individual's prerogative to engage in sexual relations on their own terms. It is an exercise of the individual's sexual agency, and includes ... the freedom to decide on the nature of the

170 *State of U.P.* v. *Chhoteylal* (2011) 2 SCC 550, 17.

171 *State of Himachal Pradesh* v. *Mango Ram* (2000) 7 SCC 224.

172 *State of Himachal Pradesh* v. *Mango Ram* (2000) 7 SCC 224, 13.

173 *State of Himachal Pradesh* v. *Mango Ram* (2000) 7 SCC 224, 13.

174 *Navtej Singh Johar* v. *Union of India*, Writ Petition (Crl.) No. 76 of 2016.

175 *Navtej Singh Johar* v. *Union of India*, Writ Petition (Crl.) No. 76 of 2016, at 132 of Justice Dipak Mishra's opinion (on behalf of himself and Justice Khanwilkar).

relationship that the individual wishes to pursue'.[176] The Court further quoted several judgments which recognized that the guarantee of human dignity forms a part of our constitutional culture. Hence, although this judgment marks a major victory for LGBT rights in India, the judgment has also sent an important message that the principle of dignity is the test to assess whether there is consent to private sexual acts within a marriage.

Therefore, the concept of consent which anchors within itself equality, freedom, and rationality, as well as natural capacities, should be built into a universal concept for any sexual activity in law as well. Hence, the grounds visited above are grounds enough for the acts constituting marital rape to be criminalized.

'Other Means of Approaching the Court': Misused and Subject to Misinterpretation

The most common argument forwarded by law-makers is that there are other means available to the aggrieved wife for approaching the court. In order to examine this claim, we must discuss the existing provisions on spousal sexual violence to see if the aggrieved wife can in fact seek any legal remedy and if the adequacy of these provisions can safeguard married women's safety and provide them with an alternate forum to complain against marital rape. The judiciary has referred to various provisions from different legislations to address the issues relating to spousal sexual violence such as the PWDVA, and cruelty in a marriage under Section 498A IPC.

Spousal sexual violence has been covered within the definition of domestic violence[177] under the PWDVA.[178] With the enactment of PWDVA,

[176] *Navtej Singh Johar* v. *Union of India*, Writ Petition (Crl.) No. 76 of 2016, 67 of Justice Dr D.Y. Chandrachud's opinion.

[177] The definition of sexual violence in the PWDVA is based on the UN Framework for Model Legislation on Domestic Violence, which reads as:

> For the purposes of this Act, any act, omission or commission or conduct of the respondent shall constitute domestic violence in case it—
>
> a) harms or injures or endangers the health, safety, life limb or well-being, whether mental or physical, of the aggrieved person or tends to do so and includes causing physical abuse, sexual abuse, verbal and emotional abuse and economic abuse; ...
>
> has the effect of threatening the aggrieved person or any person related to her by any conduct mentioned in clause (a) or clause (b); or (d) otherwise injures or causes harm, whether physical or mental, to the aggrieved person.

[178] Unlike the IPC which provides for penal provisions, PWDVA is a civil law aimed at providing emergency reliefs to women in domestic relationships. This

for the first time 'sexual abuse' within marriage has been recognized and defined. Section 3(a) of the PWDVA states that any act or conduct of the respondent shall constitute an act of domestic violence in case it 'harms or injures or endangers the health, safety, life, limb or well-being, whether mental or physical, of the aggrieved person or tends to do so and includes physical abuse, sexual abuse, verbal and emotional abuse and economic abuse'. Sexual abuse is defined as 'any conduct of sexual nature that abuses, humiliates, degrades or otherwise violates the dignity of woman'[179] squarely places spousal sexual violence as a type of domestic violence.

'Sexual abuse' as defined under the PWDVA thus recognizes the intention of violating the dignity of a woman, protects her right to a life encompassing all elements that facilitate the exercise of choice and autonomy over her mind and body. Sexual acts that humiliate, degrade, and violate the dignity of the woman clearly fall within the definition of sexual violence under the PWDVA. The Supreme Court judgment in *Bodhisattwa Gautam* v. *Subhra Chakraborty*[180] is significant here, which held that

> women have the right to be respected and treated as equal citizens. Their honour and dignity cannot be touched or violated. They also have the right to lead an honourable and peaceful life. Women, in them, have many personalities combined. They are mother, daughter, sister and wife and not playthings for centre spreads in various magazines, periodicals or newspapers nor can they be exploited for obscene purposes.[181]

Thus, though the judgment was delivered in the context of Section 375 IPC, it is equally applicable in the context of rape within marriage, where the dignity of the married woman is violated in the same way as any other woman, depriving her of personal liberty and endangering her life. Would

---

implies the institution of proceedings under the IPC require stricter evidentiary standards as well as procedural rules pertaining to the criminal law whereas PWDVA reiterates the right of women to live without violence through the remedies it offers such as right to residence, monetary compensation, maintenance, protection orders. The contention of tailoring procedures facilitating adequate addressal of sexual violence under the criminal law regime is found to be reflected in the PWDVA. While the underlying nature of the Act is to support civil action, the proceedings prescribed are those of the Criminal Procedure Code, 1973. Thus, applications for relief under the Act are made to the Magistrate.

179 Explanation I (ii) to § 3 of the PWDVA.

180 *Bodhisattwa Gautam* v. *Subhra Chakraborty* (1996) 1 SCC 490.

181 *Bodhisattwa Gautam* v. *Subhra Chakraborty* (1996) 1 SCC 490, 9.

a violation by her husband not lead to exactly the same consequences as by a stranger?

However, since the remedy under the PWDVA is a civil remedy in cases where sexual violence including forced intercourse has occurred, the court can at best grant protection order in the form of stop violence orders, compensation, and other reliefs to the aggrieved wife. PWDVA does not provide the aggrieved wife a forum to seek punishment for the crime for marital rape against her husband. The only provision in criminal law that addresses cruelty in marriage is Section 498A IPC.[182] Section 5(e)[183] of the PWDVA specifically recognizes the right of the aggrieved person to file a complaint under Section 498A IPC, seeking punitive measures. Thus, it is essential to further examine if a wife seeks her husband's punishment for marital rape under the law of cruelty under Section 498A IPC.

Section 498A[184] IPC was introduced with a view to recognize and criminalize cruelty meted out to wife by the husband and the relatives of

[182] § 498A IPC (Husband or relative of husband of a woman subjecting her to cruelty).

[183] § 5(e) of the PWDVA reads as: 'Duties of police officers, service providers and Magistrate. A police officer, Protection Officer, service provider or Magistrate who has received a complaint of domestic violence or is otherwise present at the place of an incident of domestic violence or when the incident of domestic violence is reported to him, shall inform the aggrieved person—

(e) of her right to file a complaint under section 498A of the Indian Penal Code (45 of 1860), wherever relevant: Provided that nothing in this Act shall be construed in any manner as to relieve a police officer from his duty to proceed in accordance with law upon receipt of information as to the commission of a cognizable offence'.

[184] § 498A IPC: 'Husband or relative of husband of a woman subjecting her to cruelty: Whoever, being the husband or the relative of the husband of a woman, subjects such woman to cruelty shall be punished with imprisonment for a term which may extend to three years and shall also be liable to fine. Explanation: For the purpose of this section, "cruelty" means—

(a) any *wilful conduct* which is of such a nature as is likely to *drive the woman to commit suicide or to cause grave injury or danger to life, limb or health (whether mental or physical) of the woman* (emphasis mine); or
(b) harassment of the woman where such harassment is with a view to coercing her or any person related to her to meet any unlawful demand for any property or valuable security or is on account of failure by her or any person related to her to meet such demand'.

the husband.[185] While the section is largely used in connection with cruelty related to dowry demands, it is broad enough to include most forms of cruelty such as driving the woman to attempt suicide or causing grave injury to her or adversely impacting her mental or physical health in any manner. Thus, from the face of it, sexual cruelty can be read into Section 498A IPC since sexual cruelty without a doubt gravely impacts her physical and mental health.

There is not a single case, however, which explicitly mentions sexual cruelty or sexual violence as being read within this section. There are, however, precedents that mention 'abnormal behaviour',[186] 'beating at odd hours of the night',[187] and 'continuous taunting and teasing',[188] and so on, as constituting injury, indicating cruelty under Section 498A IPC. Even if one considers the possibility that sexual abuse coupled with injuries can be prosecuted under this section, absence of case law on sexual cruelty which does not necessarily lead to physical injuries, may well be interpreted to mean that sexual abuse that can lead to mental injuries be prosecuted under this provision. The observations in *Samdeep Mohan Varghese* v. *Anjana*[189] are persuasive and can be relied upon in such instances where the court stated that a marriage is a 'partnership of equals' and the wife's preferences have to be attended to, and in case she dislikes certain acts, the husband forcing her to do the same would amount to cruelty.

It is well worth examining the concept of 'cruelty' under provisions related to divorce as a ground for seeking divorce in India.[190] The Hindu Marriage Act, 1955, lays out the circumstances under which a spouse can apply for a decree of divorce, one of which includes 'cruelty'.[191] Further, under Section 10 of the Indian Divorce Act, 1869, cruelty exists as an independent ground for divorce. In *A. Jaychandra* v. *Aneel Kumar*,[192] the Supreme Court observed that cruelty need not be physical if, from the conduct of his spouse,

[185] Section 498A IPC was introduced in the code by the Criminal Law Amendment Act, 1983 (Act 46 of 1983).

[186] *Gananath Pattnaik* v. *State of Orissa* (2002) 2 SCC 619.

[187] *Ramesh Kumar* v. *State of Chhattisgarh* (2001) 9 SCC 618.

[188] *Mohd. Hoshan* v. *State of A.P.* (2002) 7 SCC 414.

[189] *Samdeep Mohan Varghese* v. *Anjana*, MAT.APPEAL. Nos. 99 and 152 of 2009, High Court Kerala decided on 15 September 2010; https://indiankanoon.org/doc/1439693/.

[190] Including personal laws.

[191] Section 13 of the Hindu Marriage Act, 1955.

[192] *A. Jaychandra* v. *Aneel Kumar* (2005) 2 SCC 22 (2005) 2 SCC 22.

same is established and/or an inference can be legitimately drawn that 'the treatment of the spouse is such that it causes an apprehension in the mind of the other spouse, about his or her mental welfare then this conduct amounts to cruelty'.[193] In *Sobha Rani* v. *Madhukar Reddi*,[194] the Court stated that with respect to mental cruelty, the enquiry must begin as to the nature of cruel treatment, and then the impact of such treatment in the mind of the spouse, 'whether it caused reasonable apprehension that it would be harmful or injurious to live with the other'.[195] In the case of *Vinita Saxena* v. *Pankaj Pandey*,[196] the Court, going into the legal proposition of cruelty, stated that to amount to cruelty, 'there must be such wilful treatment of the party which caused suffering in body or mind either as an actual fact or by way of apprehension in such a manner as to render the continued living together of spouses harmful or injurious having regard to the circumstances of the case'.[197] It is further stated that 'spouses owe rights and duties each to the other and in their relationship, they must act reasonably'.[198]

Thus, incidents of marital rape can be a valid ground for obtaining divorce in a court of law and ordinarily it can also be prosecutable as it usually results in causing suffering to body and mind of the wife under Section 498A IPC. Judgments, however, seem to suggest that the act of cruelty is not seen as an isolated single act but the outcome of continued suffering of living together suggesting that a perpetual cycle of violence is to be suffered by the aggrieved woman in order to seek punishment under Section 375 IPC and for getting a divorce on the ground of cruelty.

Under divorce law, cases seeking divorce on grounds of cruelty, where courts have expressly recognized sexual cruelty, have confined to cases where an allegation of 'unnatural' sexual acts have been made out. In *Bini John* v. *Saji Kuruvila*,[199] it was stated that 'insistence of unnatural sex, continued compulsion for oral sex, anal sex causing pain and physical injury to make the wife to concede to such unnatural sex will certainly amount to cruelty'.[200] It must be noted, however, that claims of unnatural sexual activity have only formed a basis for divorce in these cases; cases where this has been

[193] *A. Jaychandra* v. *Aneel Kumar* (2005) 2 SCC 22 (2005) 2 SCC 22, 10.
[194] *Sobha Rani* v. *Madhukar Reddi* (1988) 1 SCC 105.
[195] *Sobha Rani* v. *Madhukar Reddi* (1988) 1 SCC 105, 4.
[196] *Vinita Saxena* v. *Pankaj Pandey* (2006) 3 SCC 778.
[197] *Vinita Saxena* v. *Pankaj Pandey* (2006) 3 SCC 778, 31.
[198] *Vinita Saxena* v. *Pankaj Pandey* (2006) 3 SCC 778, 45.
[199] *Bini John* v. *Saji Kuruvila* (1997) SCC OnLine Ker 27.
[200] *Bini John* v. *Saji Kuruvila* (1997) SCC OnLine Ker 27, 8.

recognized as a criminal act are rare. Moreover, in specific cases of marital rape, where 'unnatural' sexual acts were present and had led to injuries, it was then further prosecutable under existing penal laws such as Section 377[201] IPC, which penalizes voluntary unnatural offences.

The Criminal Law Amendment Act of 2013 has since widened the definition of rape to include within its scope acts beyond peno-vaginal penetration. Since, the scope of the definition of rape is now wide enough to cover acts of anal sex, oral sex, insertion of objects into the vagina, and so on, these acts that could in the past only be penalized as 'unnatural' sexual acts under Section 377 IPC are now covered under the definition of rape. Also, it must be noted that 377 IPC penalized unnatural sex, either voluntary or non-voluntary and consensual or non-consensual, this in any event was not the correct forum to address marital rape, since the element of force and the involuntary nature of rape itself would be trivialized under any circumstances. Also, penal–vaginal sex is in any event not considered 'unnatural', in addition to the fact that Section 377 is now an obsolete law and unconstitutional[202] on grounds that it is being incorrectly used to victimize the LGBT community.

The argument of alternate forum to address marital rape as a crime is fallacious, since none of the provisions discussed above address rape as a crime. While PWDVA is unique in unequivocally recognizing sexual violence as domestic violence, it provides a civil remedy. Section 498A IPC covers spousal sexual violence under cruelty, but its limitation is the way it has been interpreted by the courts in the requirement that sexual abuse must

[201] *Bini John v. Saji Kuruvila* (1997) SCC OnLine Ker 27, 8.(§ 377 IPC: 'Unnatural offences') and on September 6, 2018 in Navtej Singh Johar v. Union of India, Writ Petition (Crl.) No. 76 of 2016 unanimously held that § 377 IPC was unconstitutional 'in so far as it criminalises consensual sexual conduct between adults of the same sex'.

[202] Section 377 IPC was decriminalized with respect to sex between consenting adults by the Delhi High Court in 2009 in the *Naz Foundation v. Government of NCT Delhi and Others*, 160 *Delhi Law Times* 277. However, the judgment was overturned in 2013 by the Supreme Court in *Suresh Kumar Kaushal v. Naz Foundation* (2014) 1 SCC 1 which held that amending or repealing Section 377 IPC should be a matter left to the Parliament and not the judiciary. However, in 2016, the court after hearing the curative petition (C) No. 88-102/2014 submitted by the Naz Foundation, referred the matter to a five-member constitutional bench which on 6 September 2018 in *Navtej Singh Johar v. Union of India*, Writ Petition (Crl.) No. 76 of 2016 unanimously held that Section 377 IPC was unconstitutional 'in so far as it criminalises consensual sexual conduct between adults of the same sex'.

be accompanied by injury; physical injury may not necessarily follow from every case of marital rape, where absence of consent is said to constitute rape. Mental injury, though recognized under 498A IPC, is difficult to prove in a court in absence of any physical injury. Even though the courts can interpret the law of cruelty under IPC to punish the husbands committing rape on their wives, they have not done that so far; rather, they have used the marital rape exception to acquit husbands and in justifying rape within marriage.[203] Under divorce law, marital rape as an act of cruelty can only be used for the limited purpose of granting divorce. Further, a single act of forced sex is not taken to suggest a perpetual cycle of cruelty even for granting divorce. Since section 377 IPC did not cover peno-vaginal acts as 'unnatural', marital rape or any other case of heterosexual peno-vaginal rape was not covered under this section.

***

So far, the law and its implementation pertaining to domestic violence, cruelty, divorce, and rape in the IPC indicates that marital rape is unpunishable in India and the basic requirement of consent is conveniently ignored in law when it comes to any sexual activity or intercourse between a married couple.[204]

While the enormous social, intergenerational, and economic costs of sexual violence within marriage are recorded extensively,[205,206] World Bank

[203] *State v. Vikash*, decided by Special Fast Track Court, Dwarka, New Delhi on 7 May 2014. Unique Case ID No. 02405R0349722013; https://indiankanoon.org/doc/100624392/.

[204] Verma (Retd) et al., *Report of the Committee on Amendments to Criminal Law*.

[205] United Nations Study of the Secretary General, in 'Ending Violence against Women: From Words to Action', published in 2006; http://www.un.org/womenwatch/daw/public/VAW_Study/VAWstudyE.pdf.

[206] WHO Fact sheet on 'Violence against Women: Intimate Partner and Sexual Violence against Women' (updated in November 2016); http://www.who.int/mediacentre/factsheets/fs239/en/. Some of the costs of spousal sexual violence include: domestic violence prevents women from contributing productively to the family, the economy, and public life and drains resources from social services, the justice system, health care agencies, and employers; and lowers the overall educational attainment, mobility, and innovative potential of the survivors. Women may suffer isolation, inability to work, loss of wages, lack of participation in regular activities, and limited

has noted similar costs in cases of marital rape as well to record that it is equally grave and has ripple effects throughout the society.[207] Hence, the grave nature of sexual violence cannot be seen in isolation, it must necessarily include the incidence of marital rape. The rationale for criminalizing marital rape is the same as the one that guides the offense of rape in every case, namely, respect for the autonomy of the woman in body, mind, and emotions, since sex is an act which a person decides to engage in voluntarily. It is here that a woman's consent[208] becomes critical to her voluntary participation in the sexual act. Yet, it is true that legal reforms on sexual violence such as the 2013 Criminal law amendment have failed to question the asymmetrical character of marriage, reinforcing an object-like treatment of women and continue to legitimize violent structures in the private lives of women by retaining the marital rape exception.

The exception to Section 375 IPC has created paradigms where women and men are not treated as organic individuals capable of thinking, loving, having dignity, but instead reduces the human body of a wife as the only attribute of being human, that is, best being used as a consumable commodity and made to suffer as body parts for sexual exploitation. Though this exception is clearly in violation of the internationally recognized principles, the interests of the lawmakers is contrary to those principles in the domestic law. With the retention of the exception of marital rape, the law-makers have assured that women on their marriage are exposed to unlimited amount of sexual perversion at the hands of their husbands, and her body, soul, and mind becomes into an object for consumption.

Fifty-two countries including several common law countries such as the USA, New Zealand, Ireland, Malaysia, Ghana, Israel, France, Germany, Brazil, Austria, Thailand, Netherlands, Philippines, Hong Kong, Chile,

---

ability to care for themselves and their children. Women absent themselves from employment as a result of the injuries and stress and further costs arise when women lose jobs as a result of absence or reduced performance and are compelled to relocate.

[207] World Bank, *World Development Report 1993: Investing in Health* (New York: Oxford University Press, 1993).

[208] In a recent unusual but only a persuasive Order dated 6 November 2017 of the Gujarat High Court in *Nimeshbhai Bharatbhai Desai v. State of Gujarat*, Cri. Misc. Application (for Quashing and set aside FIR/ Order No. 26957/2017), the court has pertinently observed that marital rape refers to 'unwanted intercourse by a man with his wife obtained by force, threat or force, or physical violence, or when she is unable to give consent' and 'it is a non-consensual act of violence perversion by a husband against the wife where she is abused physically and sexually'.

Belgium, Sweden, and so on, have criminalized marital rape either through legislative or by judicial intervention and thus comply with the international principles of bodily integrity, integrity of a person, freedom from discrimination based on marital status, and so on, to ensure equal status in marriage and equal protection of laws. These jurisdictions have recognized that consent should not be implied by the relationship between the parties under any circumstances, including marriage. It is therefore necessary that international is not considered to be separate and apart from the domestic because gendered, sexual, and cultural dichotomies permeate the narratives of the nation-states.[209] According to the UN Women's 2011 report,[210] by April 2011, out of 179 countries in the world for which data was available, 52 countries had amended their legislations to explicitly make marital rape a criminal offence. India remains in the remaining countries who have the marital rape exception with countries such as Pakistan, Algeria, China, Iran, Egypt, and the UAE.

Thus, forced sexual intercourse is a very clear indication of discord and violence. It is a form of domestic violence in its existence and at the core of such a marriage. The marital rape exception in the IPC puts the woman in a situation where the woman is not given the space to communicate and be heard. It disregards the requirement of 'unequivocal voluntary requirement', that is, consent which mandates that sexual acts are not to be performed in callous disregard of the woman's desire to participate for specific sexual acts. This shows that there is a vast disconnect between equality and respect for obligations of those who administer the law. An affirmative model of consent should be adopted in marriages where a husband is not left to make assumptions and where sexual intercourse is understood beyond the contemporary connotation such as an 'act of passion, actuated by libido' and other regressive and reductive perceptions which is based on confused desires on account

[209] Ratna Kapur, 'Gender, Sovereignty and the Rise of a Sexual Security Regime in International Law and Postcolonial India', in *Melbourne Journal of International Law*, 14 (2) (2013); http://www.austlii.edu.au/au/journals/MelbJIL/2013/12.pdf.

[210] UN Women Report (Annexure 4), 'Progress of the World's Women 2011–2012: In Pursuit of Justice'; http://www.unwomen.org//media/headquarters/attachments/sections/library/publications/2011/progressoftheworldswomen-2011-en.pdf?la=en&vs=2835; and Ruby Mellen, 'The Rapist's Loophole: Marriage: Where and how Legal Systems Around the World Permit Violence against Women', *Foreign Policy* (March/April 2017), available at http://foreignpolicy.com/2017/03/20/decoder-the-rapists-loophole-marriage/.

of differences in gender relations. This affirmative model of consent will help in achieving equality before law and equal protection within the country in its true spirit.

Equality as envisaged by the founding members of the Constitution under Article 14 which entails within itself the equality of results to enhance its omnipotence. This dynamic nature of equality only leads to the adoption of the substantive equality model, which is distinguished from the formal equality model, where it is not the form but the substance or the effect, which serves as an aid for classification. 'If "equal" treatment of subjects, classified and treated as "similar" on the basis of "sameness" results in divergent impacts, the "substantive" equality model rings the alarm'.[211] This discussion raises the question about the possibility of gender justice. Traditional ideas of woman and family have repeatedly intervened substantive equality and deny dignity to women. Under the substantive approach to equality, the sections of Articles 15 and 16 of the Constitution pertaining to women are not exceptions, but part of the Articles' articulation of an anti-hierarchical understanding of equality.[212] The principle of substantive equality means that India is responsible for addressing the unintended consequences of such laws.

The classification of married women as created by the exception of marital rape denies a married woman autonomy and personhood, and grounds her political, economic, social, and sexual status in her husband. It is hence essential that this law should evolve and change with the needs of society. The persistent failure of laws to check discrimination against women in cases of domestic violence, sexual harassment, rape (including marital rape), sex determination, and sex selective abortions to name a few have to do in large measure the power of sexual stereotypes in conditioning the minds of functionaries in the criminal justice system. Hence, the law cannot remain hidebound and static, as it reflects the society we live in.

The state thus cannot afford to paint a picture of progress and fairness in society or root out ills such as rapes and sexual violence against women, married or otherwise, by their husbands or an unknown person, which plague our society today. All these evils are the manifestation of a misogynistic bias

[211] Catherine MacKinnon, 1991. *Difference and Dominance on Sex Discrimination*, (Kennedy and Bartlett) Ed., Feminist Legal Theory, 81.

[212] Martha C. Nussbaum, 2005. *India, Sex Equality, and Constitutional Law, constituting Women: The Gender of Constitutional Jurisprudence*, ed. Bev Baines (Cambridge University Press).

in society propagated by the lack of acknowledgement of women, especially wives, as true equals and in a way from the law of the land still treating a wife as the property of the husband and the continuation of this cycle with dysfunctional families indoctrinating their daughters towards mute acceptance and their sons towards the age-old way of objectifying and owning their wives. It is thus essential to challenge the constitutional validity of the exception of marital rape which is accepting and propagating this culture of sexism and women being limited to body parts and being used as objects.

7. *Towards Uniformity of Rights*

*Muslim Personal Law, the Domestic Violence Act, and the Harmonization of Family Law in India**

Saptarshi Mandal

The secular constitution does not recognize (...) the existence of different varieties of matrimonial violence like Hindu violence, Christian violence, Muslim violence and secular violence.

—*Justice Arvind Kumar Tripathi, Mohd. Waqar v. State of UP* (2014)

A popular perception of Indian family law, both at home and globally, is that it consists of separate bodies of law governing different religious groups. The same is often encountered in scholarly descriptions too. For instance, Archana Parashar and Amita Dhanda begin the introduction to their 2008 edited volume, *Redefining Family Law in India*, with the claim that 'Family law is synonymous with religious personal

* I would like to thank my student Avani Tewari for providing excellent research assistance towards this chapter.

laws in India'.[1] Such descriptions create an incomplete picture, for they fail to capture the hybrid nature of Indian family law where we see a dynamic interaction between group-specific laws and laws and principles of universal application. Recent family law jurisprudence is abound with examples where rights, obligations, and immunities under the group-specific law are overridden—and in the process, modified—by the common laws upholding specific state interests.

The operation of Muslim Personal Law (hereinafter, MPL), which is often mistakenly perceived as resistant to change/state intervention, helps illustrate this phenomenon. Thus, while under the dominant interpretation of the *Shariat*, a Muslim husband is not obliged to provide for the divorced wife beyond three months (*idda*, or the waiting period), courts have allowed Muslim women to seek maintenance from their former husbands even beyond three months, under a common criminal law provision, which is based on the welfare state's concern for preventing destitution and resultant criminality.[2] In the case of adoption, though Muslim law does not recognize the concept, a 2014 Supreme Court judgment held that Muslims could adopt under the common juvenile justice law, children, who were orphaned, abandoned, or surrendered, thus furthering the state's interest in the rehabilitation of such children.[3] Similarly, the Muslim husband's right to polygamy under the Shariat is restricted by the general service rule applicable to government employees mandating monogamy, which is based on the secular state's modernizing project.[4] For Muslim citizens, the exercise of judicial authority in each of these cases has modified the 'law' governing the formation, sustenance, and dissolution of their families. In other words, the entire universe of rules that a Muslim is likely to consider while contemplating marriage, divorce, or parenthood, now comprises legal rules specific to their 'own' group, as well as those that they share with other Indians.

Thus, contrary to accounts of Indian family law that portray it as a system of distinct sets of religious norms, my starting point in this chapter is to emphasize the dynamic interaction in Indian family law between group-specific norms and universal norms, between religious doctrine and governance imperatives. My argument in this chapter builds on Susanne

[1] Archana Parashar and Amita Dhanda, *Redefining Family Law in India* (New Delhi: Routledge, 2008), p. ix.

[2] *Daniel Latifi and Another* v. *Union of India* (2001) 7 SCC 740.

[3] *Shabnam Hashmi* v. *Union of India* (2014) 4 SCC 1.

[4] *Khursheed Ahmad Khan* v. *State of UP* (2015) 8 SCC 439.

and Lloyd Rudolph's suggestion that the constitutional goal of a uniform civil code be understood as 'a process rather than as a specific outcome, a process in which legal uniformity and legal pluralism jockey for dominance, not for the whole field'.[5] I use the term 'harmonization' to describe the process of legal change evidenced in Indian family law in the last two decades. I understand the term in its common sense as bringing together discordant elements for a specific purpose, without erasing the distinctiveness of the entities harmonized. The outcome of harmonization in the family law context is the application of common standards across groups, based on a common philosophy or a common characterization of a problem, while still retaining the idea of separate group-specific laws. Harmonization in Indian family law has taken place most visibly as exercises in judicial interpretation, as we saw in the examples cited earlier, but through enacting common legislations as well. The PWDVA, 2005 is one such law, that, as I discuss in this chapter, has aided in bridging group difference on a number of issues pertaining to rights and obligations within marriage. Thus, my purpose in this chapter is to illustrate how the PWDVA has contributed to, what Rudolph and Rudolph call, 'greater uniformity of rights',[6] despite separate group-specific laws.

The above account of harmonization, however, must be accompanied with the caveat that it does not characterize every aspect of family law in India, with the result that we can only talk about *zones of harmonization* in a patchy legal field. The case of divorce law can be used as an illustration here. All the matrimonial statutes (Hindu, Parsi, Christian, civil), after undergoing amendments at different points of time since the mid-1970s, now have (*a*) the same grounds for fault divorce; (*b*) divorce by mutual consent; and (*c*) the same terms of divorce for men and women (with minor exceptions). However, the extent of uniformity here is marred by one technical difference, that while the Hindu, Parsi, and civil laws allow parties to file for divorce after living separately for one year[7], it is two years under the Indian Divorce Act governing the Christians.[8] Further, Muslim divorce law

[5] Susanne Rudolph and Lloyd Rudolph, 'Living with Difference in India: Legal Pluralism and Legal Universalism in Historical Context', in *Religion and Personal Law in Secular India: A Call to Judgment*, ed. Gerald James Larson (Bloomington and Indianapolis: Indiana University Press, 2001), p. 56.

[6] Rudolph and Lloyd Rudolph, 'Living with Difference in India', p. 56.

[7] Section 13B(1), Hindu Marriage Act, 1955; Section 32B(1), Parsi Marriage and Divorce Act, 1936; Section 28(1), Special Marriage Act, 1954.

[8] Section 10A(1), Indian Divorce Act, 1869.

shares a few features with these statutes, namely, divorce by mutual consent (*mubarat*) and a few fault grounds available to Muslim women under the Dissolution of Muslim Marriage Act, 1939 (hereinafter, DMM Act), but differs on all other accounts, principally in its sex-based asymmetry.[9] Thus, the extent of harmonization in the case of divorce, though significant when seen historically, is not as much as we notice in the case of maintenance, which I describe later in this chapter. Harmonization is thus a slow and ever-incomplete process.

Three factors are key to the harmonizing role played by the PWDVA. The first is the religion-neutral framing of the Act, as well as the judges' understanding of violence against women as a universal phenomenon cutting across religious groups, as reflected in the quote at the beginning of this chapter. The second factor, also pertaining to the statutory text, is that though it is a law concerning violence, it not only proscribes acts of violence against women in the family, but is also essentially designed to protect their economic interests, which allows the Act entry into the domain of family law. The third factor is the judges' understanding that women face the same economic hardships upon marriage breakdown, irrespective of the religious group they belong to. This is reflected in the judges' obiter observations in maintenance claims made under the PWDVA, which is continuous with the preexisting jurisprudence on maintenance under both common and personal law. Thus, I argue in this chapter that the Domestic Violence Act is performing the threefold function of (*a*) furthering the process of harmonization of Indian family law, (*b*) using gender justice as the basis of harmonization through its focus on economic vulnerability of women in the event of marriage breakdown, irrespective of their group identity, and (*c*) offering a gendered justification to the protective function of family law.

[9] Muslim law provides different modes of divorce for the husband and the wife. *Talaq* or male-initiated divorce can take place either through a single pronouncement of talaq followed by no sexual contact for three months (*talaq ahasan*); three pronouncements over a period of three months with no sexual contact (*talaq hasan*); or a single irrevocable pronouncement or three pronouncements at one go (*talaq al-bidah*). Female-initiated divorce on the other hand is either with the husband's consent to being released from the marriage (*khula*); upon delegation by the husband (*talaq-i-tafweez*); through a decree by a *qazi*, that is, an Islamic judge (*faskh*) or by a state court under the Dissolution of Muslim Marriage Act, 1939.

Domestic Violence, Marriage Breakdown, and Women's Economic Vulnerability

The literature on women's economic predicament upon marriage breakdown in India repeatedly emphasizes the economic vulnerability in the aftermath of divorce or separation as a common state shared by women across religious groups. Based on a series of studies of divorced, separated, and deserted Hindu women carried out in the 1980s, Paul Amato notes that 'many live at a bare subsistence level and face continuing difficulties in providing food, clothing, and shelter for themselves and their children'.[10] Amato identifies childcare responsibilities, without adequate or any child support from the father, as one of the factors contributing to the women's economic burden post marriage breakdown. In some cases, women may also relinquish child support in order to permanently sever contact with abusive husbands. Women's natal kin—parents or siblings—are most likely to provide economic support in the initial stages, though they might be reluctant to do so indefinitely, if they feel that they have already discharged their responsibility by arranging her marriage or by providing a dowry. As a result, women are likely to set up independent households and attempt to be economically independent, but as Amato concludes, due to limited education and job skills, attaining economic self-sufficiency is difficult.[11] Munira Siganporia's study of formal and informal social support available to divorced Muslim women in Bombay and Pune, Maharashtra, bears similar findings.[12] A majority of the women interviewed had child care responsibilities; they returned to the natal home after divorce, a major consideration behind which was the lack of availability of housing; most did not get their *mehr*[13] upon divorce, or get back the dowry articles; maintenance was uncertain, even when the assurance to pay was obtained through the mediation of community bodies.

[10] R. Paul Amato, 'The Impact of Divorce on Men and Women in India and the United States', *Journal of Comparative Family Studies* XXV, 2 (1994): 210.

[11] Amato, 'The Impact of Divorce on Men and Women in India and the United States', p. 211.

[12] Munira Siganporia, 'Post-Divorce Problems and Social Support: A Study of Muslim Divorced Women of Maharashtra', in *Islam, Women and Gender Justice*, ed. Asghar Ali Engineer (New Delhi: Gyan Publishing House, 2000), pp. 127–28.

[13] *Mehr* or *mahr* is the money or property that a wife is entitled to receive from her husband in a Muslim marriage. Usually a small fraction of the amount promised is paid at the time of marriage, with the rest being paid when the marriage ends, either by divorce or death.

Lawyer and feminist activist Flavia Agnes' autobiographical account[14] bears out the difficult choice women are forced to make between enduring physical violence with the constant threat of being dispossessed from the matrimonial home on the one hand, and divorce, destitution, and being left without a shelter on the other. Patricia and Roger Jeffery write based on their research on gender relations in rural Bijnor, Uttar Pradesh, in the early 1990s, that though for most women marital bliss was 'somewhat elusive',[15] their '"exit options" often made remaining in an uncongenial marriage seem the least worst option when set beside their likely fate as a separated woman'.[16] The likelihood of living in penury and precariousness of kin support meant that irrespective of what religious group they belonged to, women as well as their natal families tried their best to avoid marriage breakdown. The authors conclude:

> Contrary to Hindu Right assertions, Hindu women in rural Bijnor are *not* less vulnerable to being left in penury by their husbands than Muslim women are. The types of problems women report, the efforts they put into achieving reconciliation, their reliance on natal kin and the centrality of kin-based mechanisms for dispute resolution, are common across the board. So, too, are the outcomes when the marriage breaks down: women's lack of entitlements in the ex-husband's household, their temporary reliance on their natal kin, and their probable remarriage in circumstances that may prove no better (and may even be worse) than the first marriage (emphasis in the original).[17]

A more recent study by Kirti Singh,[18] involving interviews with 405 divorced or separated women across 21 cities, repeats the same findings as the above. 83 per cent of the women interviewed had separated on account of domestic violence, while 13.5 per cent had been deserted by their husbands.[19] Domestic violence was a common reason for separation across

[14] Flavia, *My Story…Our Story of Rebuilding Broken Lives* (Bombay: Women's Centre, 1988).

[15] Patricia Jeffery and Roger Jeffery, *Confronting Saffron Demography: Religion, Fertility, and Women's Status in India* (New Delhi: Three Essays Collective, 2006), p. 62.

[16] Jeffery and Jeffery, *Confronting Saffron Demography*, p. 66.

[17] Jeffery and Roger Jeffery, *Confronting Saffron Demography*, p. 75.

[18] Kirti Singh, *Separated and Divorced Women in India: Economic Rights and Entitlements* (New Delhi: Sage and Ottawa: International Development Research Centre, 2013).

[19] Singh, *Separated and Divorced Women in India*, p. 28.

religious and caste groups. On the economic situation of the interviewees, the study notes:

> Despite maintenance provisions, most women are financially dependent on their natal families and 63 per cent live with natal families, usually parents. (....) Remarriage is extremely rare. The fact that 85.6 per cent of the surveyees had children living with them compounded their troubles. The miserable financial status of separated and divorced women is evident from the fact that even after separation 41.5 per cent had no income and 27.4 per cent earned less than Rs. 2000 per month.[20]

The sociology of marriage breakdown in India therefore offers ample basis to argue that protection of economic interests of the parties must be regarded as the principal function of family law in India, as well as the principal site for operationalizing gender justice.

Multiple Orderings of Maintenance and Muslim Women's Religious 'Difference'

In the absence of community of property (except in the state of Goa), the only mechanism available to women to mitigate their economic vulnerability resulting from both marriage-dependency and marriage-breakdown, is that of maintenance. Women divorced or living separately from their husbands can seek maintenance either under the group-specific matrimonial statute applicable to them or under the common anti-vagrancy provision, Section 125 of the CrPC. All the matrimonial statutes (both group-specific and civil) provide for interim maintenance during the legal proceedings and permanent maintenance at the end of the proceedings for separation or divorce. Under the former, courts are authorized to award temporary maintenance to a wife who does not have sufficient means to support herself during court proceedings and cover litigation expenses, commensurate with the means of the husband.[21] As Werner Menski[22] remarks, these provisions envisage a distinct form of legal aid, wherein instead of the state, the husband, who

[20] Singh, *Separated and Divorced Women in India*, p. 24.

[21] Section 36, Indian Divorce Act, 1869; Section 39, Parsi Marriage and Divorce Act, 1936; Section 36, Special Marriage Act, 1954; Section 24, Hindu Marriage Act, 1955.

[22] Werner Menski, *Hindu Law: Beyond Tradition and Modernity* (New Delhi: Oxford University Press, 2003), p. 514.

is also a party to the dispute, is called upon to bear the expenses for the wife's access to justice. As for permanent alimony, the matrimonial statutes provide for either a one-time payment of a lump sum amount or periodic payments throughout the life of the wife or till the wife remarries.[23]

The statutes do not specify the quantum of maintenance. While there are stray instances, such as the 1970 Supreme Court judgment in *Kulbhushan Kumar* v. *Rajkumari*,[24] where the judge held that the husband will not be liable to pay more than 25 per cent of his income as maintenance, judges generally maintain that there is no fixed formula for computing the amount of maintenance and that it depends on the specific facts and circumstances of each case. A 2011 Supreme Court judgment, *Vinny Parmar* v. *Paramvir Parmar*,[25] summarized the legal position as follows:

> The court has to consider the status of the parties, their respective needs, the capacity of the husband to pay, having regard to reasonable expenses for his own maintenance and others whom he is obliged to maintain under the law and statute. The courts also have to take note of the fact that the amount of maintenance fixed for the wife should be such as she can live in reasonable comfort considering her status and mode of life she was used to when she lived with her husband. At the same time, the amount so fixed cannot be excessive or affect the living condition of the other party. These are all the broad principles courts have to keep in mind while determining maintenance or permanent alimony.

This is the basic template for post-divorce or post-separation maintenance found under all matrimonial statutes, with major or minor statute-specific differences. Thus, the Hindu and the Parsi statutes differ from the rest in one crucial respect, that under these, either spouse can claim maintenance from the other, while under the civil and the Christian statutes only the wife can. Similarly, extramarital sexual activity on the part of the recipient during the subsistence of marriage could potentially disentitle them from permanent alimony or reduce the amount under all the statutes, except for the Christian one.

Muslim women did not have access to any means of economic support akin to permanent alimony till 1973. Following the colonial courts' interpretation

[23] Section 37, Indian Divorce Act, 1869; Section 40, Parsi Marriage and Divorce Act, 1936; Section 37, Special Marriage Act, 1954; Section 25, Hindu Marriage Act, 1955.

[24] (1971) AIR 234.

[25] (2011) 13 SCC 112.

of Islamic law, a husband was mandatorily required to pay maintenance during the waiting period of three months (*idda*) following divorce or till the end of pregnancy, if the wife was pregnant at the time of divorce. But providing for the wife beyond the waiting period was treated as optional. In 1973, the vagrancy prevention provision of the CrPC was amended to provide that a divorced wife, irrespective of religious affiliation, could seek maintenance from her former husband. Section 488 of the original CrPC enacted in 1898 provided that if a man with sufficient means neglected or refused to provide for his wife or children, a Magistrate could order him to pay a monthly amount, not exceeding Rupees 500, as maintenance. The section was particularly disfavored by Muslim husbands, for it also allowed a wife, whose husband had married again or kept a mistress, to refuse to live with him and still claim maintenance.[26] Menski writes:

> Not surprisingly, this provision was challenged with particular vigour by Muslim husbands on the ground that it conflicted with traditional *shariat* rules. While most of these petitions were turned down, it soon transpired that the fastest remedy for a Muslim husband faced with claims to maintenance from a 'disobedient' wife was simply to divorce her by *talaq*, thus freeing himself from the burden imposed by s. 488. The section thus lost much of its protective energy through the easy device of the husband's instant *talaq*.[27]

This protective dimension of Section 488 was sought to be rehabilitated and extended to all women, when the provision was repackaged as Sections 125 to 127 of the CrPC in 1973. The new sections defined the term 'wife' to include a divorced wife who had not remarried. Divorced Hindu, Christian, and Parsi women already had access to post-divorce maintenance under their respective matrimonial statutes. To them, the new amendment provided an additional layer of protection against penury. But for divorced Muslim women, the new amendment sought to vastly modify their traditional post-divorce entitlement under MPL. The innovation was resisted by the Muslim legislators, claiming that it was an interference with the Shariat.[28] The result was a compromise in the form of the new Section 127(3)(b) of the CrPC, which provided that a Magistrate could cancel an order of maintenance

[26] Proviso to Section 488(3), Code of Criminal Procedure, 1893.

[27] Werner Menski *Modern Indian Family Law* (Surrey: Curzon Press, 2001), p. 250.

[28] Rina Verma Williams, *Postcolonial Politics and Personal Laws: Colonial Legal Legacies and the Indian State* (New Delhi: Oxford University Press, 2006), pp. 128–9.

under Section 125, if they found that the wife had already received the whole amount that was 'payable to her on divorce', under the applicable customary or personal law.

In a series of early cases before the courts, where Muslim women claimed post-divorce maintenance under the new provision, husbands sought to escape liability by claiming that the meagre deferred dower (*mehr*) was the amount payable on divorce. Judges were faced with the question as to the actual scope of a Muslim woman's post-divorce entitlement in view of Section 127(3)(b).[29] In two consecutive judgments of the Supreme Court—*Bai Tahira* v. *Ali Hussain Fisalli Chothia*[30] and *Fuzlunbi* v. *Khader Vali*[31]—Justice Krishna Iyer emphasized the vision of economic justice underlying Sections 125–7, and held that the husband satisfied his obligation under the general law only if the amount paid as part of his obligation under the personal law was a substantial amount, sufficient to protect the wife from destitution. Thus, even if he had paid up the deferred mehr and maintenance as per MPL, the husband could still be held liable under the Section 125, CrPC, and his obligation towards the former wife could extend beyond the idda.

A five-judge bench of the Supreme Court affirmed this interpretation in *Mohd. Ahmed Khan* v. *Shah Bano Begum.*[32] Chief Justice, Yeshwant Chandrachud, who wrote the judgment, reasoned that (*a*) MPL, in limiting the husband's obligation to the idda, did not encounter the specific problem targeted by Sections 125–7, namely, the prevention of vagrancy, and therefore the husband's obligation under personal law and the secular law were not in conflict, but were located in separate, parallel domains; (*b*) the legislature intended the sections to override personal law, which was evident from the fact that the section allowed a wife, whose husband contracted

[29] In *Rukhsana Parvin* v. *Shaikh Mohomed Hussein Mohomed* (1977) 79 BOMLR 123, a division bench of the Bombay High Court held that on a plain reading of the two provisions, it must be concluded that Section 127(3)(b) restricted a divorced Muslim woman's right to obtain maintenance under Section 125. On the other hand, in *Hajuben Suleman* v. *Ibrahim Gandabhai*, (1977) 18 GLR 133, a division bench of the Gujarat High Court held that the words 'has received' in Section 127(3)(b) must be liberally and purposively interpreted as the wife voluntarily and satisfactorily receiving an amount upon divorce, for an order of maintenance under Section 125 to be cancelled.

[30] (1979) 2 SCC 316.

[31] (1980) 4 SCC 125.

[32] (1985) 2 SCC 556.

another marriage or kept a mistress, to refuse to live with him and yet legitimately claim maintenance, disregarding a Muslim man's right to marry up to four women under MPL; (*c*) mehr was an incident of marriage and therefore, deferred mehr could not be the 'amount payable on divorce' within the meaning of Section 127 (3)(b); and (*d*) there was no inconsistency between what Section 125 envisioned and the Shariat, for there were interpretive traditions within Islamic jurisprudence that obligated the husband to make 'provision' for the divorced wife, in excess of the maintenance paid during the idda.

The judgment and the political contestations over Muslim women's rights in its aftermath have been extensively addressed in the literature on personal law reform.[33] In response to the opposition to Shah Bano by conservative Muslim religious groups and politicians, the central government enacted the Muslim Women (Protection of Rights on Divorce) Act, 1986 (hereinafter, the MWA), to remove Muslim men and women from the purview of Section 125 CrPC. The Act provided that the former husband's economic obligations towards the wife were limited to the idda. Further, that if a divorced woman was unable to provide for herself after the idda, she could claim maintenance from her natal kin, children, or the *waqf*[34] board. But, though the Act was supposedly to undo the holding of Shah Bano, the statutory language suggested otherwise. While Section 3 (1)(a) explicitly limited the Muslim husband's post-divorce obligation to the idda, to denote the substantive aspect of the husband's obligation, the other clauses of the section used the phrase 'a reasonable and fair provision and maintenance'.[35] In Shah Bano, Justice Chandrachud had used the two terms 'provision' and 'maintenance' to denote distinct economic obligations of the husband. To that extent, instead of negating Shah Bano, the Act seemed to be codifying, following Shah Bano, the minority view in Islamic jurisprudence that required the husband to pay not only maintenance during the idda, but also make provisions for her future needs (*mata'un bil-maroof* or *mata*).

[33] Narendra Subramanian, 'Islamic Norms, Common Law, and Legal Reasoning: Muslim Personal Law and The Economic Consequences of Divorce in India', *Islamic Law and Society* 24 (2017); Rochana Bajpai, *Debating Difference: Group Rights and Liberal Democracy in India*, 24, 3 (New Delhi: Oxford University Press, 2011); Williams, *Postcolonial Politics and Personal Laws*.

[34] 'Section 3(r) of the Waqf Act, 1995 defines *waqf* as "the permanent dedication by a person professing Islam, of any movable or immovable property for any purpose recognised by the Muslim law as pious, religious or charitable". A *waqf* board is a state constituted body under this Act to regulate *waqfs* and *waqf* properties.'

[35] Section 3(1)(a).

Most high courts exploited the ambiguity in the statutory text to rule in favour of women. These high courts read the phrase 'reasonable and fair provision' in light of the title and the preamble to the MWA that claimed to protect the rights of divorced Muslim women.[36] For instance, in *Arab Ahemadhia Abdulla* v. *Arab Bail Mohmuna Saiyadbhai*[37]—the first such high court judgment—Justice M. Shah of the Gujarat High Court wrote:

> ... it seems that the Parliament intended that the divorced woman gets sufficient means of livelihood after the divorce and that she does not become destitute or is not thrown on the streets without a roof over her head and without any means of sustaining herself and her children. The word 'provision' itself indicates that something is provided in advance for meeting some needs.

Consequently, in this and a majority of the other cases under the MWA, judges granted generous amounts to the wives to see them through the post-divorce period. Thus, although divorced Muslim women were not eligible to claim maintenance from their husbands under the CrPC—the common legal recourse available to the all other Indian women—the above judicial approach meant that they were not left without economic protection. Admittedly, Muslim women were often able to secure a higher amount of maintenance than their non-Muslim counterpart under the above approach, since till 2001, there was a cap on how much a Magistrate could award under Section 125 CrPC, but none under the MWA. However, the MWA, in addition to denying them the relatively laxer procedure for obtaining maintenance under the common law,[38] also marked a separation in the civic status of Muslim women from other Indian women on the basis of religion.

Gender Justice as the Basis of Harmonization

Feminist researchers studying the adjudication of family law in the lower courts have repeatedly emphasized that notwithstanding the differences in the laws governing them, women approach the courts with the same

[36] See, Subramanian 2017, Section 2(a), Muslim Women (Protection of Rights on Divorce) Act, 1986.

[37] AIR 1988 Gujarat 141.

[38] Section 125, CrPC being a criminal law provision does not demand strict evidence of marriage—which is the domain of civil law—to grant maintenance. Under the MW Act on the other hand, to claim maintenance a woman must first establish that she was 'married according to Muslim law, ...'. Section 2(a), MW Act.

problems and struggle with similar predicaments.[39] In a series of decisions, starting with the 2001 Supreme Court judgment in *Danial Latifi* v. *Union of India*,[40] this commonality of women's experience, particularly that of women's post-divorce economic vulnerability, emerged as the basis for re-establishing Muslim women's entitlement under the CrPC. This section traces the trajectory of these decisions to illustrate how harmonization was achieved through the exercise of judicial authority on the basis of gender justice.

In 1986, Danial Latifi, the lawyer who had represented Shah Bano, had challenged the constitutional validity of the Muslim Women Act on the ground of violation of Muslim women's fundamental rights to equality before law, equal treatment of law, and life with dignity. Latifi argued in his petition that since the object behind Section 125 CrPC was to prevent destitution, denying the remedy to Muslim women without any legitimate basis, amounted to a violation of their right to equality under Article 14 and the right to life under Article 21 of the Constitution. The central government opposed the petition, arguing that personal law was a legitimate ground for exempting a group from application of the common laws and that the legislature was authorized to do so. The All India Muslim Personal Law Board (AIMPLB), which was an intervener in the case, also opposed the petition. The AIMPLB defended the 1986 Act, arguing that it was consistent with the 'social ethos' of the Muslim community that did not cast the responsibility to maintain a destitute divorced woman solely upon the former husband, but spread it over a wide net of kinsmen. Another intervener, the National Commission for Women, supported the petition, arguing that economic support envisaged by the Act was 'illusory', since it sought to hold responsible the natal kin, who are 'strangers to the marital relationship'; the legatees, who may be too young or too old; or the waqf boards that may not have the adequate means to support all the claimants.

The judgment of the five-judge bench, delivered 15 years after the petition was filed and authored by Justice Rajendra Babu, is a brilliant example of

[39] Srimati Basu, 'Separate and Unequal: Muslim Women and Un-Uniform Family Law in India', *International Feminist Journal of Politics* 10, 4 (2008): Maitrayee Mukhopadhyay. 1998. *Legally Dispossessed: Gender, Identity and the Process of Law.* Calcutta: Stree. Sylvia Vatuk. 2001. '"Where Will She Go? What Will She Do?": Paternalism toward Women in the Administration of Muslim Personal Law in Contemporary India' in G.J. Larson (ed.) Religion and Personal Law in Secular India: A Call to Judgment. Pp. 226–38. Bloomington: Indiana University Press.

[40] (2001) 7 SCC 740.

judicial craftsmanship. Similar to the high court judgments that had read the MWA liberally to establish the husband's economic obligations, the judgment in *Danial Latifi* managed to secure economic protection for divorced Muslim women, without explicitly going against the legislature and without giving the conservative Muslim organizations the opportunity to object either. The judgment prefaced the consideration of the specific constitutional challenges to the Act, with a discussion of women's economic dependency in marriage and the consequent economic vulnerability upon divorce:

> In our society, whether they belong to the majority or the minority group, what is apparent is that there exists a great disparity in the matter of economic resourcefulness between a man and a woman. Our society is male dominated both economically and socially and women are assigned, invariably, a dependant role, irrespective of the class of society to which she belongs. A woman on her marriage very often, though highly educated, gives up her all other avocations and entirely devotes herself to the welfare of the family, in particular she shares with her husband, her emotions, sentiments, mind and body, and her investment in the marriage is her entire life, a sacramental sacrifice of her individual self and is far too enormous to be measured in terms of money.

Justice Babu emphasized that while it was difficult to compensate a woman for the emotional stress of marriage breakdown, it was 'universally recognized' that her livelihood must be secured through some means. It was unlikely, the judgment noted, that Muslim law envisaged a 'different kind of responsibility', and if it did, it was based on 'distortion of social facts'. From this perspective, and in view of the stated legislative intention which was to limit the holding of *Shah Bano*, the judges found the Act to have 'unreasonably discriminated' against Muslim women, and *prima facie*, unconstitutional. But despite this finding, the judgment upheld the Act. This was achieved by disregarding legislative intention and instead opting for a more redeeming reading of the Act.

Looking at the terminology used in the MWA ('reasonable and fair provision and maintenance to be made and paid'), the judgment inferred that the legislature in fact did not intend to overturn *Shah Bano*, but on the contrary, it wanted to accord statutory recognition to *Shah Bano*'s interpretation of the husband's post-divorce obligation towards the wife, within MPL itself. The judgment held that as per the scheme of the Act, the husband was required to contemplate the future needs of the wife and make provision for them at the time of divorce. The judges reasoned that while the Act stated that such provision had to be made during the waiting period, nothing in the Act suggested that such provision was to be made *for* the waiting period alone. Further, if the husband failed to make a reasonable and fair provision for the wife within the waiting period, and if the wife fell on hard times subsequently, she could enforce her right to adequate provision against the husband anytime, as long as she did not remarry. To that extent, the judgment held, the Act was not contrary to the spirit of Section 125 CrPC, but performed the same function as the latter.

Danial Latifi practically reconstructed the MWA using gender justice as its central pillar. From the point of harmonization, the most crucial move lay in holding that though codified in a separate, group-specific statute, the underlying objective of the Act was the same as that of the common law, Section 125 CrPC. This understanding guided the judicial approach in subsequent judgments of the Supreme Court, which in turn took recourse to other creative arguments to harmonize. The 2007 judgment in *Iqbal Bano* v. *State of UP*,[41] emerged out of a Magistrate awarding a Muslim woman a meagre Rupees 450 per month as maintenance under Section 125, CrPC. The husband opposed it, arguing that he had paid the deferred mehr within the idda as per the Act, which rendered Section 125 inapplicable. Now, following *Danial Latifi*, the wife was entitled to a reasonable and fair provision for herself under the MWA. The judges held that since the same court was authorized to hear petitions under both Section 125 CrPC as well as the MWA, a relief granted under the former could be treated as a relief granted under the latter.

In 2009, another division bench of the Supreme Court decided *Shabana Bano* v. *Imran Khan*,[42] where it held, following *Danial Latifi* and *Iqbal Bano*, that a divorced Muslim woman could seek maintenance from the former husband, under Section 125 CrPC, even after the idda. In a further move towards institutional harmonization, the Court held that family courts would have exclusive jurisdiction to hear maintenance petitions whether they are under the MWA or the CrPC. The 2014 judgment, *Shamim Bano* v. *Ashraf Khan*,[43] also foregrounds gender justice, once again the wife's post-divorce economic vulnerability as the pretext for harmonization. Here the husband divorced the wife while the latter's application for maintenance under Section 125 CrPC was pending. This application was dismissed by the Magistrate. Next, she filed an application under the MWA for the

41 (2007) 6 SCC 785.
42 (2010) 1 SCC 666.
43 (2014) 12 SCC.

recovery of mehr, ornaments, and other dues, and appealed the dismissal of the first application. The Allahabad High Court dismissed the appeal, holding that post-divorce she was entitled to claim maintenance only under the MWA, and that her access to the CrPC was barred unless the husband consents to be governed by the CrPC, as per Section 5 of the Act. On appeal before the Supreme Court, the judges upheld the wife's eligibility for maintenance under the CrPC even beyond the relief obtained by her under the Act. Significantly, the judges held that a Magistrate's wide power to grant relief under the CrPC would supersede the consent requirement instituted by the MWA. Arguably, this wide interpretation was justified by the nature of the problem that it was intended to remedy. Like Justice Rajendra Babu in *Danial Latifi*, Justice Dipak Misra invoked the economic consequences of divorce on women, and the 'duty' of the law as well as of the former husband:

> When the marriage breaks up, a woman suffers from emotional fractures, fragmentation of sentiments, loss of economic and social security and, in certain cases, inadequate requisites for survival.... It is the law's duty to recompense, and the primary obligation is that of the husband'.

Thus, the story of Muslim women's entitlement to post-divorce support did not end with the enactment of the MWA in 1986, or even with *Danial Latifi* that re-signified the Act both in terms of intent and content. While these are important signposts in the history of personal law reform in India, the post-*Danial Latifi* judgments of the Supreme Court, coming from diverse benches and yet furthering the same idea, tell us that *Danial Latifi* was not a one-off instance of judicial creativity, but was part of a wider pattern of harmonizing separate laws in the interest of common priorities through the use of judicial authority. Vrinda Narain has described this as the 'transformatory'[44] role played by the Supreme Court of India by privileging the socio-economic vulnerability of Muslim women over their religious identity. Sagnik Dutta[45] has shown how the Court's approach towards the rights of Muslim women shifted over time from minority 'accommodation' to one where the judges interwove moral, religious, and secular concerns to

[44] Vrinda Narain, 'The Supreme Court of India and Maintenance for Muslim Women: Transformatory Jurisprudence', in *Routledge Handbook of Gender in South Asia*, ed. Leela Fernandes (London and New York: Routledge, 2014), p. 100.

[45] Sagnik Dutta, 'From Accommodation to Substantive Equality: Muslim Personal Law, Secular Law, and the Indian Constitution 1985–2015', *Asian Journal of Law and Society* 4, 1 (2017).

recognize Muslim women's claims to substantive equality. In this section, I have identified yet another theme underlying the judges' interpretive strategy towards harmonization, namely, the commonality in women's post-divorce economic situation.

Beyond Religious Difference: Muslim Women and Economic Support under the PWDVA

Women's economic dependency within marriage has not only directed developments in personal law reform as we have seen in the previous section, but has also determined the shape of the legal response to domestic violence. The Indian feminist understanding of domestic violence has been different from the one shaping the issue in several Western jurisdictions and at the international level, in two respects. First, as opposed to the American radical feminist understanding that theorizes violence as the key instrument used by men to *subordinate women as a class*,[46] in Indian feminist discourses domestic violence is understood in the context of the structural inequalities within the family along multiple axes including age, control over resources, and gender.[47] Second, distinct from the appeal to the deterrent or ideological functions of criminal law encountered elsewhere, feminists in India have always been sceptical about the criminal law, often advocating its use by the victims of domestic violence only for strategic purposes.[48]

Criminal law has proved to be of limited use, as what women need more critically, when faced with violence, is shelter and means to sustain themselves and their children. Many women who succeed in getting their criminal complaints registered eventually decide not to pursue them in exchange of a favourable divorce settlement or to return to their marriages in the absence of any viable alternative for support or sustenance. Additionally, for many women from poor and marginalized groups, the police itself is the authoritarian face of the state and thus do not hold up any promise of protection. As an activist recounted the Muslim women's predicament regarding the police in the aftermath of the communal riots in Bombay in 1992–3, to a researcher:

[46] Leigh Goodmark, *A Troubled Marriage: Domestic Violence and the Legal System* (New York: New York University Press, 2011).

[47] A. Suneetha and Vasudha Nagraj, 'A Difficult Match: Women's Actions and Legal Institutions in the Face of Domestic Violence', *Economic and Political Weekly* 41, 41 (2006).

[48] Geetanjali Gangoli and Gopika Solanki, 'Defining Domestic Violence and Women's Autonomy in Law', *Socio-Legal Review* 12, 1 (2016).

> While the police is generally not keen to take up cases of domestic violence, if the complainant is a Muslim woman, they rush to arrest the man. After the riots, women feel that their problems multiply after going to the police. The police, as a part of the procedure, question the neighbours, who are terrified after being subjected to torture during the riots. So many innocent Muslims have been caught under TADA. This is another reason why (Muslim) women keep quite even after being beaten by their husbands.[49]

Coming from this context, feminist demands for legislation to address domestic violence in India emphasized the need for practical support for women, rather than an ideological commitment to dismantling the notional privacy of the 'home' by treating domestic violence as just another crime. This is reflected not only in the legislative proposals made by the state, but also in feminist responses to them. In 1994, the newly established National Commission for Women prepared the Domestic Violence to Women (Prevention) Bill that proposed civil remedies against violence and dispossession from home, and for economic relief. The draft bill was widely commended by feminist activists for prioritizing economic protection for victims of violence. Hailing the bill, the Bombay based feminist NGO, Majlis, wrote:

> The excellence of the Bill can perhaps be attributed to the fact that it accurately identifies that economic dependence, lack of residence and poor access to courts encourage a woman to tolerate domestic violence. Hence it seeks to provide her with economic rights to empower her, so that she may have viable options to escape from the violence within marriage without rendering her roofless.[50]

The 1994 draft bill did not reach the Parliament, but by the end of the decade a more detailed bill—developed by Lawyers Collective Women's Rights Initiative (LCWRI)—with a more sophisticated understanding of domestic violence and providing for more extensive civil remedies was in place. Introducing an early version of the new draft bill in 2000, the Lawyers Collective noted in a pamphlet:

> The breakdown of a marriage entails no economic consequences for a man.... A man can quite simply throw out his wife from the home and wait for her to

[49] Geetanjali Gangoli, *Indian Feminisms: Law, Patriarchy and Violence in India* (Hampshire: Ashgate Publishing Limited, 2007), p. 111.

[50] Majlis, Comments on the Domestic Violence Bill for discussion (1995). Available with the author, p. 1.

make her long-winding way through the courts for what ever *[sic]* little relief she can get. He can put her in fear of loosing *[sic]* custody of her children and agree to unconscionable compromises. It is in this context that there is a felt necessity for a law on domestic violence.[51]

A 2004 booklet on the draft bill similarly noted that 'in India, the prominent manifestation of domestic violence is first for the woman to be a prisoner of the house and then to be thrown out of the same'.[52] From this perspective, the most crucial legal remedy for women facing domestic violence, lay in recognizing their rights against dispossession from home and to monetary relief such as maintenance and compensation. The PWDVA, which was finally enacted in 2005, contained both.[53]

One of the most significant achievements of the PWDVA, due in large measure to the formulation of the issue by the feminist campaign that preceded it, was that it instituted legal norms governing relationships and resources within the conjugal/familial unit by completely bypassing the set of rules hitherto governing these subjects, that is, personal law. The PWDVA provided a new code governing the material dimensions of the relationships between husbands and wives; parents and children; and members of a household in general, and in the process, modified the pre-existing codes under group-specific personal law. In the rest of this section, I will substantiate this claim by examining appellate court decisions where Muslim women sought economic support and residence under the PWDVA in order to track both the discursive and concrete changes in how claims are made and how they are addressed by judges. I will show that the PWDVA has enabled the creation of common standards on four issues: access to maintenance; access to shared residence; maintenance and residence being delinked from the question of validity of marriage; and statutory provisions superseding the terms of private agreements governing marriage.

[51] Lawyers Collective Women's Rights Initiative, *Domestic Violence (Prevention) Bill 2000: A Lawyers Collective Proposal* (New Delhi: The Gondals Press, 2000), p. 4.

[52] Lawyers Collective Women's Rights Initiative, *Only Her Word: A National Campaign for a Law on Domestic Violence* (New Delhi: The Gondals Press, 2004), p. 45.

[53] Section 17 of the Act provided a victim woman the right to reside in her matrimonial home, irrespective of the ownership of the house; she could ask for a residence order to that effect, from a Magistrate, under Section 19. Further, under Section 20, she could ask for a range of monetary reliefs.

Maintenance

As in the case of 125 CrPC, a common plea taken by husbands is that a divorced Muslim woman is entitled to seek economic support only under the MWA, but not under the PWDVA. Judges have consistently held that a woman's religious affiliation is irrelevant to her claim for maintenance and other reliefs under the PWDVA. In the 2012 judgment, *Sameer* v. *Resmina*,[54] the Kerala High Court held, 'irrespective of caste, religion etc. any person who qualifies and comes within the definition of "aggrieved person" is entitled to canvass the reliefs provided under the Act'. In another 2011 judgment, *Syed Nadeem* v. *State*,[55] a Delhi High Court judge arrived at the same conclusion. Justice Rajiv Endlaw wrote:

> [the] Muslim Women Act would not come in the way of applicability of the provisions of the Domestic Violence Act to Mohammedans; if it were to be so held, owing to the Hindu Marriage Act, 1955 also containing provisions qua maintenance, Domestic Violence Act would not apply to Hindus also, making the same otiose.

We find a different rationale for the same holding in the 2013 Rajasthan High Court judgment, *Jakir Hussain* v. *State*,[56] where the judge reasoned that the PWDVA, being a subsequent legislation and a beneficial one, would supersede the provisions of the MWA.

This judicial affirmation of the uniform application of the PWDVA is connected to the judges' understanding of the Act as an instrument to secure the interests of women in relationships of economic dependency, thus aligning the judicial understanding of the Act with the feminist vision behind it. In *Jakir Hussain*, for instance, the judge locates the Act on a progressively widening scale of economic protection made available to divorced Muslim women, from the MWA of 1986 through the generously interpreted Section 125 CrPC, to the PWDVA of 2005. The 2013 Bombay High Court judgment in *Parvin Firoz Shaikh* v. *Firoz Sharfuddin Shaikh*[57] provides another

[54] Crl. M.C. No. 3336/2011. Order dated 8 October 2012, available at https://indiankanoon.org/doc/49334599/ (accessed 30 December 2017).

[55] W.P. (Crl) 887/2011. Order dated 15 June 2011, available at https://indiankanoon.org/doc/1548842/ (accessed 30 December 2017).

[56] Crim. Misc. Petition 572/2013. Order dated 8 April 2013, available at https://indiankanoon.org/doc/165665407/ (accessed 30 December 2017).

[57] Criminal W.P. 562/2011. Order dated 27 February 2013, available at https://indiankanoon.org/doc/38885865/ (accessed 30 December 2017).

example. Here the husband opposed the order of maintenance arguing that he had divorced the wife through a single irrevocable talaq before the filing of the application under the PWDVA, and therefore he was no longer obliged to pay maintenance under the Act. The judge turned to the manner in which *talaq* was pronounced and concluded that the evidence did not bear out any 'reasonable cause' behind the talaq as required by the Supreme Court's 2001 judgment in *Shamim Ara* v. *State of U.P.*,[58] but in fact, indicated the opposite. The judge's approach centres on this unthinking divorce and its effect on the economic well-being of the wife and children:

> Talaq must be for a reasonable cause; it should not be at the whims and fancies of the husband. The object and scope of the DV Act is to ensure maintenance to those, who need such protective shelter from the person under an obligation. The petitioner (the wife) obviously has to maintain two children (born) out of the wedlock, infirm, embattled and hapless. Naturally, the whims of the husband would not be permitted to deflate the provisions of the DV Act, which provides a room to claim maintenance.

Arguably, the mode of pronouncing talaq is immaterial to a claim under the PWDVA, but it is noteworthy that the judge makes a connection between the legal position against easy divorce and the rationale behind economic support for women—both features characterizing Indian family law in general.

A 2018 Bombay High Court judgment provides another example. In *Ali Abbas Daruwala* v. *Shehnaz Daruwala*,[59] the wife filed for divorce on two counts of cruelty under the DMM Act. Subsequently, she also filed a case under the PWDVA, asking for interim maintenance for herself and the children, which was granted by the family court. On appeal, the husband argued that the family court had erred in admitting the wife's application for interim maintenance since the DMM Act, under which the wife had sought divorce, did not have provisions for ancillary reliefs such as maintenance and custody. Dismissing the appeal, Justice Bharati Dangre held that not only did Section 26 of the PWDVA allow a woman to seek relief under the Act alongside relief already sought under other laws in other cases, but the two claims of the wife, that of divorce and maintenance, arise out of the same facts—what is 'cruelty' under the DMM Act is 'domestic violence' under the

58 2002 (7) SCC 518.

59 http://www.livelaw.in/woman-governed-by-muslim-personal-law-can-invoke-provisions-of-domestic-violence-act-and-seek-relief-bombay-hc-read-judgment/ (accessed 5 July 2018).

PWDVA—and to that extent, the family court was justified in passing an order of maintenance, even though the main case was that of divorce under the DMM Act.

Shared Residence

As far as maintenance is concerned, the developing jurisprudence under the PWDVA, taking cue from the judicial treatment given to the MWA and Section 125 CrPC, is premised on the Muslim woman's 'sameness' with women from other religious groups. There is wide judicial consensus discernable in decisions, both at the trial and appellate levels, that all women have the same economic predicament in the event of marriage breakdown, and therefore religious affiliation cannot be a reason to restrict access to maintenance. But Muslim woman's 'difference' could possibly resurrect in the matter of the right to residence, with inconsistent judicial approaches to divorced Muslim women's right to reside in the former matrimonial home. In the 2008 Madhya Pradesh High Court judgment, *Razzak Khan* v. *Shahnaz Khan*,[60] a single judge bench dismissed the husband's argument that allowing a divorced woman to reside in the former husband's house would amount to *haram*, that is, sin. On a plain reading of the definitions of 'aggrieved person',[61] 'domestic relationship',[62] 'shared household',[63] and the right to residence in the shared household, the judge did not find a legal basis to deny the divorced wife's right to reside in the former husband's home that he shared with other family members.

A 2014 Allahabad High Court judgment, however, held otherwise. In *Mohd. Waqar* v. *State of UP*,[64] the husband challenged the Magistrate's order directing him to provide the divorced wife a room in the house owned by him, food from his kitchen, and maintenance. Seeking a revision, the husband contended that a divorced Muslim wife's monetary claims were limited by the MWA, and that providing food and accommodation to a divorced wife, as was ordered by the Magistrate, was illegal and contrary to MPL. The judge dismissed the argument regarding the non-applicability of the PWDVA.

[60] 2008 (4) MPHT 413.

[61] Section 2(a), PWDVA.

[62] Section 2(f), PWDVA.

[63] Section 2(s), PWDVA.

[64] Criminal Revision Petition 161/2014. Order dated 6 May 2014, available at https://indiankanoon.org/doc/17790813/ (accessed 30 December 2017).

On maintenance, he directed the Magistrate to decide the issue upon a fresh inquiry into the allegations of domestic violence and financial situation of the wife. But on the right to residence, he held that since the fact of talaq was established by the wife's own admission, the Magistrate's order directing the provision of accommodation and food was 'erroneous and illegal'.

Though not directly on point, but a 2015 judgment of the Kerala High Court suggests that judges may be willing to prioritize safety of a woman over the propriety of her staying in the former husband's house. *Muhammad* v. *Maimunabi*[65] involved an interesting situation where the divorced wife had obtained a protection order and a residence order and was staying in the former matrimonial home for many years along with her grown up children and their families. The former husband, who had remarried in the meantime and had been staying in Saudi Arabia, sought revision of the residence order to the effect that the former wife would continue to stay on the first floor of the house, while him and his current wife would stay on the ground floor. The husband even offered to construct a separate staircase to independently access the first floor. The High Court judge dismissed the application primarily on the technical ground that the husband had sought revision under Section 25 of the PWDVA, which in fact allowed only an aggrieved party to seek discharge of an order. But in dismissing the husband's appeal, the judge also agreed with the lower courts' opinion that allowing the former to enter the house 'was likely to cause disturbance to the peaceful life of the respondent and her family'.

To be sure, unlike the case of maintenance, a divorced women's right to reside in the former husband's house *in general,* is on shaky ground. A 2013 survey of lower court orders showed that Magistrates rarely granted residence orders to divorced women.[66] Further, a 2015 Calcutta High Court judgment has held that the wording of Section 17—the provision that recognizes a woman's right to reside in the shared household—indicates that divorced women are excluded from its scope.[67] Justice Joymalya Bagchi

[65] Criminal Revision Petition 781/2015. Order dated 9 February 2015, available at https://indiankanoon.org/doc/103758222/ (accessed 30 December 2017).

[66] Lawyers Collective Women's Rights Initiative, 'Staying Alive: Evaluating Court Orders', Sixth Monitoring and Evaluation Report 2013 on the Protection of Women from Domestic Violence Act, 2005 (2013), pp. 76–8.

[67] *Prabir Kumar Ghosh* v. *Jharna Ghosh*, available at https://indiankanoon.org/doc/43830489/ (accessed 30 December 2017).

interpreted the words 'woman *in a* domestic relationship' in Section 17 to mean that only women who are currently in a domestic relationship are eligible to claim the right to reside. The Punjab and Haryana High Court also seems to have adopted the same reasoning in a 2016 judgment, reportedly observing that 'where the domestic relationship ceases, the provisions under the Act cannot be invoked'.[68] These inferences are incorrect for they disregard the fact that the term 'domestic relationship' has a statutory definition, which includes both current and past relationships through marriage. But in the event, other high courts adopt this interpretation too and it emerges as the dominant legal position, then *all* divorced women will be disentitled from claiming a right to reside in the former husband's house and not just Muslim women owing to any religion-based consideration, like a conduct being *haram*.

Access to Maintenance and Shelter Delinked from Marriage

Under the matrimonial statutes governing the other religious groups, the maintenance that can be asked for at the time of divorce or separation proceedings is dependent on the existence of a valid marriage. Similarly, under the MWA too, a divorced Muslim woman is entitled to claim maintenance provided she was 'married according to Muslim law'.[69] On the other hand, validity of marriage is irrelevant for claiming maintenance under 125 CrPC since this is granted by Magistrates following criminal procedure, who do not have jurisdiction over civil matters such as validity of marriage. Maintenance claims under the PWDVA are decided following the same principle as the CrPC, but where the PWDVA goes a step ahead of the CrPC is in applying the principle to a claim for the right to reside in the shared household or in an alternative accommodation as well. In the 2017 Delhi High Court judgment, *Shabana* v. *Shahid Beg*,[70] the wife was granted maintenance and alternative accommodation by the trial court. But on appeal, the district court reversed it, accepting the husband's argument that the wife had not been correctly divorced by her previous husband, which made his own marriage with her

[68] Surender Sharma, 'Divorced Women can't File Plaint under Domestic Violence Act: HC', *Hindustan Times*, 9 June 2016, available at http://www.hindustantimes.com/punjab/divorced-women-can-t-file-plaint-under-domestic-violence-act-hc/story-jBuMg458JNUregBSXSAnIL.html (accessed 30 December 2017).

[69] Section 2(a), Muslim Women (Protection of Rights on Divorce) Act, 1986.

[70] Criminal Revision Petition 380/2016. Judgment dated 9 August 2017, available at https://indiankanoon.org/doc/55240047/ (accessed 30 December 2017).

void, and as a result, he was not obliged to pay maintenance. Hearing the wife's appeal against this decision, the High Court judge noted that the evidence clearly established that the wife and the husband were in a 'domestic relationship', had lived in a 'shared household' and she had been subjected to 'domestic violence'. These ingredients, the judge noted, were adequate for a relief under the Act, but the district judge had instead 'misdirected himself in taking it upon himself to decide whether a valid marriage existed' between the parties. A court dealing with an application under the PWDVA was not competent to decide such questions, the judge clarified. He restored the trial court's order and further increased the amount to be paid by the husband for maintenance and alternative accommodation.

Private Agreements

On Muslim family law reform, *nikahnamas*, or written marriage contracts, have been proposed have been proposed as an instrument that could effectively protect the interests of women.[71] The standing of private agreements vis-à-vis statutory rights and obligations, therefore needs to be examined. It bears going over the facts of the 1978 *Bai Tahira*[72] case, referred to earlier, where the Supreme Court had encountered the question in relation to Section 125 CrPC. Here, the parties had entered into a consent decree at the time of divorce, as per which the husband had transferred some property to the wife, and the wife had undertaken to not claim anything more from the husband or his estate. Subsequently, the divorced wife, unable to maintain herself, sought further support under Section 125 CrPC. The lower courts rejected her case on the ground that she had not established neglect by the former husband. Before the Supreme Court, the husband contested the wife's appeal pointing out, among other things, the terms of the consent decree. Writing for a three judge-bench, Justice Krishna Iyer dismissed the argument reasoning that the parties had entered into the agreement in 1962, whereas the statutory right that the wife sought to enforce came into existence much later, in 1973. Justice Iyer held that 'no settlement of claims which does not have the special statutory right of the divorcee under s. 125 can operate to negate that claim'.

Under the group-specific matrimonial statutes, judges in both colonial and independent India have *predominantly* taken the above approach and

[71] A. Suneetha, 'Muslim Women and Marriage Laws: Debating the Model Nikahnama', *Economic and Political Weekly* 47, 43 (2012).

[72] Proviso to Section 488(3), Code of Criminal Procedure, 1893.

refused to uphold private agreements if they defeated the economic interests of the wife. In the 1945 Bombay High Court judgment, *Hirabai Bharucha* v. *Pirojshah Bharucha*[73]—case under the Parsi Marriage and Divorce Act, 1936—Justice Coyajee held such a contractual clause to be invalid in view of the public policy objective underlying the statutory right to maintenance. A division bench of the same high court took the same position in a 2004 case under the Hindu Marriage Act, 1955. In *Geeta Gokarna* v. *Satish Gokarna*,[74] Justice F. Rebello held that since the authority to decide whether or not to award maintenance and how much was conferred on the judge by statute, their jurisdiction could not be ousted by a private agreement. The position under the MWA, however, departs from these. In the 1992 judgment, *Mytheen* v. *Saphiya*,[75] Justice K. Thomas of the Kerala High Court reasoned that the statutory language of Section 3 of the MWA showed that the legislature intended the Act to supersede all the other laws pertaining to the conditions of divorce, but refrained from transgressing into a Muslim couple's private right to dissolve their marriage, extra-judicially (through *khul*' or *mubarat*).[76] The judge held that it was the duty of the court to uphold a valid agreement. Thus, if the wife had received an amount in 'full and final settlement of her claims' at the time of divorce and undertaken not to make any future claims, she could not seek a 'reasonable and fair provision' under the MWA at a later point.

Broadly speaking, the difference in judicial approach to the question of private agreement when it comes to maintenance depends on whether maintenance is understood as a matter of public interest or private right. In a 2017 judgment, the Bombay High Court addressed the question with respect to the PWDVA. In *Aiyaz Kasmali Hamirani* v. *State of Maharashtra*,[77] the parties had executed an agreement, in which they undertook to refer any difference or dispute between them and any question pertaining to the marriage, to arbitration. The relevant clause in the agreement provided that such

[73] AIR 1945 Bombay 537.

[74] AIR 2004 Bombay 345.

[75] Criminal Revision Petition 95/1991 and 535/1992. Judgment dated 12 July 1993. Kerala High Court.

[76] *Khul* is the mode of divorce where a wife offers to compensate the husband if he agrees to divorce her, and the same is accepted by the husband. When both parties mutually agree to dissolve the marriage and one makes the offer which the other accepts, it is referred to as *Mubarat*.

[77] Criminal Revision Petition 166/2015. Judgment dated 15 June 2017, available at https://indiankanoon.org/doc/61894416/ (accessed 30 December 2017).

questions or disputes shall be resolved by the relevant MPL and other applicable laws, but that the forum shall be the Reconciliation and Arbitration Board for Western India. While the arbitration process for divorce was underway, the wife approached the family court under the PWDVA, which allowed her interim maintenance. The husband opposed the relief arguing that the jurisdiction of the court was waived by virtue of the agreement and by the fact that the wife had herself submitted to the jurisdiction of the Board. The family court, the session's court, and on further appeal, the High Court too dismissed the husband's case. The High Court held that since the PWDVA was a benevolent legislation that provided women 'a platform to seek redressal and protection against domestic violence', accepting the husband's argument would amount to denying women that protection.

***

In this chapter, I have described and traced the evolution of the legal framework governing maintenance, and argued that the PWDVA performs a key function in this journey of legal change by bridging group-difference on a number of issues pertaining to rights and obligations within marriage. The following table (Table 7.1) provides a schematic representation of the legal trajectory that I have described in this chapter. The last row signifies the essence of harmonization: the borders of the boxes are in bold lines, indicating that groups are still relevant; but all the boxes are shaded with the same pattern signifying that the substantive rights and the institutional forum where they can be sought are common across groups.

I will conclude this chapter with a recent lower court judgment under the PWDVA that illustrates the degree of harmonization achieved with respect to economic support for women in the event of marriage breakdown in Indian family law, as of 2017. The Delhi District Court judgment in *Bilal Qureshi* v. *Shaista Qureshi*,[78] was in response to the husband's appeal against a trial court order awarding interim maintenance to the wife. The wife had filed an application under Section 12 of the PWDVA citing ill treatment by the husband and the in-laws: her jewelry was taken away; she was taunted for bringing insufficient dowry at the time of marriage; the husband and in-laws were unhappy that she gave birth to a girl and refused to bear the pregnancy related expenses; she was turned out of the matrimonial home; she was not allowed to meet the daughter and was threatened with 'dire consequences'

[78] Criminal Appeal No. 05/2017. Judgment dated 4 May 2017, available at https://indiankanoon.org/doc/96709194/ (accessed 30 December 2017).

Table 7.1 Women's Access to Maintenance on Marriage Breakdown

	Hindu	Muslim	Christian	Parsi	Civil
Till 1973	Hindu Marriage Act, 1955	Muslim Personal Law	Indian Divorce Act, 1869	Parsi Marriage and Divorce Act, 1936	Special Marriage Act, 1954
1973 to 1985(s. 125 CrPC: wife includes divorced wife)					
1986 to 2001(Muslim Women Act, 1986)					
2001 to 2005 (*Danial Latifi v. Union of India*)					
2006 onward (Domestic Violence Act, 2005)					

Source: Author.

whenever she attempted to meet her. In response to the wife's prayer that she did not have any source of income and had to turn to her natal family for support, the trial court had directed the husband to pay her Rupees 7,000 per month as interim maintenance.

The husband appealed the order, adopting a common strategy, wherein he argued that he had already divorced the wife by pronouncing talaq, which made the PWDVA inapplicable, and that he had limited financial means, as a result of which, he was unable to pay maintenance as per the trial court's order. Judge Hemani Malhotra's brief judgment, delivered on 4 May 2017, focuses only on the second issue, noting that the argument regarding talaq was irrelevant to a claim under the PWDVA. The judge turned to two Delhi High Court judgments dealing with maintenance under the Hindu Marriage Act, which had held that since in India, individuals, particularly those who were self-employed or worked in the unorganized sector, hardly revealed their actual income in order to avoid paying tax, courts should look at the lifestyle of the parties to assess their means.[79] In this case, the husband's business cards and his health club membership were taken to indicate that his economic means were higher than what he had claimed on record. Judge Malhotra therefore dismissed the appeal against the order of interim maintenance.

This rather mundane case perfectly illustrates my argument in this chapter regarding, (a) the dynamic interaction between group-specific and common elements in Indian family law, (b) the harmonizing function performed by the Domestic Violence Act, and (c) gender justice serving as the ground for harmonization. A Muslim woman approaches the state legal system seeking economic relief. She does so not under her 'own' group law, but under a law dealing with domestic violence that is applicable across religious groups. The husband opposes it using a group-specific and a group-neutral defense, but the judge rejects both of them. Instead, she frames the problem as a common one facing women in pursuit of maintenance, namely, husbands suppressing their actual incomes. The judge here uses an idea propounded under a statute governing the Hindus to grant to grant relief to the Muslim petitioner, in a case filed under a common law.

[79] *Bharat Hegde v Saroj Hegde*, 140 (2007) Delhi Law Times 16; *Radhika v. Vineet Rungta*, 110 (2004) Delhi Law Times 111.

SECTION III

Expectations from the Law and Its Enforcement

8. *Analysing Orders Granted under the PWDVA, 2005*

Aparna Chandra

Methodology

The aim of this chapter is twofold: one, to describe the trends and patterns of usage of the PWDVA; and two, to examine judicial approaches towards adjudication under the Act. The overall objective is to explore whether the law is being used and implemented in a manner true to the objects and purposes of the Act.

This chapter is based on an empirical analysis of orders from 14 states passed under the PWDVA between 1 April 2012 and 31 March 2013.[1]

[1] Andhra Pradesh, West Bengal, Uttarakhand, Tripura, Himachal Pradesh, Jharkhand, Kerala, Maharashtra, Odisha, Assam, Delhi, Sikkim, Mizoram, Nagaland. Since the volume of cases for Sikkim, Mizoram, and Nagaland were very small compared to the other states, these orders were clubbed together and studied to make comparison possible. In the rest of the report, these three states are collectively referred to as the North East states.

Approximately 7,000 orders from these states were made available to Lawyers Collective by the Supreme Court of India. A group of researchers at the Centre for Constitutional Law, Policy and Governance, National Law University, Delhi, first reviewed all the orders to remove insubstantial orders, that is, those orders which provided no details about the case. The bulk of such orders consisted of one-line adjournments, which provided no information to enable any analysis. After removing the insubstantial orders, around 4,200 orders remained. A quarter of these were selected randomly from each state, while ensuring that all districts of each state were represented in the final sample. Cumulatively, 1,055 cases were analysed. These cases consist of orders passed by magistrate courts, orders passed on appeal, as well as orders passed in cases where the parties have reached a settlement.

One key element of the PWDVA is that it recognizes that domestic violence takes place in a variety of familial settings, and is not limited to matrimonial violence. However, previous Monitoring and Evaluation Reports by Lawyers Collective have found that the law is rarely used in contexts other than the marital one. To investigate whether there are any distinct concerns, challenges, patterns of usage and implementation of the law in such cases, we studied all cases where the aggrieved person filed the complaint against a person other than her marital family. All cases filed against members of the natal family, against descendants, and against domestic partners are covered in this dataset. The entire dataset contains 89 such orders. The numbers indicate that the law continues to be used predominantly by women complaining of domestic violence against their marital relations. Very rarely is the law used to seek relief against a member of the natal family, descendants, or against partners in domestic relationships in the nature of marriage.

Each case that was studied was coded along 95 parameters. Given the large number of parameters, and the generally short length of orders passed under the Act, the dataset returned a number of null observations, where the data were either unavailable or irrelevant. These have been coded in the dataset as 'NA', and subtracted from the total number of observations for each variable.[2] While, due to the number of parameters, a high number of null observations was expected, it is concerning that in a significant number of cases basic information about the case like who is filing, against whom, alleging what, and asking for what relief, was also missing.

[2] The total number of cases before magistrates' courts in the dataset is 757. Subtracting the number of null observations from this gives us the number of cases where data is available and relevant for each variable. In studying each parameter, this number has been used as the basis to determine percentages of observations (Tables 8.1 and 8.2).

Table 8.1 Total Number of Cases Studied

Court	Andhra Pradesh	West Bengal	Uttarakhand	Tripura	Himachal Pradesh	Jharkhand	Kerala	Maharashtra	North East	Odisha	Assam	Delhi	Total
Magistrate Court	131	98	66	49	118	26	78	15	14	81	40	41	757
Appeals	27	23	27	2	17	8	4	3	1	10	8	7	**137**
Compromise	13	7	26	12	51	4	16	12	7	2	8	3	**161**
Total	**171**	**128**	**119**	**63**	**186**	**38**	**98**	**30**	**22**	**93**	**56**	**51**	**1,055**

Source: Author.

Table 8.2 Total Number of Cases against a Non-Marital Relation

Court	Andhra Pradesh	West Bengal	Uttarakhand	Tripura	Himachal Pradesh	Jharkhand	Kerala	Maharashtra	North East	Odisha	Assam	Delhi	Total
Magistrate Court	4	15	3	2 2	6	4	13	0	0	20	0	8	75
Appeals	2	4	1	0	1	0	0	0	0	0	0	1	**9**
Compromise	0	0	0	0	2	1	1	0	0	0	1	0	**5**
Total	**6**	**19**	**4**	**2**	**9**	**5**	**14**	**0**	**0**	**20**	**1**	**9**	**89**

Source: Author.

Apart from many orders having little data, in 64 of the 757 magistrate court cases (amounting to 8.5 per cent of the dataset), no reasons for granting or denying relief were provided in the order. Since an order is a public record of a decision of a court, and involves an exercise of public, often coercive, power, accountability requires that the order narrate the basic facts of the case and the reasoning behind the decision—aspects that are often missing from court decisions.

Further, given the nature of queries and parameters, in many instances, the dataset contains multiple observations for a single variable. An example is the variable 'relationship between the Respondent and the Aggrieved Person'. The aggrieved person may have filed the complaint against the husband as well as her in-laws. The data were coded in a way that ensured that in such cases, the same variable for a single case can return two (or multiple) observations. For this reason, in some of the following tables, the sum of all entries exceeds the total number of cases.

With these preliminary observations on methodology and content, in the next part of this chapter, I will begin by describing the patterns of usage of the legislation in the Magistrates' courts. Findings of the study regarding the profile of users, the nature of violence they complain of, and the types of reliefs they claim, are detailed in this part. In the next sub-part, I describe the adjudicatory practices under the Act before magistrates' courts. Findings relating to the reliefs granted, reasons therefore, and evidence relied on to grant the relief, are described in this part. So also, the procedures used by courts in delivering interim and final orders, and the use of allied mechanisms like that of protection officers, service providers, shelter homes, and so on, are examined here. In Part III, I describe the findings relating to appellate court orders and settlement orders. In Part IV, on the basis of the findings of the previous parts, I conclude with observations on best practices in adjudication under the Act, as well as areas of continuing concern and caution.

Magistrates' Courts

Patterns of Usage

The PWDVA sought to provide immediate relief and support to aggrieved persons through the mechanism of interim and ex-parte interim orders. To study whether the various procedures envisaged under the law are being used effectively to provide urgent relief to an aggrieved person, interim as well as final orders were examined as part of this study (Table 8.3).

Table 8.3 Nature of Orders

Nature of Order	Andhra Pradesh	West Bengal	Uttarakhand	Tripura	Himachal Pradesh	Jharkhand	Kerala	Maharashtra	North East	Odisha	Assam	Delhi	Total
Final	90	19	23	24	59	11	19	11	2	25	12	7	**302**
Exparte Final	16	7	5	5	15	2	7	0	0	7	3	6	**73**
Interim	18	56	20	12	35	13	10	1	7	35	7	23	**237**
Exparte Interim	4	15	10	4	3	0	42	0	4	12	11	5	**110**
Section 31	0	0	2	3	1	0	0	1	1	0	1	0	**9**
NA	3	1	6	1	5	0	0	2	0	2	6	0	**26**
TOTAL	**131**	**98**	**66**	**49**	**118**	**26**	**78**	**15**	**14**	**81**	**40**	**41**	**757**

Source: Author.

1. *Profile of Users*

a. **Religion:** The data indicate (Tables 8.4 and 8.5) that the PWDVA is primarily being used by married, divorced/separated, or widowed women against that marital relations. The PWDVA is a secular law, and applies to all persons regardless of their religious identity or applicable personal law. Consistent with this, the data indicate that women of all religious identities use the law roughly in the same proportion as their presence in the general population of the country.[3]

b. **Relationship between Parties** (Tables 8.6 and 8.7): As Table 8.6 indicates, 63.2 per cent cases were filed against the husband. In-laws were respondents in 73.4 per cent cases. Most cases in this group were filed against both the husband and the in-laws. However, cases filed only against in-laws were predominantly by widows.

   PWDVA is a gender specific legislation in that a case can only be filed by a woman, and (during the time period covered by this study) only against her male relatives.[4] The only exception is that where the aggrieved person files against her marital family or domestic partner, female relatives of the husband/partner can also be made respondents.[5] Therefore, an aggrieved person could not file a case against the female members of her natal family in the relevant time period. However, 33.6 per cent respondents in cases against non-marital family members were filed against women. Typically, in these cases, female relatives were made a party along with male relatives who fall within the definition of respondents under the Act. Surprisingly, in a large number of such cases, courts passed orders against the female relatives as well.

c. **Residential Status of the Aggrieved Person:** When the aggrieved person complains against her marital relations, she tends, by that time, to reside outside her marital home (Table 8.9). Of the 455 cases where this information was relevant and available, in only 13 per cent

[3] As a methodological point, the religion of the parties was noted only when this detail was specifically mentioned in the order or the order indicated the personal law under which parties married each other. Names of parties was not used as a proxy to determine their religion.

[4] In *Harsora* v. *Harsora*, Civil Appeal No. 10084 of 2016, decided on 6 October 2016, the Supreme Court held that Section 2(q) of the PWDVA is unconstitutional to the extent that it limits respondents to 'adult males'. In effect the judgment paved the way for a wider category of female relatives to be included as respondents under the Act.

[5] Section 2(q), PWDVA. See *Harsora* v. *Harsora*, Civil Appeal No. 10084 of 2016, decided on 6 October 2016.

of the cases was the woman still residing in the shared household at the time of filing the complaint. This indicates that a majority of the users of the law find it convenient to file cases only after they leave the shared household. The issue becomes significant because, as we shall see, judges often find the aggrieved person not residing in the shared household as a reason to deny her relief under the law.

d. **Length of Relationship:** An important finding of the study was that 45 per cent of cases were filed by women against their marital relations and partners after more than seven years of marriage/relationship (Table 8.10). Only 7.7 per cent of the cases involved marriages less than a year old. An oft repeated criticism of domestic violence laws is that such laws are misused by women who escalate ordinary issues relating to 'adjustment' within the marital home, into complaints of domestic violence. However, if 45 per cent of the cases of matrimonial violence are filed by women who have been in a relationship for longer than seven years, then the notion that a bulk of the claims are due to 'adjustment' issues, is patently false. Women file domestic violence complaints only after investing a significant amount of time (apart from other tangible and intangible resources like emotions) into the relationship. To think of these decisions as whimsical, impulsive, or the complaints as non-serious therefore appears to be derived from stereotypes about women's decision-making processes, and is not supported by empirical data.

e. **Duration of Violence:** Along the same lines, in 40.4 per cent cases women allege that they have filed the PWDVA complaint after enduring more than five years of violence. In 69.1 per cent of the cases, before filing the case under the PWDVA, the woman had made some complaint to a state authority regarding the violence. In 80.1 per cent cases, she had attempted conciliation, generally with the help of family members or the local panchayat. These data (Table 8.11) further serve to debunk the myth that domestic violence laws are used by trigger happy, maladjusted women, who file these cases on a whim, or in an effort to seek vengeance upon family members. Instead, the picture that emerges is of women investing a significant amount of time in the relationship, enduring long periods of violence, seeking help from family and community members, and even approaching the state for help, before cases under the PWDVA are filed.[6]

[6] This is not to state, of course, that women *should* put up with violence for a certain amount of time before they complain, or that their complaints should be taken seriously only if they have suffered for long durations. The only claim here is that the general myth surrounding the use of domestic violence laws is falsified by the data presented.

Table 8.4 Religion of the Aggrieved Person

Religion of the Aggrieved Person	Andhra Pradesh	West Bengal	Uttarakhand	Tripura	Himachal Pradesh	Jharkhand	Kerala	Maharashtra	North East	Odisha	Assam	Delhi	Total
Buddhist	0	0	0	0	0	0	0	1	0	0	0	0	**1**
Christian	6	0	0	0	0	0	5	0	0	0	0	0	**11**
Hindu	40	24	15	1	35	8	18	2	0	20	0	17	**180**
Muslim	6	6	1	2	0	5	4	0	0	1	3	4	**32**
Parsi	0	0	0	0	0	0	0	0	0	0	0	0	**0**
Sikh	0	1	0	0	2	0	0	0	4	0	0	0	7
Any Other	0	0	0	0	0	0	0	0	0	0	0	0	**0**
NA	79	67	50	46	81	13	51	12	10	60	37	20	**526**
TOTAL	**131**	**98**	**66**	**49**	**118**	**26**	**78**	**15**	**14**	**81**	**40**	**41**	757

Source: Author.

Table 8.5 Religion of the Respondent

Religion of the Respondent	Andhra Pradesh	West Bengal	Uttarakhand	Tripura	Himachal Pradesh	Jharkhand	Kerala	Maharashtra	North East	Odisha	Assam	Delhi	Total
Buddhist	0	0	0	0	0	0	0	1	0	0	0	0	**1**
Christian	6	0	0	0	0	0	6	0	0	0	0	0	**12**
Hindu	40	24	15	1	35	7	18	2	0	19	0	17	**178**
Muslim	6	6	1	2	0	5	4	0	0	1	3	4	**32**
Parsi	0	0	0	0	0	0	0	0	0	0	0	0	**0**
Sikh	0	1	0	0	2	0	0	0	4	0	0	0	7
Any Other	0	0	0	0	0	0	0	0	0	0	0	0	**0**
NA	79	67	50	46	81	14	50	12	10	61	37	20	**527**
TOTAL	**131**	**98**	**66**	**49**	**118**	**26**	**78**	**15**	**14**	**81**	**40**	**41**	757

Source: Author.

Table 8.6 Respondent's Relationship with Aggrieved Person

Respondent/ Relationship with A.P.	Andhra Pradesh	West Bengal	Uttarakhand	Tripura	Himachal Pradesh	Jharkhand	Kerala	Maharashtra	North East	Odisha	Assam	Delhi	Total
Husband/ Ex-husband	87	22	35	28	53	18	50	10	2	63	20	34	**422**
In-Laws	203	25	53	15	53	6	31	18	0	57	5	27	**490**
Husband's First Wife	0	0	0	0	0	0	0	0	0	1	0	0	**1**
Husband's Second Wife/ Subsequent Wife	6	0	1	0	0	0	0	1	0	0	0	0	**8**
Son(s)	0	3	2	1	1	0	9	0	0	0	0	2	**18**
Father and Step Father	3	1	0	0	2	1	2	0	0	0	0	1	**10**
(Female Relative Natal Family- Mother, Sister, Daughter, DIL)	3	1	0	0	1	0	8	0	0	0	0	0	**15**
Other relatives	6	1	0	0	0	0	6	0	0	2	0	1	**16**
Live-in partner	2	0	0	1	0	0	0	0	0	0	0	0	**3**
NA	1	11	13	10	13	1	9	0	0	13	15	3	**89**
TOTAL	**314**	**65**	**104**	**55**	**123**	**26**	**115**	**29**	**2**	**137**	**40**	**68**	**1078**

Source: Author.

Table 8.7 Respondent's Relationship with Aggrieved Person (Non-Marital Relations)

Respondent/ Relationship with A.P.	Andhra Pradesh	West Bengal	Uttarakhand	Tripura	Himachal Pradesh	Jharkhand	Kerala	Odisha	Delhi	Total
Father/Step Father	0	1	0	0	1	2	2	2	1	**9**
Son(s)	1	12	3	1	5	1	9	9	6	**47**
Brother	0	4	0	0	0	1	0	6	1	**12**
Brother-in-Law	1	0	0	0	0	0	0	0	0	**1**
Son-in-Law	0	1	0	0	0	0	1	0	0	**2**
Domestic Partner	1	0	0	1	0	0	0	0	0	**2**
Daughter-in-Law	0	2	0	0	4	0	4	8	3	**21**
Daughter(s)	0	0	0	0	1	0	1	0	0	**2**
Mother/Step Mother	0	0	0	0	0	0	3	0	0	**3**
Sister	2	1	0	0	0	0	0	6	1	**10**
Sister-in-Law	0	1	0	0	0	0	0	6	1	**8**
Other Relatives	1	4	0	0	0	0	3	3	1	**12**
TOTAL	**6**	**26**	**3**	**2**	**12**	**4**	**23**	**41**	**14**	**131**

Source: Author.

Note: The total number of entries in Tables 8.6 and 8.7 are higher than the total number of Magistrate cases because an aggrieved person can file against multiple relatives in a single case.

Table 8.8 Marital Status of the Aggrieved Person

Marital Status of the Aggrieved Person	Andhra Pradesh	West Bengal	Uttarakhand	Tripura	Himachal Pradesh	Jharkhand	Kerala	Maharashtra	North East	Odisha	Assam	Delhi	Total
Separated/ Divorced	6	1	2	0	2	0	0	0	0	1	0	2	**14**
Married	108	56	43	27	98	22	56	15	14	62	19	34	**554**
Relationship in the nature of marriage	1	0	0	0	0	0	0	0	0	0	0	0	**1**
Unmarried	1	0	0	1	1	0	0	0	0	2	0	0	**5**
Widow	10	8	5	0	1	1	6	0	0	2	0	2	**35**
NA	5	33	16	21	16	3	16	0	0	14	21	3	**148**
TOTAL	**131**	**98**	**66**	**49**	**118**	**26**	**78**	**15**	**14**	**81**	**40**	**41**	**757**

Table 8.9 Respondents' Residential Status

If Respondent is Husband/In-Law Residential Status of the Aggrieved Person	Andhra Pradesh	West Bengal	Uttarakhand	Tripura	Himachal Pradesh	Jharkhand	Kerala	Maharashtra	North East	Odisha	Assam	Delhi	Total
Living separately	40	11	10	3	23	9	8	6	6	20	2	12	150
Residing in the Natal Home	61	32	23	2	53	10	12	6	1	26	12	8	246
Residing in the Shared Household	6	6	11	1	9	0	11	0	3	4	0	8	59
NA	24	49	22	43	33	7	47	3	4	31	26	13	302
TOTAL	131	98	66	49	118	26	78	15	14	81	40	41	757

Source: Author.

Table 8.10 Length of Marriage/Relationship

Length of marriage/ Relationship in the nature of marriage before complaint was filed	Andhra Pradesh	West Bengal	Uttarakhand	Tripura	Himachal Pradesh	Jharkhand	Kerala	Maharashtra	North East	Odisha	Assam	Delhi	Total
1-3 years	19	6	5	2	16	3	1	5	1	7	1	2	**68**
3-5 years	13	2	8	2	6	0	0	0	0	5	1	4	**41**
5-7 years	10	4	4	0	7	7	1	3	4	3	0	2	**45**
Above 7 years	49	13	9	3	26	5	6	4	2	13	4	12	**146**
Upto 1 year	5	8	0	0	8	1	0	0	0	2	0	1	**25**
NA	35	65	40	42	55	10	70	3	7	51	34	20	**432**
TOTAL	**131**	**98**	**66**	**49**	**118**	**26**	**78**	**15**	**14**	**81**	**40**	**41**	757

Source: Author.

Table 8.11 Duration of Violence

Duration of violence before PWDVA complaint made	Andhra Pradesh	West Bengal	Uttarakhand	Tripura	Himachal Pradesh	Jharkhand	Kerala	Maharashtra	North East	Odisha	Assam	Delhi	Total
Upto 6 months	3	1	1	0	3	0	0	2	0	2	0	2	**14**
6 months–1 year	8	8	0	1	9	2	1	3	0	1	0	0	**33**
1–3 years	26	7	7	1	16	2	2	3	0	7	0	4	**75**
3–5 years	11	2	6	4	6	2	1	0	0	4	1	2	**39**
>5 years	34	8	8	2	23	5	3	4	6	11	1	4	**109**
NA	49	72	44	41	61	15	71	3	8	56	38	29	**487**
TOTAL	**131**	**98**	**66**	**49**	**118**	**26**	**78**	**15**	**14**	**81**	**40**	**41**	757

f. **Pending Litigation:** Close to half the cases filed under PWDVA (46.9 per cent), also have Section 498A, IPC cases pending. Nearly a quarter of the cases (23.4 per cent) have pending maintenance cases under Section 125 CrPC or the relevant personal laws, and 14.4 per cent cases have pending divorce cases (Table 8.15).

2. *Types of Violence Alleged and Reliefs Sought*

a. **Types of Violence Alleged:** Aggrieved persons allege physical abuse, verbal and emotional abuse, and economic abuse in roughly the same proportion (Table 8.16). Sexual abuse is alleged in a very small number of cases. While the reasons for this could vary from the continuing lack of societal recognition of sexual abuse as a form of violence, to women's reluctance to report such abuse due to a culture of shame and silence surrounding sexual violence; the PWDVA is the closest metric for estimating the potential impact of criminalization of marital rape. We know from the National Family Health Survey 2005–6 that about 8.5 per cent married women report having faced sexual violence from their current husbands.[7] This number is one indicator of the prevalence of sexual violence in the society in general. In this light, the low number of allegations of sexual abuse under the PWDVA signifies under-utilization of the Act to seek relief from sexual violence, and not an under-occurrence of such abuse. These low reporting figures also indicate that fears that criminalization of marital rape will lead to rampant misuse are overstated, since, even where women do have the option to report sexual violence, they rarely do so.[8]

Note again, that since one case can (and often does) involve allegations of multiple types of violence, the sub-parameters above do not correspond to the total number of cases where violence of a particular type (physical, verbal or emotional, sexual or economic) was alleged. So, also the sum of the types of violence is greater than the total number of cases before the Magistrates' courts.

[7] Ministry of Health and Family Welfare, Government of India, *National Family Health Survey 2005–06*, Chapter 15.

[8] Of course, there are many other stronger, more principled, arguments for why the marital rape exemption in Section 375, IPC should be removed. Most importantly, such a law is at odds with a Constitution that recognizes the right to bodily integrity, sexual autonomy, equality, and right to life with dignity of women.

Table 8.12 Prior Complaints

Prior to the present complaint had the AP ever complained of DV before any state authority?	Andhra Pradesh	West Bengal	Uttarakhand	Tripura	Himachal Pradesh	Jharkhand	Kerala	Maharashtra	North East	Odisha	Assam	Delhi	Total
No.	24	4	3	2	8	5	2	7	0	4	0	1	**60**
Yes and the matter is ongoing	14	7	2	1	4	0	0	1	0	6	0	0	**35**
Yes and the matter was settled	9	2	4	0	19	5	0	0	4	3	0	0	**46**
Yes but present status not known.	14	6	4	1	11	1	0	0	1	2	0	0	**40**
Yes but the complaint was not entertained/ rejected	2	0	1	2	2	1	0	0	0	3	0	0	**11**
Yes under the PWDVA itself and an order was issued	1	0	1	0	0	0	0	0	0	0	0	0	**2**
NA	67	79	51	43	74	14	76	7	9	63	40	40	**563**
TOTAL	**131**	**98**	**66**	**49**	**118**	**26**	**78**	**15**	**14**	**81**	**40**	**41**	757

Source: Author.

Table 8.13 Attempts to Reconcile

Was any attempt made at compromise or reconciliation either before or after filing the complaint?	Andhra Pradesh	West Bengal	Uttarakhand	Tripura	Himachal Pradesh	Jharkhand	Kerala	Maharashtra	North East	Odisha	Assam	Delhi	Total
No	22	0	0	2	8	1	1	0	0	1	1	7	**43**
Yes	59	10	8	8	41	8	8	3	4	16	3	7	**175**
NA	50	88	58	39	69	17	69	12	10	64	36	27	**539**
TOTAL	**131**	**98**	**66**	**49**	**118**	**26**	**78**	**15**	**14**	**81**	**40**	**41**	**757**

Source: Author.

Table 8.14 Entity Mediating the Reconciliation Attempt

Who mediated the reconcilliation attempt?	Andhra Pradesh	West Bengal	Uttarakhand	Tripura	Himachal Pradesh	Jharkhand	Kerala	Maharashtra	North East	Odisha	Assam	Delhi	Total
Court referred	1	1	0	3	3	0	0	0	1	4	1	4	18
Family	15	3	1	2	2	2	1	2	0	5	1	0	34
NGO	0	0	0	0	0	0	0	0	1	1	0	0	2
Panchayat	31	0	2	0	13	1	0	0	0	0	1	1	49
PO	1	1	0	0	4	0	0	1	1	0	0	0	8
Police	2	0	0	0	5	2	1	0	0	2	0	1	13
Any Other	2	0	3	2	3	2	4	0	1	2	0	0	19
NA	79	93	60	42	88	19	72	12	10	67	37	35	614
TOTAL	131	98	66	49	118	26	78	15	14	81	40	41	757

Source: Author.

Table 8.15 Pending Litigation

Pending Litigation	Andhra Pradesh	West Bengal	Uttarakhand	Tripura	Himachal Pradesh	Jharkhand	Kerala	Maharashtra	North East	Odisha	Assam	Delhi	Total
Divorce	4	2	0	0	1	1	3	0	1	3	0	1	**16**
Maintenance	5	5	2	3	4	0	2	1	0	4	0	0	**26**
Property suit	2	0	0	0	0	0	1	0	0	0	0	2	**5**
Custody and Guardianship	0	0	0	0	0	0	0	0	0	0	0	1	**1**
Restitution of conjugal rights under Hindu Marriage Act	6	2	2	2	0	0	0	0	0	2	0	0	**14**
Section 498-A IPC	25	8	2	3	4	2	1	1	0	6	0	0	**52**
Any Other	4	1	4	0	1	3	2	0	0	1	0	0	**16**
NA	91	84	59	44	108	20	69	13	13	68	40	37	**646**
TOTAL	**137**	**102**	**69**	**52**	**118**	**26**	**78**	**15**	**14**	**84**	**40**	**41**	**776**

Source: Author.

Table 8.16 Type of Abuse Alleged

Abuse Alleged	Andhra Pradesh	West Bengal	Uttarakhand	Tripura	Himachal Pradesh	Jharkhand	Kerala	Maharashtra	North East	Odisha	Assam	Delhi	Total
Physical Abuse	**95**	**43**	**52**	**10**	**82**	**14**	**29**	**10**	**10**	**37**	**11**	**25**	**418**
Verbal and Emotional Abuse	**99**	**39**	**53**	**7**	**74**	**12**	**24**	**14**	**9**	**41**	**11**	**26**	**409**
Doubting AP's Character	22	0	6	1	17	1	6	2	0	1	1	0	57
Dowry Related Abuse	46	11	20	3	24	6	0	5	0	21	9	16	161
Abuse Related to Child Bearing	15	2	3	0	7	0	0	3	0	3	0	0	33
Restrictions on Liberty	8	2	3	0	13	1	0	0	1	0	0	1	29
Caste based abuse	1	0	0	0	1	0	0	0	0	1	0	0	3
Threatening to kill the AP	19	2	8	0	11	0	2	1	0	6	0	3	52
Marriage related threats	18	4	6	2	4	0	0	2	0	6	1	0	43
Others	62	33	48	3	48	8	20	13	8	22	4	13	282
Sexual Abuse Alleged	7	4	2	1	5	1	2	**0**	**0**	3	**0**	1	**26**

(Cont'd)

Table 8.16 (*Cont'd*)

Abuse Alleged	Andhra Pradesh	West Bengal	Uttarakhand	Tripura	Himachal Pradesh	Jharkhand	Kerala	Maharashtra	North East	Odisha	Assam	Delhi	Total
Economic Abuse Alleged	**114**	**48**	**39**	**14**	**74**	**20**	**37**	**9**	**3**	**48**	**9**	**25**	**440**
Maintenance and Necessity	64	34	35	8	55	9	13	8	4	31	3	18	282
Alienation/ Dis possession (Abuse Regarding Propoerty and Shelter)	111	41	44	11	57	24	33	8	0	37	8	17	391
Restriction on Economic Independence -AP is not allowed to work or join her job after the marriage	2	0	1	1	1	0	0	0	0	0	0	0	5
Any Other	1	2	2	0	3	0	2	1	1	1	0	1	14

Source: Author.

Verbal and emotional abuse alleged by aggrieved persons include, (*a*) doubting the aggrieved person's character by casting aspersions on her character, questioning her child's legitimacy, and claiming that the aggrieved person is not worthy of being the respondent's wife; (*b*) dowry-related abuses, including insults for not bringing enough dowry; (*c*) abuses regarding child-bearing, such as insults for not having a male child or bearing a female child, or coercing the aggrieved person to abort her child; (*d*) restrictions on the aggrieved person's liberty, such as not allowing her to visit her parents, not allowing her to meet her children, forcing her to get married, or not allowing her to marry the person of her choice; (*e*) threats to kill the aggrieved person; (*f*) caste-based abuses; (*g*) divorce or re-marriage related threats, like threatening the aggrieved person with divorce, or threatening to re-marry; and, (*h*) other abuses, such as using abusive words, ridiculing the aggrieved person's disability, threatening to dispossess the aggrieved person from her matrimonial home, or treating her like a domestic help.[9]

Economic abuse alleged by aggrieved persons include (*a*) abuse relating to maintenance and necessities, such as not providing the aggrieved person with basic necessities, or money for her maintenance, desertion by the husband leading to denial of necessities, cutting off electricity to the premises occupied by the aggrieved person, or not providing support for the educational needs of the children; (*b*) abuse relating to alienation of or dispossession from property, such as dispossession from the matrimonial or the family home, denial of share in the property, alienation of investments, movable or immovable property, especially the aggrieved person's stridhan, not returning her stridhan, stopping the payment of rent for the shared household, and eviction from rented accommodation in collusion with the landlord; (*c*) restriction on economic independence, like not allowing the aggrieved person to work or join her job after the marriage.

b. **Motives for Violence:** Many orders also contain allegations about the reason why the respondent has been committing the acts of violence. While these reasons are based on the personal experience of the aggrieved persons rather than any independent determination of the respondent's motive, these data present a picture of the causes of domestic violence (Table 8.17). Of the 355 cases for which this data was available, 73.8 per cent cases cited dowry as the reason for

[9] It should be noted that considering treatment as a domestic help as an abuse points to a larger systemic concern about the treatment of domestic help in general, and highlights the need for law to protect their interests.

violence. Alcoholism and a second marriage or adulterous relationship were other significant reasons cited for violence.

c. **Reliefs Sought**: Complaining of physical, verbal, emotional, economic, and sometimes sexual abuse, aggrieved women seek a variety of relief under the Act. Monetary relief, residence orders, and protection orders are the most sought after reliefs, while temporary custody is sought in a limited number of cases. Compensation for injuries, mental trauma, and emotional distress is not sought with the same regularity as the other reliefs (Table 8.18 to 8.24).

As expected, the most frequently sought protection order is to restrain the respondent from committing further acts of domestic violence.

Residence orders sought predominantly comprise orders restraining the respondent from changing the status quo with respect to the aggrieved person's right to residence. This includes restraining the respondent from dispossessing the aggrieved person from the shared household, or otherwise disturbing her possession of the shared household, restraining the respondent or his relatives from entering any portion of the shared household in which the aggrieved person resides, restraining the respondent from alienating or disposing off the shared household, and restraining the respondent from renouncing his rights in the shared household. Similarly, orders are sought from courts directing the respondent to secure the same level of alternate accommodation for the aggrieved person or pay the rent for the same. Where the aggrieved person has already been disposed from the property, orders are sought to restore status quo ante, and direct the respondent to return to the possession of the aggrieved person her property, and direct the respondent to pay the rent or EMI of the house, in case he has stopped doing so.

Monetary relief is the most frequently claimed remedy under the Act. Orders are sought for the aggrieved person's maintenance, including orders directing the respondent to pay monthly or lump sum maintenance for the aggrieved person and/or her children; restitution for loss such as loss of earnings, expenses incurred for medical treatment, litigation expenses, and relief for the loss caused due to the destruction, damage, or removal of any property from the control of the aggrieved person. Other types of monetary reliefs sought include direction to the respondent's employer or a debtor to pay to the aggrieved person or to deposit with the court a portion of the salaries or debt, to be adjusted towards the monetary relief payable by the respondent.

Table 8.17 Alleged Motives for Violence

Alleged Reasons for Violence	Andhra Pradesh	West Bengal	Uttarakhand	Tripura	Himachal Pradesh	Jharkhand	Kerala	Maharashtra	North East	Odisha	Assam	Delhi	Total
Alcoholism	15	3	4	0	28	0	13	0	2	4	0	2	**71**
Desertion	4	0	0	0	0	0	0	0	0	3	0	3	**10**
Dowry	82	27	21	4	41	9	5	9	0	39	8	17	**262**
Relating to child birth	10	1	2	0	10	0	1	2	0	1	1	0	**28**
Second Marriage or Adultrous Relationship	13	6	4	3	3	8	7	1	0	10	3	3	**61**
Any Other	4	5	2	0	0	2	3	1	0	3	1	0	**21**
NA	34	60	39	43	57	11	56	4	12	32	31	23	**402**
TOTAL	**162**	**102**	**72**	**50**	**139**	**30**	**85**	**17**	**14**	**92**	**44**	**48**	**855**

Source: Author.

Table 8.18 Protection Order Sought

Protection Order Sought	Andhra Pradesh	West Bengal	Uttarakhand	Tripura	Himachal Pradesh	Jharkhand	Kerala	Maharashtra	North East	Odisha	Assam	Delhi	Total
No. of Cases in which Protection Order was Sought													
No. of Cases in which Protection Order Sought	73	35	20	2	49	6	40	11	5	27	9	5	**282**
Types of Protection Orders Sought													
Prohibit the Respondent from aiding or abetting in the commission of acts of DV	3	2	2	0	3	0	2	4	0	2	0	0	**18**
Restrain the Respondent from entering the place of employment of the AP the children's school or any other place frequented by the AP	2	1	1	0	0	0	0	4	0	1	0	0	**9**

Protection Order Sought	Andhra Pradesh	West Bengal	Uttarakhand	Tripura	Himachal Pradesh	Jharkhand	Kerala	Maharashtra	North East	Odisha	Assam	Delhi	Total
Restraining the Respondent from alienating any assets operating bank lockers or bank accounts used by both the parties	4	0	0	0	1	0	0	2	0	0	0	0	7
Restraining the Respondent from alienating the AP's Stridhan	2	1	1	0	1	0	0	0	0	0	0	0	5
Restraining the Respondent from communicati ng in any manner including personal oral or written or electronic or telephonic contact with the AP or any of her relatives	5	1	0	0	0	0	0	5	0	0	0	0	**11**

(Cont'd)

Table 8.18 (*Cont'd*)

Protection Order Sought	Andhra Pradesh	West Bengal	Uttarakhand	Tripura	Himachal Pradesh	Jharkhand	Kerala	Maharashtra	North East	Odisha	Assam	Delhi	Total
Restraining the Respondent from entering the premise of the AP	3	0	1	0	1	1	4	4	0	3	0	1	**18**
Restraining the Respondents from committing any further acts of DV	31	12	12	0	27	0	25	2	2	14	8	3	**136**
Restrict the Respondent from misbehaving with the AP her dependants and other relatives in any manner	12	0	1	0	2	0	0	2	0	0	0	0	**17**
Any Other	30	22	7	2	21	5	10	0	3	9	0	1	**110**
NA	58	63	46	47	69	20	38	4	9	54	31	36	**475**
TOTAL	**150**	**102**	**71**	**49**	**125**	**26**	**79**	**27**	**14**	**83**	**39**	**41**	**806**

Source: Author.

Table 8.19 Residence Orders Sought

Residence Order Sought	Andhra Pradesh	West Bengal	Uttarakhand	Tripura	Himachal Pradesh	Jharkhand	Kerala	Maharashtra	North East	Odisha	Assam	Delhi	Total
No. of Cases in which Residence Order was Sought													
No. of Cases in which Residence Order Sought	72	37	25	10	44	8	56	11	3	22	12	17	**317**
Types of Residence Orders Sought													
Restraining/Maintaining Status Quo	44	12	21	2	10	3	27	7	2	14	7	14	**163**
New/Separate Accommodation	19	10	5	2	12	2	2	9	0	3	3	7	**74**
Restoring Status Quo Ante	14	8	3	7	6	2	3	2	0	0	2	1	**48**
Any Other	16	19	4	1	21	4	8	0	1	11	1	1	**87**
NA	59	61	41	39	74	18	22	4	11	59	28	24	**440**
TOTAL	**152**	**110**	74	51	123	29	62	22	14	87	41	47	**812**

Source: Author.

Table 8.20 Monetary Relief Sought

Monetary Relief Sought	Andhra Pradesh	West Bengal	Uttarakhand	Tripura	Himachal Pradesh	Jharkhand	Kerala	Maharashtra	North East	Odisha	Assam	Delhi	Total
No. of Cases in which Monetary Relief was Sought													
No. of Cases in which Monetary Relief Sought	110	58	41	9	75	19	44	14	3	53	22	33	**481**
Types of Monetary Relief Sought													
Maintenance	130	78	52	11	92	29	44	24	2	70	40	56	**628**
Restitution	30	15	10	0	10	3	0	18	0	15	2	2	**105**
Others	26	7	5	1	14	1	5	3	2	10	0	0	**74**
NA	21	40	25	40	43	7	34	1	11	28	18	8	**276**
TOTAL	**207**	**140**	**92**	**52**	**159**	**40**	**83**	**46**	**15**	**123**	**60**	**66**	**1,083**

Source: Author.

Table 8.21 Extent of Monetary Relief Sought

Extent of Monetary Relief Sought	Total	West Bengal	Uttarakhand	Tripura	Himachal Pradesh	Jharkhand	Kerala	Maharashtra	North East	Odisha	Assam	Delhi	Total
Below 500	0	0	0	0	0	0	0	0	0	0	0	0	**0**
500–999	0	0	0	0	0	1	0	0	0	0	0	0	**1**
1,000–4999	10	6	3	3	3	4	5	0	0	9	3	0	**46**
5,000–9999	32	15	5	1	21	6	11	1	0	14	3	4	**113**
10,000–49,999	34	18	22	0	17	5	2	9	0	13	2	8	**130**
50,000–99,999	3	0	1	0	1	1	0	1	0	1	0	1	**9**
Above 1 Lakh	12	2	3	0	0	0	0	2	0	3	0	1	**23**
Above 1 Crore	0	0	0	0	0	0	0	0	0	0	0	0	**0**
NA	53	59	37	46	78	9	42	2	14	48	32	27	**447**
TOTAL	**144**	**100**	**71**	**50**	**120**	**26**	**60**	**15**	**14**	**88**	**40**	**41**	**769**

Source: Author.

Table 8.22 Temporary Custody Sought

Temporary Custody Sought	Andhra Pradesh	West Bengal	Uttarakhand	Tripura	Himachal Pradesh	Jharkhand	Kerala	Maharashtra	North East	Odisha	Assam	Delhi	Total
					No. of Cases in which Temporary Custody was Sought								
No. of cases in which Temporary Custody was sought	5 5 5 5 5	2	4	1	5	1	25	1	1	2	0	3	**50**
					Types of Temporary Custody Sought								
Temporary custody of the minor child	2 5 5 5	0	1	0	4	1	0	1	0	1	0	3	**13**
Visitation Rights	0 5	0	0	1	0	0	0	0	0	0	0	0	**1**
Any Other	3	2	3	0	1	0	1	0	1	1	0	0	**12**
NA	126	96	62	48	113	25	77	14	13	79	40	38	**731**
TOTAL	**131**	**98**	**66**	**49**	**118**	**26**	**78**	**15**	**14**	**81**	**40**	**41**	757

Source: Author.

Table 8.23 Compensation Order Sought

Compensation Order Sought	Andhra Pradesh	West Bengal	Uttarakhand	Tripura	Himachal Pradesh	Jharkhand	Kerala	Maharashtra	North East	Odisha	Assam	Delhi	Total
					No. of Cases in which Compensation Order was Sought								
No. of cases in which Compensation Sought	66	20	12	1	22	6	32	10	0	18	8	4	**199**
					Types of Compensation Sought								
Compensation claimed for mental torture and emotional distress caused due to acts of DV.	40	5	6	0	16	3	5	9	0	9	7	4	**104**
Compensation claimed for physical injuries caused by the acts of DV.	19	1	5	0	5	2	1	6	0	2	5	3	**49**
Any Other	22	15	6	1	6	3	7	1	0	9	0	0	**70**
NA	65	78	54	48	96	20	46	5	14	63	32	37	**558**
TOTAL	**146**	**99**	**71**	**49**	**123**	**28**	**59**	**21**	**14**	**83**	**44**	**44**	**781**

Source: Author.

Table 8.24 Extent of Compensation Sought

Extent of Compensation Sought	Andhra Pradesh	West Bengal	Uttarakhand	Tripura	Himachal Pradesh	Jharkhand	Kerala	Maharashtra	North East	Odisha	Assam	Delhi	Total
Below 500	0	0	0	0	0	0	0	0	0	0	0	0	**0**
500–999	0	0	0	0	0	0	0	0	0	0	0	0	**0**
1,000–4999	0	0	0	0	0	0	0	0	0	1	0	0	**1**
5,000–9999	0	0	0	0	0	1	0	0	0	0	0	0	**1**
10,000–49,999	1	0	1	0	3	1	0	0	0	2	1	0	**9**
50,000–99,999	4	2	0	0	2	0	3	1	0	1	1	1	**15**
Above 1 Lakh	42	7	7	0	11	2	4	9	0	8	1	3	**94**
Above 1 Crore	0	0	0	0	0	0	0	0	0	0	0	0	**0**
NA	84	89	58	49	102	22	71	5	14	69	37	37	**637**
TOTAL	**131**	**98**	**66**	**49**	**118**	**26**	**78**	**15**	**14**	**81**	**40**	**41**	757

Source: Author.

Temporary custody is sought in a limited number of cases, and primarily deal with the custody of minor children.

While compensation is not sought as frequently as some of the other reliefs, in the cases where the aggrieved person does ask for compensation, she most often seeks it for mental trauma and emotional distress caused due to acts of domestic violence.

Adjudication under the Act

Reliefs Granted, Reasoning, and Evidence

Monetary relief is not only the most sought after remedy, but is also the relief that was most likely to be granted rather than denied, compared to other reliefs. Courts granted monetary relief in 84.5 per cent of the cases where it was sought, compared to 75.6 per cent for protection orders, 70.1 per cent for residence orders, and only 50.7 per cent for compensation orders (Tables 8.25 to 8.33).

The most frequently granted protection order is to restrain the respondent from committing further acts of domestic violence (Table 8.26). Maintaining status quo and restraining the respondent from disposing the aggrieved person from the shared household is the most frequently granted residence order. In close to half the cases (46.8 per cent) where residence order is granted (Table 8.27), the respondent is directed to secure alternative accommodation for the aggrieved person. Orders to pay maintenance to the aggrieved person form the bulk of orders relating to monetary relief. Restitution for losses incurred was granted in only 8 per cent cases, even though restitution was sought in 21.8 per cent cases where the aggrieved person petitioned for monetary relief. Therefore, though on the one hand, courts have the highest acceptance rate for monetary relief, they have the lowest acceptance rate for compensation orders, as well as a low rate of grant of restitution. This indicates that judges generally see the PWDVA as a tool for protecting women from present or future violence or economic abuse. They do not give adequate attention to the restitutive justice aspect of the law.

Table 8.25 Order of the Court

Order	Andhra Pradesh	West Bengal	Uttarakhand	Tripura	Himachal Pradesh	Jharkhand	Kerala	Maharashtra	North East	Odisha	Assam	Delhi	Total	Acceptance Rate
Total No. of Cases	131	98	66	49	118	26	78	15	14	81	40	41	757	
Protection Order														
Granted	33	26	20	8	54	4	48	3	7	20	10	5	238	75.6
Denied	34	9	5	3	10	1	6	0	1	5	0	3	77	
NA	64	63	41	38	54	21	24	12	6	56	30	33	442	
Residence Order														
Granted	38	24	17	8	36	8	40	7	2	18	12	10	220	70.1
Denied	33	13	10	4	12	1	8	1	1	2	1	8	94	
NA	60	61	39	37	70	17	30	7	11	61	27	23	443	
Monetary Relief														
Granted	86	45	29	12	80	20	33	10	3	48	29	29	424	84.5
Denied	30	9	11	2	7	1	3	0	1	7	2	5	78	
NA	15	44	26	35	31	5	42	5	10	26	9	7	255	
Temporary Custody														
Granted	4	1	1	1	5	0	1	0	3	1	1	2	20	69.0
Denied	0	2	2	2	1	0	0	0	0	0	0	2	9	
NA	127	95	63	46	112	26	77	15	11	80	39	37	728	
Compensation Order														
Granted	24	5	7	2	10	4	7	3	0	8	3	1	72	50.7
Denied	38	5	3	2	5	2	6	1	0	6	0	2	70	
NA	69	88	56	45	103	20	65	11	14	67	37	38	625	

Source: Author.

Table 8.26 Types of Protection Order Granted

Protection Order Granted (Section 18)	Andhra Pradesh	West Bengal	Uttarakhand	Tripura	Himachal Pradesh	Jharkhand	Kerala	Maharashtra	North East	Odisha	Assam	Delhi	Total
Prohibit the Respondent from aiding or abetting in the commission of acts of DV	2	8	3	1	7	3	1	0	1	4	0	0	**30**
Restrain the Respondent from entering the place of employment of the AP the children's school or any other place frequented by the AP	2	3	2	0	0	0	0	1	0	0	0	0	**8**
Restraining the Respondent from alienating any assets operating bank lockers or bank accounts used by both the parties	0	4	0	1	2	0	0	0	1	0	0	0	**8**

(Cont'd)

Table 8.26 (*Cont'd*)

Protection Order Granted (Section 18)	Andhra Pradesh	West Bengal	Uttarakhand	Tripura	Himachal Pradesh	Jharkhand	Kerala	Maharashtra	North East	Odisha	Assam	Delhi	Total
Restraining the Respondent from alienating the AP's Stridhan	0	1	0	0	2	0	0	0	0	0	0	0	**3**
Restraining the Respondent from communicating in any manner including personal oral or written or electronic or telephonic contact with the AP or any of her relatives	2	2	1	0	5	0	0	2	1	0	0	0	**13**
Restraining the Respondent from entering the premise of the AP	2	3	2	3	1	1	6	0	0	1	0	2	**21**
Restraining the Respondents from committing any further acts of DV	29	18	18	8	50	3	42	0	4	17	10	2	**201**

Restrict the Respondent from misbehaving with the AP her dependants and other relatives in any manner	5	4	0	3	2	0	0	0	0	0	0	0	**14**
Any Other	2	1	0	0	1	0	5	1	3	1	0	1	**15**
NA	98	72	46	41	64	22	32	12	7	61	30	36	**521**
TOTAL	**142**	**116**	72	57	134	**29**	**86**	**16**	**17**	**84**	**40**	**41**	**834**

Source: Author.

Table 8.27 Types of Residence Order Granted

Residence Order Granted (Section 19)	Andhra Pradesh	West Bengal	Uttarakhand	Tripura	Himachal Pradesh	Jharkhand	Kerala	Maharashtra	North East	Odisha	Assam	Delhi	Total
Restraining/ Maintaining Status Quo	18	12	20	8	18	6	36	1	4	11	4	7	**145**
New/ Separate Accommodation	29	12	3	2	20	3	2	6	0	9	13	4	**103**
Restoring Status Quo Ante	5	5	1	1	8	1	1	0	0	0	4	0	**26**
Any Other	1	3	1	0	1	1	2	0	0	0	2	0	**11**
NA	93	74	49	41	82	18	38	8	12	63	28	31	**537**
TOTAL	**146**	**106**	**74**	**52**	**129**	**29**	**79**	**15**	**16**	**83**	**51**	**42**	**822**

Source: Author.

Table 8.28 Types of Monetary Relief Granted

Monetary Relief Granted (Section 20)	Andhra Pradesh	West Bengal	Uttarakhand	Tripura	Himachal Pradesh	Jharkhand	Kerala	Maharashtra	North East	Odisha	Assam	Delhi	Total
Maintenance	83	42	30	12	75	18	33	8	2	44	32	29	408
Restitution	2	3	2	0	8	3	0	9	1	4	0	2	34
Others	4	0	0	0	1	0	0	0	0	1	1	0	7
NA	45	53	37	37	38	6	45	5	11	33	11	12	333
TOTAL	134	98	69	49	122	27	78	22	14	82	44	43	782

Source: Author.

Table 8.29 Amount of Income of Respondent Proved

Amount of income of Respondent proved	Andhra Pradesh	West Bengal	Uttarakhand	Tripura	Himachal Pradesh	Jharkhand	Kerala	Maharashtra	North East	Odisha	Assam	Delhi	Total
Below 500	0	0	0	0	0	0	0	0	0	0	0	0	**0**
500-999	0	0	0	0	0	0	0	0	0	0	0	0	**0**
1,000-4999	5	2	0	1	7	0	1	1	0	1	0	1	**19**
5,000-9999	5	2	1	0	3	3	1	0	0	1	1	7	**24**
10,000-49999	9	7	3	0	10	2	6	0	0	6	0	9	**52**
50,000-99999	1	1	2	0	0	0	0	0	0	2	0	0	**6**
Above 1 Lakh	2	0	0	0	0	0	0	1	0	2	1	1	**7**
Above 1 Crore	0	0	0	0	0	0	0	0	0	0	0	0	**0**
NA	109	86	60	48	98	21	70	13	14	69	38	23	**649**
TOTAL	**131**	**98**	**66**	**49**	**118**	**26**	**78**	**15**	**14**	**81**	**40**	**41**	757

Source: Author.

Table 8.30 Quantum of Monetary Relief Granted

Quantum of Monetary Relief Granted	Andhra Pradesh	West Bengal	Uttarakhand	Tripura	Himachal Pradesh	Jharkhand	Kerala	Maharashtra	North East	Odisha	Assam	Delhi	Total
Below 500	0	0	0	0	0	0	0	0	0	0	3	0	**3**
500-999	5	1	0	0	4	2	2	0	0	2	6	0	**22**
1,000-4999	53	33	21	9	67	13	21	6	2	34	16	11	**286**
5,000-9999	16	7	5	2	9	1	9	2	0	8	3	6	**68**
10,000-49999	7	6	4	0	2	4	1	1	1	2	1	4	**33**
50,000-99999	1	0	2	0	0	1	0	0	0	1	0	0	**5**
Above 1 Lakh	4	0	0	0	0	0	0	1	0	0	0	0	**5**
Above 1 Crore	0	0	0	0	0	0	0	0	0	0	0	0	**0**
NA	46	53	36	38	38	6	45	5	11	35	12	20	**345**
TOTAL	**132**	**100**	**68**	**49**	**120**	**27**	**78**	**15**	**14**	**82**	**41**	**41**	**767**

Source: Author.

Table 8.31 Temporary Custody Granted

Temporary Custody Granted (Section 21)	Andhra Pradesh	West Bengal	Uttarakhand	Tripura	Himachal Pradesh	Jharkhand	Kerala	Maharashtra	North East	Odisha	Assam	Delhi	Total
Children to spend their vacations with the Respondent	0	0	0	0	0	0	0	0	0	0	0	0	**0**
Joint custody granted to the parents	0	0	0	0	0	0	0	0	0	0	0	0	**0**
Respondent granted visitation rights once a week/ month	0	0	0	0	0	0	0	0	1	0	0	0	**1**
Temporary custody granted to the AP's inlaws	0	0	0	0	0	0	0	0	0	0	0	0	**0**
Temporary custody of the minor child given to the AP	3	1	0	0	4	0	1	0	2	1	0	1	**13**

Temporary custody of the minor child given to the father	0	0	0	0	1	0	0	0	0	0	0	0	**1**
Any Other	1	0	1	1	0	0	0	0	1	0	1	1	**6**
NA	127	97	65	48	113	26	77	15	10	80	39	39	**736**
TOTAL	**131**	**98**	**66**	**49**	**118**	**26**	**78**	**15**	**14**	**81**	**40**	**41**	**757**

Source: Author.

Table 8.32 Compensation Order Granted

Compensation Order (Section 22)	Andhra Pradesh	West Bengal	Uttarakhand	Tripura	Himachal Pradesh	Jharkhand	Kerala	Maharashtra	North East	Odisha	Assam	Delhi	Total
Compensation granted for mental torture and emotional distress caused due to acts of DV.	16	4	5	0	7	4	4	1	0	4	3	1	**49**
Compensation granted for physical injuries caused by the acts of DV.	9	2	2	0	3	0	1	1	0	0	0	1	**19**
Any Other	4	1	1	1	1	0	1	1	0	1	0	0	**11**
NA	110	93	60	48	109	22	73	13	14	76	37	40	**695**
TOTAL	**139**	**100**	**68**	**49**	**120**	**26**	**79**	**16**	**14**	**81**	**40**	**42**	774

Source: Author.

Table 8.33 Quantum of Compensation Granted

Quantum of Compensation granted	Andhra Pradesh	West Bengal	Uttarakhand	Tripura	Himachal Pradesh	Jharkhand	Kerala	Maharashtra	North East	Odisha	Assam	Delhi	Total
Below 500	0	0	0	0	0	0	0	0	0	0	0	0	**0**
500-999	0	0	0	0	0	0	0	0	0	0	0	0	**0**
1,000-4999	1	1	1	0	1	0	1	0	0	0	0	0	**5**
5,000-9999	2	3	2	1	1	2	0	0	0	4	2	0	**17**
10,000-49999	5	0	3	0	8	2	4	2	0	3	0	0	**27**
50,000-99999	3	1	1	1	0	0	0	0	0	1	1	0	**8**
Above 1 Lakh	13	0	0	0	0	0	1	1	0	0	0	0	**15**
Above 1 Crore	0	0	0	0	0	0	0	0	0	0	0	0	**0**
NA	107	93	59	47	108	22	72	12	14	73	37	41	**685**
TOTAL	**131**	**98**	**66**	**49**	**118**	**26**	**78**	**15**	**14**	**81**	**40**	**41**	757

Source: Author.

Examining the reasons that courts give (Table 8.34) for granting or denying the relief asked for, provides an interesting window into the operation of the law. To enable speedy access to relief, especially physical protection, securing shelter, and economic sustenance, the PWDVA provides for relief based on prima facie satisfaction that domestic violence has taken place. If courts were to insist on a very high standard of proof, or very detailed procedural requirements, an aggrieved person in urgent need of support may not be able to effectively access the remedies under the Act. Consistent with this approach, the data reveal that courts routinely grant reliefs on the basis of prima facie satisfaction that domestic violence has taken place or is likely to take place. This is especially true for the grant of protection orders.

In 24.7 per cent of the cases where the judge denied a protection order, it was because the parties were residing separately because of which the court believed that there was no imminent threat of domestic violence. This reasoning has to be juxtaposed with the finding above that most women tend to file complaints under the PWDVA only after leaving the shared household (Tables 8.35 to 8.37). Further, merely because the parties are not residing in the same location does not mean that the threat of violence has been removed. Recognizing this, the Act defines a 'domestic relationship' as one where the parties are living or *have lived together* in a shared household.[10] The Act has application in both instances.

A bulk of the residence orders are also granted on the basis of prima facie satisfaction. In a small number of cases, the fact that the aggrieved person left on her own or that she is residing in her natal home, are given as reasons for denying residence orders. However, the Act defines a shared household as one where the person aggrieved 'lives or *at any stage has lived* in a domestic relationship'.[11] In addition, Section 17, PWDVA, provides every woman in a domestic relationship the right to reside in the shared household. Therefore, the reasoning that a woman who has left on her own or who is currently residing in her natal home is not entitled to a residence order goes against the text and spirit of Section 17. In light of the finding above that most women are able to file their complaint under the PWDVA only upon leaving the shared household, the interpretation taken by judges in these cases will serve to nullify one of the central provisions of the Act.

[10] Section 2(f).

[11] Section 2(s), PWDVA.

Table 8.34 Reasons for Granting Protection Order

Reason for grant of Protection Order	Andhra Pradesh	West Bengal	Uttarakhand	Tripura	Himachal Pradesh	Jharkhand	Kerala	Maharashtra	North East	Odisha	Assam	Delhi	Total
Being prima facie satisfied that DV has taken place or is likely to take place	24	16	16	7	38	4	38	2	2	11	8	4	**170**
There is a threat to the life of the AP and her children	4	2	1	0	1	0	2	0	0	1	0	1	**12**
Any Other	1	2	0	0	1	0	4	0	4	1	0	0	**13**
NA	103	78	49	42	78	22	34	13	8	68	32	37	**564**
TOTAL	**132**	**98**	**66**	**49**	**118**	**26**	**78**	**15**	**14**	**81**	**40**	**42**	**759**

Source: Author.

Table 8.35 Reasons for Denial of Protection Order

Reason for Denial of Protection Order	Andhra Pradesh	West Bengal	Uttarakhand	Tripura	Himachal Pradesh	Jharkhand	Kerala	Maharashtra	North East	Odisha	Assam	Delhi	Total
AP is not residing with the Respondent imminent threat of DV is not present	9	4	3	0	2	0	0	0	0	1	0	0	**19**
DV not proved	14	4	4	1	6	0	3	0	1	2	0	1	**36**
Limitation Period Lapsed.	0	0	1	1	0	0	0	0	0	0	0	0	**2**
The parties are divorced and residing separately	1	0	1	0	0	0	0	0	0	0	0	0	**2**
Any Other	11	1	0	1	2	1	2	0	0	2	0	1	**21**
NA	97	89	61	46	108	25	72	15	13	76	40	38	**680**
TOTAL	**132**	**98**	**70**	**49**	**118**	**26**	77	**15**	**14**	**81**	**40**	**40**	**760**

Source: Author.

Table 8.36 Reasons for Grant of Residence Order

Reasons for Grant of Residence Order	Andhra Pradesh	West Bengal	Uttarakhand	Tripura	Himachal Pradesh	Jharkhand	Kerala	Maharashtra	North East	Odisha	Assam	Delhi	Total
AP being the wife of the Respondent is entitle to being provided with the rent for her accommodation or a separate accommodation	12	2	0	0	1	1	1	4	0	2	0	2	**25**
AP will need the Stridhan for her day-to-day life	2	0	0	0	0	0	1	0	0	0	0	0	3
AP being the wife of the Respondent is entitle to stay in the matrimonial home	7	1	3	0	2	1	0	0	0	2	0	0	**16**

(Cont'd)

Table 8.36 (*Cont'd*)

Reasons for Grant of Residence Order	Andhra Pradesh	West Bengal	Uttarakhand	Tripura	Himachal Pradesh	Jharkhand	Kerala	Maharashtra	North East	Odisha	Assam	Delhi	Total
Being prima facie satisfied that DV has taken place or is likely to take place	10	9	8	6	20	5	18	0	1	3	6	0	**86**
Every woman in a domestic relationship has a right to reside in the SH whether or not she has any right title or beneficial interest in the same.	0	0	1	0	2	0	0	0	0	0	0	0	**3**
Husband is the Co-owner of the property	0	0	0	0	0	0	0	0	0	0	0	0	**0**
Marriage not disputed	5	2	4	0	10	2	0	0	0	3	5	3	**34**

Property belongs to the FIL MIL BIL etc.	0	0	0	0	0	0	0	0	0	0	0	0	**0**
Property belongs to the husband or taken on rent by the husband	2	0	0	0	0	0	1	0	0	0	0	0	**3**
Property belongs to the Joint Family of which the husband is a member	0	1	0	0	1	0	0	0	0	0	0	0	**2**
Property belongs to the Joint Family of which the Respondent is a member	0	1	0	0	0	0	0	0	0	0	0	0	**1**
The property belongs or is rented by the Respondent	1	0	1	0	0	0	0	0	0	0	0	0	**2**
Any Other	1	0	1	0	2	0	2	1	1	3	0	2	**13**
NA	100	83	51	43	88	19	54	10	12	69	33	33	**595**
TOTAL	**140**	**99**	**69**	**49**	**126**	**28**	**77**	**15**	**14**	**82**	**44**	**40**	**783**

Source: Author.

Table 8.37 Reasons for Denial of Residence Order

Reasons for denial of Residence Order	Andhra Pradesh	West Bengal	Uttarakhand	Tripura	Himachal Pradesh	Jharkhand	Kerala	Maharashtra	North East	Odisha	Assam	Delhi	Total
AP has failed to provide any details of her stridhan	2	2	1	0	1	0	1	0	0	0	0	2	**9**
AP has left the SH on her own	2	0	4	0	0	0	0	0	0	0	0	0	**6**
AP is not able to prove the property is a joint family property	2	0	3	0	0	0	0	0	0	0	0	0	**5**
AP is staying at her parental home and not in immediate need of a relief	2	4	1	0	0	0	1	0	0	0	0	0	**8**
Application is for enforcement of property rights and court does not have jurisdiction over title disputes	0	0	0	0	0	0	0	0	0	0	0	1	**1**
DV not proved	10	6	3	0	5	0	1	0	1	1	0	1	**28**

Property is owned by the FIL MIL BIL etc	0	0	1	0	0	0	0	0	0	0	0	0	**1**
Relying on the Batra v. Batra Judgment	2	0	1	0	1	0	0	0	0	0	0	0	**4**
Respondent makes an offer that the AP can come back	0	0	1	0	1	0	0	0	0	0	0	0	**2**
The property in question is not a SH	7	0	0	0	0	0	3	0	0	0	0	1	**11**
Any Other	9	2	0	4	6	1	3	1	0	1	1	5	**33**
NA	98	85	56	45	106	25	70	14	13	79	39	33	**663**
TOTAL	**134**	**99**	**71**	**49**	**120**	**26**	**79**	**15**	**14**	**81**	**40**	**43**	**771**

Source: Author.

Monetary relief, likewise, is granted on a prima facie finding of domestic violence, and on finding that the woman is unable to maintain herself (Table 8.38). This is consistent with the overall focus of courts on maintenance as opposed to restitution under the Act. The PWDVA creates a rights-based framework for securing the bodily integrity, autonomy, basic needs, and dignity of women. However, in nearly a quarter of the cases where monetary relief was granted (23.6 per cent, n=100), the courts' rationale for providing the relief sought was that it is the moral duty of the husband to maintain his wife and children and provide for their basic needs. Instead of locating the relief in the right of the woman to be free from domestic violence and abuse, judicial reasoning in these cases re-inscribes patriarchal notions of the family upon the law.

Finally, looking at the reasons for denial of compensation orders indicates that this is one area where courts ask for higher proof of injuries or mental trauma or distress caused to the aggrieved person (Table 8.39). Since aggrieved persons are often not able to produce such proof, compensation for domestic violence is denied to them. Seeking specific proof of mental trauma even where the court finds that domestic violence has in fact taken place, indicates a lack of understanding of the impact of domestic violence upon a woman.

Enough observations were not available to draw any conclusions regarding the reasons for the grant or denial of temporary custody orders.

Consistent with the rationale that placing a high burden of proof on an aggrieved person will defeat the objectives of the law, since the aggrieved person may not have the resources or may not be in the condition to meet a high burden, courts give significant weightage to the aggrieved person's affidavit or testimony in granting relief. The study shows that documentary evidence is not generally insisted on. This approach cuts across the different kinds of reliefs claimed by aggrieved persons, and covers evidence in support of a protection order, evidence to support residence in a shared household, and evidence of income for monetary relief.[12] In cases involving monetary relief, however, since the quantum of income is generally disputed and reliable evidence of income is difficult to obtain, courts use two strategies to determine income. One, they rely on 'guesswork' (22.2 per cent), or on their appreciation of the standard of living of the parties

[12] The study had very few observations on the kinds of evidence accepted by courts in support of temporary custody orders. Therefore, no conclusion can be drawn from these data (Tables 8.40 to 8.47).

based on conspicuous consumption patterns (3.7 per cent); and two, they use the Minimum Wages Act as the default income standard (6.4 per cent). Only in 4.8 per cent cases do courts base their opinion on the DIR. Courts are more likely to rely on the income stated by the respondent (7.4 per cent) than to seek independent verification through protection officers. This is one area where the mechanism of protection officers can be effectively used to supplement adjudicatory processes. However, as will be discussed in detail later, courts have not made full use of the potential of this mechanism.

Like the other reliefs, courts tend to rely on affidavits and testimonies of the aggrieved person in granting compensation orders. However, this finding should be correlated with the concern raised above that courts often deny compensation orders on the ground that documentary proof of injuries or mental or emotional trauma was not provided by the aggrieved person. Therefore, the finding is more mixed for compensation orders as compared to the others.

Procedures under the Act

The PWDVA aims to create an easily and speedily accessible system for immediate and sustained relief from domestic violence, and for this purpose, provides for procedural flexibility[13] as well as a range of institutional mechanisms to aid in holistic support to victims of violence. Multiple agencies like protection officers, NGOs working as service providers, the police, shelter homes, and providers of medical services are all empowered to facilitate access to reliefs and remedies tailored to the specific circumstances of the aggrieved person.

The data reveal that courts regularly use the procedural flexibility provided under the Act to simplify the adjudicatory process (Table 8.48). Of the 237 cases of interim orders, for example, in at least 46 per cent cases courts decided on interim relief on the basis of an oral hearing of parties. Only in 3.8 per cent cases did they insist on evidence being led before the decision on interim relief.

In delivering final orders too, in close to half the cases (49 per cent), courts took evidence on oath subject to cross examination, which helps to both increase the pace of the proceedings, as well as to reduce the burden on the aggrieved parties.

[13] See example, Section 28(2).

Table 8.38 Reasons for grant of Monetary Relief

Reasons for grant of Monetary Relief	Andhra Pradesh	West Bengal	Uttarakhand	Tripura	Himachal Pradesh	Jharkhand	Kerala	Maharashtra	North East	Odisha	Assam	Delhi	Total
AP has no source of income to maintain herself and her minor child	17	12	10	1	21	8	3	3	1	10	7	8	**101**
Being prima facie satisfied that DV has taken place or is likely to take place	15	11	10	4	20	5	11	0	0	7	8	4	**95**
Divorced Muslim wife is entitled to claim maintenance from her husband till she remarries (relying on ShabanaBano vs. Imran Khan)	0	0	0	0	0	0	0	0	0	0	0	0	**0**

It is the moral duty of the husband to maintain his wife and children and provide for their basic needs	31	4	8	0	22	2	3	2	0	11	1	16	**100**
Litigation expense granted to the AP to help with the cost of litigation	0	1	0	0	0	0	0	1	0	0	0	1	**3**
Medical expense are granted when the AP can show proof of injury	1	0	0	0	0	0	0	0	0	1	0	0	**2**
No proof of income but granted as an obligation of husband	10	4	5	3	8	3	2	1	1	2	1	1	**41**

(Cont'd)

Table 8.38 (*Cont'd*)

Reasons for grant of Monetary Relief	Andhra Pradesh	West Bengal	Uttarakhand	Tripura	Himachal Pradesh	Jharkhand	Kerala	Maharashtra	North East	Odisha	Assam	Delhi	Total
Percentage of Husband's income given to AP was decided considering husband's dependents	2	0	0	0	0	0	0	0	0	0	0	0	**2**
Percentage of Husband's income given to AP was decided considering requirement of children	1	0	0	0	0	0	0	0	0	0	0	0	**1**
Percentage of Husband's income given to AP was decided considering the needs of the AP	0	0	0	0	0	0	0	0	0	0	0	0	**0**

Refusal on the part of the husband to maintain the AP and her child inspite of having sufficient income is held to be an economic abuse	2	1	0	0	0	0	0	1	0	0	0	0	**4**
The respondent is able bodied hence capable of working	6	4	0	0	16	0	0	0	0	0	2	1	**29**
The respondent is employed and earning sufficiently	9	2	2	2	2	1	0	1	0	1	0	1	**21**
Widowed DIL has a right to be maintained by her FIL	1	0	0	0	0	0	0	0	0	0	0	0	**1**
Any Other	0	0	0	0	0	0	0	0	0	0	0	0	**0**
NA	57	65	41	40	51	8	56	7	12	51	23	15	**426**
TOTAL	152	104	76	50	140	27	75	16	14	83	42	47	**826**

Source: Author.

Table 8.39 Reasons for denial of Monetary Relief

Reasons for denial of Monetary Relief	Andhra Pradesh	West Bengal	Uttarakhand	Tripura	Himachal Pradesh	Jharkhand	Kerala	Maharashtra	North East	Odisha	Assam	Delhi	Total
AP is getting maintenance under Section 125 CrPC	7	2	1	0	3	0	0	0	0	0	0	3	**16**
AP was staying away from the matrimonial home on her own volition	1	0	3	0	0	0	0	0	0	1	0	0	**5**
Domestic Violence not proved.	10	4	3	0	4	0	2	0	0	1	0	0	**24**
Limitation Period Lapsed.	0	0	2	1	0	0	0	0	0	0	0	1	**4**
Medical expense denied as AP did not submit any medical reports	8	0	0	0	0	0	0	0	0	0	2	0	**10**
No maintenance can be claimed against the In-laws	3	1	1	0	0	0	0	0	0	0	0	0	**5**
No proof of earning of the husband submitted in the court by the AP	1	0	3	0	0	0	0	0	0	1	0	0	**5**

Sufficient income being earned by the AP herself	3	0	1	0	0	0	0	0	0	0	0	0	**4**
Taking into consideration the ability of the respondent to pay and his other liabilities.	1	0	3	0	1	0	0	0	0	0	0	0	**5**
Any Other	3	2	1	1	0	1	1	0	1	4	0	1	**15**
NA	101	89	55	47	111	25	75	15	13	74	38	36	**679**
TOTAL	**138**	**98**	**73**	**49**	**119**	**26**	**78**	**15**	**14**	**81**	**40**	**41**	**772**

Source: Author.

Table 8.40 Reasons for Grant of Compensation Order

Reasons for Grant of Compensation Order	Andhra Pradesh	West Bengal	Uttarakhand	Tripura	Himachal	Jharkhand	Kerala	Maharashtra	North East	Odisha	Assam	Delhi	Total
Being prima facie satisfied that DV has taken place or is likely to take place	8	1	4	2	2	2	3	1	0	2	0	0	**25**
Respondent has caused AP mental shock emotional abuse	11	2	2	0	4	1	0	1	0	3	0	0	**24**
Respondent has caused the AP economic abuse and deprivation of her access to the Respondent's SH	2	0	2	0	2	0	0	0	0	1	0	1	**8**
Any Other	3	0	2	0	1	1	1	0	0	0	0	0	**8**
NA	111	95	59	47	110	22	72	14	14	75	39	40	**698**
TOTAL	**135**	**98**	**69**	**49**	**119**	**26**	**76**	**16**	**14**	**81**	**39**	**41**	**763**

Source: Author.

Table 8.41 Reasons for Denial of Compensation Order

Reasons for Denial of Compensation Order	Andhra Pradesh	West Bengal	Uttarakhand	Tripura	Himachal Pradesh	Jharkhand	Kerala	Maharashtra	North East	Odisha	Assam	Delhi	Total
AP has not submitted any medical report to prove injuries caused by acts of DV	8	0	0	0	0	0	0	1	0	1	0	1	**11**
AP is unable to prove that she suffered any mental torture and emotional distress	16	1	0	0	2	0	1	1	0	1	0	2	**24**
Domestic Violence not proved	10	2	2	0	2	1	1	0	0	1	0	0	**19**
Limitation Period Lapsed.	0	0	0	1	0	0	0	0	0	0	0	0	**1**
Any Other	12	2	1	1	1	1	4	0	0	3	0	0	**25**
NA	93	93	63	47	113	24	72	14	14	75	40	39	**687**
TOTAL	**139**	**98**	**66**	**49**	**118**	**26**	**78**	**16**	**14**	**81**	**40**	**42**	**767**

Source: Author.

Table 8.42 Reasons for Grant of Temporary Custody

Reasons for Grant of Temporary Custody	Andhra Pradesh	West Bengal	Uttarakhand	Tripura	Himachal Pradesh	Jharkhand	Kerala	Maharashtra	North East	Odisha	Assam	Delhi	Total
Being prima facie satisfied that DV has taken place or is likely to take place	1	1	0	0	1	0	0	0	1	0	0	0	**4**
Mother is the natural guardian of the child	3	0	0	0	1	0	0	0	0	0	0	0	**4**
The best interest of the child is taken into consideration	0	1	0	0	1	0	0	0	0	1	0	0	**3**
The child wants to stay with his/her mother	0	0	0	0	0	0	0	0	0	0	0	0	**0**

Under Hindu Minority and Guardianship Act 1956 the custody of a minor who has not completed 5 years of age shall ordinarily be with the mother	0	0	0	0	0	0	0	0	0	0	0	0	**0**
Under the Muslim Personal Law (Sunni Law) a mother is entitled to the custody of a male child till 7 years of age and a female child till she attains puberty.	0	0	0	0	0	0	0	0	0	0	0	0	**0**

(Cont'd)

Table 8.42 *(Cont'd)*

Reasons for Grant of Temporary Custody	Andhra Pradesh	West Bengal	Uttarakhand	Tripura	Himachal Pradesh	Jharkhand	Kerala	Maharashtra	North East	Odisha	Assam	Delhi	Total
Visitation rights granted to the Respondent keeping in mind the best interest of the child	0	0	0	0	0	0	0	0	1	0	0	0	**1**
Any Other	0	0	0	0	2	0	0	0	0	0	0	1	**3**
NA	127	97	66	49	113	26	78	15	13	80	40	40	**744**
TOTAL	**131**	**99**	**66**	**49**	**118**	**26**	**78**	**15**	**15**	**81**	**40**	**41**	**759**

Source: Author.

Table 8.43 Reasons for denial of Temporary Custody

Reasons for denial of Temporary Custody	Andhra Pradesh	West Bengal	Uttarakhand	Tripura	Himachal Pradesh	Jharkhand	Kerala	Maharashtra	North East	Odisha	Assam	Delhi	Total
Children do not wish to stay with the AP	0	0	0	0	0	0	0	0	0	0	0	0	**0**
Custody given to the Respondent in the best interest of the child.	0	0	0	0	0	0	0	0	0	0	0	0	**0**
Directed the AP to file a petition under the Guardian and Wards Act	0	0	0	0	0	0	0	0	0	0	0	1	**1**
Domestic Violence not proved.	0	0	0	0	0	0	0	0	0	0	0	0	**0**
Limitation Period Lapsed.	0	0	0	1	0	0	0	0	0	0	0	0	**1**
Any Other	0	0	2	1	1	0	0	0	0	0	0	1	**5**
NA	131	96	64	47	117	26	78	15	14	81	40	39	**748**
TOTAL	**131**	**96**	**66**	**49**	**118**	**26**	**78**	**15**	**14**	**81**	**40**	**41**	755

Source: Author.

Table 8.44 Evidence Accepted by the Court in Support of the Protection Order Granted

Evidence accepted by the court in support of the Protection Order granted	Andhra Pradesh	West Bengal	Uttarakhand	Tripura	Himachal Pradesh	Jharkhand	Kerala	Maharashtra	North East	Odisha	Assam	Delhi	Total
Affidavit of AP	7	5	0	3	4	0	31	0	2	1	1	0	**54**
Testimony of AP	20	15	0	3	35	2	13	0	1	0	5	3	**97**
Other Testimonies	20	7	0	4	20	3	2	0	1	1	5	0	**63**
DIR	2	8	0	1	6	1	4	0	1	1	0	1	**25**
Documentary Evidence	2	1	0	0	2	0	0	0	0	0	0	0	**5**
Any Other	0	1	8	0	0	0	0	1	2	6	0	1	**19**
NA	104	75	58	43	71	24	38	14	8	72	33	37	**577**
TOTAL	**155**	**112**	**66**	**54**	**138**	**30**	**88**	**15**	**15**	**81**	**44**	**42**	**840**

Source: Author.

Table 8.45 Evidence Accepted by the Court in Support of Residence in Shared Household

Evidence accepted by the court in support of residence in Shared Household	Andhra Pradesh	West Bengal	Uttarakhand	Tripura	Himachal Pradesh	Jharkhand	Kerala	Maharashtra	North East	Odisha	Assam	Delhi	Total
Documentary Proof	2	1	0	1	2	0	1	0	0	1	0	0	**8**
Affidavit or Testimony of AP	22	12	11	5	18	2	31	2	1	15	9	5	**133**
Admission of the Respondent	11	2	4	0	1	3	3	2	0	1	1	3	**31**
DIR or Home Visits by PO	0	3	0	1	5	1	2	0	0	3	0	1	**16**
Testimonies of Other Witnesses	2	1	0	0	5	2	0	0	0	4	4	0	**18**
Any Other	0	0	2	0	0	0	1	0	0	2	0	0	**5**
NA	108	83	57	43	94	22	48	11	13	63	31	33	**606**
TOTAL	**145**	**102**	**74**	**50**	**125**	**30**	**86**	**15**	**14**	**89**	**45**	**42**	**817**

Source: Author.

Table 8.46 Evidence Accepted by the Court in Support of Income

Evidence accepted by the court in support of income	Andhra Pradesh	West Bengal	Uttarakhand	Tripura	Himachal Pradesh	Jharkhand	Kerala	Maharashtra	North East	Odisha	Assam	Delhi	Total
AP's Affidavit or Testimony	17	10	4	3	8	4	6	2	0	8	7	7	**76**
Respondent's Admission	7	0	0	0	1	1	2	0	0	2	0	1	**14**
Documentary Proof	7	1	3	1	2	1	1	1	1	3	0	4	**25**
Other Oral Evidence	3	0	0	0	3	2	0	0	0	1	3	0	**12**
Based on Standard of Living	2	0	0	0	0	0	0	1	0	0	0	4	7
DIR	0	3	1	1	0	0	1	0	0	2	0	1	**9**
No proof of income hence Minimum Wages Act used to fix the salary of the respondent.	1	0	0	0	4	0	0	0	0	0	0	7	**12**
The Court feels it necessary to indulge in some guesswork	12	3	3	1	10	0	1	4	0	3	0	5	**42**
Any Other	1	2	0	0	2	0	0	0	0	3	0	0	**8**
NA	86	80	55	44	85	21	68	8	13	58	31	19	**568**
TOTAL	**142**	**101**	**67**	**50**	**120**	**30**	**79**	**17**	**14**	**82**	**43**	**51**	**796**

Source: Author.

Table 8.47 Evidence Accepted by the Court in Support of Compensation Granted

Evidence accepted by the court in support of compensation granted	Andhra Pradesh	West Bengal	Uttarakhand	Tripura	Himachal Pradesh	Jharkhand	Kerala	Maharashtra	North East	Odisha	Assam	Delhi	Total
Admission of the Respondent	1	0	0	0	0	0	0	0	0	0	0	0	**1**
Affidavit of AP	9	1	2	1	1	1	2	1	0	2	0	0	**20**
DIR	0	2	0	1	2	0	0	0	0	0	0	0	**5**
FIR	0	0	0	0	0	0	0	0	0	0	0	0	**0**
NA	121	95	64	48	115	25	76	14	14	79	40	41	**732**
TOTAL	**131**	**98**	**66**	**50**	**118**	**26**	**78**	**15**	**14**	**81**	**40**	**41**	**758**

Source: Author.

Table 8.48 Procedure for Ex-Parte and Interim Orders

Procedure for ex-parte and Interim Orders	Andhra Pradesh	West Bengal	Uttarakhand	Tripura	Himachal Pradesh	Jharkhand	Kerala	Maharashtra	North East	Odisha	Assam	Delhi	Total
Ex-parte order granted on the basis of affidavit alone	3	5	8	2	1	1	26	0	1	3	3	2	**55**
Ex-parte Order granted on the basis of DIR only	0	2	5	1	2	1	2	0	1	3	0	2	**19**
Ex-parte Order granted on the basis of the application	5	6	9	5	7	2	13	0	2	7	4	3	**63**
Interim Order granted on the basis of affidavit after hearing the Respondent	3	6	2	1	3	4	1	0	3	5	1	3	**32**
Interim Order granted on the basis of application and	11	17	9	5	20	5	10	1	3	9	5	14	**109**

hearing the parties													
Interim Order granted on the basis of evidence subject to cross-examination	0	1	0	0	1	0	0	0	0	0	0	0	**2**
Interim Order granted on the basis of Oral Evidence	2	2	0	0	1	0	0	0	0	2	0	0	**7**
Any Other	2	13	0	3	5	1	2	1	1	0	1	1	**30**
NA	106	47	42	33	80	14	26	13	4	55	26	18	**464**
TOTAL	**132**	**99**	**75**	**50**	**120**	**28**	**80**	**15**	**15**	**84**	**40**	**43**	**781**

Source: Author.

Table 8.49 Procedure for Final Orders

Procedure for Final Orders (Final-Oral/ written Cross Examination)	Andhra Pradesh	West Bengal	Uttarakhand	Tripura	Himachal Pradesh	Jharkhand	Kerala	Maharashtra	North East	Odisha	Assam	Delhi	Total
Evidence of the parties are taken on oath subject to cross-examination	59	11	11	5	45	8	4	1	1	5	8	4	**162**
Final Order granted on the basis of affidavit alone	2	0	1	1	2	0	6	0	0	0	0	2	**14**
Final Order granted on the basis of affidavit along with oral arguments	25	2	12	4	3	2	7	0	0	6	0	2	**63**
Final Order granted on the basis of evidence led by the complainant.	6	5	3	0	6	2	4	4	0	6	2	2	**40**

Final Order granted on the basis of testimony of the AP	18	7	3	2	14	1	1	1	0	6	3	2	58
Any Other	1	0	1	6	7	2	1	1	1	2	1	1	24
NA	26	77	43	32	46	12	56	8	12	57	28	29	426
TOTAL	137	102	74	50	123	27	79	15	14	82	42	42	787

Source: Author.

An attempt was made to study the procedures under Section 31 of the Act, which deals with breach of court orders. However, since only nine orders pertained to this section, no meaningful conclusions could be drawn from the study.

While courts are using the procedural innovations under the Act, they are not fully utilizing the services of other agencies. While the reasons for this may vary from unavailability of protection officers due to vacancies or overburdening to lack of knowledge of judicial officers regarding the mechanisms under the Act, the fact remains that judicial orders reveal a lack of integration of these mechanisms into the adjudicatory and remedial processes.

Take, for example, protection officers. Section 9, PWDVA, lists out a range of duties and functions for protection officers, first amongst which is assisting the Magistrate in the discharge of her functions. The protection officer is also charged with facilitating an aggrieved person's access to the system by helping her file applications before the court. However, the study reveals that women use protection officers to file applications in only 16 per cent of the cases (Table 8.50). In the remainder, they approach the court directly. This data should be a cause for reflection on why users of the Act do not, by and large, prefer to use the services of a protection officer. One reason might be that women approach protection officers for pre-litigation counselling and settlement, and approach the court only as a last resort. However, even in such a case, one would expect a well-functioning system to see more cases being filed in court through protection officers.

The limited use of protection officers to file applications is mirrored in the negligible use of the DIR mechanism in the adjudicatory process. 69.1 per cent of the orders do not even mention DIRs.

While the non-mention of DIRs does not indicate that DIRs were not called for or submitted, the lack of mentions does indicate that the DIR process is not being treated as an integral part of the adjudicatory process.

In cases where the services of the protection officer are utilized, at the pre-trial stage, they are generally involved in preparing the application under Section 12, PWDVA and in preparing DIRs (Table 8.52).

During trial, protection officers are generally involved in filing court directed DIRs and in the service of notice (Table 8.51). As discussed, their services could be utilized for gathering information about the financial status of the respondents. However, this is a rare occurrence.

After trial, protection officers are sometimes called upon to assist with the enforcement of orders. However, due to a high number of null observations, no conclusions can be drawn regarding the frequency of such use, or the general role played by protection officers after the trial is over (Tables 8.53 and 8.54).

Table 8.50 Application Filing Procedure

Application filed by	Andhra Pradesh	West Bengal	Uttarakhand	Tripura	Himachal Pradesh	Jharkhand	Kerala	Maharashtra	North East	Odisha	Assam	Delhi	Total
AP through SP	0	0	0	0	0	0	0	0	0	0	0	0	**0**
Another Person	0	0	0	0	0	0	1	0	0	1	0	0	**2**
AP	94	76	58	35	89	23	48	11	13	55	25	40	**567**
AP through PO	30	8	2	13	25	1	3	4	1	18	1	0	**106**
AP through Police	0	0	0	0	0	0	0	0	0	0	0	0	**0**
NA	6	14	5	1	4	2	26	0	0	6	14	1	79
TOTAL	131	98	66	49	118	26	78	15	14	81	40	41	757

Source: Author.

Table 8.51 Filing of DIR

Filing of DIR	Andhra Pradesh	West Bengal	Uttarakhand	Tripura	Himachal Pradesh	Jharkhand	Kerala	Maharashtra	North East	Odisha	Assam	Delhi	Total
DIR called for	0	13	6	3	0	0	0	1	0	3	8	1	**35**
DIR considered while granting order	4	24	9	3	12	5	3	0	0	14	2	13	**89**
DIR filed after the application (at the direction of the court)	0	3	2	2	2	1	0	0	0	2	7	1	**20**
DIR filed with the application	12	9	5	6	21	1	3	0	3	3	1	0	**64**
DIR not mentioned in the order	103	46	35	27	68	16	70	5	10	43	21	21	**465**
Any Other	1	0	3	1	1	4	0	0	0	0	0	0	**10**
NA	12	5	7	7	16	0	3	9	1	16	2	6	**84**
TOTAL	**132**	**100**	**67**	**49**	**120**	**27**	**79**	**15**	**14**	**81**	**41**	**42**	**767**

Source: Author.

Table 8.52 Role of the Protection Officer at the Pre-Trial Stage

At the Pre-Trial Stage (Role of PO)	Andhra Pradesh	West Bengal	Uttarakhand	Tripura	Himachal Pradesh	Jharkhand	Kerala	Maharashtra	North East	Odisha	Assam	Delhi	Total
Counseling both the parties	2	0	0	0	2	0	0	0	0	0	0	0	**4**
Counseling the AP	2	0	0	0	0	0	0	0	0	0	0	0	**2**
Filling the DIR	10	24	10	8	21	4	2	0	3	1	1	2	**86**
Preparing a Safety Plan	0	0	0	0	0	0	0	0	0	0	0	0	**0**
Preparing an application u/s 12	22	6	1	5	18	1	2	1	0	10	0	0	**66**
Refer the AP to SP/MF etc	0	0	0	0	0	0	0	0	0	0	0	0	**0**
Any Other	2	4	1	0	1	0	0	0	0	0	0	0	**8**
NA	99	67	54	41	87	22	75	14	11	70	39	39	**618**
TOTAL	**137**	**101**	**66**	**54**	**129**	**27**	**79**	**15**	**14**	**81**	**40**	**41**	**784**

Source: Author.

Table 8.53 Role of the Protection Officer at the Trial Stage

At the Trial Stage (Role of PO)	Andhra Pradesh	West Bengal	Uttarakhand	Tripura	Himachal Pradesh	Jharkhand	Kerala	Maharashtra	North East	Odisha	Assam	Delhi	Total
Assist in the enforcment of order	0	2	1	2	2	0	0	0	0	6	1	1	**15**
Conduct a Home Visit	0	1	0	0	0	0	0	0	0	1	0	1	**3**
Counseling both the parties	2	1	0	0	1	0	0	0	0	0	0	0	**4**
Counseling the AP	0	1	0	0	0	0	0	0	0	0	0	0	**1**
File a report on the Financial Status of the Respondent	0	0	0	0	0	0	0	0	0	2	0	0	**2**
Filing Court directed DIR	0	16	7	2	2	1	0	0	0	7	8	1	**44**
Regain the custody of AP's children and enforcing visitation rights (Interim Order)	0	0	0	0	0	0	0	0	0	1	0	1	**2**

Restore possession of personal effects (interim Order)	0	0	0	2	1	0	0	0	0	0	0	2	**5**
Service of Notice	1	12	5	13	3	0	0	0	0	15	4	1	**54**
Any Other	0	2	0	4	2	0	0	0	0	2	0	0	**10**
NA	128	66	58	30	109	25	78	15	14	49	30	34	**636**
TOTAL	**131**	**101**	**71**	**53**	**120**	**26**	**78**	**15**	**14**	**83**	**43**	**41**	**776**

Source: Author.

Table 8.54 Role of Protection Officer at the Post-Trial Stage

At the Post-Trial Stage (Role of PO)	Andhra Pradesh	West Bengal	Uttarakhand	Tripura	Himachal Pradesh	Jharkhand	Kerala	Maharashtra	North East	Odisha	Assam	Delhi	Total
Assist in the enforcement of orders.	12	6	0	2	4	1	0	0	0	1	0	0	**26**
Regain the custody of AP's children and enforcing visitation rights	0	1	0	0	0	0	0	0	0	0	0	0	**1**
Reporting to the police for breach of orders	0	0	0	0	0	0	0	0	0	0	0	0	**0**
Restore possession of personal effects	1	0	0	1	0	0	0	0	0	0	0	0	**2**
Submit report of breach to the Magistrate	0	0	0	0	0	0	0	0	0	0	0	0	**0**

Take police assistance in enforcement of Orders	0	1	0	0	0	0	0	0	0	0	1	0	2
Any Other	2	2	0	0	0	0	0	0	0	0	0	0	4
NA	116	90	66	46	114	25	78	15	14	80	39	41	724
TOTAL	**131**	**100**	**66**	**49**	**118**	**26**	**78**	**15**	**14**	**81**	**40**	**41**	**759**

Source: Author.

While protection officers and their services find some, albeit limited, mention in court orders, service providers are virtually non-existent in the judicial record. Except for four mentions, two for assisting in the enforcement of court orders, one for filing a DIR, and one other, court decisions are completely silent on service providers. Likewise, there is no mention of shelter homes or medical service providers in the orders. Again, while the absence of reference to them does not indicate that they are playing no role under the Act, it does point to the lack of integration of these mechanisms with the adjudicatory process. To the extent that the PWDVA seeks to create a unified, single window mechanism for holistic relief and protection of the aggrieved person, this lack of integration goes against the objectives of the law.

Data about the role of the police was also very limited. To the extent that it was available, it indicated some trends towards police officers counselling aggrieved persons to compromise matters before the filing of a case (n=5), assisting in the enforcement of ex-parte and interim orders during the trial (n=17), and in the enforcement of final orders after trial (n=12).

Appeals and Revisions

The dataset contains 137 orders pertaining to appeals and revisions (Table 8.55). About half of these (48.3 per cent) were appeals against interim orders. Since the purpose of the interim order process is to allow for immediate relief and protection for the aggrieved person, the frequent use of the appellate process at this stage is a matter of concern. These data therefore point to the need for considering whether appeals against interim orders should be limited or eliminated in cases under the PWDVA. As a related point, in some cases, particularly in Delhi, it was noticed that Section 482, CrPC, powers of the High Court was being invoked to quash complaints under the PWDVA. Given the need for urgency, and the often unequal access to higher courts of an aggrieved person (who is more likely to have limited resources), compared to the respondent, using high courts' inherent powers to quash proceedings is likely to disadvantage aggrieved persons and create additional barriers to accessing relief under the Act.

To understand the impact of filing of appeals upon the reliefs ordered by the trial court, we studied the extent to which stay was granted pending appeal (Table 8.56). While the number of observations are too few to make definitive statements, the caution mentioned above, of placing barriers in the way of accessing reliefs under the Act, apply with equal force to this issue. Courts should therefore be circumspect in ordering a stay on the order of the trial court pending appeal.

Table 8.55 Appeal against Interim or Final Order

Appeal against Interim or Final Order	Andhra Pradesh	West Bengal	Uttarak hand	Tripura	Assam	Jharkhand	Kerala	Maharashtra	North East	Odisha	AssamQ	DelhiQ	Total
Final Order	17	5	12	0	11	3	1	3	0	0	5	3	**60**
Interim Order	10	16	11	0	5	3	1	0	1	5	2	2	**56**
NA	0	2	4	2	1	2	2	0	0	5	1	2	**21**
TOTAL	27	23	27	2	17	8	4	3	1	10	8	7	137

Source: Author.

Table 8.56 Effect of the On-Going Appeal on the Lower Court Order

Order pending the disposal of the Appeal	Andhra Pradesh	West Bengal	Uttarakhand	Tripura	Assam	Jharkhand	Kerala	Maharashtra	North East	Odisha	Assam	Delhi	Total
Stay issued on the relief decreed by the lower court.	1	0	1	0	0	0	0	1	0	2	0	0	**5**
Stay was refused. Decree of the Lower Court to have effect	3	4	1	0	0	0	0	1	0	0	0	0	**9**
Relief granted by Lower Court limited (circums cribed) pending disposal of appeal	3	2	0	0	1	1	0	0	0	2	0	0	**9**
Any Other	3	1	1	0	1	0	2	0	1	1	0	0	**10**
NA	17	16	24	2	15	7	2	1	0	5	8	7	**104**
TOTAL	27	23	27	2	17	8	4	3	1	10	8	7	**137**

Source: Author.

Finally, appeals were dismissed in 43.7 per cent of the cases and allowed (35 per cent) or partly allowed (21.4 per cent) in the remainder (Table 8.57). Without access to comparators in other areas of law, it is difficult to know whether this rate of reversal of lower court decisions is at par or at variance with the overall system. Certainly, however, that more than half the cases appealed are reversed fully or partly on appeal,[14] may point to concerns regarding the quality of adjudication.

Settled Cases

A total of 161 orders in the dataset pertained to cases where the parties had settled the matter. By and large, these orders contained very little information regarding the case, and therefore a high percentage of the variables returned null observations. From the remainder, it appears that parties settle matters regardless of the nature of violence alleged against the respondent. Most of these cases are settled either through the court or through court adjunct mechanisms like Mediation Centres and Lok Adalats. The terms of the settlement reveal that in about a third of the cases (31.3 per cent) parties agreed to reconcile their differences. However, the remaining cases by and large focus on maintenance for the aggreived person, agreement for divorce, and agreement to withdraw all pending litigation against the respondent. Given the nature of violence alleged, and the fact that a vast majority of these cases are settled through the court or allied mechanisms, protection officers can be used to determine whether the terms of the settlement are fair to both parties, whether there is continuing threat to the aggreived person, and whether the terms are being adhered to by the respondent. However, the data reveals, that as in other contexts, protection officers are rarely called upon to provide inputs in cases of settlement between parties (Tables 8.58 to 8.62).

Judicial Attitudes

The rights and reliefs under the Act do not depend upon the religious identity or personal law of the respondent. However, in previous Monitoring and Evaluation Reports, certain cases came to light where the case was decided on the basis of the personal laws of the parties. To study this, we examined whether judges explicitly rely upon the personal law of the parties in deciding upon the relief available. This was found to be the case in only three orders within the dataset.

[14] It is important to note that Section 29, PWDVA does not give the sessions court any discretion in admission of appeals. Therefore, appeal is a statutory right under the Act.

Table 8.57 Result of the Appeal

Result of the Appeal	Andhra Pradesh	West Bengal	Uttarakhand	Tripura	Assam	Jharkhand	Kerala	Maharashtra	North East	Odisha	Assam	Delhi	Total
Appeal Allowed	9	4	13	0	4	1	3	2	0	3	1	4	44
Appeal partly allowed	8	6	5	0	3	1	0	0	1	2	1	0	27
Appeal dismissed	10	12	8	1	8	6	1	1	0	2	4	2	55
NA	0	1	1	1	2	0	0	0	0	3	2	1	11
TOTAL	27	23	27	2	17	8	4	3	1	10	8	7	137

Source: Author.

Table 8.58 Nature of Violence Alleged

Nature of Violence	Andhra Pradesh	West Bengal	Uttarakhand	Tripura	Assam	Jharkhand	Kerala	Maharashtra	North East	Odisha	Assam	Delhi	Total
Physical Abuse	0	1	0	0	8	0	0	6	1	0	0	0	**16**
Verbal and Emotional Abuse	0	0	1	0	4	0	0	5	1	0	0	0	**11**
Economic abuse	0	1	1	1	9	0	0	2	1	0	0	0	**15**
Sexual Abuse	0	0	0	0	0	1	0	0	0	0	0	0	**1**
NA	13	6	25	11	39	3	16	7	5	2	8	3	**138**
TOTAL	13	8	27	12	60	4	16	20	8	2	8	3	**181**

Source: Author.

Table 8.59 Authority involved in the settlement

Authority affecting the settlement	Andhra Pradesh	West Bengal	Uttarak hand	Tripura	Assam	Jharkhand	Kerala	Maharashtra	North East	Odisha	Assam	Delhi	Total
Gram Panchayat	0	0	0	2	0	0	0	0	0	0	0	0	2
Lok Adalats	9	0	0	0	8	0	2	2	0	1	0	0	22
Magistrate Court	2	0	1	7	15	1	1	0	2	1	0	0	30
Mediation Centre	0	0	7	0	3	0	1	4	4	0	0	1	20
Any Other	2	2	1	1	6	1	7	2	0	0	0	1	23
NA	0	5	17	2	19	2	5	4	1	0	8	1	64
TOTAL	13	7	26	12	51	4	16	12	7	2	8	3	161

Source: Author.

Table 8.60 Result of the Settlement

The case resulted in	Andhra Pradesh	West Bengal	Uttarakhand	Tripura	Assam	Jharkhand	Kerala	Maharashtra	North East	Odisha	Assam	Delhi	Total
Out of Court Settlement	8	4	11	7	11	1	6	1	2	1	6	0	**58**
Settled through the Court	3	0	8	2	11	1	2	8	2	1	1	1	**40**
Withdrawn by the AP or not pressed by the AP	1	3	6	3	26	2	1	0	1	0	0	2	**45**
Any Other	0	0	0	0	1	0	0	0	0	0	1	0	**2**
NA	1	0	1	0	2	0	7	3	2	0	0	0	**16**
TOTAL	13	7	26	12	51	4	16	12	7	2	8	3	**161**

Source: Author.

Table 8.61 Terms of Settlement

What are the Terms of Settlement?	Andhra Pradesh	West Bengal	Uttarakhand	Tripura	Assam	Jharkhand	Kerala	Maharashtra	North East	Odisha	Assam	Delhi	Total
Reconciliati on between the parties	2	0	6	1	7	1	0	0	2	1	0	1	**21**
Assurance by the Respondent that he would stop the violence	0	0	2	0	9	0	0	0	2	0	0	0	**13**
A one time lump sum amount is paid to the AP	4	0	4	2	1	1	0	2	2	0	1	0	**17**
Respondent agrees to pay a certain amount as maintenance to the AP	1	0	3	0	12	0	0	1	0	0	1	0	**18**
Mutual consent divorce the Respondent agrees for a final settlement amount as the divorce settlement	1	0	0	0	0	0	0	2	0	0	0	0	**3**
AP agrees to withdraw all pending litigation against the Respondent	2	0	1	2	3	0	0	2	0	0	0	0	**10**
Any Other	1	0	0	0	3	0	1	1	0	0	0	0	**6**
NA	3	7	13	9	27	2	15	8	2	1	6	1	**94**
TOTAL	**14**	**7**	**29**	**14**	**62**	**4**	**16**	**16**	**8**	**2**	**8**	**2**	**182**

Source: Author.

Table 8.62 Filing of DIRs in Settlement Cases

Filing of DIR	Andhra Pradesh	West Bengal	Uttarakhand	Tripura	Assam	Jharkhand	Kerala	Maharashtra	North East	Odisha	Assam	Delhi	Total
DIR called for	0	1	1	0	0	0	0	2	0	0	0	0	**4**
DIR considered while granting order	0	1	1	0	3	0	0	0	0	0	1	0	**6**
DIR filed after the application (at the direction of the court)	0	1	1	1	2	0	0	0	0	1	0	0	**6**
DIR filed with the application	0	0	0	3	1	1	0	0	4	0	0	0	**9**
DIR not mentioned in the order	11	3	4	3	36	2	15	3	3	0	2	0	**82**
Any Other	0	0	0	0	0	0	0	0	0	0	1	0	**1**
NA	2	1	19	5	9	1	1	7	0	1	4	3	**53**
TOTAL	**13**	**7**	**26**	**12**	**51**	**4**	**16**	**12**	**7**	**2**	**8**	**3**	**161**

Source: Author.

However, a more common concern was regarding the judicial reasoning on why an aggrieved person is entitled to relief. A rights-and-equality-oriented approach to protection against economic abuse should understand women's right to economic sustenance both within larger socio-economic structures which deny women access or equal opportunity to find employment outside the home, as well as the recognition of women's contribution towards the generation of family income through their employment at home. However, as mentioned previously, courts tend to locate their maintenance decisions on a husband's or son's 'moral duty' to maintain the wife or mother, rather than on her entitlement to economic support for the services she performs.

Another concern evident in a subset of cases is that while a range of reliefs were asked for, the courts' decision only focused on granting maintenance. This indicates an approach amongst some judges at least of viewing the legislation as a corollary to Section 125 CrPC, rather than as a comprehensive law on domestic violence.

***

Based on the tabulation and percentage distribution analysis described earlier the following emerge as adjudicatory practices under the law that ought to be emulated widely:

1. Tabulation of data relating to cases against non-marital relations reveals that the percentage distribution of observations therein is not very different from the data in the general pool of cases. Therefore, it appears that granting of relief under the Act does not depend on the type of relationship between the aggrieved person and the respondent.
2. Courts routinely use the procedural flexibility under the Act to reduce procedural and evidentiary burdens upon aggrieved persons, and facilitate their access to immediate relief under the Act.
3. By and large, courts do not rely on the personal laws of parties (at least explicitly) in determining the relief that an aggrieved person is or is not entitled to.

At the same time, the study reveals certain areas of concern regarding adjudication under the PWDVA:

1. While a majority of aggrieved persons leave the shared household before filing a case under the PWDVA, courts often deny relief to a women on the ground that she is no longer residing in the shared household. This goes

against express provisions of the law, and also does not account for the fact that violence does not require continuing residence in the shared household.

2. Complaints under the Act are routinely filed against female non-marital relatives. Courts also often grant relief in such cases, going against the express restrictions on the scope of the law.
3. Some judges tend to treat PWDVA as primarily a maintenance law rather than a comprehensive legislation on domestic violence. In such cases, while a range of reliefs are asked for, the courts' decision only focuses on granting maintenance.
4. As a related point, courts are more likely to grant monetary relief relating to the future maintenance of the aggrieved person, rather than restitution for losses incurred in the past. So also, judges appear to be more reluctant to grant compensation orders as compared to other orders, and tend to place higher evidentiary burdens on women in such cases, requiring specific proof of injuries or mental trauma, even when domestic violence itself is proved.
5. Many judges locate the grant of remedies under the Act, especially monetary relief, within patriarchal frameworks of the moral responsibility of male family members to maintain their female relatives. In a constitutional paradigm which recognizes women's equality, but is also sensitive to existing socio-economic and legal structures that continue to deny women equality in reality, a more nuanced understanding of the basis for reliefs under the Act is required. Locating the relief in the right of the woman to be free from domestic violence and abuse, as well as the recognition of women's contribution towards the generation of family income through their employment at home, are more equality-oriented bases for judicial reasoning.
6. The study finds that the judicial process, by and large, lacks the multi-agency approach to addressing domestic violence envisaged under the PWDVA. The services of Protection Officers are not utilized fully, or even regularly. The absence of any mention of DIRs in a significant number of cases suggests that the DIR process is not fully integrated into the judicial process. Where information required for decision making under the Act is lacking, as for example, details of the financial status of the respondent, courts rely more on guesswork than on reports by Protection Officers. Similarly, in cases where parties reach a settlement, and the court orders a consent decree, the services of Protection Officers can be utilized to determine whether the terms of the settlement are fair to both parties, whether there is continuing threat to the aggrieved

person, and whether the terms are being adhered to by the respondent. Presently, such an approach is lacking.

7. The judicial record is virtually silent on service providers under the Act as well as shelter homes and medical facilities, indicating once again, that at the very least, there is a lack of integration of these mechanisms with the adjudicatory process. To the extent that the PWDVA seeks to create a unified, single window mechanism for holistic relief and protection of the aggrieved person, this lack of integration goes against the objectives of the law.
8. The regular use of the appellate process against interim orders is a cause of concern since it places additional barriers in the way of urgently accessing reliefs under the Act. Similarly, permitting recourse to Section 482, CrPC for quashing of complaints under the Act is likely to hinder the ability of the system to provide immediate relief to aggrieved persons. For the same reasons, courts should be circumspect in ordering a stay on trial court proceedings or reliefs pending appeal.

9. *Long Road to Justice*

Implementation of the Protection of Women from Domestic Violence Act (2005) in Haryana[1]

MONICA SAKHRANI, TRUPTI JHAVERI PANCHAL, RADHIKA CHAKRABORTY, MANISHA KANDE

The PWDVA was introduced in 2006, after several years of advocacy by the women's movement. Hailed as a landmark piece of legislation, it expanded the definition of 'domestic relationship' to include non-marital relationships and familial relationships, recognizing multiple and diverse needs of survivors by mandating a supportive network of protection officers and service providers, and foregrounded the importance of speedy justice for survivors.[2] Prior to the implementation of the

[1] The findings and analysis in this chapter have been taken from a four-state study on the implementation of the PWDVA—'Quest for Justice: A Study of Implementation of Protection of Women from Domestic Violence Act 2005' (2014).

[2] I. Jaising, 'Bringing Rights Home: Review of the Campaign for a Law on Domestic Violence', *Economic and Political Weekly*, 44 (2009): 50–7.

PWDVA, women facing domestic violence had access only to criminal law through Section 498A of the IPC that addressed cruelty to married women. The PWDVA presented a much-needed civil recourse with supportive redressal mechanisms. However, nearly a decade into its enactment, strong implementation of the PWDVA is not yet a reality, as women struggle with judicial delays, inadequate court orders, and a fractured and sparse service network.

This study seeks to understand and evaluate the implementation of the PWDVA in Haryana, from the standpoint of the survivors of domestic violence. It explores how women encountered the law, and the processes and challenges they have undergone in their quest for justice. It also examines the implementation of the PWDVA across the country in order to identify and recommend best practices. This report is drawn from a study on the implementation of the PWDVA in four states of India (Haryana, Maharashtra, Odisha, and Tamil Nadu) and presents an analysis on the findings from Haryana.

In Haryana, gaps in civil society organizations and grassroots level work on violence against women has impacted the implementation of the PWDVA.[3] Added to the poor sex ratio[4] the low Female Literacy Rates,[5] Prem Chowdry has identified shifts in gender regimes introduced by the Green Revolution in the 1960s, which marked an increased pressure on women's labour and severely increased wage differentiation in a region that experienced a sudden influx of capital and income, suggesting that rapidly changing patterns of consumption and increasing urbanization added to women's lack of control over expenditure. She also argues that the introduction of women's inheritance rights and women's increased investment in claiming their shares in property have created potential for violent conflict between her natal and affinal kin, making control over women a more pressing concern for rural men.[6] The poor status of women in the region and shifts in gender politics

[3] Special Cells for Women and Children, 'Paving New Pathways: Special Cells for Women and Children in Haryana, 2008–2014', Government of Haryana, 2016.

[4] Amongst the lowest in the major states in India, B. Yadav, 'Haryana's "Setting Daughters"', *Economic and Political Weekly* 36, 45 (2001): 4257–9.

[5] 66.8 per cent as compared to the male literacy rate at 85.4 per cent. 'Census of India 2011', Ministry of Home Affairs, Government of India, 2011.

[6] Prem Chowdhry, *The Veiled Woman: Shifting Gender Equations in Rural Haryana 1880–1990* (New Delhi: Oxford University Press, 1994); Prem. Chowdhry, 'Infliction, Acceptance and Resistance: Containing Violence on Women in Rural Haryana', *Economic and Political Weekly* 47, 37 (2012): 43–59.

make Haryana an important site for exploring the implementation of laws addressing violence against women.

Haryana has adopted a unique implementation model for the PWDVA. Protection-cum-Prohibition Officers (PPOs) who hold charge both under the PWDVA and the Prohibition of Child Marriages Act, were appointed in 2006 in recognition of the intersections of these forms of gender violence.[7] The PPO model in Haryana as a unique intervention and presents an opportunity to highlight and evaluate the effectiveness of innovation in implementation strategies for the PWDVA. While studies have been conducted in several other states on the implementation of the PWDVA, no major study has been conducted on implementation in Haryana. Literature from Delhi, Odisha, and Gujarat points towards major gaps in implementation,[8] and national monitoring and evaluation of the PWDVA has highlighted inadequate protocols for developing stakeholder network and to address judicial biases and gaps in budgetary allocation in various states.[9]

The findings from the present study indicate that in Haryana, a dismal number of women have been able to obtain relief under the PWDVA. Women who were interviewed cited delays and protracted procedures as the main constraints faced by them. The stakeholder network was found to be fractured and sparse: while protection officers (PO) have been appointed by the state government, little else has been done by way of creating supportive services and notification of service providers (SP) under the PWDVA. This report highlights gaps in the implementation of the law and presents recommendations for their redressal based on the study conducted in Haryana.

Studies on violence against women reflect that women survivors often do not approach the legal system. This study thus sought to locate factors that

[7] Special Cells for Women and Children, 'Paving New Pathways.

[8] M. Bhatia, 'Domestic Violence in India: Cases under the Protection of Women from Domestic Violence Act, 2005', *South Asia Research* 32, 2 (2012): 103–22; Civil Society Resource Facility, 'A Report on the Status of PWDVA in Orissa, 2010–2011 Oxfam (unpublished report on file with the researchers, 2010); Centre for Social Justice, 'A Fact File on the Implementation of the Protection of Women from Domestic Violence Act, 2005 in the state of Gujarat, Oxfam' (unpublished report on file with the researchers, 2009).

[9] Lawyers Collective, *Staying Alive: Fourth Monitoring & Evaluation Report on the Protection of Women from Domestic Violence Act, 2005* (New Delhi: Lawyers Collective and ICRW, 2011); (Lawyers Collective 2011, 2013); *Staying Alive: Evaluating Court Orders. Sixth Monitoring and Evaluation Report on the Protection of Women from Domestic Violence Act 2005.*

affect women's access to justice through the legal system, and understand the relationship between legal rights and alternate dispute redressal mechanisms that survivors turn to. While the study locates itself within the framework of law and court processes,[10] the intent was to understand women's experiences with these processes as rights-bearers and how they navigated the legal system. Accordingly, the study examines the micro-processes in the implementation of the PWDVA, understanding how women and stakeholders use and perceive the law, and where they see the law as lacking, is crucial for its effective implementation.

The primary objectives of the study include:

1. To study the manner in which the PWDVA is being implemented
2. To identify the needs and expectations of women facing domestic violence from the legal system
3. To identify the factors that lead to the exercise of legal rights by women facing domestic violence
4. To suggest steps in advocating for the implementation of the law and access of rights by women facing domestic violence

Methodology

The Study was commissioned by the Ministry of Women and Child Development, Government of India and carried out by the TISS, Mumbai. The aim of the study was to study the implementation of the PWDVA from the standpoint of the woman who is subjected to domestic violence.

Universe of the Study and Research Design

Hissar and Fatehbad districts in Haryana were selected for study on the basis of purposive sampling of districts based on NCRB Crime against Women statistics. Based on the data from amongst the highest and lowest incidence of crimes under Section 498A and Section 304B (2006–10), these two districts were chosen for data collection. The court records of all the cases filed in the magistrates' courts in the two districts chosen as the sample were the universe of the *secondary data*. All cases filed from 2006[11] up to the completion of data collection in 2012 were included in the study.[12]

[10] The ones mandated under the PWDVA.

[11] The year PWDVA can into force.

[12] All the records made available to the research team were included as a part of the study.

The aim was to understand how the law unfolded itself in its implementation through the voices of women and key stakeholders under the Act, as well as what alternate redressal mechanisms women had accessed.

The study also aimed to look at the factors that led to the women accessing the legal system as well as the barriers to the same. To achieve this end, primary data were collected employing qualitative methodology through semi-structured interviews and interview guides from three groups of interviewees:

1. Women survivors of violence who had accessed the PWDVA.
2. Women survivors of violence who had accessed alternate justice mechanisms.
3. Key stakeholders such as POs, SPs, police officials, NGO/CBO workers, panchayat members, Legal Service Authority, lawyers handling these cases, and experts including Magistrates to gain an understanding of the nature of implementation of the Act.

The semi-structured interview guides for interviews with women, both those who had filed cases under the PWDVA and those who had accessed alternate dispute resolution mechanisms, included details about the demographic profile, their experience of violence, help-seeking behaviour, their knowledge of law, their reasons for approaching court, their experience with court, and their current demographic profile and living status. The interviews thus sought to capture their subjective experiences with the judiciary, as well as their assessment of the judicial response to their case and suggestions in order to make the judiciary more responsive to the needs of the women.

Stakeholders were interviewed in order to understand their experience of discharging their duties as outlined in the Act, and to gain information regarding the nature of cases they handled, and the challenges they faced in working with other stakeholders and women survivors. Thus, interviews were conducted with POs, SPs, police officials, lawyers, legal aid officials, and also local caste panchayat members, especially in Haryana where caste panchayats act as parallel bodies of justice delivery, which women often access before they access the formal legal system.

The main sources of data in Haryana were as follows:

1. **Court Records of cases filed under the PWDVA—filed in the Hissar and Fatehbad district:** 970 court records were studied in the Hissar (681) and Fatehbad (289) district of Haryana. A nearly equal proportion of cases were collected from rural (466) and urban (504) courts.

2. **In-depth interviews:** 49 women were interviewed who had filed court cases under PWDVA in the two districts of Hissar and Fatehbad.
3. **In-depth interviews:** 47 women were interviewed who had not filed cases under PWDVA but accessed alternate dispute mechanisms in the two districts of Hissar and Fatehbad.
4. **In-depth interviews:** 47 stakeholders including lawyers, police officials, POs, and SPs from Hissar and Fatehbad were interviewed.

Scope of the Study and Challenges of Legal Research

Conducting legal research on a large scale comes with various challenges. Legal data are static and the information available was dependent on what court records had been maintained, and on the access granted to researchers. As centralized court records for cases filed under PWDVA were not available, all courts in districts were contacted for data collection. The individual courts also did not maintain records of the cases filed under the Act and therefore the investigators were dependant on the court staff for the records of the cases. Therefore, no verification could be done as to whether all the cases filed in the particular court had been examined by the researchers.

In addition to this, the cases filed under Section 26 of the PWDVA, which permits applications under the PWDVA to be filed in any pending proceeding between the parties, were not looked at as these were not separately numbered but were interlocutory applications. As the majority of the cases were filed as separate proceedings (this was confirmed by inquiring with the lawyers filing cases under the PWDVA in most of the districts), it was decided that the records of the magistrates' courts where the proceedings were filed would be perused for the purposes of the study. The judgments of the four high courts and the Supreme Court were also studied.

The study sought to bring further depth to court data by conducting interviews with women in order to understand their experiences of the Act. The two datasets were found to speak to each other, with interviews providing depth to the patterns observed through the court data. However, in the absence of any centralized record of PWDVA complaints, it was not possible to create a sampling frame using court records. Thus, a purposive sampling process was followed for identifying women for the interviews. Thus, the data provided in the interviews may be subject to sampling bias. Care should be applied while generalizing the findings. However, it must be mentioned that the findings of the interviews corroborated the findings of the secondary data.

One challenge in this study was that the court data were based on the contradictory claims of the parties. While in the adversarial system, it is expected that allegations of violence by the applicant are bound to be denied by the respondents, the description of the facts relating to violence depended on the case of the women applicants. It is the woman's voice which has been the basis of this study. However, the complexities of the court cases, creativities of legal drafting, the unsubstantiated nature of truth claims by the parties, and the contradictory findings of the facts by the trial and appellate courts were challenges faced during the study.

Key Findings

Who uses the PWDVA?

From court data as well as individual interview data collected through this study, it becomes possible to create a profile of women experiencing violence and approaching this Act. As per secondary data from courts, 71 per cent of women filing cases under the PWDVA were between the age group of 18 to 35—the reproductive age of women and a majority of cases were filed by married women.

Though the definition of domestic relationship has been broadened by the PWDVA, most cases were filed by married women (92.7 per cent), and were largely filed against their husband (24.8 per cent) and/or marital family (64.2 per cent), as per court records. Most women identified themselves as married to their partners due to social stigma surrounding non-marital intimate relationships. Unmarried women comprised 5 per cent of cases from the court records, whereas 0.1 per cent were separated, 0.3 per cent were divorced, and 6.4 per cent were widowed. No women were identified as

Table 9.1 Profile of Woman Complainants under the PWDVA

	Court records (970)	Interviewed data (49)
Age (18–35)	693 (71.4%)	43 (87%)
Age (More than 60)	24 (2.5%)	1 (2%)
Religion (Hindu)	933 (96.2%)	46 (93.9%)
Religion (Sikh)	31 (3.2%)	3 (6.1%)
Marital status (Married)	899 (92.7%)	46 (93.9%)
Case filed against (Husband and In-laws)	623 (64.2%)	

Source: Authors.

being in a live-in relationship in either dataset from Haryana. A large majority of the women interviewed, who had filed cases under the PWDVA, were married (93.9 per cent), whereas (6.1 per cent) were widowed. This shows that the Act is primarily being used by married women to file cases against their marital family, and that after married women, widowed women comprise the most significant percentage of those using the Act. However, we can also see that over 8 per cent of the persons using the Act are non-married persons, which is a significant figure.

Out of the 970 court cases studied, 144 cases had one or more applicants who were children, reflecting that the Act to some extent is being harnessed to secure the rights of children as well.

As the drafting of complaints does not mandate details about the socio-economic status of women, many complaints do not mention details like education and occupation unless they are deemed as necessary to the case by the official filing/drafting the Domestic Incident Report (DIR) or the application. Educational information was available for 168 women, of which 130 women were non-literate and 20 were graduates. From the interview data, it emerged that education levels displayed more variation, from literate (22.4 per cent) to primary and secondary (32.6 per cent), matriculation (18.4 per cent) and higher secondary education/graduation (8.2 per cent), and professional education (6.1 per cent).

97.3 per cent of women applicants as per court data identified themselves as homemakers, and 69.4 per cent of the women interviewed identified themselves as homemakers. Thus, it appears that the majority of women using the PWDVA were financially dependent on their marital or natal family.

The court records revealed that 27.6 per cent of women who registered cases in the court were married for two to five years, followed by 23 per cent of women who were married for 11 to 20 years. The interview data also reveal that 26.5 per cent of women respondents who had filed cases under the PWDVA had been married for two to five years and another 26.5 per cent for six to 10 years. This shows that women undergo violence for a significant number of years before filing cases under the PWDVA.

In interviews, 93.9 per cent of women who filed cases under the PWDVA reported that their family had arranged their marriage. All women interviewed reported that dowry had been given at the time of marriage, and court records showed that 802 out of 970 women reported the exchange of dowry (82.7 per cent). 57 per cent of women who did not go to court reported dowry as cause of violence in the interviews, and 63 per cent of those who went to court reported dowry as a cause of violence.

Why do Women Seek Legal Redressal under PWDVA?

Court records revealed that in 26 per cent of cases women faced violence within two years of marriage. It was also revealed that 10.5 per cent of women faced violence within a year of marriage, followed by 17.3 per cent of women who faced violence between three to five years of marriage. This indicates that within the first five years of marriage, women faced regular occurrences of violence. According to the court records, in a majority of cases (98.1 per cent) women have experienced three or more types of violence, from their husband, in laws, intimate partner, and other members of the marital family. The percentage of violence faced by the women from their natal family is very low (.4 per cent). Interview data reveal that 91.8 per cent of women who filed cases under the PWDVA faced violence from both their husband and in-laws.

Before filing cases under the PWDVA, women also sought help from other avenues. Interview data from women who approached the court to file a case under the PWDVA, revealed that most women (61.2 per cent) sought help from their parents, followed by those who sought help from their family along with their panchayat member (28.6 per cent). Few women also sought help from their marital family and the PO. 83.7 per cent of women interviewed reported satisfaction with the external help they sought. From interview data, it emerged that a majority of women filing cases under the PWDVA primarily sought to stop the violence they were experiencing (41). Women also sought to end dowry demands (14), reconcile (10), and obtain monetary help (four).

A majority of women said that they chose to take legal action because they had been thrown out of their home (42.9 per cent). 22.4 per cent of women said that they went to court because they experienced excessive violence. Other reasons cited were that they 'saw no other choice' (10.2 per cent), that the lawyer suggested this course of action (8.2 per cent), this course of action was suggested by the natal family (4.1 per cent), or that settlement was not possible (4.1 per cent).

Many women cited a lack of awareness about legal provisions for relief from domestic violence; only 24.5 per cent of women from interview data said that they had been aware of the PWDVA before filing a case, and only 16.3 per cent of women cited awareness about the laws available to women to address domestic violence. 18.4 per cent of women said they were aware of the existence of Section 498A. Most women thus said that only their lawyer suggested that they file a case under the PWDVA (53.1 per cent). 30.6 per cent of women said that this measure was suggested by both their lawyer and family. Thus, it is not surprising that a majority of women interviewed said that the decisions about what relief to seek under the PWDVA was influenced by their lawyer. In only four cases did their lawyer have no role in the decision about reliefs sought. A few women (14) said that their family also influenced their decision. Only two women said that they made the decisions themselves.

Most lawyers interviewed agreed that what women need from the PWDVA most are protection orders, followed by shelter and maintenance orders. One suggested that women need a block-level protection officer. One lawyer emphasized the need for a shelter home in the district, and others cited the need for police services.

From court records, we see that women experienced multiple forms of violence, most for many years, before they approach the legal system. 98.8 per cent of women reported some form of physical violence, including beating (96 per cent), being overburdened with work (46.3 per cent), instigations of violence (34.6 per cent), and violence during pregnancy (12.7 per cent), amongst others. 46.7 per cent of women reported experiencing sexual violence, including being forced to have sexual intercourse (44 per cent), being forced to watch pornography (6.4 per cent), and being used to entertain others (3.2 per cent). 99.4 per cent of women reported experiencing emotional violence, such as abusive behaviour (99 per cent), being denied medical treatment (77 per cent), being prevented from meeting their natal family (58 per cent), and aspersions on their character (38 per cent). Economic violence

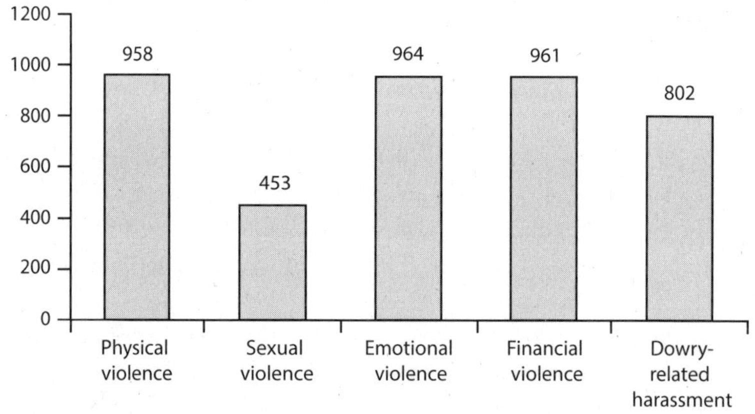

Figure 9.1 Multiple forms of violence.
Source: Authors.

Table 9.2 Multiple Forms of Violence Experienced by Women

Physical violence	Beating	Burns	Beating children	Violence during pregnancy	Causing miscarriage	Driven to commit suicide or threaten to kill	Instigating of violence	Overburden with work	Any other	
958 (98.8)	931 (96)	14 (1.4)	102 (10.5)	123(12.7)	18 (1.9)	11 (1.1%)	337 (34.7)	449 (46.3)	75 (7.7)	
Sexual violence	Forced to have sexual intercourse	Force to watch porn	Forcibly using you to entertain others	Any other act of sexual violence	Any other					
453(46.7)	427(44)	62 (6.4)	31(3.2)	26(2.7)	14(1.4)					
Emotional violence	Abusive behaviour	Aspersion on character	Adultery	Alcoholism/ drug abuse	Not giving medical treatment when sick	Not allowing to visit or meet parents	Any other			
964 (99.4)	960 (99)	371 (38.2)	159(16.4)	405(41.8)	747(77)	563(58)	36(3.7)			
Economic violence	Not giving money for expenses	Not giving enough food	Demanding money	Demanding house	Not allowing to work	Taking away salary or money	Disposing of streedhan	Dispossession from SH	Sale or dispose of shared household	Any other
961 (99.1)	941 (97)	769 (79.3)	767(79.1)	220(22.7)	412(42.5)	21(2.2)	564(58.1)	654(67.4)	46(4.7)	

Source: Authors.

was also widespread, with 99.1 per cent of women reporting violence such as being denied money for expenses (97 per cent), being denied money for food (97.9 per cent), money being demanded from them (79 per cent), and dispossession from the shared household (67.4 per cent). 82.7 per cent of women reported dowry-related harassment. When interviewed, a PO shared that in her experience, most women who approach her have been thrown out of their houses and are in dire need of shelter, and fear for their safety. Interviews with women, both women who had filed PWDVA cases

Box 9.1

Case Study 1

Anjali had been married for nearly 10 years at the time of data collection. Violence started 20 days after her marriage and took the form of beating, constant demands for dowry, verbal and mental abuse, and economic abuse. This was perpetrated by her husband and in-laws. She shared that her relationship with her husband was strained, as he was not satisfied with the dowry given at the time of marriage. He asked for a bike and 1 lakh rupees in cash for start a bigger cycle repair shop. He made a suicide attempt six months after their marriage, citing his reason as her not bringing cash from her parents. Her father had given a buffalo as a part of the dowry, but her husband and in-laws taunted her, saying 'Bhains to humare yaha thi, Bike kyun nahi di' [we already have buffaloes, why didn't you bring a bike]. She shared that her father-in-law had 'wrong intentions', implying that he sexually harassed her. She also faced violence from the entire family for giving birth to a girl child, and was not given proper food during her pregnancy. In 2007, her husband beat her with a belt and iron rod and she was admitted to a hospital. Her father intervened many times but nothing changed. She shared '1-2 mahine sasural mein rehti hoon, phir pihar aana padta hai' [I stay for one or two months in the marital home, but then I have to return to the natal home]. Anjali approached the police a few times and approached the women's cell in 2013. Although she wanted to register a complaint, her husband was repeatedly counselled and no complaint was registered. She shared that the police told her 'Rehena to usi ghar mein hai, aise se bulakar samjha denge' [you have to stay in that house eventually; it is better if we call him and counsel him]. After March 2013, her husband and in laws refused to live with her, and then Anjali, on consultation with a lawyer, employed by her father, had filed a case under PWDVA a month before data collection. She is hopeful that the lawyer will deliver on the assurances and she will get relief under the Act.

and women who had not filed cases, suggest that both sets of women faced similar forms and kinds of violence. Women in interviews shared incidents of violence, and highlighted the everyday nature of the violence they faced.

Put together, this paints a shocking and dismal picture of the severity and nature of violence experienced by complainants. Most women do not first approach the court but attempt family or community-based interventions, failing which, they approach the legal system and file a case through a lawyer.

PWDVA Processes and the Role of Stakeholders

Under the PWDVA, a wide network of stakeholders was envisioned to provide a variety of reliefs that women survivors of violence may need. Under the Act, POs, SPs, medical relief, and shelter homes are to be appointed as stakeholders bound to provide assistance to women facing violence. The stakeholder network is one of the hallmarks of the Act, as it places responsibility on the state to create multiple forms of support for women facing violence. However, in Haryana this network was found to be lacking.

Protection Officer

The PO, as designated under the P.WDVA, was intended to 'provide a bridge between the woman and the court and the other functionaries/services within the Act. Protection Officers work as officers of the court and render assistance to the court in dispensing justice'.[13] The PO thus was envisioned as the first point of contact for the survivor of violence, and as the nodal functionary who would file the DIR, provide referrals to other services, and support her through the court processes. While POs remain to be appointed in other states,[14] the government of Haryana has institutionalized a network of PPOs (under the PWDVA and the Prohibition of Child Marriage Act, 2006 (PCMA)) in each district of Haryana. Thus, the network of POs is strong in this state.

Most women who were interviewed (63.3 per cent) said they were aware about the presence of the PO, and 59.2 per cent of them said that the PO had helped file the DIR. 57.1 per cent of them reported a satisfactory experience

[13] Lawyers Collective, *Manual on the Best Practices under the Protection of Women from Domestic Violence Act, 2005* (New Delhi: Lawyers Collective, 2013b).

[14] M. Sakhrani and T. Panchal, 'Quest for Justice', Ministry of Women and Child Development, Tata Institute of Social Sciences and Government of India, Mumbai, 2014.

with the PO. A PO of Fatehbad reported that in the last year the POs of the district had handled 206 cases out of which 148 cases were referred to by the court, 23 by the police, 2 by others, and in which 33 of the women had approached directly. They shared that at a time a PO would be handling approximately seven cases. Thus, we see that women often have gone directly to court rather than first approaching the PO.

Interviews revealed that the POs face difficulties, and one PO shared that her main concerns were a heavy workload, long hours, and inadequate pay. The PO also shared that due to a heavy workload (the POs in Haryana hold additional charge and are also POs under the PCMA), she was unable to go to court to follow up on cases as the lawyers would take over, and her role ended at referring women to free legal aid to file the case. She would in some urgent cases file the case herself, but was unable to follow up after the summons were served. The PO, while aware that her role involved referral, cited a dearth of shelter homes and the limited availability of qualified service providers as a major obstacle.

Service Providers and Legal Aid

All women interviewed who had filed cases under the PWDVA were unaware of the presence of any SP. Most lawyers had not worked with service providers or any other organizations in their PWDVA cases. The PO of Fatehbad interviewed reported a negative experience with the single SP in the district. The police officers interviewed were also unaware of the shelter homes in their district. However, some police officers shared that the police had established a 'protection home' in their district. Only 28.6 per cent of women interviewed, who had filed cases under the PWDVA, were aware of their right to legal aid, and only one had approached the legal service authority, and reported an unsatisfactory experience with legal service authority. One woman reported that though she was aware of her right to legal aid, '*sarkari vakil mein dam nahin hota*' [government lawyers don't have any strength]. Most lawyers interviewed said that women came to them through the legal service authority, and one PO shared that she had not had a negative experience with the legal service authority and that she regularly referred women to them, and they handled cases well. Court data also reflected the lack of service providers as stakeholders in the supportive network for women. It thus seems evident that the service provider network needs to be strengthened in these districts. These gaps are critical, as the need for supportive services is one of the key tenets of the Act.

Police

Of the women interviewed, 49 per cent sought help from the police, but of these 15 women reported dissatisfaction with the help received from the police, and only six reported satisfaction with police help. Women shared that the police, when first approached, counselled them and their husband rather than registering a complaint. One woman said that the police told her '*yadi tume ghar basana hai to, kuch to sahan bhi karna hoga*' [if you want to establish a home for yourself, then you have to tolerate some things], and another that the police told her that '*rehena to usi ghar mein hai, aise se bulakar samjha denge*' [you have to stay in that house eventually, it is better if we call him and counsel him], even though she wanted to file a complaint. One lawyer who had worked with the police said that the police in one case assisted in enforcing the execution of a residence order, and another shared a similar experience. Another said that police officials are not sensitive to issues of violence against women; however, one PO had very positive feedback about the police. Police officials interviewed said that they had not received any training dealing with the PWDVA. A few were not aware of the Act at all. Most said that they followed court directions in cases of domestic violence, and referred women to the PO for counselling and mediation. As a police official suggested, there is the need for grassroots awareness about the provisions of the PWDVA to be developed. Even the police officials of the Women's Cell, which sees the maximum number of domestic violence cases come through, cite lack of awareness of the Act and said that they refer such cases to the PO, and have little involvement with them. There is also generally less awareness about the role of the police under this Act, and this has not been spelled out clearly in the Act itself.

DIR and the Role of Stakeholders

The first step of the implementation of the PWDVA was envisioned to be the DIR. This report was to function as a record of the history of violence that a woman was facing, which could be presented as evidence in court. While filing of a DIR in itself did not initiate court proceedings (which would be initiated only after the filing of form II), the DIR was intended to be a legal record and affirmation of the violence a woman had faced. The POs and SPs (as notified under the Act, and including hospitals, shelter homes, Special Cells, and so on), are empowered to file the DIR.

From court records, it emerged that a DIR was filed in 781 cases (80.5 per cent). The DIR was filed by the PO in 773 cases, and by the SP in only two cases. Interviews with lawyers confirmed that in most cases the PO files the DIR. This is also linked to the dearth of service providers in the area. Most lawyers said that the aggrieved woman does not determine the contents of the DIR, but is usually aware of the contents. One lawyer went so far as to claim that illiterate women often did not know the contents of the DIR, but educated women did. From court data, it was also observed that in 69.8 per cent of cases, the DIR was sent to court within three days of it being filed. In 8.2 per cent of cases it was sent to court within one month of being filed.

The PO interviewed at Fatehbad said that the DIR is filed only in cases when the woman desires to go to court, and so in most cases when the DIR is filed the case does end up in court.

It was envisioned that the DIR would be the basis on which the PO or SP would help women initiate court proceedings, as the PWDVA itself includes filing of a DIR in the duties of a PO or SP. However, it was observed through court data that the DIR, rather than being filed before court proceedings, was in 67.5 per cent of cases, filed between one to six months after a case under the PWDVA was filed. Further, in 83.5 per cent of cases, the DIR is filed only after being ordered by the courts.

Thus, it appears that in these two districts of Haryana, women first approach the court through lawyers, and not through the PO, after which the court directs the PO to file a DIR. Further, lawyers interviewed largely said that the DIR was not used by the court in delivering orders, and that the courts usually waited for evidence to be presented before they passed orders. This was confirmed by one PO interviewed, who said that the courts did not consider the DIR to be evidence. The DIR thus must be harnessed as a more effective tool for POs and SPs to help women towards filing cases under the PWDVA, rather than being filed retrospectively when the case is already in process, and must be accepted by the court as grounds on which to file an interim order. Thus far, it is only being filed as a formal/procedural measure, and one which ends up prolonging the process.

Court Response to Cases Filed under the PWDVA

Through the following sections, it becomes evident that women have received very little relief under the PWDVA, and that the relief sought far outweighs the orders granted. Delays in judicial proceedings further led to delays in relief, as many cases were still pending. A quick comparison of orders claimed and granted at the time of data collection, shows us that in very few cases had orders been granted to women. The subsequent graph suggests that final protection orders had been granted in as few as 4 per cent of cases, and final residence orders were granted in as few as 4.5 per cent of cases.

It becomes evident from the data available that the relief women were being provided by the courts was inadequate in comparison to the violence women reported. The following tables presents a comparison of the types of violence experienced by women and the relief they were given by the courts, and display that the number of women who report severe forms of violence have received extremely few protection and residence orders, even interim ones, to address their situation.

As is evident from the preceding table, the physical violence experienced by women is severe and widespread, but the orders delivered do not match the demand for them. Of the 931 women who experienced severe violence such as beating and sought protection orders, only 43 received interim protection orders and 40 received final protection orders. Of the 102 women who reported beating of children and sought protection orders, only 12 received interim relief and 8 received final orders.

Interim relief is an important provision under the Act. Recognizing that women require immediate and urgent help in securing their safety, the Act makes a provision for interim and ex-parte protection orders, and interim residence orders; however, as is evident, the judiciary seems to hesitate in delivering these orders. Women also reported experiencing sexual violence and emotional violence in high numbers (46.7 per cent and 99.4 per cent, respectively). Yet as we see, even interim orders, which are meant to provide immediate support and relief to women, were fully or partly granted in a mere 24.3 per cent of cases.

Interim Relief Sought and Interim Relief Granted

Interim relief was sought in a total of 822 cases out of 970 (84.7 per cent), and granted in only 236 cases—around 28 per cent of the cases in which it was sought. If the seeking and grant of interim reliefs is disaggregated according to type of area (rural or urban), we see that interim relief was granted in more rural cases (32.9 per cent) than urban, where only 24.8 per cent of applicants received interim relief. If the data are disaggregated district-wise, we see that in Fatehbad, 39.2 per cent of applicants who had sought interim orders were granted the same, while in Hissar only 26.1 per cent of clients who sought interim orders were granted interim orders.

Table 9.3 Physical Violence and Orders Claimed and Granted

Type of violence	Protection order claimed	Protection order granted- Interim	Protection order granted- Final	Residence order claimed	Residence order granted- Interim	Residence order granted – Final
Beating	931	43	40	886	49	42
Burns	14	0	0	13	0	0
Beating children	102	12	8	102	6	7
Violence during pregnancy	123	7	3	119	10	7
Causing miscarriage	18	1	0	18	2	0
Driven to commit suicide or threaten to kill	11	0	0	10	0	0
Instigation of violence	337	22	13	325	27	16
Overburdened with work	449	9	11	417	10	9

Source: Authors.

Table 9.4 Interim Relief Sought and Granted (Urban and Rural areas)

	Fully or Partly Granted	Refused	Not Passed	Not Available	
Urban- Interim relief sought	106	9	312	0	427
	24.8%	2.1%	73.1%	0.0%	100.0%
Rural- Interim relief sought	130	5	260	0	395
	32.9%	1.3%	65.8%	0.0%	100.0%

Source: Authors.

Table 9.5 Interim Relief Sought and Granted (Per District)

	Fully or Partly Granted	Refused	Not Passed	Not Available	
Fatehbad- Interim Relief sought	65	6	95	0	166
	39.2%	3.6%	57.2%	0.0%	100.0%
Hissar- Interim Relief Sought	171	8	477	0	656
	26.1%	1.2%	72.7%	0.0%	100.0%

Source: Authors.

These data thus show that many women (15.3 per cent) did not seek any interim relief under the Act. The law is intended to work for providing speedy remedy for violence, and does not determine civil rights of parties. The non-seeking of interim reliefs thus shows an underutilization of the law; which is based not on the civil jurisprudence of property claims but on the domestic violence law of different jurisdictions (including the West). Further, the non-passing of interim reliefs, especially orders to stop violence and removal from shared household, reveals judicial reluctance to grant reliefs which do not fall within the ambit of conventional civil jurisprudence and do not require more than a prima facie proof of violation of rights, even in cases where there are allegations of serious violence.

Protection Orders Sought and Protection Orders Granted

The following chart compares the extreme discrepancy between the number of protection orders sought and the number of protection orders granted. In a total of 956 cases, protection orders were sought. In a total of 822 cases, interim relief was sought. Interim orders were granted in 28.7 per cent of these cases. It is observed that the most common order to be

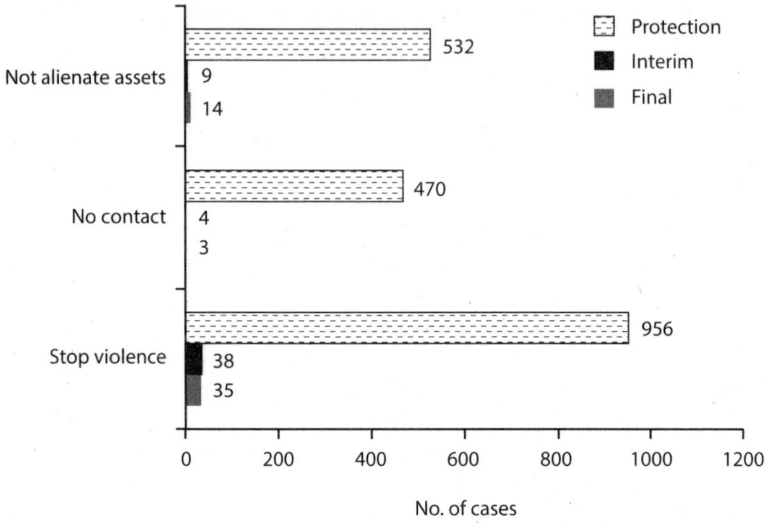

Figure 9.2 Protection Order Sought, Interim Protection Order Granted, and Final Protection Order Granted
Source: Authors.

Table 9.6 Economic Violence and Orders Claimed and Granted

Area	POs Claimed	FPOG* Granted		Total
		No	Yes	No
Urban	Number	475	29	504
	% within POs claimed	94.2%	5.8%	100.0%
Rural	Number	455	11	466
	% within POs claimed	97.6%	2.4%	100.0%

Source: Authors.
Note: *Final Protection Order Granted

granted was the Stop Violence order, both for interim as well as final relief. However, the low number of interim relief orders granted is a cause for concern.

If the data are disaggregated by type of area (rural and urban), we see that the number of protection orders granted in urban areas exceeded the number granted in rural areas (29 granted in urban, and 11 in rural). Data disaggregated by district showed no major variation across districts.

Residence Orders Sought and Residence Orders Granted

As the following chart demonstrates, women were granted very few residence orders, even as compared to protection orders. A majority of women asking for residence orders asked for right to shared household (654); however, only 14 women were granted this interim order, and 21 the final order. When asked what violence they were facing, 654 women reported dispossession from shared household. The debate about women's right to the shared household has been complicated by several court rulings.[15]

Most women had not mentioned in their court applications whose name the shared household was in (674 per cent). A majority had mentioned that it was in their husband's name (19.9 per cent of all applications), followed by those who mentioned that it was in their in-law's name. This is presumably because post-recent court rulings, establishing right to shared household, has become more complex. In the *S.R. Batra and Anr.* v. Smt *Tarun Batra* judgment, the Supreme Court maintained that the right to residence was restricted to property belonging directly to the husband.[16]

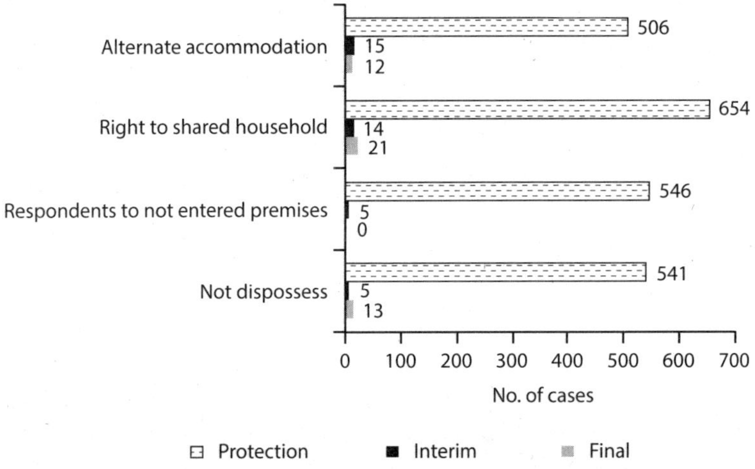

Figure 9.3 Residence Order Sought, Interim Residence Order Granted, and Final Residence Order Granted
Source: Authors.

15 Sakhrani and Panchal, 'Quest for Justice', pp. 121–3.

16 Lawyers Collective, in their 6th *Staying Alive* Report (on monitoring and evaluation of the implementation of PWDVA), has extensively studied the negative

With the Supreme Court judgment, lack of proof of husband's share in the property, and the lack of shelter homes provided by the state, women are faced with the choice of either staying in a violent home or being dependent on their natal families. The reluctance to grant reliefs under the Act could also be caused by the judgments of the higher courts that discourage grant of reliefs.

Monetary Relief Sought and Monetary Relief Granted

A significant finding of the study was that monetary relief was the most commonly granted relief but also that the monetary relief granted was extremely disproportionate to the monetary relief sought and also that even this was not always granted. Monetary relief was sought in 898 cases, and granted in only 94 cases. Monetary relief granted largely ranged between Rs 1,000 per month and Rs 5,000 per month; whereas most women (404) asked for relief between Rs 5,000 and Rs 10,000 per month. Four women were granted monthly maintenance below Rs 1,000 per month, 44 women were granted monthly maintenance between 1,000 and 2,000, and 20 women were granted maintenance between Rs 2,000 and 3,000. Only 10 women were granted maintenance above Rs 5,000 per month. It could be suggested that as Magistrates are accustomed to dealing with matters under section 125 of the CrPC of all reliefs prayed for they are most likely to grant monetary reliefs. However, these reliefs are much lower than what women want and are just a token amount.

In the subsequent table, we see that women have not been granted monetary relief in proportion to the relief they have asked for. From the following table, it can be inferred that no applicants have been granted monetary relief in the form of monthly maintenance over Rs 10,000.

In comparing, the alleged income of the respondent and the monetary relief granted, we see that the alleged income of most respondents does not exceed Rs 30,000. We also see that the monetary relief granted does not correspond directly to a portion of the respondent's alleged income: in that even in cases where the respondent's alleged income is over 15,000, women have still been granted sums such as Rs 1,000–2,000.

---

impact of the *Batra* v. *Batra* judgment on the judiciary's willingness to grant right to residence as a part of PWDVA, and suggests that after this judgment, courts are willing to grant residence orders when the husband is the owner/has rented the house, but are not willing to do so when ownership rests with the in-laws.

Table 9.7 Monetary Relief Sought and Monetary Relief Granted

		Monetary Relief granted								Total
		Not granted	Not applicable	below 1,000	1,000–2,000	2,001–3,000	3,001–4,000	4,001–5,000	More than 5,000	
Monthly Maintenance Sought	INA	26	0	0	0	0	0	0	0	26
	<2,000	8	0	0	1	0	0	0	0	9
	2,001–5,000	164	0	1	11	8	1	1	0	186
	5,000–10,000	360	0	2	23	7	4	4	4	404
	10,001–20,000	211	0	1	8	4	4	2	6	236
	20,001–30,000	37	0	0	0	1	0	0	0	38
	30,001–50,000	19	0	0	0	0	0	0	0	19
	50,001–1 lakh	5	0	0	0	0	0	0	0	5
	> 1 lakh	1	0	0	0	0	0	0	0	1
	no	18	0	0	1	0	0	0	0	19
	NA	0	27	0	0	0	0	0	0	27
Total		849	27	4	44	20	9	7	10	970

Source: Authors.

Table 9.8 Alleged Income of Respondent and Monetary Relief Granted

Alleged income of key respondent	Monetary relief granted								
	Not granted	NA	Below 1,000	1,000–2,000	2,001–3,000	3,001–4,000	4,001–5,000	More than 5,000	Total
< 2000	0	0	0	1	0	0	0	0	1
2,000–5,000	11	0	0	1	1	0	0	0	13
5,001–10,000	68	0	0	6	4	2	1	1	82
10,001–15,000	84	0	1	6	2	3	3	0	99
15,001–25,000	189	1	0	7	4	0	1	3	205
25,001–30,000	123	0	1	4	1	3	1	3	136
>30,000	137	0	0	6	1	0	1	1	146
INA	237	26	2	13	7	1	0	2	288
Total	849	27	4	44	20	9	2	10	970

Source: Authors.

Compensation Sought and Granted

The PWDVA also makes a provision for women to seek compensation for the harms they have experienced. However, while many women have asked for compensation, a negligible number of women have been granted any compensation at all. As seen in the table below, whether compensation was asked for by the applicant, was cross tabulated with compensation granted by the court to find out if the applicant received compensation. Out of 970 applicants, 675 applicants asked for compensation. It was discovered that out of 675, only 11 applicants received compensation from the court. This signifies that though applicants have asked for compensation under the PWDVA, very few of them received it. In Lawyers Collective's analysis of judgments across the country, they suggest not only that 'in cases where reasons for the denial of Compensation Orders are mentioned, Courts appear to mainly deny Compensation where the woman is unable to prove mental torture, emotional distress or physical injuries due to acts of domestic violence', but also that 'judges are reluctant to grant Compensation Orders even if Protection Orders are granted and acts of domestic violence are proven'.[17] They also point out that there is no uniformity across the country when it comes to the quantum of compensation granted (for example, they found that in Andhra Pradesh it ranged from 1 lakh and above, while in Bihar it ranged from Rs 1,000–5,000).[18] Compensation is also often clubbed with monetary relief/maintenance, and is given as a lumpsum. As Lawyers Collective's analysis of judgments under PWDVA finds:

> Courts seldom grant Compensation and where it is granted it is not based on the realities of domestic violence suffered by the aggrieved woman. Courts tend to tie the reliefs of Maintenance and Compensation together and grant a lump sum indicating a lack of understanding on part of the judiciary of the objectives of the Act and defeating the purpose of incorporating different reliefs which speak to the different needs of the aggrieved woman.[19]

[17] 'Staying Alive: Evaluating Court Orders. Sixth Monitoring and Evaluation Report on the Protection of Women from Domestic Violence Act 2005', New Delhi: Lawyer's Collective and ICRW, 2013.

[18] Lawyers Collective, *Staying Alive: Evaluating Court Orders. Sixth Monitoring and Evaluation Report on the Protection of Women from Domestic Violence Act 2005* (New Delhi: Lawyers Collective and ICRW, 2013a).

[19] Lawyers Collective, *Staying Alive*, 2013a, p. 151.

Table 9.9 Compensation Claimed and Granted

Compensation Sought	Compensation Granted			
	Not Granted	Yes	NA	Total
Yes	664	11	0	675
No	0	0	295	295
Total	664	11	295	970

Source: Authors.

A chi square test was done to understand whether the compensations asked for differed from the compensations granted. The chi-square value was 970.000 at two degree of freedom (p=0.000). Thus, the test showed that there was a significant statistical relationship between the compensation asked and compensation granted.

If we disaggregate the data on compensation asked according to type of area (rural or urban), we see that in rural areas, more women got compensation (10) than in urban areas (only one woman).

Exparte Reliefs

Exparte relief, as stipulated by the PWDVA, may be granted 'if the Magistrate is satisfied that the application prima facie discloses that the respondent is committing, or has committed an act of domestic violence or if there is likelihood that the respondent may commit an act of domestic violence'. The rationale behind granting ex-parte relief was the urgency experienced by a woman living in a household where there is violence. However, ex parte relief was granted in only 37 cases. One lawyer said that ex-parte orders are not passed by Magistrates as they wait for evidence to be presented; again reflecting a reluctance to move beyond traditional civil jurisprudence in which the rights of the accused are kept as central; however, it must be understood that protection orders are not a violation of the rights of the accused (as he has no right to commit violence).

Other Court Processes

Women also filed cases under other provisions outside of the PWDVA to seek relief. 52 women had filed a case for maintenance, eight applicants and 13 respondents had filed for divorce, six respondents and one applicant had filed for restitution of conjugal rights, and 103 applicants had other pending court proceedings. Thus, while the PWDVA was envisioned as a one-window approach for domestic violence, a number of women are also turning to other laws for relief. However, there is no evidence of forum shopping. Many women are looking at PWDVA remedies within the structure of marriage itself. We see that data on 498A cases filed by these women shows that 13.2 per cent of women had filed 498A cases alongside PWDVA cases.

Appeal Filed

Of the 31 cases in which an appeal was filed, 12 were filed by the aggrieved party and 19 were filed by the respondent/s. Of these, of cases filed by the aggrieved party, three were pending without stay, four were dismissed, two were allowed, and in two cases the order had been modified. Of the cases filed by respondents, one was pending with stay granted, seven were dismissed, four were allowed, and in six cases the order had been modified. In all of these cases, the maintenance had even been reduced by the appeals court. This reduction shows that the trial court orders, though inadequate, are still more sensitive to the women than the appellate court orders—which often reverse or water down the few remedies that are granted. This also would tend to send a strong message to the trial court judges to desist from giving remedies in domestic violence matters.

Mediation and Settlement

Mediation was conducted in 46 out of the 970 cases. Of this, it was successful only in 16 cases, and was successfully conducted but not effected in 18 cases. Settlements were negotiated in 17 cases, of which 14 settlements were negotiated successfully.

Timelines of Cases

The PWDVA states that, 'the magistrate shall endeavour to dispose of every application made under sub-section (1) within a period of sixty days from the date of its first hearing'. However, from the available court records, it appears that out of the 970 cases studied, only in 11 of cases (1.1 per cent) was the final order passed within the stipulated period of 60 days. In 27 cases, the Final Order was passed within two to six months of filing the case and in 29 cases the order was passed within six months to one year of filing the case. A further 24 final orders were passed as late as one to two years after the case was filed, and five were passed within two to four years of filing the case. In only 329 cases had evidence been led in court, and in 301 cases evidence had not yet been led.

Out of a total of 970 cases, 312 were pending. Further, in 363 cases the case was withdrawn before the final order was passed. In only 61 of these cases were interim orders passed (16.8 per cent). While it is difficult to determine the exact reasons for why women withdraw cases, it is clear that of the reasons in delays in judicial proceedings, women tire of the expense and energy and withdraw cases, preferring alternate redressal mechanisms. Lawyers reiterated these problems in interviews (as discussed previously). Further, 163 cases were dismissed for the non-appearance of the aggrieved party. Two possible reasons for this can be presented—that women tired of waiting for a response from the court and the lack of response made them lose patience with the process or secondly, that women achieved their desired result by filing the case and hence dropped out of the system. While the PO claims that the latter is true, the former reason is more likely as there is a distinct finding of low court response, and the lawyers reiterate this reason: the POs do not follow up on the cases, so lawyers in this case might have more insight. Further, given the lack of any other services, especially shelter homes in the state, the reason for any kind of out of court settlement or sheer fatigue and inability to cope with the demands of the legal system would be considerably high. This is also reflected in the interviews of the women who had approached the court.

As seen in Table 9.10, the date of filing case by the applicant was cross tabulated with the number of pending final orders to understand how long cases have been pending for. Out of 970 cases, 312 cases were pending at the final stage. It was observed that out of 360 cases filed in 2010, 90 were

Table 9.10 Year of Filing Case and Whether Final Order is Pending

Year of filing case	Final order pending		
	Yes	No	Total
2007	2	11	13
2008	6	42	48
2009	27	122	149
2010	90	270	360
2011	185	207	392
2012	0	2	2
INA	2	4	6
Total	312	658	970

Source: Authors.

pending at the final stage. In 2011, 392 cases were filed, out of which 185 were pending at the time of data collection. Under the Act, the court proceedings should be completed within 60 days from the date of filing. This implies that though applicants continued to file cases from 2007 under the PWDVA, a large number of cases were still pending at the time of data collection.

A chi square test was done to understand whether the date of filing case was differed from final order pending. The chi-square value was 73.656 at six degree of freedom (p=0.000). The test showed that there was a significant statistical relationship between the date of filing case and final order pending.

In the four-state study, of the large number of cases that have been withdrawn, the largest is in Haryana: 216 in Hissar and 147 in Fatehbad. The largest number of cases that have been dismissed due to default (as the applicant abandons the case and does not appear in court) is also in Haryana—163 out of the total of 164. This large-scale withdrawal and dismissal for default could indicate disillusionment with the delays and lack of reliefs being granted by the courts. Thus, it is crucial to remember that a large number of women are dropping out of the system.

The interim order was envisioned as providing immediate relief to women who have filed cases under the PWDVA, as women facing violence need pressing reliefs and help with the violence they are facing. However, only 8 interim orders were granted within one month of the case being filed, and only 18 within two months of the case being filed, out of the 970 applicants who had prayed for reliefs. 728 women had as yet not received even interim relief orders. Most interim orders, when granted, were passed within six

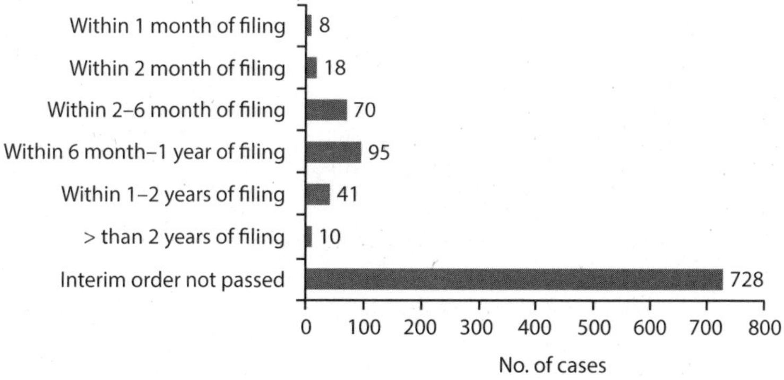

Figure 9.4 Period within which interim order was passed
Source: Authors.

months to one year of filing the case, followed by cases in which the interim order was passed within two to six months of filing the case. Given the fact that Magistrates are urged to dispose of cases within 60 days, this delay in passing even interim orders should be addressed.

If the data on the time period of passing interim and final orders are disaggregated by district, we see a slight difference between Hissar and Fatehbad. From Table 9.11, we see that in Fatehbad, the majority of cases in which a final order was passed (5.2 per cent), the order was passed within two to six months of filing the case, whereas in Hissar, the highest percentage was 2.5 per cent, filed within one to two years of filing the case. Indeed, in Hissar, five final orders were passed as late as within two to four years of filing the case, and three even passed more than four years after filing the case. We see the same pattern in the passing of interim orders: a majority of interim orders in Hissar were passed within six months to one year of filing the case (11.3 per cent), whereas in Fatehbad, a majority of orders were passed within two months to six years of filing the case (12.5 per cent). Thus, it seems that there are more delays in the passage of orders in Hissar than Fatehbad.

Thus, we see that the PWDVA, which was meant to provide speedy reliefs to women facing domestic violence, in fact entails lengthy and

Table 9.11 Time Period between Interim Order and Filing of Case (Per District)

District		Frequency	Percent
Fatehbad	Within 60 days of filling the case	7	2.4
	Within 2 to 6 months of filling the case days of filling the case	15	5.2
	Within 6 months to 1 year of filling the case	14	4.8
	Within 1 year to 2 years of filling the case	7	2.4
	Not applicable	246	85.1
	Total	289	100.0
Hissar	Within 60 days of filling the case	4	.6
	Within 2 to 6 months of filling the case days of filling the case	12	1.8
	Within 6 months to 1 year of filling the case	15	2.2
	Within 1 year to 2 years of filling the case	17	2.5
	Within 2 to 4 years of filling the case	5	.7
	more than 4 years	3	.4
	Not applicable	625	91.8
	Total	681	100.0

Source: Authors.

long-drawn out judicial procedures. With most women unaware of or disconnected from the support stakeholder networks (as discussed previously), women are made to live with violence without any relief under the PWDVA due to judicial delays.

From all stakeholders and functionaries interviewed other than women, it appeared that lawyers had the most hands-on experience with court proceedings. Many lawyers believed that Magistrates did not deal sensitively

Box 9.2

Case Study 2

Preeti had been married to her husband for 10 years at the time of data collection. She came from an agricultural family, and her husband too was a farmer. Her marital family had a large house and was financially comfortable. She shared that the violence started 10 days after marriage, and that her husband demanded a bike and 50,000 rupees in cash as dowry. He was unkind to her, and her in-laws did not treat her well. Her mother-in-law accused her of ruining their family's reputation: '*Isne to samaj mein humari naak katwa di*'. (She has brought us social dishonour). Her husband began to beat her every day, and violence increased when she gave birth to a girl. She sought help from her parents, to bring an end to the beating and dowry demands. Her father paid 20,000 rupees to her husband, but even this did not help. The decision to file a case was made in 2009, when her husband and brother-in-law beat her and threw her out of the marital home. Further, her husband and in-laws were not ready to compromise or resolve the issue at the panchayat meeting organized by her father. She shared that what she wanted from the law was protection, residence in the marital home, maintenance, and an end to the violence. She approached the court through a lawyer, who charged them Rs 10,000. She was unaware of free legal aid. Preeti had a good experience with the PO, who read out all documents to her and supported her through the process. However, she shared that the lawyer was not able to handle her case well, and succeeded only in obtaining a maintenance order for her, without a protection and residence order. She shared that she struggled to follow court procedure; and despite obtaining the maintenance order her husband did not give her any money at all. She said that nothing changed in her life, and said '*Court mein jakar keval perishani hi mili*' [one gets only trouble from going to court]. She shared that for her the cost of going to court was loss of health, weakness, body pain, and more worries about her future and her daughter. She is living with her parents and does household work at their home.

with women's issues, and deal with domestic violence as simply a routine case. Two lawyers said that most Magistrates think that domestic violence allegations are false, and one said that Magistrates think that domestic violence applications are filed only to pressure respondents.

Lawyers also cited the issue of long trials and extremely lengthy processes. One said that because of long trials, cases often end in compromise. Another issue with the court process as cited by lawyers was that only maintenance interim orders were passed, with insufficient amounts provided, and that courts often wait to pass orders only after evidence is presented. Lawyers also largely reported dissatisfaction with the final order passed, in that it did not meet the complete requirements of the applicant. Nearly all said that the passage of final orders was not speedy and often difficult, and that final orders are rare, as most Magistrates pass only protection or maintenance interim orders, if at all.

Why Do Women Choose Not to Approach the Court?

The profile of women who do not file cases under PWDVA but access alternative redressal mechanisms, does not differ significantly from the profile of women who do use the PWDVA. Neither does the kind or degree of violence differ. Women who did not file cases under the PWDVA cited a variety of reasons for their decision not to do so. Interview data suggested that a majority of women took assistance from other sources, such as their family (44), PO (40), panchayat member (21), and the police (10). This indicates that although women did not go to court, they took help from multiple available resources. 85.1 per cent of these women were satisfied with the help they got. However, other institutions exhibit a significant patriarchal bias in their approach to women. From interviews with panchayat members, it emerged that women are not permitted to join the caste panchayat, and in most cases nor are they allowed to speak before the panchayat, they may approach the panchayat as a complainant but a man must speak on their behalf. The express motive of the panchayat is not to address violence, but to save the family; as expressed by one member '*ghar kisi bhi halat mein tutna nahi chahiye*' [under no circumstances should the family be broken]. The panchayat refers cases to the police to create pressure on the man, but would not refer a case to court. Most panchayat members were vehement in their assertion that the court and police were not the correct solution. Many panchayat members interviewed also shared that in custody cases they generally awarded custody to the man, as women usually do not have a source of income to support the child. One panchayat member mentioned that this was also because then the child would obtain rights to their father's property. Thus, the community also discourages women from seeking legal redressal.

When asked why they did not seek help under the PWDVA, women cited a variety of reasons. A majority of women (25.5 per cent) said that they tried to solve the matter through police intervention. Others (19.1 per cent) cited a lack of knowledge about the law. 57.4 per cent of women approached the police station for help. Only 25.5 per cent of these women were aware of the PWDVA and their rights under the PWDVA, which suggests that lack of knowledge of their legal rights might be a factor in their decision not to approach the court. One woman shared that she did not go to court because she wanted to save her family—'*ghar basana tha*'.

Box 9.3

Case Study 3

Neelu came from a family of agricultural workers, with her mother and brother the chief earners. She shared that the violence started one year after her marriage. She shared that her husband would drink excessively, and become abusive and beat her. Her marital family was not supportive and never intervened to get her husband to stop drinking. A year after marriage, she and her husband shifted to a rented house. She faced financial violence and verbal abuse as well. Although she has never sought medical help, her health was severely affected by the violence. She was dependant on her mother and brother for financial support, and they continued to send money to her for household expenses.

She first approached her mother and brother for help, who suggested resolving the issue through meetings with the husband. However, due to an escalation of violence she approached the PO for help, and interventions work was carried out at the Special Cell. She said that one month after the intervention however, the violent behaviour recurred. She did not turn to the law because her mother and brother did not allow her to file a case, and she had no support because of which she was unable to file. She shared that in retrospect, she believed she should have gone to court and would advise other women to go to court for relief. She is currently living with her natal family. Neelu shared that she is worried about her children and their future.

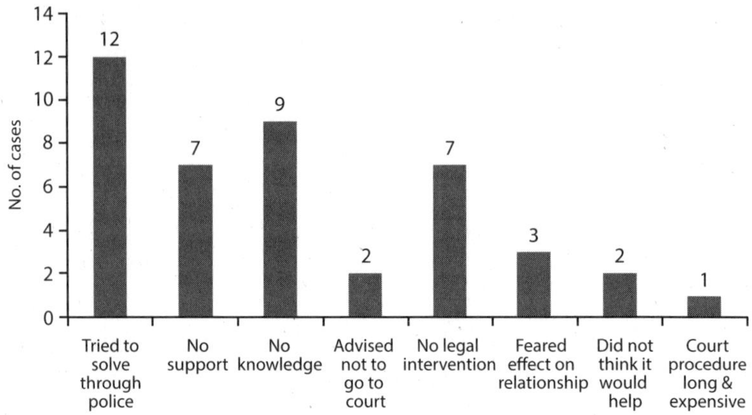

Figure 9.5 Reason for not Filing Complaint under PWDVA.
Source: Authors.

It was heartening to note that 97.9 per cent of these women said that they were aware of the presence of the PO, and had approached the PO, and 88.6 per cent expressed satisfaction about the help they got from the PO. This is a significant step towards the implementation of the PWDVA. However, while there was awareness about the PO, only seven women were aware of their right to legal aid, and 85.1 per cent of women were unaware of this right. Further, women were equally unaware of other laws available to them (83 per cent were unaware).

Another important factor was the role of the police. Of the women interviewed, who had approached the police, only 14 expressed satisfaction with police help. Six women reported that the police lodged a non-cognizable offence (NC) instead of an FIR (as is mandated for cases of domestic violence).

Women's Experience with PWDVA Processes

From the interviews conducted, women who have filed cases under the PWDVA have reported varying levels of satisfaction with the PWDVA implementation processes. Only 4.1 per cent of women were satisfied with the orders they received, as a majority, 65.3 per cent had as yet received no court orders. 28.6 per cent women were dissatisfied with the orders they received.

Women after having undergone the process of filing a case under the PWDVA, expressed that they expected to get the reliefs they prayed for

(39), and to get faster relief (18). Thus, it seems that most women had experienced judicial delays, and specifically desired the reliefs that they had prayed for and had not necessarily been granted. As becomes clear from the evidence presented above, judicial delays are a major cause for concern, and only a fraction of women praying for relief are receiving it in a timely manner. Most women cited the lengthy procedure as a challenge. 14 women expressed that they had not faced any challenges in their experience with the PWDVA. When asked about their experience with the Magistrate, it was surprising that a majority of women, 59.2 per cent, had not had any contact or interaction with the Magistrate trying their case. Apart from this, 24 women reported a negative experience with the Magistrate.

85.5 per cent of women said that they were unable to follow the happenings at court, which could be linked to the high number of cases being dismissed due to non-appearance of applicant (163), and high number of cases withdrawn (363). 49 per cent of women stated that they had faced financial difficulties due to their decision to take the case to court; also connected to the high number of withdrawn and dismissed cases.

From interviews, it emerged that many women did not have a positive experience at the court, with many reporting that they did not get relief (28.6 per cent), that there were multiple procedures to be undertaken/followed (12.2 per cent), that the process was negative, too long, and was delayed (8.2 per cent). Most women shared that the process had not really had an impact on their lives, whereas some described an extremely negative impact.

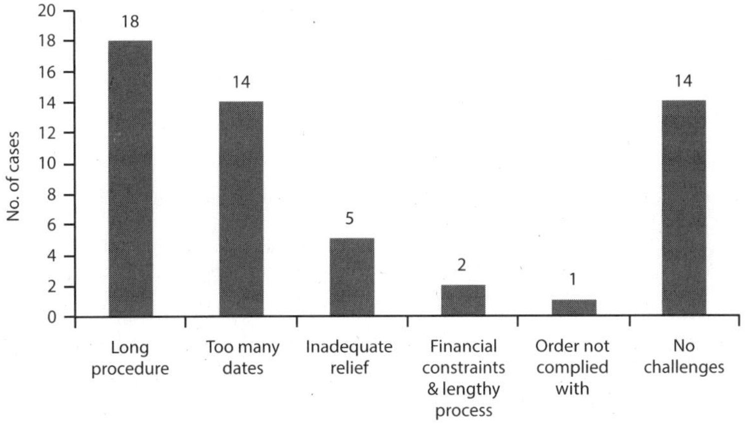

Figure 9.6 Challenges Faced.
Source: Authors.

A few women mentioned that the reputation of their family had been negatively affected, but many shared that the court proceedings had worsened their relationship with their husband or marital families, and that their husbands had become more adamant about refusing support/maintenance/residence. 17 women stated that the court proceedings had no positive impact on their lives, and nine women said their life had become worse after filing a case. Thus, the very experience of filing a case is a traumatic one, which has multiple social, financial, and emotional implications for a woman. In this social climate, where breaking out of a marital relationship is so stigmatized and has so many negative repercussions for women, it is vital that women get speedy and substantial relief, as many were left with a sense that filing a case had only worsened their situation.

Lawyers suggest that major challenges that women face are extremely lengthy trials, and that women do not get the reliefs they seek. One lawyer pointed out that court proceedings are lengthy and too complex for lay persons, and that women depend on lawyers who might misguide them. Others cited expenses as a major challenge for women. One lawyer suggested that women's relatives pressurize them to compromise due to the lengthy trial process. Lawyers mentioned that trials continued for as long as three months to four years. Some lawyers cited that service of summons was not done effectively.

It is food for thought that only 12.2 per cent of the women interviewed stated that the situation of violence in their lives has changed after this intervention, and that for 87.6 per cent of women, their experience of violence has not altered after court proceedings. This calls for introspection on the effectiveness of the current mechanisms to end domestic violence through the PWDVA.

***

A culture of silence surrounds domestic violence. It is often dismissed or tacitly condoned, as a 'family matter', not 'suitable' for public discussion or legal remedy. Further, women are discouraged or unable to seek help due to a variety of factors, ranging from financial dependence on perpetrators, social pressure, lack of alternatives, fear of estrangement from loved ones, feeling guilt/shame, and feeling responsible for the violence. Women also often face eviction from their familial homes, lack of financial resources, and lacking the means to follow up on complaints.[20] Before the introduction of

[20] S. Sarvanan, 'Violence against Women in India: A Literature Review', Institute of Social Studies Trust, 2000.

the PWDVA in 2006, laws that addressed violence against women were identified as inadequate in confronting the wider spectrum of women's needs—such as shelter, monetary reliefs, immediate protection from violence, and medical and psychosocial support. Section 498A of the IPC, a result of years of campaigning against dowry-related violence, was limited in its scope by requiring women's very lives to be in danger in order for redressal to be sought, and did not provide civil reliefs. Other provisions pertaining to sexual violence did not adequately address women's requirements for breaking out of the cycle of domestic violence, and it was out of this felt need that the PWDVA emerged.[21]

The PWDVA, a unique law that addressed women's needs rather than taking a retributive or punishment-based approach, was heralded as a major step forward for survivors of domestic violence; however, its implementation must still see significant improvement. The networks that it was envisaged to set up remain fractured and few, widespread information about the law is still lacking, and tardy judicial proceedings entail that the immediacy and effective reliefs envisioned when the law was drafted, still have not come into practice. Lawyers Collective argues that there is a need to strengthen the autonomy of the POs and appoint and train more POs where needed, and stresses the need for training to counter biases and problematic counselling by untrained stakeholders which may go against the best interests of the applicant. They suggest that an understanding of the secular nature of the Act is growing, but delays in judicial proceedings often result in women not getting the immediate benefits the Act promises. These findings have largely been corroborated by the present study, which also finds the delays in judicial proceedings, inconsistent and fragmented reporting formats, and an under-developed stakeholder network to be a major obstacle in the effective implementation of the PWDVA.

Haryana, apart from its poor sex-ratio and gender-asymmetrical literacy rates, is also known for the strong caste panchayat presence, which perpetuates oppressive gender regimes and provide interventions for women facing violence that often privilege family structures and patriarchal values (see Ganesh 2008). However, the Haryana government in 2006 took proactive initiative and institutionalized Special Cells for Women and Children within police stations across each district in Haryana. Each cell comprised two trained social workers who provided socio-legal support to women facing violence. These social workers were also appointed as full-time PPOs

21 Jaising, 'Bringing Rights Home'.

under the PWDVA and the PCMA, 2006. Thus, the Special Cells for Women and Children in Haryana is a project that is instrumental to the implementation of the PWDVA, and one of the cogs in what should be a wide network of stakeholders in a state. The POs provide important services to women who do not choose to file cases under the PWDVA as well, and offer counselling and mediation to survivors of domestic violence. The PO network in Haryana is the only stakeholder system under the PWDVA so far that has been well developed. Thus, apart from the courts, currently the POs are the primary state provision for addressing domestic violence. Feedback from women, lawyers, and police officials for POs is very positive, and it is crucial that their network be further strengthened.

Despite the presence of a strong network of POs, the other parts of the stakeholder network in Haryana appear to be severely lacking. There are few SPs, and most stakeholders interviewed stressed the need for provisions such a shelter homes in all districts. The crux of the PWDVA is its foundational stakeholder network, including service providers, shelter homes, medical facilities, and POs. Currently in Haryana, only the PO network is well developed, and it is vital that more SPs and shelter homes are appointed for each district. Further, the role of the police under the Act must be clarified and spelt out. The police officers interviewed had minimal dealings with the Act and did not see it as coming under their purview.

There seems to be a low awareness amongst women about the right to free legal aid, despite provisions for the right to legal aid being in place. Most lawyers interviewed did take remuneration from their clients and many women as well as lawyers stated that financial burdens of pursuing a case often became significant for women and impeded their ability to see cases through. Thus, free legal aid networks must be strengthened and women should be given information about these services. In this regard, the link between free legal aid services and POs must also be strengthened. Most POs are unable to follow up on the later stages of cases due to their workload, and lawyers become key players in the courts. Most women interviewed also reported a limited or negligible awareness about the law and their rights under various laws for women facing violence. Awareness drives for women regarding the PWDVA should be undertaken.

The DIR was envisioned as one of the key pegs of the PWDVA. However, from interviews with lawyers, POs, and from court data, it seems that the DIR has been reduced to a formality and is not considered as evidence in court—though the PO plays an active role in filing the DIR, the court waits for evidence before granting orders. Further, in most cases, women go directly to the court through lawyers, and the PO is directed to file the DIR by the court only after court proceedings have begun. In their current form, the DIRs do not provide complete information and details about the respondent and the applicant. It is important that the DIR is as accurate and reliable a record of the woman's experience and expectations as possible. The DIR must be used as an effective and comprehensive testimony of the woman's experience of violence, and must not be reduced to a mere formality. It is thus vital that the DIR be used as grounds to pass interim orders, and thus be used to reduce delays and enable speedy relief to women. It is also advised that the forms under the Act be revamped accordingly, so as to maximize the usefulness of the DIR. It is vital that the DIR provides important information such as the narrative of violence, the needs of women, and the role, liability, and means of the respondent. Similarly, Form V (Safety Plan) appears also to be a formality more than a reality. Thus, these forms must be revamped and effectively harnessed as tools in securing justice for women.

As this study reveals, there is a serious gap between what women expect and need from the law, and what the judicial system delivers. It is the duty of the state to rectify this situation and deliver timely and effective justice. Tardy judicial proceedings were a major impediment to women securing justice under the PWDVA in Hissar and Fatehbad. Overwhelmingly, from stakeholders as well as women, what was reported as the most challenging part of the quest for justice was severe judicial delays. Cases from as early as 2007 remained pending at the time of data collection, and the high number of withdrawals and dismissals for non-appearance of aggrieved party are testament to how women tire of the lengthy court proceedings. In an act that stipulates a 60-day period for disposal of cases, delays of over one year are worryingly common. These delays thus violate the very spirit of the law, and must be addressed. It is also important that training programmes be conducted for members of the police and the judiciary. Magistrates and police officials alike must be trained in sensitively dealing with cases of domestic violence. The trend of appeals courts reducing reliefs is also a cause of concern in terms of the message it sends to the lower judiciary in the handling of the cases before them.

The low rate of interim reliefs being provided reveals that even though the Act provides for interim and ex parte reliefs to provide immediate support for women, most women are not getting this relief at all and are forced to live with violence without support from the state during the course of the trial. This was corroborated by interviews with lawyers and POs. Women thus turn to alternate mechanisms for justice. Many women turned to their panchayat for support; yet, interviews with panchayat members revealed a family-centric perspective rather than a woman-centric one, and an emphasis not on stopping violence but on saving families. Panchayat members reported that in most cases they were approached by male members of the family. In many panchayats, women do not even participate in the panchayat meetings. A lack of SPs means that women must turn to familial/community-based patriarchal structures for justice, which might not be focused on securing her interests.

Lawyers emphasized that the benefit of the PWDVA was that it was a multi-relief Act, under which women could get all the relief they need under the same roof. However, in practice, women are not able to obtain relief under this Act. Many lawyers suggested that a summary trial, as stipulated in the Act, must be undertaken in practice. Several lawyers suggested a separate court for issues pertaining to domestic violence so that women can get speedy relief and some suggested that the cases be handled by the family courts. One suggested sensitization programmes for Magistrates. Others cited the need for a referral network such as free shelter homes and medical aid for survivors of violence.

One PO who was interviewed stressed that the PWDVA while a useful Act, is not implemented in its spirit. She said that there is no implementation machinery, and because of this there is no real impact on the incidence of domestic violence in her district. A women's rights activist in Haryana shared that 'the act is a good attempt, well-thought-out, and progressive and creative. The implementation needs to be improved. Right now, we see shortfall due to improper implementation; if it is implemented in its spirit, only then will we be able to see its shortcomings'.[22] This sentiment rings true through this study, as only when implementation takes place and becomes widespread, can the mechanisms of the act and its provisions be deliberated and improved. At this stage, the relief women receive is so scant that infrastructure and basic timely delivery of justice, in keeping with the spirit of the Act, must be the key thrust.

The PWDVA was envisaged as a multi-agency response to the needs of the survivor, and was not meant to be a law that was to be litigated in courts unless there was failure to address the needs of the woman. The safety plan was meant to be prepared and executed by the PO, who was envisaged as the single window for delivery of services and needs of the woman; and the court order was meant to protect the woman's civil rights. Unfortunately, apart from appointing POs, the state has done little else to redress women's needs. The family as an institution has traditionally been the primary provider of welfare

22 Interview with the activist on file with authors.

in India. The PWDVA has the potential to revolutionize this lacuna on the part of the state and provides an alternate in situations where the family in fact becomes the cause of the woman's distress. However, the gaps in the system and judicial delays leaves the legal system unable to deliver these entitlements.

References

Bhatia, M 2012, Domestic Violence in India: Cases under the Protection of Women from Domestic Violence Act, 2005 *South Asia Research*, 32 (2): 103–22.

Centre for Social Justice 2009, *A Fact File on the Implementation of the Protection of Women from Domestic Violence Act, 2005 in the State of Gujarat*, Oxfam (Unpublished report on file with the researchers).

Chowdhry, P 1994, *The Veiled Woman: Shifting Gender Equations in Rural Haryana 1880-1990*. New Delhi: Oxford University Press.

——— 2005, Crisis of Masculinity in Haryana: The Unmarried, The Unemployed, and the Aged *Economic and Political Weekly* 40 (49): 5189–98.

——— 2012, Infliction, Acceptance and Resistance: Containing Violence on Women in Rural Haryana. *Economic and Political Weekly* 47 (37): 43–59.

Civil Society Resource Facility 2010, *A Report on the Status of PWDVA in Orissa, 2010-2011, Oxfam* (Unpublished report on file with the researchers).

Ganesh, I M 2008. *Next Steps, Special Cell Strategy and Vision*. Mumbai: Special Cell for Women and Children, TISS Mumbai.

Jaising, I 2009, Bringing Rights Home: Review of the Campaign for a Law on Domestic Violence *Economic and Political Weekly*, 44(44): 50–7.

Kothari, J 2005, Criminal Law on Domestic Violence: Promises and Limits, *Economic and Political Weekly*, 12 November, pp. 4843–9.

Lawyers Collective 2011, *Staying Alive: Fourth Monitoring & Evaluation Report on the Protection of Women from Domestic Violence Act, 2005* New Delhi: Lawyer's Collective and ICRW.

——— 2013a, *Staying Alive: Evaluating Court Orders. Sixth Monitoring and Evaluation Report on the Protection of Women from Domestic Violence Act 2005*. New Delhi: Lawyer's Collective and ICRW.

——— 2013b, *Manual on the Best Practices under the Protection of Women from Domestic Violence Act, 2005*. New Delhi: Lawyer's Collective.

Sakhrani, M and Panchal, T 2014, Quest for Justice, Mumbai: Tata Institute of Social Sciences and Government of India, Ministry of Women and Child Development

Sarvanan, S 2000, Violence Against Women in India: A Literature Review. Institute of Social Studies Trust.

Special Cells for Women and Children 2016, *Paving New Pathways: Special Cells for Women and Children in Haryana, 2008-2014*. Haryana: Govt of Haryana.

Yadav, B 2001. 'Haryana's "Setting Daughters"', *The Economic and Political Weekly* 36 (45): 4257–59.

10. *Nature of Services Available to Women Survivors*

One Stop Crisis Centres—Review and Recommendations

PADMA BHATE-DEOSTHALI,
SANGEETA REGE

Setting the Context

Domestic violence is one of the most common forms of violence experienced by women in India. The latest estimate by the World Health Organization (WHO) (2013) states that one in three women experience some form of violence. This is just the tip of the iceberg, as there is underreporting of violence due to high level of acceptance of domestic violence and the stigma attached to women who report and complain about domestic violence. It is the feminist movement in India that brought domestic violence into the public domain, much like in most other countries where the movement against violence against women has been led by feminist groups. One of the known interventions in domestic violence, started by women's groups, was the consciousness-raising (CR) activities that provided a space for women to share their experiences with women in similar situations, develop links between their personal experiences and the political context in which these are structured. Domestic violence interventions in the form of support groups, crisis interventions services, shelter, legal aid amongst others, are three decades old. Most of these interventions focus on psycho-social and legal support. The emphasis on each of these differs based on the genesis of the services. The counselling services set up by women's groups emphasize on social support for empowerment, while those set up by trained social workers/counsellors emphasize on psychological and social support (Rege and Aarthi, 2012).

The chapter presents the existing evidence on One Stop Centres (OSC) in terms of their location, objectives, and impact. It presents a landscape of services for responding to Violence Against Women (VAW) and presents evidence on OSCs. It argues for an evidence-based approach in setting up of responses for survivors of domestic violence.

PWDVA Mandate for a Comprehensive Response

Domestic violence could take any form—physical, emotional, sexual, and/or financial—within the household. The abuser/s could be a woman's husband and/or other members of the natal or marital families. Such violence cuts across boundaries of class, caste, religion, community, and nation. It is rooted in the social, economic, political, and cultural structures that place women in unequal and vulnerable positions. Domestic violence is often used as a tool to subjugate and control them. Such behaviour is generally perceived to be routine within families and has been historically accepted as such.

One of the most significant milestones in the domestic violence movement is the enactment of the Protection of Women from Domestic Violence Act (PWDVA). The drafting of the act and the advocacy for its enactment was led by the Lawyers Collective through a nation-wide consultative process involving feminists, social workers, activists, lawyers, and other stakeholders. The PWDVA is a unique law as it recognizes the dynamic situation of women facing domestic violence and their multiple needs; it was drafted based on evidence of several years of service provision by organizations responding to domestic violence. The appointment of and role of PO was envisioned based on the experience of many years of case work with survivors of domestic violence. Up until the passing of the PWDVA survivors of domestic violence could only file under the criminal law provision under 498A IPC which resulted in most cases in the immediate arrest of the partner. The arrest resulted in women being thrown out of their marital homes or in escalation of violence. Moreover, women only wanted the violence to stop, but there was nothing in law that could help them. The PWDVA and the response model envisaged within it was a response to this critical gap in women's access to justice. For the first time, women who reported domestic violence could also access reliefs such as right to residence, protection order, interim maintenance amongst others reliefs.

The response model envisaged under the law lists a number of stakeholders such as POs, SPs, medical facilities, thus recognizing that women experiencing domestic violence may go to any of these at different points in time. So the entry and access to the law was kept open and the reliefs under the law were over and above what was being offered by counselling centres.

Further, the law extends its provisions to relationships in the nature of marriage, and most importantly, provides a comprehensive list of various forms of violence such as physical, emotional, sexual, and financial for the first time in India. By doing so, it recognizes that behaviour that was hitherto considered 'normal' or a 'part and parcel' of married life was now recognized as a form of domestic violence punishable by law, for example, recognizing the deeply entrenched son preference and its impact on women, the law categorizes 'insult for not having a male child' as a form of emotional abuse. Similarly, forced sexual intercourse by a husband or intimate partner is recognized as sexual violence, thus providing women who are victims of marital rape a recourse to legal redressal. Despite this recognition of marital rape in PWDVA in 2005, the amendments to the rape law in 2013 did not include rape by husband as part of the definition of rape due to the misogynist and patriarchal attitudes of parliamentarians. However, forced sexual intercourse by the husband living separately, whether under a decree of separation or otherwise, is recognized as rape. This is an important aspect to be mentioned here, as there is evidence of a large number of women experiencing sexual violence in marriage and for them, the PWDVA is the only legal recourse. Dilaasa crisis intervention centre reports that 42 per cent of women registered with them report sexual violence within marriage (Bhate-Deosthali et al. 2012).

The entire infrastructure envisaged under the PWDVA such as protection officers and SPs was to enable women to effectively use the law and offer an alternative worldview, strengthen their capacities to stop violence without blaming themselves or compromising their lives to preserve their marriage. As seen in the annual monitoring reports compiled by Lawyers Collective over the years, this infrastructure has been developing in different ways with varied effectiveness across states. Despite the strong demand by women's groups under the AMAN network that has been consistently demanding better implementation of the PWDVA, the state has not made adequate provisions for the same. The Umbrella Scheme of 2012 which allocated approximately Rs 1,100 crores for the setting up of POs office and training of all stakeholders exists only on paper.

Domestic Violence—Extent and Consequences

There is sufficient evidence from India that domestic violence is widespread. Despite lack of accurate evidence base, it is well accepted that domestic violence is the most pervasive form of gender based VAW affecting their health and well-being. The estimates from community-based studies vary from 18 per cent to 70 per cent (Daga et al. 1999; Rao 1997; Mahajan 1990; Visaria 1999; Khot et al. 2004). The variations related to the prevalence can be attributed to differences in the methodology, the manner in which questions are asked, the extent of rapport established, and ways in which data are analysed. The National Family Health Survey (NFHS)-3 indicated a lifetime prevalence rate of domestic violence at 34 per cent among women of reproductive age (15–49 years). According to NFHS-3 data, 19 per cent of women experienced physical or sexual violence in last 12 months preceding the survey. On an average, amongst married women who reported violence in the last 12 months, 42 per cent reported some kind of injury; 40 per cent cuts, bruises, or aches; 10 per cent reported eye injuries, sprains, dislocations, or burns; 7.5 per cent reported deep wounds, broken bones or teeth, or other serious injury; and 2 per cent reported severe burns. Most abused women seek help from their families and friends, very few go to institutions such as the police (1.5 per cent), medical personnel (0.5 per cent), or social service organizations (0.05 per cent). But these data are 10 years old; no new national household survey has been conducted since then. The National Crime Records Bureau (NCRB) recorded 8,455 dowry deaths and 1,18,866 cases of cruelty by husbands. These data cover only those women who mustered the courage to report at the police stations. A comparison of National Family Health Scheme and NCRB data indicate the reluctance among women in approaching redressal mechanisms.

Living in abusive relationships and abusive families is known to affect survivors' mental and physical health. There is growing evidence on the range of physical and mental health consequences of domestic violence—both immediate as well as long-term (Garcia-Moreno et al. 2005). It impacts women's health in myriad ways, directly and indirectly, and can lead to chronic debilitating conditions, including death. A study among 2,199 pregnant women in North India indicated that child birth among mothers who had faced domestic violence are 2.59 times more likely to lead to pre-natal and neo-natal mortality (Koski et al. 2011). Physical and sexually intimate partner violence is associated with miscarriage, and reproductive health services should be used for screening of spousal violence and link to assistance (Johri et al. 2011).

In addition to injuries, disability and mental health consequences of violence include symptoms such as crying easily, inability to enjoy life, fatigue and thoughts of suicide, depression, feelings of anger and helplessness, self-blame, anxiety, phobias, panic disorders, eating disorders, low self-esteem, nightmares, hyper vigilance, heightened startle response, memory loss, and nervous breakdowns (Deosthali et al. 2009; Garcia-Moreno et al. 2005). Further, a study reported that the gamut of mental health consequences for women facing violence can range from mental stress, anxiety, depression, disturbed sleep, psychosomatic disorders, and suicidal behaviour (Kumar et al. 2005). A study by Choudhary and Patel (2008) on effects of spousal violence on women's health in Goa shows that spousal violence is a causal factor for attempted suicide and sexually transmitted infections among women. One way in which women attempt suicide in India is by burning themselves; other common methods include consumption of poisonous substances such as pesticides, insecticides, or kerosene.

Tracing the Evolution of Responses to Domestic Violence in India

The feminist movement in India brought the issue of VAW into the public domain in the 1970s. The rape of Mathura (in 1972), a tribal girl, by two policemen in the police station became the starting point of the anti-rape struggle in India that began in Mumbai in 1979–80 and expanded to other cities. The years after that witnessed agitation, mass campaigns, public education, legal reform, and advocacy to raise awareness about these forms of violence. Violence within the family drew serious attention, given the large number of dowry deaths or bride-burning cases in the country at that time, and later, the issue of physical abuse and battering was also brought to the fore. There was also a realization that women often faced domestic violence unrelated to dowry demands. The gaping silence and social stigma around domestic violence was also being broken during this period.

NGO Response

In addition to raising awareness about VAW, autonomous women's groups, along with non-governmental organizations (NGOs) such as Vimochana, Women's Centre, and Saheli, were the first to establish some kind of infrastructure and services to care for and provide support to women survivors of domestic violence. These were autonomous women's groups that provided counselling and shelter to women survivors of domestic violence. They also organized awareness drives on the issue of bride burning, dowry deaths, and domestic violence through street plays and campaigns.

Government Response

The State also responded to the growing pressure created by the sustained campaigns taken up by these groups on the issue of domestic violence. During the 1980s and 1990s, the establishment of free legal cells, family counselling centres, family courts, and special cells at police stations in the city of Mumbai were some steps taken to provide redress to survivors of domestic violence.

Health Sector Response

Research evidence indicated that large numbers of women were accessing health facilities for treatment of health consequences of domestic violence, but the health system was treating only the physical symptoms and injuries. Dilaasa—a joint initiative by Centre for Enquiry into Health and Allied Themes (CEHAT and the Municipal Corporation of Greater Mumbai—was set up in 2001 with the aim to sensitize the public health system on domestic violence as a public health issue and set up a hospital-based crisis centre for provision of services for domestic violence survivors. The hospital staff has been trained to recognize domestic violence, to document present and past incidents of violence, provide treatment, and refer them for crisis intervention services to Dilaasa. This model has been replicated in several settings.

Since then, there has been consistent work by health and women's groups to sensitize the health system on issues related to VAW. The health policy in India recognized gender-based violence as an issue only in 2017 after this consistent engagement since 2000. The first ever policy directive issued by the Ministry of Health (MoH) was in 2014, on the guidelines and protocols for medico-legal care for survivors/victims of sexual violence. But there has been no such directive for responding to domestic violence, which is extremely common and requires a public health response, despite the PWDVA mandating a role for medical facilities. The 2017 policy provides an opportunity for the MoH to issue specific guidelines for responding to domestic violence in tune with the PWDVA.

Evidence from Existing Response Models Akin to the OSC Model

In India, OSCs have been conceptualized and set up in different settings such as health, police, and courts. The following section presents the existing models that appear to be working and must be sustained through adequate allocation, capacity building, and monitoring exercises. Learnings from these can inform the new OSCs being set up by the Ministry of Women and Child Development (MWCD).

Crisis Centres Located within Health Facilities

Table 10.1 provides a glimpse into models set up in tertiary- and secondary-level hospitals. Dilaasa was set up in 2000 in Mumbai and has been replicated in several places.

It has established strong linkages for ensuring

- o police support by telephone calls to police stations when survivors want to register a complaint;
- o social support such as shelters, children's institutions, hostels, financial aid, income generation/skill building amongst others;
- o legal support lawyers—voluntary as well as NGOs and SLSA;
- o support during court trials—public prosecutors;
- o in case of children, strong linkages with Child Welfare Committees (CWCs) have been fostered.

Figure 10.1 Models set up in tertiary- and secondary-level hospitals.
Source: CEHAT(2012) Comprehensive health care response to sexual assault, report, CEHAT Mumbai. Available at http://www.cehat.org/go/uploads/Publications/R87%20Establishing%20a%20Comprehensive%20Health%20Sector%20Response%20to%20Sexual%20Assault.pdf; Bhate Deosthali Padma, Manghnani Poornima, Malik Seema (2005) Establishing Dilaasa: Documenting the Challenges. Report, CEHAT Mumbai. Available at http://www.cehat.org/go/uploads/Dilaasa/estabdilaasa.pdf.

Table 10.1 Models Set up in Tertiary- and Secondary-level Hospitals

Name	Location	Staffing	Services	Funding	Components
Dilaasa	11 peripheral hospitals in Mumbai	–social workers deputed to the centre or hired for the centre	–DV and rape –Medical –Police, legal and social support through strong referral mechanism	Ministry of Health	Training of health professionals police and counsellors
Bhoomika	21 centres across 21 district hospitals in the state	Social workers hired for the centre	Counselling for DV Referral to state legal aid for legal services	NRHM	
IOHLYNT	Based in Shillong civil hospital	Deputation of social worker from dept. of social welfare	Psycho social support Police aid Referral to PO and legal aid Emergency shelter	DWCD, NRHM	Training of HCP Training of police personnel
Sukoon	Five centres in district hospitals	Health resource centre	Psycho social support Links with police stations, and POs	NRHM and DHS	Training of hospital staff
Dilaasa Women's Crisis Centre	1 crisis centre in North Goa district hospital Plans for 1 crisis centre in South Goa district hospital	Supported by NMEW and DHS	Psycho social support Linkages with PO, legal aid Emergency shelter services	NMEW, WCD	Training of health care providers at the level of hospitals and community health centres awareness programs in communities

Source: WHO & CEHAT (2015) National Consultation on Health Sector Responses to VAW. Report (unpublished). Mumbai: CEHAT.

An external evaluation of Dilaasa found it to be an evidence based and a sustainable hospital-based model for responding to domestic violence and sexual violence. It has been set up as a department of the hospital, the OSC has to present aggregate data on how many women and children received services every month, nature of health consequences, and the like. A monitoring committee oversees the activities of the hospital-based OSC.

The pathway for women to these centres is unique as they are identified by health providers and referred to the centre, and women arriving at the centre thereafter, read IEC material that has been put up at the facility level for creating awareness about domestic violence. Some efforts are being made at the primary level through training of ASHA workers. However, this approach raises several ethical and practical issues as the secondary- and tertiary-level of health systems do not have the required skill and infrastructure for responding to domestic violence.

Crisis Centres Located within Police Stations

In Mumbai, special cells for women and children were set up in 1984; located within the police stations, these were started as a project of the TISS. These were established to enable women to access reforms in laws such as Section 498A IPC, to protect women against cruelty within marital families and harassment pertaining to dowry demands. The special cell engages in counselling women when they approach police stations and helps facilitate police procedures. An important area of the work of the special cell is to sensitize police personnel to the issue of VAW and to ensure comprehensive services from the police station for women who come to the police. After women reach the police stations, the police officer puts the woman in touch with the special cell worker, the worker then coordinates for additional services as required by the women, such as coordination for health services, legal aid, and shelter facilities. Another important component of the special cell's work is making home visits to assess the situation of the woman and carrying out joint meetings with perpetrators. The special cell workers are expected to coordinate with women and visit civil and criminal courts to assist them with legal proceedings.

The special cell started in 1984 in one police station of Mumbai and was replicated in two additional police stations in Mumbai by 1994. In 2001, the Government of Maharashtra entered into a formal collaboration with TISS, Mumbai and the United Nations Development Fund for Women (UNIFEM) and the special cells were replicated in seven districts of Maharashtra. At the completion of the collaboration contract, the Department of Women and Child Welfare took over the special cell programme and replicated it in 16 districts of Maharashtra. The period between 2009 and 2013 also saw the expansion of special cell in other states such as Delhi, Orissa, Gujarat, Haryana, Madhya Pradesh, Andhra Pradesh, and Rajasthan. In each of these states, the special cells have been established by different agencies, some by the state and some by the NGOs. Special cells operating in different states either with the support of NGOs or Women and Child Departments (WCD) have not yet sought to seek the OSC funds for cells in the police station (Dave 2014). These cells have been providing services to survivors of violence for several years. It is not clear why these have not been designated as OSCs. The role of the various ministries such as WCD and Home is in question, as these cells are under WCD but located in police stations.

Rape Crisis Centre at the Delhi Commission of Women

The Delhi Commission has been implementing the Rape Crisis Cell Programme for Women since 2005 to provide legal assistance in cases of sexual assault through collaboration with crisis intervention centres (CIC) in each of its districts. The CIC are outsourced to NGOs. After a case of rape or sexual assault is reported, the concerned investigation officer or the station house officer (SHO) must inform a CIC counsellor. The CIC counsellor arrives at the police station and performs all immediate crisis-response activities like counselling of the victim, informing her of her legal rights, and helping her with procedures to be followed, including the medico-legal certificate (MLC) examination. The rape crisis centre (RCC) lawyer provides legal assistance and support to the victims of sexual assault in courts. These lawyers support the victim during court proceedings, oppose bail applications of the accused/s, and move applications seeking victim compensation. The programme regularly takes up cases of extreme brutality, violation, and inaction of authorities (that is, police or hospitals). The RCCs are funded through the state women and child department and Central Social Welfare Board. There is no information pertaining to recognizing RCCs as OSC under the MWCD scheme, neither has the Delhi Commission for Women sought funds from MWCD to support RCCs.

Court-Based One Stop Centre (OSC)

In order to facilitate humane psychological, medical treatment to the victims of crime during the investigation, crime, and thereafter, it is important to have support services at the level of the court. It is a known fact that there is a complete absence of support to navigate the court procedures, understand the court procedures and its implications, and provide support and handholding throughout the court proceedings. This necessitates the establishment of a court-based OSC. Such an OSC has been established by the Delhi State Legal Services Authority (DLSA) and has been functional since 31 March 2016. One judicial assistant and one orderly are posted in the centre. Psychological/emotional counsellors sit for a few hours on weekends or come in when the centre has prior notice of a victim. The centre is primarily used for recording of statements of minors and victims of sexual offences by Magistrates under Section 164 CrPC.

The role of the court OSC is to assist the survivor of VAW right from the investigation to completion of the trial. The OSC assists in disbursal of compensation, witness protection, and any other services as required by the survivor. The OSC works in close coordination with the public prosecutor and makes provision for counsellors to accompany the survivor to courts. The counsellors and the lawyer assigned to the survivor are familiar with the court proceedings and communicate the progress of the case to the survivor from time to time

The above section presents the various OSCs located in different systems such as police, health, and judiciary. They are providing women-centred services to survivors and there is an urgent need to strengthen these structures, instead of creating new ones. The centres can be part of a strong referral system so that women have multiple places to go to for support and counselling through their struggle for justice.

Understanding the Origins of OSC

OSC as a method for responding to rape or domestic violence have been operational in the West since the 1970s and in South Asia for more than a decade. Several OSC models in countries such as England and Wales, Rwanda, Zambia, Australia, South Africa, Malaysia, Phillipines, and Bangladesh have different histories and origin. The Australian rape crisis centre was the outcome of the feminist movement and is based in a community set-up. This centre receives survivors who seek services for healing from the consequences of rape and for those who wish to engage in group therapy. The entire programme is volunteer-led, where volunteers undergo six-week training. The rape crisis centres in England and Wales runs a Sexual Assault Referral Program (SARC) which operates as centres to provide emergency medico-legal services, however, in some places they are not able to provide medical treatment and care, in which case they are referred to hospitals for treatment. The SARC centres, after carrying out medico-legal service, refer for medical aid and psycho-social services as the focus is on the collection of forensic evidence in a sensitive manner. USA has models that include hospital-based services for domestic violence and rape through the department of social workers at the hospital and a team of volunteers trained to provide on-site support for rape survivors 24x7. The way in which this operates is that the hospital calls a hotline number as soon as a rape victim comes to the hospital and a volunteer on duty comes in and facilitates the entire medical examination and also provides basic support. The ones in South Africa are located in hospitals but linked to the public prosecutor's office and so focus on the judicial outcome. The ones in Rwanda are located in the police station with the same focus on support for the judicial process. These services have been focused on domestic violence or rape, thus having two separate services running in the same facility to respond to these two forms of VAW. Recognizing the need to set up OSCs to respond to all forms of violence within low resource setting, the initiatives in South Asia seek to provide comprehensive service to all survivors primarily located in hospitals. Malaysia, Phillipines, and Bangladesh set up such models that focused on training of health professionals on identifying violence amongst patients and carried out service provision to survivors. Many of these models were dependent on NGOs for providing counsellors and thus the quality and availability was subject to availability of NGO members. This dependence posed a barrier in integrating these into the existing health-care services.

OSC as the State Response to VAW

The OSCs became a buzzword in the context of the Justice Verma Committee (JVC) Report and the Justice Usha Mehra Committee Report. Recommendations of these reports were in response to the mass agitations following the brutal physical and sexual assault on a young woman in the capital city and her subsequent death in December 2012. The JVC was set up to review the existing law and infrastructure, and make recommendations. The JVC Report 2013 highlighted the institutional biases towards rape within the police, health, and judiciary that prevent access to and delivery of justice and made recommendations for changes in law and at all levels of the criminal justice system. The Usha Mehra Committee also made recommendations for setting up crisis centres for rape survivors and inter-sectoral collaboration. The Government of India was compelled to take swift action, which resulted in several positive changes in a span of one year. Amendment of the rape law, setting up of a telephonic help line by the chief minister's office in Delhi, and gender sensitive protocols for medico-legal care were some of the concrete steps taken by the government. The Government of India also launched a 10 billion rupees fund called the Nirbhaya Fund and was expected to support all the initiatives to be undertaken to increase the safety of women and mitigate VAW. In the same vein, the MWCD Union of India launched a new scheme namely Nirbhaya Centres which adopted the OSC model. Despite existing models of OSC such as Dilaasa, the scheme did not build on it. The model is a joint initiative of CEHAT and the Municipal Corporation of Greater Mumbai. An external evaluation carried out in 2010 has recommended its upscaling, as this had integrated a health response to VAW within the hospital. The initial focus of the OSC scheme was to only focus on survivors of rape. But considering that an OSC necessitated creation of an entire infrastructure, personnel, and response mechanisms, it was important to expand the scope of these interventions to all forms of violence against women and children. Civil society and women's groups' consistent dialogue with MWCD led the department revising its proposal to extend the response at these centres to all forms of VAW.

The OSCs, as these are now called, are being set up one per state with a centre–state sharing of funding resources. The OSCs, as envisaged under the MWCD scheme, do address domestic violence and sexual violence. The SOP that have been issued for the functioning of these centres provides clear direction on linking up with the PWDVA infrastructure. The establishment of OSCs is based on a survivor-centred approach to providing services. It would be useful to trace the origin of this model. The Umbrella Scheme of 2012 made provision for setting up of hospital-based crisis centres in 100 hospitals on the lines of Dilaasa. The hospital-based crisis centres were envisaged as having strong linkages with the police and the courts. Where a woman decides to take police assistance and wants to get a FIR registered, the centres shall have the provision of calling the required police station and record the FIR at a place where the woman is comfortable, followed by the statement under Section 164. Such a centre is expected to provide the necessary linkages and support to survivors in accessing justice.

Objectives

The key aim of an OSC is to provide multiple services such as emotional support, police aid, shelter services, and legal aid as well as rehabilitation services under one roof. But this is highly resource intensive and poses challenges in low- and middle-income countries. Personnel from various systems such as the police, health, and social justice cannot always be expected to be deputed full time at these centres due to huge human resource crunch and other systemic problems. For example, in centres where there are one police personnel deputed full time, their role is limited to informing the woman about police procedures and does not extend to registering an FIR at the centre. This information can be provided by the centre staff and the local police can then be called to file the FIR. What has been found to be useful and effective is to set up strong referral mechanism with multiple SPs so that women are able to access services easily.

Review of the Existing OSC under the MWCD Scheme

The MWCD OSC scheme did not take into account the existing models of response such as hospital-based, police, and court OSCs, instead, the scheme proposed the setting up of the new structure under the MWCD close to a hospital if possible. But it was left to the states to decide on the location of OSCs. The OSC aims to provide integrated support and assistance under one roof to women affected by the violence of all forms. MWCD developed specific guidelines on 17 March 2015 for setting up OSC scheme. The location of the OSC was proposed to be in a government hospital or within a radius of 2 km if the space of 132 sq. m was not available in the hospital or within a medical facility. In the absence of space in the hospital, OSC was proposed to be built within hospital premises or within a 2 km radius on a separate piece of land. The revised guidelines of August 2016 gave first preference to the hospital or medical facility or staff quarters with the provision of five rooms with a total carpet area of 132 sq. m. If that is not possible, then government institution like Nari Niketan was preferred site of location of OSC. In the first OSC scheme roll out, 36 OSC were proposed, one OSC was to be established in every State/UT on a pilot basis in a hospital, or within a 2 km radius of a hospital. The OSC is expected to have a full-time administrator, a full-time case worker, on call psychologist, on call health worker, police constable stationed at the OSC, and an on call state legal aid authority lawyer.

The finance ministry created a fund called 'Nirbhaya' in 2014 with a corpus of Rs 1,000 crores, with the same amount being added annually. One of the schemes funded by the Nirbhaya Fund is the OSC Scheme. The OSC scheme in its initial stages set out to set up one OSC per state.

However, between June 2016–17, such OSC had been set up in different states. These are: Chhattisgarh (Raipur), Andhra Pradesh (Vijaywada), Haryana (Karnal), Odisha (Bhubaneshwar), Chandigarh, Pondicherry, Goa (Bambolim), Karnataka (Udupi), Rajasthan (Jaipur), Diu (for Daman and Diu and Dadar and Nagar Haveli), Uttarakhand (Haridwar), Uttar Pradesh (Banda), Andaman and Nicobar Islands (Port Blair), Arunanchal Pradesh (Paptimpare), Kerala (Thiruvananthapuram), Meghayala (Shillong), and Nagaland (Dimapur).

The MWCD has carried out an evaluation of its centres and is in the process of upscaling them. The authors have reviewed the report, and based on the date presented, several issues have emerged that require deliberation so that the roll out can be better informed.

Several of these OSCs are located in the vicinity of hospitals or within the hospitals, but there is no coordination between the police, OSC staff, and hospitals. When a woman reporting violence comes to the hospital with health consequences she gets treated, but does not receive a referral to the OSC located within the same premises. Women reaching OSC for services and those wanting to file a police complaint cannot avail of the medico-legal and police post of the hospital. These women are taken to another police station to record a complaint. A coordinated approach requires that when a woman accessing OSC services decides to register a complaint, the police on duty of the hospital should coordinate with the specific police station so that the police can reach the OSC to record the complaint. The police facilitation officer (PFO), although deputed at the centre, cannot file FIRs and so the woman still has to go the police station to file one. So, it is not useful to have someone from the police department round the clock at the OSC. There is a need for better coordination of local police with the OSC where, once a call is made from the OSC, the police must immediately facilitate recording of FIR. The FIR must be recorded at the OSC based in a hospital at the behest of the woman.

Medical staff deputed at the OSC is either on call or round the clock. The profile of the medical staff is that of auxiliary nurses and their role is to accompany the woman to the nearest hospital and access medical care. Nurses and auxillary nursery and midwifery (ANMs) have no mandate to 'treat' or carry out medico-legal documentation of cases of violence. Thus, the full time or part time auxiliary nurse does not have a role at the level of the OSC. OSC has no mechanism for coordinating with the POs and SPs under the PWDVA. The infrastructure created for the implementation of the PWDVA thus remains a parallel mechanism, if proper linkages are not created. This is essential as most women reporting violence are facing domestic violence.

The current profile of women reaching Nari Niketan shelter-based OSC shows that women who are destitute and in need of shelter are brought by the police to this OSC. Thus, OSC ends up operating as a shelter rather than carrying out coordinated service delivery.

Outsourcing of services: there is a tendency and push for outsourcing of services and we need to demand that full-time staff is recruited at the OSC in order to ensure accountability and ownership. The budget for payment to people on call should be better utilized to offer quality services.

Interventions: there is a concern with regard to the approach adopted by OSCs to enable women to deal with violence. Invariably the abusive person (often the husband) is called to the OSC and a joint meeting is conducted to verify true/false cases. Often, women are not prepared for these joint meetings and calling the husband may jeopardize their safety and mobility. These methods tantamount to victim blaming and also question the veracity of the woman. There is no protocol for carrying out crisis intervention or for a feminist approach to counselling in the current OSCs.

The MWCD has now issued standard operating procedures (SOP) that clearly lay down the quality of counselling, the pathways to care, and the linkages to other systems such as the PWDVA infrastructure of POs, SPs, as well as the legal service authority for assisting women in accessing justice and other social support. The SOP document is available on the MWCD website and is a robust document that lays down the roles and responsibilities of each functionary, the quality of services to be provided, the ethical principles to be adhered to, the referral agencies, and the linkages with other programmes and schemes of the state.

Despite the several limitations pointed out about setting up rape crisis centres, the Delhi government went ahead and implemented this recommendation and set up rape crisis centres in few hospitals in Delhi such as Ram Manohar Lohia and Safdarjung. These have merely marked out separate room for examination and collection of medical evidence in instances of sexual assault survivors. No effort has been made to provide comprehensive services such as counselling support, shelter services, and referrals to legal aid. They are asked to go to the Delhi commission women. The existing hospital team of counsellors and psychologists has not been assigned any role here and the focus is evidence collection, and counselling is outsourced. (CBGA 2017).

Way Forward

The entire campaign to end VAW after the Delhi rape incident demanded a change in institutional responses to VAW. OSCs are set up as one mechanism of creating an institutional response, but in reality the functions and activities of OSC have been outsourced to different agencies thus making non-state players accountable for an institutional response. There is a danger in essentializing OSCCs as the only response to VAW. VAW is a complex reality and its roots are deeply entrenched in society. Therefore, there is a need to look at the different structures and increase competencies of those structures. The OSC centres which are stand-alone centres with on call staff are not integrated within any of the systems/institutions and therefore accountability of these centres will be a huge challenge. The SOPs that have been issued by the MWCD for setting standards for intervention services are women-centred, but for its implementation, rigorous training and monitoring is required. The state must make provision for the same and ensure that women survivors of violence are not further blamed or victimized. The OSCs must therefore be equipped to coordinate support for women from various agencies in a way that women are not shunted from one place to another.

In India, the two existing models, namely, the Special Cell for Women and Children located in the police station, and Dilaasa, integrated into the public hospital system, have shown positive results and there should be an effort to upscale these models. The court based OSC should be reviewed as it is well documented that the legal battle is long, intimidating, and tiring, and support at the level of the courts can help women to continue with the legal system. There is a need to understand that crisis intervention services need to be set up within different institutions such as the health department, police stations, and courts that survivors have to access for justice and care.

Over the last three decades, there has been a demand for the state to set up services for survivors of domestic violence. However, one of the main concerns of the feminist groups has been the quality of services being offered by many of the state-run centres. With their focus on 'preserving marriage', 'reconciliation', compromise, they fail to question domestic violence and often minimize it as a 'conflict' or a 'quarrel' within the home. This is due to the complete lack of a feminist perspective and women centred approach in their response. Feminist interventions locate the roots of VAW within structures and institutions that are gender unequal. It questions abuse and puts the onus of abuse on the perpetrator, rather than the victim. The SOP of the OSCs and the training of OSC teams by the National Institute of

Public Cooperation and Child Development (NIPCID) do include feminist perspective in responding to VAW. It is important that women's groups be involved in the monitoring of these centres so that they are able to provide support and empowerment to survivors of domestic violence and sexual violence, and help them in their access to justice and in improving their well-being.

References

Bhate-Deosthali, P. et al., 'Addressing Domestic Violence within Healthcare Settings', *Economic & Political Weekly*, 47, 17 (2012): 67.

Chowdhary, N., & Patel, V. 'The Effect of Spousal Violence on Women's Health: Findings from the Stree Arogya Shodh in Goa, India', *Journal of Postgraduate Medicine* 54, 4(2008): 306.

CEHAT. 'Establishing a Comprehensive Health Sector Response to Sexual Assault' (Rep). (2012).

Daga, A. et al., 'Domestic Violence against Women: An Investigation of Hospital Casualty Records Mumbai', *Journal of Family Welfare* 45,1(1999): 1–11.

Dave, A. *Women Survivors of Violence: Genesis and Growth of a State Support System*, New Delhi: Orient Blackswan. 2015.

Deosthali, P., Maghnani, P., and Malik, D. S, 'Establishing Dilaasa: Documenting the Challenges', Mumbai: Centre for Enquiry into Health and Allied Themes. 2007.

Nadkarni, Vimla, Roopashri Sinha, Leonie D'Mello (eds), 'Establishing Dilaasa: A Public Hospital Based Crisis Centre', *NGOs, Health and the Urban Poor*. Mumbai: Rawat Publications, 2009. pp. 140–60.

García-Moreno, C. et al., 'WHO Multi-Country Study on Women's Health and Domestic Violence against Women: Initial Results on Prevalence, Health Outcomes and Women's Responses', World Health Organization. 2005.

Johri, M. et al., 'Increased risk of miscarriage among women experiencing physical or sexual intimate partner violence during pregnancy in Guatemala City, Guatemala: Cross-sectional Study'. *BMC Pregnancy and Childbirth* 11, 1(2011): 49.

Khot, A. et al., 'Domestic violence: Levels, correlates, causes, impact, and response', A Community-based Study of Married Women from Mumbai Slums. Mumbai: Centre for Enquiry into Health and Allied Themes, 2004.

Koski, A. D. et al., 'Physical violence by partner during pregnancy and use of prenatal care in rural India', *Journal of health, population, and nutrition* 29, 3(2011): 245–54.

Kumar, S. et al., 'Domestic Violence and Its Mental Health Correlates in Indian Women', *The British Journal of Psychiatry* 187, 1(2005): 62–5.

Mahajan, A. 'Instigators of Wife Battering', in S. Sood (ed.), *Violence against Women*, Jaipur: Arihant Publishers, pp. 1–10, 1990.

Nadkarni, Vimla, Sinha, Roopashri , D'Mello, Leonie (eds). 'Establishing Dilaasa: A Public Hospital Based Crisis Centre', NGOs, *Health and the Urban Poor*. Mumbai: Rawat Publications, 2009. pp. 140–60.

Rao, V, 'Wife-beating in rural South India: A qualitative and econometric analysis', *Social Science & Medicine* 44,8(1997): 1169–80.

Verma, J. S., Seth, L., Subramanian, G., and Justice J.S Verma Committee (Rep). (2013). Report of the Committee on Amendments to Criminal Law. Retrieved from http://www.prsindia.org/uploads/media/Justice%20verma%20committee/js%20verma%20committe%20report.pdf.

Visaria, Leela . 'Violence against Women: A Field Study', *Economic and Political Weekly*, 35(20): 1742–51, 2000.

World Health Organization, 'Responding to Intimate Partner Violence and Sexual Violence against Women: WHO Clinical and Policy Guidelines', 2013.

Yee, A. 'Reforms Urged to Tackle Violence against Women in India', *The Lancet* 381, 9876(2013): 1445–6.

11. *Changing Contours of Fiscal Policy and Budgets to Address Violence against Women*

An Analysis of Two States

Kanika Kaul

Despite the adoption of several legislative and policy measures, the incidence of violence against women in the country continues to be unacceptably high. While the work of women's rights organizations, activists, lawyers, and other stakeholders has focused on strengthening the legislative and policy framework, linking services, seeking accountability of institutions, and changing mindsets, the budgetary dimensions of the state's response to the issue require equal attention if we are to ensure a comprehensive response mechanism for women facing violence.

The recent years have witnessed important changes in planning and budgetary processes followed in the country thus far. These developments, including the constitution of the National Institution for Transforming India (NITI) Aayog in place of the Planning Commission, restructuring of the Union Budget in 2015–16, following the Union Government's acceptance of the 14th Finance Commission (FFC) recommendations and measures undertaken for rationalization of Centrally Sponsored Schemes (CSS) have marked gender implications.

They also have a bearing on public financing of government programmes in a range of sectors, including those meant to address violence against women.

Interventions to address violence against women are implemented by both the union government and states. Union government interventions towards the issue, led primarily by the MWCD, have, for long, been characterized by low budgetary outlays, poor implementation, and low coverage. A look at schemes to address violence against women by state governments in two states, that is, Madhya Pradesh and Jharkhand, reflects a low priority towards the issue in the state budgets. The increased fiscal autonomy available to states following the acceptance of the FFC recommendations does not appear to have translated into higher budgetary priority for the issue.

Looking ahead, in the new fiscal architecture, NITI Aayog must take measures to strengthen a gender focus in policies and programmes. An important means to achieve this end would be a reiteration of the government's commitment to Gender Responsive Budgeting by both the union government and states. With increased autonomy to determine their expenditure priorities as a result of devolution of greater untied funds (following the recommendations of FFC), states must step up their priority for interventions specifically meant to address violence against women. However, given the criticality of the issue, the union government must also continue to supplement the efforts of states in this domain.

Among the several impediments constraining the State's efforts to eliminate and address the occurrence of violence against women, bottlenecks in the domain of budgets are an important constraint. It is hoped that the priority accorded to the issue of violence against women in the policy framework translates into a higher priority for the issue in government budgets in the years to come.

Violence against women is a complex issue entrenched in deeply patriarchal social norms, addressing which requires a multi-dimensional approach. The work by women's rights organizations, activists, lawyers, and other stakeholders has focused on strengthening the legislative and policy framework, linking services, accountability of institutions, and changing mind sets. However, the budgetary and governance dimensions of the state's response to the issue require equal attention if we are to ensure a comprehensive response for women, in light of the high levels of violence against women in the country.

The last decade has witnessed a surge in the incidence of violence against women in the country. The rate of total cognizable crimes against women (crime per 1 lakh female population) for the country as a whole increased from 14.1 in 2005 to 53.9 in 2015[1] (NCRB). Significant developments in the legislative and policy spheres such as the enactment of the PWDA, the adoption of the 11th and 12th Five Year Plans (2007–12 and 2012–17), recommendations of the Justice Verma Committee (2013), among others during the same period notwithstanding, violence against women in the country continues to be unacceptably high.

The high incidence of violence against women in the country necessities an examination of government interventions to address the same. It is important to analyse the extent to which government schemes, meant to operationalize legislative and policy commitments on the issue, recognize and address the different forms of violence and the extent to which these interventions are backed by adequate budgetary outlays. This is particularly important in light of the fact that a large number of women subjected to violence do not have access to any other form of support and rely largely or entirely on State instituted support mechanisms for both immediate rescue and relief as well as for long-term rehabilitative measures.

Under the federal fiscal architecture in India, government interventions, both, in critical sectors like health, education, sanitation, and so on, on which women's reliance tends to be higher than that of men, as well as interventions specifically aimed at addressing violence against women are supported by both the union government and states. The role of each of the two levels of government in this domain is important. The union government's programmatic framework is essential to ensure a basic level of services, especially in backward states, where, given the scarcity of resources, the states' ability to provide funds for interventions to address violence against women may be limited. At the same time, states play an important role in addressing particular forms of violence specific to the region or state through appropriately designed interventions.

The recent years have witnessed important changes in planning and budgetary processes followed in the country thus far. The dissolution of the Planning Commission and the constitution of the NITI Aayog, the union government's acceptance of the recommendations of the FFC, the subsequent restructuring of the Union Budget, and rationalization of CSS are important

[1] The latest year for which crime data is provided by NCRB is 2015.

developments that have a bearing on public financing of government interventions in a range of sectors, including those addressing violence against women. Against this backdrop, it is important to analyse the implications of the changing contours of the fiscal policy brought about as a result of these recent developments on public provisioning for interventions for women. It is also pertinent to, at this current juncture, analyse the interventions specifically aimed at addressing violence against women by both the union government and states, and asses the adequacy of these interventions and what each of the two levels of governments could do to strengthen the existing programmatic framework of the government to address violence against women.

This chapter is presented in three sections. The first section describes some of the key changes in the country's planning and budgetary processes in recent years and highlights the likely implications of these on financing of interventions that are important from the perspective of women. The second and the third sections discuss the budgetary allocations for women at the level of the union government and in two states, namely, Madhya Pradesh and Jharkhand, particularly with reference to interventions instituted to address violence against women. The chapter concludes with a discussion on some of the key points that emerge from the analysis presented.

Recent Changes in the Country's Fiscal Architecture: Implications for Women

The recent years have been characterized by significant developments in the fiscal policy landscape in the country. Much of the analysis following these developments has focused on the implications of these on centre–state fiscal relations and the financing of important government schemes and programmes from here on, particularly in the social sectors. Though the outcomes of these changes would affect all sections of population, some of these changes have marked gender dimensions. An analysis of financing of government interventions to address violence against women must be foregrounded in such an analysis. The following section describes some of these key developments and the likely implications for women.

Abolition of the Planning Commission and Constitution of the NITI Aayog

The abolition of the Planning Commission in 2014 and the establishment of the NITI Aayog in its place in 2015 marked a significant departure from the planning and budgeting processes followed in the country thus far. The need for a body such as the NITI Aayog has been argued for on the grounds that 'with an increasingly open and liberalized economy and given the new realities of the global economy, we needed to rethink the tools and approaches to conceptualizing the development process'.[2] The completion of the 12th Five Year Plans (FYP) in 2016–17, thus, brought an end to the era of FYP, followed subsequently by the merger of Plan and Non-Plan heads of expenditure in expenditure budgets of the union government and several states. As the country makes a transition from the planning processes led by the Planning Commission to a still evolving new framework, it is worth reflecting on the likely implications of this change, for an important function that the Planning Commission played a significant role in, that is, planning and budgeting for the marginalized sections of population, particularly women.

For over six decades preceding the dissolution of the Planning Commission, the various FYPs had been the main policy formulation processes through which the thrust for greater attention to gender issues was introduced and institutionalized for both the union government as well as for states. For instance, the fifth FYP recognized the need for paying greater attention to women's issues (following the publication of 'Towards Equality' in the mid-1970s) Das and Mishra (2006) have traced some of the significant efforts in the FYPs with regard to the institutional architecture to address gender issues and channelising of financial resources for women. The seventh FYP pushed for constitution of the Department of Women and Child Development under the Ministry of Human Resource Development and assigned it the responsibility of monitoring the impact on women in 27 important schemes of the Government of India. Likewise, the ninth FYP introduced the Women's Component Plan, and the 12th FYP laid emphasis on Gender Responsive Budgeting (GRB). In doing so, the Planning Commission provided policy direction and suggested new schemes/programmes as required.

It has been argued that the dissolution of the Planning Commission does not mean the end of planning processes itself. Rao (2015) highlights that though the planning led by the NITI Aayog would be distinct from the planning process under the Planning Commission, as per the Cabinet resolution for the notification of the NITI Aayog, it has the responsibility

[2] Government of India, 'Draft Three Year Action Agenda', Press Information Bureau, New Delhi, 25 April 2017. Available at, http://pib.nic.in/newsite/PrintRelease.aspx?relid=157727.

of strategic planning. Henceforth, the development agenda to be pursued by the union government henceforth will be guided by a Fifteen-Year Vision, Seven-Year Strategy (which will lay down the schemes, programmes and strategies to achieve the long-term vision) and a Three-Year Action Agenda to be developed by the NITI Aayog (which outlines proposals for policy changes within a shorter timeframe). While the first two are still in the process of formulation, a draft version of the Three-Year Action Agenda has been shared in the public domain.

The discussion on women in the Action Agenda presented by NITI Aayog is centred around four areas, namely, GRB, economic participation, women's safety, and women's well-being index. Though other sections also include some discussion on women, these are not too substantive. Not only is the range of issues highlighted in the document narrow, but the discussion on these is also not too in-depth. The document highlights some dimensions of the issues but does not present a vision or a roadmap of what the government intends to achieve over the next three years. What would go a long way in bringing about a strong gender perspective in the policies, plans, and programmes that would be developed by the NITI Aayog is the constitution of a subgroup of chief ministers devoted to addressing gender issues on the lines of the subgroups of chief ministers on skill development, rationalization of CSS, and Swachh Bharat Mission.

Another question that merits some discussion pertains to the role of the MWCD in the new institutional architecture. With the end of the five-year planning process, it would be important for MWCD to draw the attention of all ministries and state governments towards gender issues and mainstreaming the required measures through appropriate policies and programmes across sectors. However, this requires a stronger MWCD that is able to effectively engage with other union ministries and work towards making their interventions more gender responsive.

A key strategy adopted by the union government (and also highlighted in the Three-Year Action Agenda) to make policies, programmes, and budgets more responsive to gender based challenges is GRB. Unlike the Scheduled Caste Sub-Plan for Scheduled Castes and Tribal Sub-Plan for tribal population which were Plan strategies and hence limited to the Plan component of the budget, GRB has been applicable over the entire budget (that is, both Plan and Non-Plan). Moreover, the Planning Commission did not play a supervisory role in the implementation of the strategy. Hence, the abolition of the Planning Commission and the subsequent merger of Plan and Non-Plan heads of expenditure does not raise concerns about the future of GRB. However, its implementation has been weak, owing to a narrow interpretation of the strategy and its limited adoption by concerned departments/ministries. The NITI Aayog, in conjunction with the Ministry of Finance (MOF) and MWCD, must take necessary steps to strengthen the implementation of the strategy by union departments/ministries.

Restructuring of Union Budget in 2015–16 Following Acceptance of the FFC Recommendations

The union government plays a critical role in provisioning of resources for social sector schemes, including even some that are state subjects. Women, typically concentrated at the lower end of the income spectrum with limited access to resources, tend to rely on public provisioning of essential services to a greater extent than men. It follows, therefore, that a reduction in union government spending on social sectors would have a disproportionately adverse impact on women unless states indeed compensate with additional budget outlays from their untied funds.

Among the most significant developments in the domain of fiscal policy in recent years is the union governments' acceptance of the recommendations of the FFC.[3] The recommendations, which will be in implementation for the period 2015–16 to 2019–20, will have a significant bearing on public financing of government interventions in a range of sectors.

The most significant recommendation of FFC pertains to the increase in the magnitude of states' share in the divisible pool of central taxes. For the period 2015–16 to 2019–20, the states' share in the divisible pool of central taxes has increased to 42 per cent.

Following the implementation of the recommendations of FFC, important changes in the form of restructuring of expenditure were introduced in the Union Budget in 2015–16. On account of an increase in the devolution of Centre's tax receipts to states, Union Budget's outlays for a number of social sector schemes were substantially reduced in 2015–16 (BE). It was expected that states would compensate for such reductions through higher allocations to these schemes with the help of the increased untied funds they would receive from the Centre. Additionally, eight CSS were delinked from support from the Centre, that is, they were discontinued. States could continue to implement these from the enhanced resources available to them,

[3] The Finance Commission is required to recommend the distribution of the net proceeds of taxes of the Union between the Union and the states, and the allocation between the states of the respective shares of such proceeds.

Key Recommendations of the 14th Finance Commission

- **Tax devolution:** The share of taxes of the Centre to states is recommended to be increased from 32 per cent to 42 per cent, an increase in 10 percentage points from the 32 per cent recommended by the 13th Finance Commission.
- **Horizontal devolution of resources:** FFC has also proposed a new horizontal formula. Relative to the 13th Finance Commission, the FFC has incorporated two new variables—2011 population and forest cover, while the criteria of fiscal discipline has been excluded.
- **Sector specific grants:** No recommendation regarding sector-specific grants for states.
- **Grants to local governments:** Distribution of grants to states for local bodies (urban and rural) based on the 2011 population with a weight of 90 per cent, and area with a weight of 10 per cent has been recommended. Total size of this grant for all states is to be Rs 2,87,436 crore.

resulting from the recommendations of the FFC. Union government's support for schemes of national priority, those that are legal/constitutional obligations (such as Mahatma Gandhi National Rural Employment Guarantee Act (MGNREGA)) and some programmes for the benefit of socially disadvantaged, however, was not reduced.

The situation with regard to union government's allocations to social sectors presents a slightly different picture in 2016–17 and 2017–18. Table 11.1 presents the budgetary outlays for some important social sector ministries in the union government.

A look at the allocations to union ministries between 2014–15 and 2017–18 presents a mixed picture. Though allocations to most ministries have increased in absolute terms as a proportion of the Union Budget, allocations to Ministry of Human Resource Development, Ministry of Social Justice, Ministry of Housing and Urban Poverty Alleviation, and MWCD, the nodal ministry for women's development and empowerment have declined. The priority to the Ministry of Minority Affairs and the Ministry of Tribal Affairs has remained unchanged over the last four years. In the case of most other union ministries such as Ministry of Health and Family Welfare (including Ayurvedic, Yoga and Naturopathy, Unani, Siddha and Homeopathy (AYUSH)), Ministry of Urban Development, Ministry of Rural Development, Ministry of Drinking Water and Sanitation, after a fall in allocations in 2015–16, the priority to these ministries has increased in subsequent years.

Table 11.1 Budgetary Outlays for Select Union Ministries

Department/Ministry	2014–15		2015–16		2016–17		2017–18
	BE	AE	BE	AE	BE	RE	BE
Health and Family Welfare (including AYUSH)							
In Rs crore	39,238	3,2154	24,282	35,190	39,533	40,995	50,281
As a proportion of Union Budget	2.1	1.93	1.22	1.97	2	2.04	2.34
Human Resource Development							
In Rs crore	82,771	68,875	69,075	67,239	72,394	73,599	79,686
As a proportion of Union Budget	4.61	1.93	3.89	3.75	3.66	3.65	3.71
Minority Affairs							
In Rs crore	3,734	3,089	3,739	3,655	3,827	3,827	4,195
As a proportion of Union Budget	0.2	0.19	0.21	0.2	0.19	0.19	0.2
Social Justice and Empowerment							
In Rs crore	6,846	5,381	6,524.82	5,753	6,566	6,569	6,908
As a proportion of Union Budget	0.38	0.32	0.36	0.32	0.33	0.33	0.32
Tribal Affairs							
In Rs crore	4,498	3,852	4,819	4,480	4,827	4,827	5,329
As a proportion of Union Budget	0.25	0.23	0.27	0.25	0.24	0.24	0.25
Women and Child Development							
In Rs crore	21,194	18,539	10,382	17,249	17,408	17,640	22,095
As a proportion of Union Budget	1.18	1.11	0.58	0.96	0.88	0.88	1.03

Table 11.1 (*Cont'd*)

Department/Ministry	2014–15		2015–16		2016–17		2017–18
			Urban Development				
In Rs crore	20,009	13,254	19,217	18,419	24,523	32,550	34,212
As a proportion of Union Budget	1.11	0.8	1.08	1.03	1.24	1.62	1.59
			Rural Development				
In Rs crore	83,852	67,311	71,695.08	77,369.2	86,055.8	96,060	105,448
As a proportion of Union Budget	4.67	4.05	4.03	5.34	4.35	5.94	4.91
			Housing and Urban Poverty Alleviation				
In Rs crore	6,009	2,728	5,634	1,761	5,411	5,285	6,406
As a proportion of Union Budget	0.33	0.16	0.32	0.10	0.27	0.26	0.30
			Drinking water and Sanitation				
In Rs. crore	15,267	12,091	6,244	11,081	14,010	16,512	20,011
As a proportion of Union Budget	0.85	0.73	0.35	0.62	0.71	0.82	0.93

Source: Union Budget documents, various years.

A more nuanced assessment of the implications of the restructuring of Union Budget expenditure could be made by analysing budgetary outlays for some of the important social sector schemes of Government of India. Table 11.2 captures the allocations to some major schemes of the union government between 2014–15 and 2017–18.

As is reflected in Table 11.2, following the restructuring of the Union Budget in 2015–16, allocations to several important schemes including the National Health Mission, Swachh Bharat Mission, Pradhan Mantri Awas Yojana, and MGNREGA have increased, which is a welcome measure. However, this has been accompanied by reductions in allocations to important schemes including Sarva Shiksha Abhiyan, Mid-Day Meal, Integrated Child Development Services (ICDS), and National Rural Drinking Water Programme. Though outlays for the Maternity Benefit Programme have been enhanced in 2017–18 (BE) to expand the coverage of the scheme from 53 districts to cover all districts, the wage loss compensation provided under the scheme, which was approved by the Cabinet in May 2017, is restricted to only the first birth. Besides reduced outlays for some schemes, eight major union government schemes, that is, schemes that were in implementation until 2014–15 have also been discontinued.[4]

The changes in the union government expenditure for important social sector schemes as discussed earlier, following the acceptance of the FFC recommendations, must be seen in light of the already low levels of union government allocations for these interventions. There has been a persistent gap between the estimated fund requirements by departments/ministries and the funds approved by the Planning Commission (in the FYP) and Ministry of Finance (in the Annual Budgets). The inadequacy of Union Budget outlays and its implications for the implementation of a number of social sector schemes has also been regularly highlighted by the Department Related Parliamentary Standing Committees in their reports over the years.

In the new framework of centre–state fiscal relations, with a greater proportion of untied funds, every state government now has a bigger opportunity to prioritize (through adequate financial resources) interventions across sectors that would address gender concerns, as well as programmes specifically aimed at addressing violence against women.

[4] Backward Regions Grant Funds, Rajiv Gandhi Panchayat Sashaktikaran Abhiyaan, Scheme for setting up of 6,000 Model Schools, National Mission on Food Processing (one of the eight schemes—modernization of police force was subsequently re-introduced in 2016–17).

Table 11.2 Union Budget Outlays for Major Social Sector Schemes

	2014–15		2015–16		2016–17		2017–18
	BE	AE	BE	AE	BE	RE	BE
			Sarva Shiksha Abhiyan				
In Rs crore	28,258	24,097	19,800*	21,661	22,500	22,500	23,500
As a proportion of Union Budget	1.57	1.45	1.11	1.21	1.14	1.12	1.09
			Mid-Day Meal				
In Rs Crore	13,215	10,524	7,775*	9,145	9,700	9,700	10,000
As a proportion of Union Budget	0.61	0.63	0.43	0.51	0.49	0.48	0.47
			Core ICDS/Anganwadi Services				
In Rs Crore	18,391	16,684	8,449	15,489	14,850	14,736	16,745
As a proportion of Union Budget	1.02	1.00	0.47	0.86	0.75	0.73	0.78
			National Health Mission				
In Rs Crore	22,731	19,752	18,875	18,972	19,037	20,037	21,941
As a proportion of Union Budget	1.27	1.19	1.06	1.06	0.96	0.99	1.02
			National Rural Drinking Water Programme				
In Rs Crore	11,000	9,243	2,611	4,370	5,000	6,000	6,050
As a proportion of Union Budget	0.61	0.56	0.11	0.24	0.25	0.30	0.28
			Swachh Bharat Mission (Rural)				
In Rs Crore	4,260	2,841	3,625	6,703	9,000	10,500	13,948
As a proportion of Union Budget	0.24	0.17	0.20	0.37	0.45	0.52	0.65
			Pradhan Mantri Awas Yojana**				
In Rs Crore	16,000	11,105	10,025	10,116	15,000	16,000	23,000
As a proportion of Union Budget	0.89	0.67	0.56	0.56	0.76	0.79	1.07

(Cont'd)

Table 11.2 (*Cont'd*)

	2014–15		2015–16		2016–17		2017–18
	BE	AE	BE	AE	BE	RE	BE
Maternity Benefit Programme (formerly known as IGMSY)							
In Rs Crore	400	343	438	233	400	634	2,700
As a proportion of Union Budget	0.02	0.02	0.02	0.01	0.02	0.03	0.13
Mahatma Gandhi National Rural Employment Guarantee Scheme							
In Rs Crore	33,989	32,977	34,699	37,341	38,500	47,499	48,000
As a proportion of Union Budget	1.89	1.98	1.95	2.09	1.95	2.36	2.24

Source: Compiled by CBGA from Union Budget documents, various years.
Note: *The total Union Budget allocation for SSA and Mid-Day Meal (MDM) are Rs 22,000 crore and Rs 9,236.4 crore, respectively. These figures are the part of the schemes financed from Prarambhik Siksha Kosh (education cess).
** Formerly known as Indira Awas Yojana.

However, the actual response from states could be very diverse. For instance, states like Jharkhand, Kerala, and Andhra Pradesh are among states that have reiterated a strengthening of GRB and interventions for women. However, very few states in all have made such pronouncements in the last three budgets. Analysis by the Centre for Budget and Governance Accountability (CBGA) (2016) for 10 state budgets in 2015–16 and 2016–17 indicate clearly that the one social sector which has not been prioritized to any greater extent in most states is social welfare (which includes the budgets of Women and Child Development). This is probably attributable to the fact that addressing gender issues does not yet have a strong political backing. This is discussed in greater detail in subsequent sections.

Recommendations of the Sub-Group of Chief Ministers on Rationalization of CSS

The Union Cabinet accepted major recommendations of the subgroup of chief minsters on Rationalization of CSSs in 2016. Given the long-standing contention of states that greater autonomy is required in the design, implementation, and financing of schemes, a subgroup of chief ministers was formed to suggest and lay down the guiding principles for rationalization of CSS and the revised fund sharing pattern (between Union and states) in CSSs.

A major recommendation by the subgroup pertains to a new classification of schemes as 'Core' and 'Optional'. Core schemes, it is recommended, would have compulsory participation by states, whereas for Optional schemes, states could choose some or all of them. Among the sectors in which CSSs are implemented, the subgroup suggested identification of the priority sectors that shall comprise of essential interventions as the National Development Agenda for realizing VISION 2022, as mentioned in Box 11.1. Another major recommendation by the Sub Group pertains to a new classification of schemes as 'Core' and 'Optional'. Core Schemes, it is recommended, would have compulsory participation by states, whereas for Optional schemes, states could choose some or all of them. Amongst the Core schemes, those for social protection and social inclusion should form the Core of the Core and be the first charge on available funds for the National Development Agenda.

The report also suggested a change in funding pattern of the union government schemes henceforth. This is important as it determines the burden of expenditure to be borne by the union government and states, respectively, for schemes under various categories and would be indicative of the sectors/schemes that the union government and states would prioritize in the coming years. The funding pattern for schemes would remain unchanged for schemes classified as Core of the Core. For core schemes, the centre–state funding pattern would be 60:40 (90:10 for the North Eastern and Himalayan states). For Optional schemes, the centre–state fund sharing

Box 11.1 Key Priority Areas in National Development Agenda for Realizing VISION 2022

- Poverty elimination: Livelihoods, jobs, and skill development
- Drinking water and Swachh Bharat Mission
- Rural connectivity: Electricity, access, roads and communication
- Agriculture, education (including Mid-Day Meal)
- Health, nutrition, women and children, and so on
- Housing for all: Rural and urban
- Urban transformation
- Law and order: Justice delivery systems
- Others, which may include wildlife conservation and greening

pattern would be 50:50 (80:20 for North Eastern and Himalayan States). Expenditure for all CSSs in union territories would be borne entirely by the union government.

The indicative list of Core of the Core schemes put forth by the subgroup includes MGNREGA, National Social Assistance Programme, National Programme for Persons with Disabilities, Scheme for Development of Scheduled Caste (CSS component), Umbrella Scheme for Education of ST Children, Multi Sector Development Programme for Minorities, Scheme for Providing Education to Madrasas/Minorities, and Welfare of Other Backward Classes.

While all schemes categorized as Core of the Core are critical for the development and empowerment of women and girl children, the omission of important schemes exclusively for women from this category of highest priority schemes is a concern. Though the quantum of funds allocated to these schemes is not adequate, the expenditure on important union government schemes for women such as the one stop centres, Beti Bachao Beti Padhao

Box 11.2 Issues Raised by MWCD for Consideration of the Subgroup of Chief Ministers on Rationalization of Centrally Sponsored Schemes

- Reiterate common priority of women and children, with monitorable outcomes—for instance, on gender, child sex ratio, nutrition.
- Formalize regular dialogue and interaction process between MWCD and states.
- Mobilize enhanced state resources for women and child issues.
- State plans to be reviewed with gender and child perspectives; similarly GOI to monitor plans and progress (including XIII Plan midterm appraisal) through the same perspectives.
- Corporate social responsibility, including Public Sector Undertaking (PSU) funds to focus on women and child issues.
- Collect, analyse gender disaggregated data, and project/disseminate, use to monitor progress.
- Place safety and security of women with highest priority.
- Poverty Task Force to integrate concepts of gender and child poverty; social inclusion indices to factor in gender and child.
- Reinforce Beti Bachao, Beti Padhao through state policies for the girl child and women; and specific interventions such as property rights, affirmative action, 50 per cent reservation for women in Panchayati Raj Institutions/ Urban Local Bodies (PRIs/ULBs).

Yojana, and several others is at present borne entirely by the union government. However, in times of shrinking resources, it is the Core of the Core schemes that will have the first charge on available resources. Thus, omission of some important schemes for women from this category of highest priority schemes is a concern. A review of the list of schemes categorized as Core of the Core and including important schemes of MWCD in this list would serve to ensure that these schemes are prioritized and are protected even if union government expenditure in other sectors reduces.

The report also includes recommendations on other important issues like salary/honoraria component under CSS for ASHAs, anganwadi workers, contract teachers under Sarva Shisksha Abhiyan (SSA), rationalization of cost norms in schemes, release of funds, and local body grants. Several other important issues pertaining to women and children were also raised for the consideration of the Sub- group by MWCD, as described in Box 11.2.

Union Government Outlays for Addressing Violence against Women

Under the federal fiscal architecture in India, states account for a larger proportion of budgetary spending on public provisioning of essential services like health, education, water, and sanitation on which women's reliance tends to be higher than that of men. Nonetheless, the union government provides budgetary resources for a number of flagship programmes in sectors like health, education, water, sanitation, rural employment, and nutrition, in addition to a number of other schemes and programmes across social sectors.

Before assessing the budgetary allocations to union government schemes to address violence against women, it may be worth briefly looking at overall union government spending on interventions for women. The Government of India adopted GRB in 2005–6. Since then, among other measures adopted to institutionalize the strategy, the union government has been presenting a Gender Budget Statement (GBS) each year. The GBS presents the magnitude of expenditure, reported by departments/ministries for the benefit of women. The GBS is presented in two parts. Part A reports the allocations for schemes/programmes exclusively for women. Part B reports those schemes/programmes in which at least 30 per cent of the allocations (but less than 100 per cent) are for the benefit of women. Figure 11.1 presents allocations in Part A as a proportion of Union Budget.

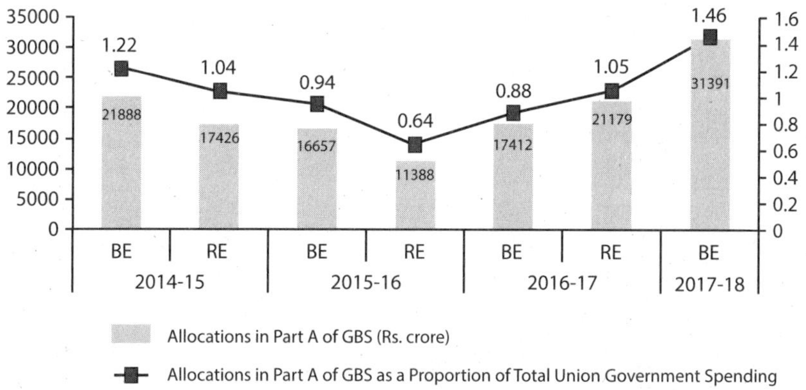

Figure 11.1 Allocations to Part A of Gender Budget Statement, Union Government
Source: Union budget documents, various years.

Of the total 56 ministries in the union government, merely 16 ministries/departments reported in Part A of the GBS in 2017–18. It is worth noting that over 70 per cent of the allocations reported in Part A of the GBS in 2017–18 is by Department of Rural Development, that is, Pradhan Mantri Awas Yojana, which is an important scheme for women but its reporting in Part A, that is, as a scheme benefitting women alone is questionable. The other departments which report notable allocations in Part A of the GBS in 2017–18 are MWCD (14 per cent) and Ministry of Petroleum and Natural Gas (11 per cent). The latter reports the scheme for liquefied petroleum gas (LPG) connection to poor households; the reporting of such an intervention benefiting women alone too is questionable

Union government interventions for addressing violence against women are led primarily by MWCD, although other ministries that play an important role in this domain (such as Ministry of Home Affairs) have also instituted some interventions.

The key schemes of MWCD to address violence against women pertain to provision of help-line, one stop centres, shelter homes, and schemes for combatting trafficking. Kaul and Shrivastava (2017) have analysed the allocations and utilization of key Union Government schemes to address violence against women for the period of the 12th FYP as presented in Figure 11.2 allocations to them for the period of the 12th FYP.

The Working Group on Women's Agency and Empowerment for the 12th FYP had presented estimations of the budgetary resources required for some of the major schemes pertaining to women. Against this requirement, Figure 11.2 presents the funds allocated and utilized.

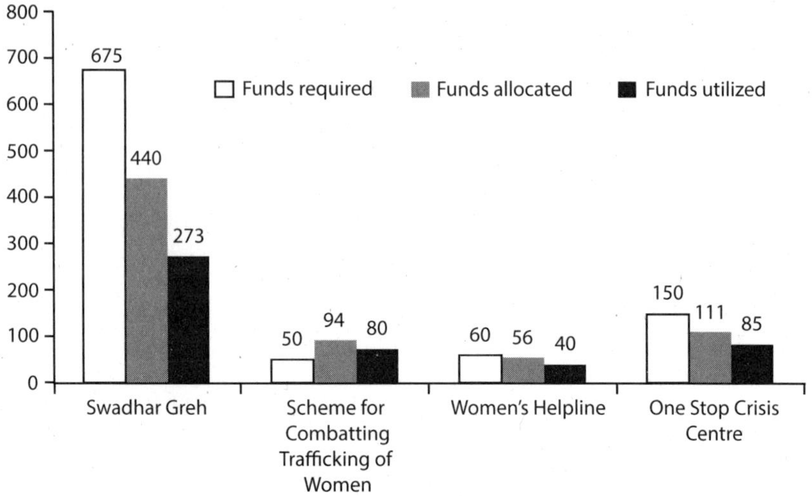

Figure 11.2 Budgetary Allocations and Utilization to Key Union Government Schemes to Address Violence against Women during 12th FYP (Rs crore)
Source: Safety of Women in Public Spaces in Delhi: Governance and Budgetary Challenges, 2017.
Notes: Recommended by Working Group on Women's Agency and Empowerment for 12th FYP.
* Includes actual expenditure for 2012–13, 2013–14, 2014–15, 2015–16, and revised estimates for 2016–17.

As can be seen in Figure 11.2, the implementation of these schemes has been constrained, as reflected in the outcomes listed as follows:

Low budgetary outlays: As against the recommended outlays, the allocations of funds to important schemes (except for Scheme for Combatting Trafficking of Women) have been lower than the estimated requirements. The utilization of the allocated funds too has been low, further widening the gap between the funds required and the funds spent.

Non-operationalization of schemes: Two important schemes, that is, Women's Helpline and one stop centres were introduced in Union Budget 2012–13. However, despite funds being allocated to these schemes each year, the implementation of the schemes was not initiated until 2015–16. The allocations to two other important schemes, 'Financial Assistance and Support Services to Victims of Rape: A Scheme for Restorative Justice' and scheme for 'Assistance to states for implementation of Domestic Violence Act, 2005' introduced in Union Budgets 2006–7 and 2012–13, respectively, remained entirely unutilized. These schemes were eventually discontinued in Union Budget 2015–16.

Low coverage and capacity: One of the manifestations of the low magnitude of public spending on these interventions is the low coverage of these schemes. For instance, as of 2014, the total number of Swadhar Greh in the country was merely 551. Several states such as Sikkim, Nagaland, Haryana, and Arunachal Pradesh have only one Swadhar Greh each.[5] Likewise, the coverage of one stop centres has been scaled down from one per district, that is, 660 to 186 cross the country.[6]

From the analysis presented, it is clear that the implementation of MWCD's schemes to address violence against women need to be far more substantive for any discernible change to take place. Though the analysis in this section covers only the last five years, it is worth noting that the concerns highlighted above have persisted for many preceding years also. Recent developments in budgetary processes notwithstanding, these concerns continue to persist. It is, therefore, important to not only step up the priority to the issue in the Union Budget but also address other bottlenecks impeding their effective implementation.

Operationalization of Nirbhaya Fund

Following the public outcry in the wake of the brutal gang rape of a 23-year-old woman in Delhi in December 2012, the Union finance minister, in the Budget Speech in 2013–14 announced the introduction of Nirbhaya Fund. It is a non-lapsable corpus fund, which supports implementation of initiatives that aim to enhance safety and security for women in the country.

As per guidelines issued by MOF in February 2015, MWCD is the nodal Ministry to appraise schemes under Nirbhaya Fund and also to review and monitor the progress of sanctioned schemes in conjunction with the line ministries/departments. MOF (DEA) had issued guidelines in October 2015 by which an Empowered Committee of Officers was constituted under the Chairmanship of Secretary, MWCD for appraising and approving various schemes/projects proposed by the departments/ministries to be funded from the Nirbhaya Fund.[7]

[5] 'Swadhar Greh Scheme', Lok Sabha Unstarred Question No. 3841, answered on 24 March 2017.

[6] Rajya Sabha Unstarred Question No. 2542, answered on 23 March 2017.

[7] Press Information Bureau, 'Clarification Regarding Utilisation of Nirbhaya Fund', 27 January 2017.

Total magnitude of Nirbhaya Fund: The total magnitude of the Fund is Rs 3,100 crore as of 2017–18. The Nirbhaya Fund received Rs 1,000 crore in 2013–14, Rs 1,000 crore in 2014–15, Rs 550 crore in 2016–17 and 2017–18 each, respectively.[8]

Proposals received: As of March 2017, 16 proposals amounting to Rs 2,349 crore have been received by various union departments/ministries and states. Of the 16 proposals received, 15 proposals amounting to Rs 2,048 crore have been appraised and recommended, which are as follows:[9]

Department/ Ministry/State	Name of the Proposal	Cost of Proposal (in Rs crore)
Ministry of Home Affairs	Emergency Response Support System	321.7
	Creation of Central Victim Compensation Fund	200
	Creation of Investigative Units for Crime against Women	324
	Organized Crime Investigative Agency	83.2
	Cyber Crime Prevention against Women and Children	244.3
	Proposal for providing facility of Social Workers/Counsellors at the District and Sub-Divisional Police Station Level in Delhi, Delhi Police	6.2
	New building with women centric facilities for Special Unit for Women and Children (SPUWAC) and Special Unit for North East Region (SPUNER) at Nanakpura, Delhi Police	23.6
Ministry of Railways	Integrated Emergency Response Management System	500

[8] 'Utilisation of Nirbhaya Fund', Rajya Sabha Unstarred Question No. 3995, answered on: 06 April 2017.

[9] 'Utilisation of Nirbhaya Fund', Rajya Sabha Unstarred Question No. 3995, answered on: 06 April 2017.

Department/ Ministry/State	Name of the Proposal	Cost of Proposal (in Rs crore)
Ministry of Electronics and Information Technology	Development and Field Testing of panic Switch based safety Device for Cars and Buses for aiding Women's Safety, MeiTY	3.5
Ministry of Women and Child Development	One-Stop Centre	119.7
	Universalization of Women Helpline, MWCD	69.5
Government of Andhra Pradesh	Abhaya Project Proposal for safety of women and girl child	138.5
	Implementation of Mahila Police Volunteers (MPVs) at Village level in two districts of Anantapur and Kadapa on pilot basis	2.3
Govt. of Rajasthan	Chirali Proposal, Women Empowerment Directorate	10.2
Government of Haryana	Mahila Police Volunteers for Karnal and Mohindergarh District	1.3

Budgetary Outlays for Addressing Violence against Women at the State Level: An analysis of Madhya Pradesh and Jharkhand

An analysis of public spending to address violence against women must necessarily take into account interventions being implemented by states. With the increase in share of untied resources available to states following the acceptance of the FFC recommendations in 2015–16, states have more autonomy to determine their expenditure priorities. Moreover, it is worth noting that though violence against women is rampant and persists throughout the country, specific forms of violence may vary from region to region. Thus, in addition to a minimum set of programmes supported by the union government, the role of states is critical to address particular forms of violence that may be specific to the region or state.

Subsequent to the adoption of GRB by the union government in 2005–6, a number of states undertook steps to institutionalize the strategy. However, as is the case with GRB at the Union level, the implementation of the strategy in most states suffers from limitations. Yet, it provides a useful opportunity to assess the priority accorded to women in the respective state budgets.

In the context of violence against women, the effective implementation of GRB should enable states to recognize the vulnerability of women to violence across sectors and institute appropriate mechanisms, backed by adequate budgetary outlays to address the same. In the following section, an attempt has been made to examine the extent to which the implementation of the strategy has led to introduction of interventions to address the various different forms of violence against women, budgetary resources allocated for these, and the utilization of allocated resources for two states, that is, Madhya Pradesh and Jharkhand.

Madhya Pradesh

Madhya Pradesh was the first state in the country to adopt GRB in 2007–8. Each year since 2007–8, the state has been presenting a GBS, which captures the magnitude of budgetary resources earmarked for women. The GBS is presented in two parts—Part A enlists those scheme and programmes which are exclusively for women, while Part B presents those schemes in which some proportion of the benefit accrues to women. It is worth noting that the entire allocations to schemes being reported in Part B are included in the GBS presented by the state, leading to a slightly misleading picture.

The analysis in this section focuses on interventions reported by departments in Part A of the GBS. Figure 11.3 presents the allocations under Part A of the GBS in Madhya Pradesh from 2014–15 to 2017–18.

It is evident from figure 11.3 that while allocations to schemes meant exclusively for women have increased in absolute terms in the four-year period, when seen as a proportion of total expenditure by the state government, the allocations have remained more or less stagnant at around 1.5 per cent. Of the 52 departments in the state, the number of departments that are reporting in Part A of the GBS, that is, departments that implement programmes exclusively for women has increased from 10 to 14 between 2014–15 and 2017–18. Over 80 per cent of the Rs 2,618 crore reported in Part A of the GBS in 2017–18 (BE) is reported by the Department of Women and Child Development and the Department of Social Justice, indicating that the other departments have small or no interventions at all meant exclusively for women.

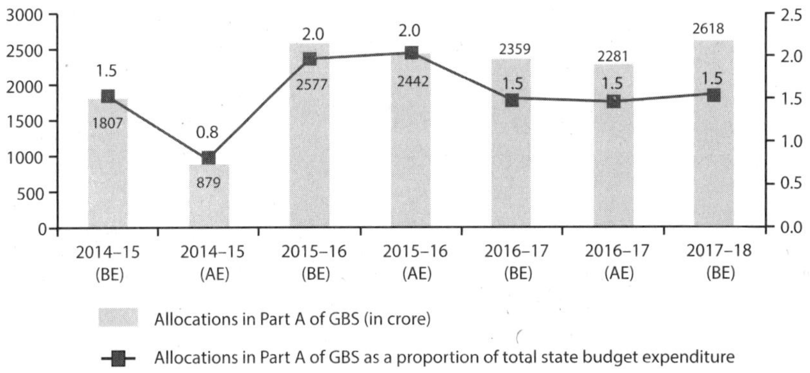

Figure 11.3 Allocations in Part A of GBS of Madhya Pradesh
Source: Budget documents, Government of Madhya Pradesh, various years.

It is important to note that enhancing women's safety and reducing their vulnerability to violence requires due recognition of the issue in a range of sectors including health, transport, policing, law, and urban development, among others. Effective implementation of GRB should enable departments to recognize these and other gender concerns in their respective sectors of concern and analyse the adequacy of the funds for these specific gender responsive interventions and their utilization.

Schemes for Addressing Violence against Women

Madhya Pradesh has a high rate of violence against women; the rate of total cognizable crimes in the state stood at 65.5 against 53.9 for the country as a whole in 2015 (NCRB 2015). The recognition of this high level of violence against women has led to policy pronouncements to address the issue. The 12th FYP of Madhya Pradesh highlights 'environment free of violence against women' as an important approach while, reducing the incidence of violence against women and providing quality care services to victims of violence is a monitorable target in the 12th FYP.

Against this backdrop, it is worth examining the extent to which schemes for addressing violence against women are prioritized in the state budget in Madhya Pradesh.

Most schemes for women in distress are implemented by the Department of Women and Child Development. These include both union government schemes and schemes by the Government of Madhya Pradesh.

Important schemes of MWCD to address violence against women are implemented in Madhya Pradesh. While some of these schemes are fully supported by the union government, for others, states are required to contribute their share in a pre-decided fund sharing pattern. Table 11.3 presents the allocations and expenditure under these schemes in the state between 2014–15 and 2017–18.

As can be seen in Table 11.3, four schemes of MWCD have been implemented in the state focusing on important, but a limited set of concerns, pertaining to women in distress. Until 2016–17, most of these schemes were not implemented in the state owing to delays in their operationalization by the union government, even though the funds to these schemes were allocated in the three preceding years. An important scheme of MWCD, Ujjwala, for prevention of trafficking and rescue, rehabilitation, and re-integration of victims of trafficking and commercial sexual exploitation has not been implemented in the state for four years between 2014–15 and 2017–18.

The budgetary outlays for these schemes are also meagre. Except for the allocations for Beti Bachao Beti Padhao and one stop centres in 2017–18 (BE), the allocations to these important interventions are hardly sufficient to meet the needs of distressed women in a populous state like Madhya Pradesh where just the reported cases of rape, kidnapping and abduction, and dowry deaths were 4391, 4547, and 66, respectively, in 2015 (NCRB 2015). As of 2015, the number of Swadhar Homes (a scheme that provides shelter, food, clothing, and medical treatment for women in difficult circumstances) in Madhya Pradesh were reported to be merely 15 (in addition to 16 Short Stay Homes).[10]

Table 11.3 Outlays for Key Union Government Schemes to Address Violence against Women in Madhya Pradesh (in Rs Crore)

	2014–15		2015–16		2016–17		2017–18
	BE	AE	BE	AE	BE	RE	BE
Mahila Helpline	–	–	–	–	3	.0007	1.1
Beti Bachao Beti Padhao	–	–	–	0.5	1.0	0.6	6.5
One Stop Centre	–	–	–	–	1.1	1.2	5.3
Swadhar Greh	–	–	–	–	1	1	1.5

Source: Budget documents, Government of Madhya Pradesh, various years.

[10] Statement referred in reply of part (b) of Lok Sabha un-starred Question No. 3841 for 24.03.2017 regarding number of Swadhar Grehs presently functional in

Table 11.4 Outlays for Key Schemes of Government of Madhya Pradesh to Address Violence against Women (in Rs Crore)

	2014–15		2015–16		2016–17		2017–18
	BE	AE	BE	AE	BE	RE	BE
Centres for safety and assistance to women facing domestic violence	4.5	1.9	3	1.3	3.0	2.6	2.5
Shaurya Dal	–	–	4.9	2.5	5.9	5.9	5.9
Usha Kiran	4.1	2.3	3.1	2.2	3.0	2.3	2.9
Mukhya Mantri Mahila Sashaktikaran Yojana	2	0.32	2	0.9	2	1	1
Beti Bachao Abhiyan	6	3.50	6	3.3	6.2	6	9.2

Source: Budget documents, Government of Madhya Pradesh, various years.

In addition to union government schemes, the Department of Women and Child Development also implements schemes of the state government for women in distress. Table 11.4 captures the allocations and expenditure for these schemes.

The state government plays a more proactive role than the union government in providing resources for addressing violence against women. The key schemes by the state government to address violence against women pertain to arresting the declining child sex ratio (Beti Bachao Abhiyan), assistance to women facing domestic violence (centres for safety and assistance to women facing domestic violence and Usha Kiran), vocational training for women facing violence (Mukha Mantri Mahila Sashaktikaran Yojana), and building community-led institutions for bringing systemic changes in the societal mindset to prevent violence against women (Shaurya Dal).

The Economic Survey 2016–17, Government of Madhya Pradesh, provides some information on the implementation of these schemes. The Beti Bachao Beti Padhao Yojana is being implemented in six districts of the state, that is, Gwalior, Datiya, Murena, Bhind, Reeva, and Tikamgarrh. The Usha Kiran Yojana for the implementation of PWDVA initiated in 2008 is being implemented in a revised mode since 2016. As per the scheme, it is planned to have an 'Usha Kiran Centre' in each district of the state. These centres

the country, State/UTs wise and number of women beneficiaries State/UTs wise accessible at http://164.100.47.190/loksabhaquestions/annex/11/AU3841.pdf.

will provide police assistance, counselling, medical aid, and rehabilitative services to women facing any form of violence. 453 Child Development Project Officers (CDPO) and Block level Women Empowerment Officials have been appointed as POs under the Act.

The state government has also constituted 'Shourya Dals' with the objective of creating a violence-free environment in Madhya Pradesh. Each group comprises five male and female members. These groups act as a bridge between the government and people. Over 60,000 such groups have been established. Additionally, the Mukhyamantri Mahila Sashaktikaran Yojana provides vocational training to ensure livelihood opportunities to women in distress. The number of women the scheme intends to reach out to in 2017–18 and 2018–19 is 1,500 and 2,000, respectively.

In view of the very limited investment by the union government in addressing violence against women, the spending by the state government on these interventions is critical to ensure adequate resources for such interventions. However, apart from the allocations to Beti Bachao Abhiyan, none of the other interventions have substantive allocations. In fact, the outlays for three schemes, that is, centres for safety and assistance to women facing domestic violence, Usha Kiran, and Mukhya Mantri Mahila Sashaktikaran Yojana, have witnessed a decline in absolute terms between 2014–15 and 2017–18. The utilization of funds for all the interventions has also been poor; less than half of the allocated funds being utilized across years in several of these schemes.

Jharkhand

The rate of total cognizable crimes in Jharkhand is 40.2 as of 2015. The total number of reported crimes against women in the state was 6,518 in 2015, which constitutes 2 per cent of the total number of reported crimes against women in the country (NCRB 2015). Before assessing the budgetary provisions for addressing violence against women in the state, it may be worth briefly looking at the overall picture vis-à-vis financing of interventions for women in the state.

The state of Jharkhand is one of the latest ones to adopt GRB. Among other measures to institutionalize the strategy, the state has been presenting a GBS since 2016–17. Based on the reporting in the GBS, it can be inferred that the total expenditure on schemes/programmes meant specifically for women was Rs 1,580 crore and Rs 3,090 crore in 2016–17 (BE) and 2017–18 (BE), respectively. As a proportion of the total expenditure by the state government, this constitutes 2.5 per cent and 4 per cent, respectively.

Of the 32 departments in the state, a total of 13 departments have reported allocations meant exclusively for women in the GBS in 2017–18.

Of the Rs 3,090 crore that is earmarked for schemes exclusively for women in 2017–18 (BE), the Department of Food, Public Distribution and Consumer Affairs reports the highest proportion, that is, 27 per cent, followed by the Department of Women, Child Development and Social Security which reports 23 per cent, Rural Development which reports 19 per cent, and the Department of school education, which reports 18 per cent, among others. However, the reporting by departments in Part A of the GBS requires further scrutiny, as the inclusion of several interventions in Part A of the GBS (such as Pradhan Mantri Ujjwala Yojana and Antodaya Ann Yojana) as schemes benefiting women exclusively is questionable.

The nodal department for the development and empowerment of women in Jharkhand is the Department of Women, Child Development and Social Security. Though the allocations to the Department have been increasing in absolute terms each year, between 2014–15 and 2017–18, as a proportion of the state budget, it has been fluctuating, as can be seen in Figure 11.4.

The department is also the nodal department for implementation of interventions for addressing violence against women in the state. These

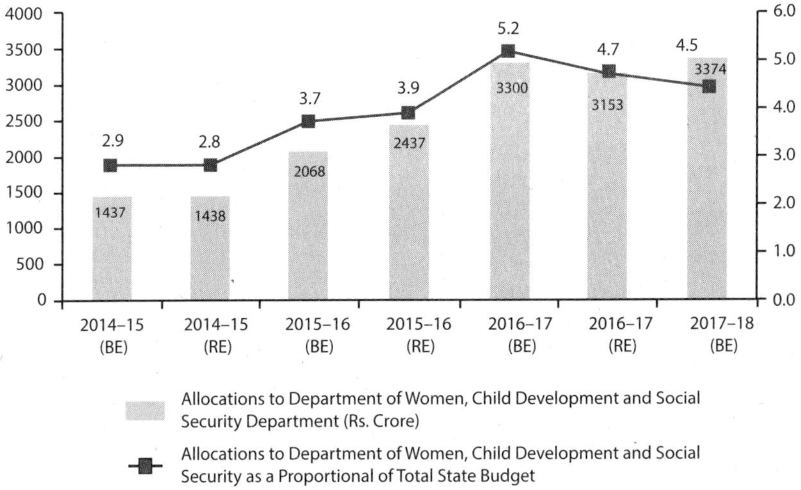

Figure 11.4 Budgetary Outlays for Department of Women, Child Development and Social Security in Jharkhand

Source: Budget documents, Government of Jharkhand, various years.

include schemes of MWCD to address violence against women as well as those by Government of Jharkhand. MWCD schemes implemented by the department include both, those that are completely supported by the union government and schemes in which states are required to contribute funds according to a pre-determined fund sharing pattern.

The implementation of most of the important schemes of MWCD to address violence against women in the state was initiated recently; these schemes were not operationalized until 2015–16. The Economic Survey 2016–17, Government of Jharkhand, presents information about various schemes and programmes to address violence against women in the state. A helpline for women has been set up in Ranchi, implemented by Xavier Institute of Social Service. The Beti Bachao Beti Padhao Yojana is being implemented in Dhanbad district of Jharkhand. Plans to start one-stop centres in Ranchi, Jamshedpur, and Dhanbad are also in the pipeline. These centres will provide free medical facilities with legal and general counselling to women in difficult circumstances and will be linked to each other. Jharkhand also has two Swadhar Greh in the districts of Palamu and Bokaro with a total capacity of 50.

However, as reflected in the Table 11.5, the budgetary allocations to these schemes too are low, leaving little scope for their effective functioning.

Table 11.5 Outlays for Key Union Government Schemes to Address Violence against Women in Jharkhand (in Rs Crore)

	2014–15		2015–16		2016–17		2017–18
	Budget Estimates (BE)	Actual Expenditure (AE)	BE	AE	BE	Revised Estimates (RE)	BE
Women's Helpline	–	–	–	0.35	0.5	0.5	0.69
Beti Bachao Beti Padhao	–	–	–	0.05	1.05	1.05	0.52
One Stop Centre	–	–	–	0.10	0.15	0.72	1.34
Swadhar Greh	0.8	–	0.8	–	0.8	0.8	1.6
Ujjwala	–	–	–	–	–	–	1.37

Source: Budget documents, Government of Jharkhand, various years.

It can be seen in Table 11.5 that only two of the abovementioned schemes have allocations exceeding Rs 1 crore in 2017–18 (BE). The allocations to Swadhar Greh, which has been in implementation for quite a few years, had remained unutilized in 2014–15 and 2015–16, while Ujjwala, a scheme for prevention of trafficking and rescue, rehabilitation, and re-integration of victims of trafficking and commercial sexual exploitation, did not receive any allocations between 2014–15 and 2016–17.

The Government of Jharkhand also has several schemes of its own for addressing violence against women; some of these key schemes pertain to (*a*) provision of a helpline for women, (*b*) shelter facilities for women in distress, (*c*) financial assistance to rape victims/survivors, women facing domestic violence, pension under Scheduled Castes and the Scheduled Tribes (Prevention of Atrocities) Rules, 1995, and promotion of inter-caste marriage between SC/ST and general category individuals through financial aid, (*d*) creating awareness against the practice of witchcraft through use of media. Table 11.6 presents budgetary outlays and expenditure for these schemes between 2014–15 and 2017–18.

As reflected in Table 11.6, schemes by Government of Jharkhand to address violence against women hardly have any allocations. Some of the abovementioned schemes of the state government had not received allocations in 2016–17 and 2017–18. The only state government scheme with substantive allocations is the scheme for eradication of witchcraft. The Economic Survey, 2016–17, also reports that the state government has taken several steps to eliminate witch hunting, such as launching a helpline to report incidences of witchcraft, and identification of areas where the incidence of the practice is high. The Government of Jharkhand has also undertaken several measures to combat human trafficking, including establishing Anti Human Trafficking Units and a helpline for incidents related to women and child trafficking. The state has, however, not instituted a separate scheme for implementation of PWDVA, 2005. As of 2014, the state had appointed 136 POs;[11] these officials hold additional charge, that is, they perform their responsibilities as POs in addition to other responsibilities assigned to them.

The above analysis underscores the need to significantly step up the priority for interventions to address violence against women in the state budget. There is a need for state government towards this end to be more substantive in terms of both the range of interventions as well as the budgetary outlays for them.

[11] 'Protection Officers under PWDVA', Lok Sabha Unstarred Question No. 1252, answered on: 18 July 2014.

Table 11.6 Outlays for Key Schemes of Government of Jharkhand to Address Violence against Women (in Rs Crore)

	2014–15		2015–16		2016–17		2017–18
	BE	AE	BE	AE	BE	RE	BE
Women's Helpline	0.90	0.14	0.90	0.27	–	–	–
Running of After Care Home/ NariNiketan/Short Stay Home-cum-Training Centre for Deserted and Estranged Women	0.50	0.26	2.50	1.13	–	–	–
Eradication of witchcraft practice	0.15	0.10	0.15	0.12	0.5	0.5	4.0
Assistance to victim of rape/ domestic violence/SC ST (prevention of Atrocity) and beneficiaries of Inter cast Marriage	–	–	–	–	–	–	4.2
Financial assistance to women and adolescent girls who are victims of rape and domestic violence	.10	–	–	.12	.20	.11	0
Establishment of rehabilitation centres for rescued adolescent girl/anti trafficking efforts	.50	.50	.50	.50	–	–	–

Source: Budget documents, Government of Jharkhand, various years.

A look at the budgets in both Madhya Pradesh and Jharkhand clearly brings out the need to step up public expenditure on addressing violence against women. An effective response mechanism requires resources for both immediate rescue and relief as well as long-term rehabilitative measures. The current interventions towards the issue present a limited set of interventions characterized by low capacity and coverage. The increase in the autonomy to states to design their expenditure priorities following the acceptance of FFC recommendations in 2015–16 has not translated into higher budgetary priority to the issue. State governments are also well positioned to implement interventions to address the different forms of violence specific to their states/region. Hence, besides union government programmes, adequate spending by states is of utmost importance to establish a comprehensive well-funded response mechanism to address the occurrence of violence against women.

***

The chapter has focused on analysing two important questions. At a broad level, it seeks to build an understanding of the implications of some of the recent changes in the country's planning and budgetary processes from a gender perspective. More specifically, it assesses the priority to address violence against women in the Union Budget and in the budgets of the states of Madhya Pradesh and Jharkhand.

A close examination reveals that changes in fiscal policy brought about as a result of developments in planning and budgetary processes in the last few years have marked gender implications. The analysis following the changes in the fiscal architecture has focused largely on its implications for centre–state fiscal relations and financing of government interventions in the social sectors. Henceforth, policy decisions in this domain must necessarily be informed by these gender dimensions. In the new institutional architecture that has evolved, NITI Aayog must take steps to continue efforts in gender mainstreaming of plans and policies that were initiated in the preceding FYPs. It also follows that, in the new fiscal regime, an important means to incorporate a gender lens in plans, policies, and programmes would be through a renewed impetus on GRB, both in the union government as well as in the states.

The analysis in the chapter also clearly indicates that the importance accorded to the issue of violence against women in the policy discourse is yet to translate into budgetary priorities, both at the level of the union government as well as in states. The increased autonomy available to states following the acceptance of the FFC recommendations does not seem to have led to an increased priority for the issue in the budgets of the two states discussed in the chapter, that is, Madhya Pradesh and Jharkhand. Government interventions by both the union government and states need to be prioritized to a much greater extent if the state's response mechanism is to adequately address the various forms of violence.

The changes in the country's fiscal architecture, brought about as a result of the recent developments, have generated intense discussions about the role of the union government and states in provisioning of services in the social sector. In the new framework of centre–state relations, it must be noted that though states should play an increasingly prominent role in implementing interventions to address violence against women, given the criticality of the issue, the union government must continue to support the efforts of states in this domain; violence against women should be a priority for both levels of governments. It is also important that states step up budgetary priority for essential services which are important from a gender perspective and in which union government expenditure has decreased such as drinking water and education. The response of states may vary from state to state and it would be worth tracking and assessing states' budgetary priorities over a period of time.

It should also be mentioned that while the focus of the present chapter is on the interventions by MWCD and the nodal departments for women at the state level, an analysis of government interventions to mitigate and address violence against women must also take into account interventions in other sectors as well. Violence against women is a cross-cutting issue. It follows, therefore, that enhancing women's safety requires a wider range of measures to be instituted by an array of departments/ministries in sectors like urban and rural development, health, sanitation, transport, police, law, and education among others.

Violence against women is a violation of women's right to live with freedom and dignity. It is obligatory on the State to eliminate it and provide an effective response in case of its occurrence. Several factors constraining the State's efforts in this regard have been bottlenecks in the domain of budgets and governance. Addressing these necessarily requires a re-orientation of our programmes and budgets to reflect greater priority towards women. It is hoped that the priority accorded to the issue of violence against women in the policy framework translates into a higher priority for the issue in government budgets in the years to come.

References

Centre for Budget and Governance Accountability (2016), 'Comparative Analysis of Priorities in State Budgets for 2015–16', Working Paper 1. A Working Paper Series by CBGA, Understanding the Changes in India's Fiscal Architecture, New Delhi.

Das Subrat and Yamini Mishra (2006), 'Women's Component Plan and Gender Budgeting in India: Still a Long Way to Go!', Yojana.

Government of Madhya Pradesh (2012), 'Twelfth Five Year Plan 2012–2017 and Annual Plan 2012–2013', Planning, Economics And Statistics Department, Government of Madhya Pradesh.

Government of India, (2017), 'Three Year Action Agenda 2017–18 to 2019–20', NITI Aayog, Government of India.

Kaul Kanika and Saumya Shrivastva, (2014), 'Lost in Implementation', 20th June, Daily News and Analysis.

——— (2017), *Safety of Women in Public Spaces in Delhi: Governance and Budgetary Challenges Centre for Budget and Governance Accountability*, New Delhi.

Rao, M. Govinda (2015), 'Abolition of Planning Commission doesn't mean planning process is over', 7 February, *Business Standard* http://www.business-standard.com/article/economy-policy/abolition-of-planning-commission-doesn-t-mean-planning-process-is-over-m-govinda-rao-115020700539_1.html.

Shah Rajeev, Ratna (2014), 'Reorienting the Plan Process and Revitalising the Planning Commission', *Economic and Political Weekly*, Vol XLIX, No. 37.

Editors and Contributors

Editors

Indira Jaising is senior advocate in the Supreme Court of India. She is the founder secretary of the Lawyers Collective and executive director of the Lawyers Collective Women's Rights Initiative. From the start of her legal career, she has been dedicated to the protection of human rights, she has argued several cases relating to discrimination against women, the poor and working class, and environmental protraction. She became the first woman to be designated as a senior advocate by the High Court of Bombay in 1986. In 2005, she was awarded the Padma Shri for her contribution in the field of public affairs. In 2009, she became the first woman to be appointed as the additional solicitor general of India. She has also served as an expert member of the United Nations Committee on the Elimination of Discrimination against Women.

Pinki Mathur Anurag is director-Technical, Lawyers Collective Women's Rights Initiative. She has been with the Lawyers Collective since 2005, and has been responsible for the legal aid cell, advocacy and research in

Mumbai. Pinki's primary academic interests lie in exploring the evolution of international law in response to violence against women. She compiled and authored *The Best Practices Manual on the PWDVA* (The Lawyers Collective and UN Women, South East Asia), and has contributed to the annual monitoring and evaluation of the PWDVA. She is currently working on a book on the representation of the Feminist Movement in the 21st Century.

Contributors

Asmita Basu is programme director, Amnesty International, India. She has over 15 years' experience of research, programme implementation, and capacity development in the fields of gender and human rights. Her major work has been in the area of drafting laws and reviewing law/policy implementation on violence against women and women's equality rights particularly in India, Bangladesh, and Lao PDR. As part of the Lawyers Collective, she was involved in drafting of the PWDVA. She was also involved in implementing one of India's largest violence against women prevention projects ('Safe Cities Initiative'), supported by DFID in Madhya Pradesh. She is a CEDAW expert for UN Women in the Asia–Pacific region and has contributed as an expert to a number of UN global initiatives on women and child rights.

Padma Bhate-Deosthali, MSW, is an independent researcher and trainer working on gender, health, and human rights. She has worked on health services research including standards of care in the private health sector and its unregulated growth, integrating gender in medical education, women's work and health, violence and health. She was a member of the Steering Group of the GDG-WHO for developing Policy and Clinical practice guidelines for responding to violence against women and a member of the National Committee under the Ministry of Health and Family Welfare for drafting the 'Guidelines and Protocols for medico-legal care for victims/survivors of sexual violence', 2014. She coordinated the setting up of Dilaasa, the first public hospital-based crisis centre in India.

Radhika Chakraborty is an independent researcher whose research interests include violence against women, gender-based violence and the law, displacement, and diaspora. She has previously worked as a researcher at the Resource Centre for Interventions on Violence Against Women at the Tata Institute of Social Sciences Mumbai, which works with state systems to institute socio-legal services for women survivors of violence, as well as with

SHRAM (Strengthen and Harmonize Research and Action on Migration), a research repository on migration in Asia. She has a master's degree in women's studies, and a BA in English literature.

Uma Chakravarti is a feminist historian who taught at Miranda House, Delhi University, from where she took early retirement in 1998. She has been associated with the women's movement and the movement for democratic rights since the late 1970s. She writes on Buddhism, early Indian history, the nineteenth century, and on contemporary subjects. She also makes films about the past when it is too depressing to live in the present.

Aparna Chandra is research director, Centre for Constitutional Law, Policy and Governance. She works on constitutional law, human rights, gender and the law, and judicial process reform. Aparna previously worked at the National Judicial Academy, India; the National Law School of India University, Bangalore; and as a Tutor in Law at Yale Law School, USA. She received her BA LLB (Hons) degree from National Law School, Bangalore in 2006, where she graduated with the first rank. She holds LLM and JSD degrees from Yale Law School where she was a Lillian Goldman Scholar from 2010–12.

Brototi Dutta is a lawyer with over 10 years of experience in policy research and advocacy, and legal writing on gender and human rights issues. Brototi started her career with Lawyers Collective and worked with the organization on a wide range of issues including domestic violence, sexual violence, and sexual harassment. She currently teaches at the Centre for Law and Policy Research, Bangalore. She has also worked with the Ministry of Women and Child Development as a senior consultant, and with the UN Women in India. She has co-authored a *Handbook for Judges on Domestic Violence law*, and written policy papers and opinion pieces on women's issues. Brototi is currently with the Centre for Law and Policy Research, Bangalore. Her research interests primarily revolve around feminist engagements with the law, including how courts and social norms interact to develop narratives of and about women, sexuality and issues of consent and choice, and gender and its inter-sectionalities.

Manisha Kande is a research officer at the Resource Centre for Interventions on Violence Against Women, Tata Institute of Social Sciences, Mumbai, India. Her research has focused on violence against women, the special cells for women in Maharashtra, and state-based socio-legal services for women survivors of violence. She has an MSW and BSW from Nirmala Niketan College of Social Work, Mumbai.

Kanika Kaul works with the Centre for Budget and Governance Accountability, specializing in research and capacity-building efforts on Gender Responsive Budgeting. She also works on other issues relating to women such as fiscal policy measures for prevention and redressal of violence against women. Her areas of interest also include drinking water and sanitation, analysing these from the perspective of disadvantaged sections of population, particularly women. She was previously involved in coordinating CBGA's work as the secretariat of the network of civil society budget groups, People's Budget Initiative. Formerly, she has worked with The Hunger Project, engaging with a network of grass roots organizations across the country to strengthen women's participation in rural local self-governance.

Saptarshi Mandal is assistant professor at the Jindal Global Law School, Sonipat, Haryana. He teaches, researches, and writes in the areas of family law, disability and mental health law, law and society, and feminist legal studies. Previously, Saptarshi worked as law researcher, trainer, and programme officer with several national and international NGOs in New Delhi, such as the Lawyers CollectiveWomen's Rights Initiative, Multiple Action Research Group, Partners for Law in Development and Amnesty International. He was the lead author of the 257th Report of the Law Commission of India (2015) on reform of the law governing guardianship and custody of children. His work has been published in the *Indian Law Review, Hong Kong Law Journal, Australian Feminist Studies, Indian Journal of Gender Studies, NUJS Law Review*, and the *Economic and Political Weekly*, among others.

Trupti Jhaveri Panchal is assistant professor in School of Social Work at Tata Institute of Social Sciences, Mumbai, and is engaged in teaching, research, and field action work. She is also the project director of two Field Action Projects, namely, Resource Centre for Interventions on Violence Against Women (RCI-VAW) and Special Cell for Women and Children (Maharashtra) units located in police system, which provide socio-legal services and a multi-agency coordinated response for women survivors of violence. Her areas of interest is violence against women, working with State, feminist praxis models, social work academia/education and training, gender, sexuality and law, issues of masculinity. Her research projects include Child Sexual Abuse, Implementation of Prohibition of Child Marriage

Act, 2006, and Implementation of Protection of Women from Domestic Violence Act, 2005 in India.

Sangeeta Rege is currently the coordinator of CEHAT. She has been leading initiatives for health system response to violence against women. She has also led CEHAT's PIL on advocating for gender-sensitive health care for survivors of sexual assault. Integrating gender in medical education has been an area of interest and she has been leading this project. She has a master's degree in social work and has 16 years of experience in the area of training, research, and advocacy on issues of violence and health.

Monica Sakhrani is a Mumbai-based lawyer and was previously with the Centre for Social Justice and Governance, Tata Institute of Social Sciences. She is the author of *Citizens Guide to Criminal Law* and co-editor of the *Handbook on Law of Domestic Violence* along with Indira Jaising. She was one of the principal investigators on the four-state study on the Implementation of the Protection of Women from Domestic Violence Act, 2005, along with Trupti Panchal.

Ajita Sharma is a practising lawyer at the chambers of senior advocate, Indira Jaising, Supreme Court of India. Currently, she works on a wide range of constitutional law and Human Rights issues. Ajita has an LLB from Jindal Global Law School at O.P. Jindal Global University, Sonipat, India, (2014) and a post graduate degree in law from the College of Law at the University of Illinois, Urbana-Champaign, USA (2015). She has been awarded with pro bono notation award (2015), scholarships (2014–15), fellowship (2009), and studentships (2009–14) in these law schools. Ajita is deeply committed to the goals of achieving substantive equality, gender justice, affirmative action, and reformation.

Index